# ORACLE9i™
# PROGRAMMING

## A PRIMER

# ORACLE9*i*™
# PROGRAMMING

## A PRIMER

Rajshekhar Sunderraman
GEORGIA STATE UNIVERSITY

Boston San Francisco New York
London Toronto Sydney Tokyo Singapore Madrid
Mexico City Munich Paris Cape Town Hong Kong Montreal

*Senior Acquisitions Editor:* Maite Suarez-Rivas
*Project Editor:* Katherine Harutunian
*Marketing Manager:* Nathan Schultz
*Senior Production Supervisor:* Jeffrey Holcomb
*Composition and Art:* Windfall Software, using ZzTEX
*Copyeditor:* Rachel Wheeler
*Proofreader:* Norma Emory
*Cover Designers:* Lynne Reed and Joyce Consentino Wells
*Cover Photo:* © 2003 Eye Wire, Getty Images
*Prepress and Manufacturing:* Hugh Crawford

Access the latest information about Addison-Wesley titles from our World Wide Web site: http://www.aw.com/cs



Library of Congress Cataloging-in-Publication Data

Sunderraman, Rajshekhar.
Oracle9i programming : a primer / Rajshekhar Sunderraman.
p. cm.
Includes bibliographic references and index.
ISBN 0-321-19498-5
1. Oracle (Computer file) 2. Relational databases. I. Title: Oracle 9i programming.
II. Title.
QA76.9.D3S9255 2003
005.75′85—dc21 2003048228

This book was composed with the ZzTEX typesetting system on a PC. The text is set in ITC Berkeley Oldstyle and the open-face titles in Monotype Old Style Bold Outline. The monospaced computer program font is ZzTEXMono Regular. The book was printed on Lynx Opaque Plus.



ISBN 0-321-19498-5
2345678910—HAM—06050403

To

My mother
`Saraswathi Sunderraman`
for her love and hard work

My father
`Sqn. Ldr. Rajagopala Sunderraman`
for his love and encouragement

My wife
`Radhika`
for her love and caring

My children
`Nandita` and `Naveen`
for their love and innocence

Oracle is one of the most widely used database systems in the world. It runs on virtually all platforms ranging from Windows-based PCs to UNIX servers. It also comes with an array of programming tools and environments and provides access to the database from a variety of high-level programming languages.

In recent years, more and more universities in the United States and elsewhere are using Oracle in their database courses as the primary vehicle to illustrate database concepts and principles. This has resulted in the need for a concise book on Oracle programming to supplement the traditional text in the database courses. The main motivation for writing this book is to satisfy this need. This book can also be used by nonacademic professionals interested in learning about Oracle programming.

In this current edition, three new chapters covering PL/SQL Web Programming, Java Servlet programming, and XML have been added, while one old chapter, Embedded SQL in C and C++, has been retired. The embedded SQL chapter will be made available on the Web for download for those users of the book who still need it. Oracle's recent database servers, starting from version 8*i*, have provided increasing support for database access on the Internet. This support has been vital to many application developers who have, in the recent past, been developing three-tier Web applications that are invoked from a Web browser. PL/SQL, the mainstay procedural language, has been enhanced with a Web Toolkit that allows dynamic Web pages to be developed with ease. Java Servlet and Java Server Pages technology from Sun Microsystems has been embraced by Oracle, and there is strong support for developing Web applications using this technology in Oracle9*i*. XML, the newest technology used in current data-interchange applications, is also being well supported by Oracle9*i*, including built-in XML parsers, XML data type for database columns, and support for importing XML data into and exporting XML data from an Oracle9*i* database. The three new chapters added in this edition cover these new technologies in detail.

The topics covered in this book are Oracle SQL, PL/SQL, Web application development using PL/SQL, database access in Java using JDBC and SQLJ, Web application development using Java Servlets and Java Server Pages, and Oracle support for XML. SQL and PL/SQL are two languages at the core of the Oracle database engine and are essential to learn before working with Oracle databases. Java has become a de facto language for many to program database applications in, and knowledge of JDBC and SQLJ is critical in developing applications that access Oracle databases. With the proliferation of the Internet, more and more applications that access Oracle databases are being made available over the Web. Learning the PL/SQL Web Toolkit and PL/SQL Server pages along with Java Servlets and Java Server Pages is becoming essential to programming such applications. The XML standard is making a major impact in current-day distributed and networked environments, and learning XML in the context of Oracle databases is proving to be an important skill for computer professionals.

Three sample databases are introduced early in the book, and most of the chapters use these databases for illustration purposes. These are the grade-book database, the mail-order database, and the portfolio database.

The grade-book database contains data typically tracked by an instructor of a course and includes information about students, courses being taught, which student is enrolled in which course, grading components for courses, and the individual's scores in these grading components. An application that allows instructors to update the database and students to access their grades is presented in the text.

The mail-order database contains data relevant to a mail-order company that sells items to customers. A variation of this database is used in the Web shopping application that allows users to shop on the Web for items. The users have the ability to search for items, add and update a shopping cart, and check out.

The portfolio database contains data about companies, their share prices, and members who have an account with the brokerage company. An application that allows members to sign on to the system, obtain stock quotes, place bids, and so on is developed in the text.

Several application programs are developed in their entirety in the different programming environments discussed in the text.[1] Other application programs are shown in part in the text, and the corresponding complete applications are available for download from the publisher's web site.

---

1. The programs and applications presented in this book have been included for their instructional value. They have been tested with care but are not guaranteed for any particular purpose. The publisher does not offer any warranties or representations, nor does it accept any liabilities with respect to the programs or applications.

## Book Use

This book is suitable as a supplemental text for an introductory database course that covers the relational model and uses Oracle as the database system for the course projects and assignments. Course projects can be developed using Embedded SQL in C or C++, JDBC or SQLJ. Web projects can be developed using the PL/SQL Web Toolkit, PL/SQL Server Pages, Java Servlets, or Java Server Pages. An entire chapter is devoted to suggestions for course projects. These course projects are typically assigned in introductory database courses where a team of students start with a problem statement, write the problem specifications, design the database, create the database in Oracle, and write application programs that access the database. Some of the chapters also have review problems for readers to go over to consolidate their understanding of the concepts presented in these chapters.

This book is also appropriate for nonacademic individuals interested in learning about Oracle. They can find materials on SQL, PL/SQL, PL/SQL Web Toolkit, PL/SQL Server Pages, Pro*C/C++, JDBC, Java Servlets, Java Server Pages, SQLJ, and XML all in one text. This book can be considered a starting point in the exploration of what Oracle has to offer.

## Supplements

The supplements for this book can be found at the following URL:

http://www.aw.com

Please follow the link to Supplements Central. These supplements include:

- Pro*C/C++ chapter that will not be in the book.
- All the code to the three running examples in the book (Grade Book, Mail Order, and Portfolio Database). In the book, there are mostly code fragments.
- All the code to a couple of other projects to be assigned as exam/homework /quizzes.
- Solutions to end-of-chapter exercises.

All of the code to a couple of other projects and solutions to end-of-chapter exercises are available online for qualified instructors. Please contact your Addison-Wesley representative for information.

# Acknowledgments

First of all, I would like to acknowledge Maite Suarez-Rivas, Katherine Harutunian, and Jeffrey Holcomb at Addison-Wesley for working with me closely and diligently to get this book out in time. The staff at Addison-Wesley is always a pleasure to work with. The reviewers for the Oracle8 edition, Akira Kawaguchi (City College of New York), Louis Mazzucco (SUNY Cobleskill), Mark Barnard (Marquette University), Willie Favero (Professional) and Ashesh Parekh (Professional) deserve special mention, as they made very useful and critical observations to improve the presentation and content of this book.

Special thanks also go out to Laurian Chirica at CalPoly, San Luis Obispo; James Geller, New Jersey Institute of Technology; Chad Peiper, University of Illinois at Urbana-Champaign; Bina Ramamurthy, Suny at Buffalo; Ahmet Ugur, Central Michigan University; and X. Sean Wang, George Mason University, for providing useful criticism in the newer chapters in the current Oracle9*i* edition.

I would also like to acknowledge all my students who have diligently worked on various projects using Oracle over the past several years at Wichita State University and Georgia State University. In particular, I would like to acknowledge the effort put forth by Krissy Echols, Veena Pujari and Radhika Venkataraman, in designing and implementing the investment portfolio database application discussed in the SQLJ chapter and to Radhika Venkataraman in particular for her effort in designing and implementing the Web Shopping application discussed in the Java Servlets chapter. I would also like to express my appreciation to my colleague, Erdogan Dogdu, for helping me with the PSP and JSP sections.

Finally, I would like to acknowledge the support my family has shown to me during the writing of this edition of the book. Thank you, Radhu, for all the hard work and understanding and thanks, Nannu and Nammi, for your excellent cooperation and constant encouragement during the writing of this book.

# CONTENTS

# CHAPTER 1

# The Relational Data Model

The relational data model presents a logical view of a database in which the user perceives the data to be organized in tabular form. This is a simple and intuitive view of data that hides all the complex details of how the data are actually stored and accessed within a computer. Moreover, over the years, very sophisticated and efficient structures and algorithms have been developed to implement database systems based on the relational model. As a result, relational databases are being used overwhelmingly in the industry and anywhere else there is a need to manage large amounts of data.

In this chapter, the basic concepts and foundations of the relational data model are presented. The chapter also presents three sample relational databases that will be used throughout this book.

## 1.1 The Relational Database

The relational data model has a strong mathematical foundation based on set theory. We thus begin here a brief mathematical definition of a relational database.

A *relation scheme* is a finite sequence of unique attribute names. For example,

```
EMPLOYEES = (EMPID, ENAME, ADDRESS, SALARY)
```

is a relation scheme with four attribute names.

Each attribute name, `A`, is associated with a *domain*, dom(`A`), a set of values. This domain includes a special value called `null`. For example, dom(`EMPID`) could be the set of all possible integers between 1000 and 9999 and the special `null` value.

Given a relation scheme R = A1, . . . , An, a *relation* r on the scheme R is defined as any finite subset of the Cartesian product

dom(A1) × · · · × dom(An)

Assuming appropriate domains for the EMPLOYEES relation scheme, a sample relation under this scheme could be

```
{ (1111,'Jones','111 Ash St.',20000),
  (2222,'Smith','123 Elm St.',25000),
  (3333,'Brown','234 Oak St.',30000) }
```

Each of the elements of a relation is also referred to as a *tuple*.

A *relational database scheme*, D, is a finite set of relation schemes:

{R1, . . . , Rm}

A *relational database* on scheme D is a set of relations:

{r1, . . . , rm}

where each ri is a relation on the corresponding scheme Ri.

## 1.2 Integrity Constraints

In addition to the data content, a relational database consists of *integrity constraints*, a set of conditions that must be met or satisfied by the data content at all times. The relational database is referred to as a *valid* database if its data content satisfies all the integrity constraints specified in its definition. Individual relations are referred to as *valid* if they satisfy all the constraints imposed on them. Three basic and important types of constraints are discussed here.

### Primary Key

A *super key* for a relation scheme R is any subset K of R that satisfies the property that in every valid relation under the scheme R, it is not possible to have two different tuples with the same values under K. A *candidate key* for R is any *super* key for R such that none of its proper subsets is also a super key. In all cases, a relation scheme must have at least one candidate key. The *primary key* for a relation scheme R is one of the candidate keys chosen by the designer of the database. For the EMPLOYEES relation scheme, the EMPID attribute by itself is the primary key. It is not always the case that the primary key is a singleton. In many situations, the primary key consists of more than one attribute. The primary key attributes are required to satisfy the **not null** constraint—i.e., that no tuple can have a **null** value under the primary key attributes. This property of primary keys is often referred to as the *entity integrity rule*.

## *Referential Integrity Constraint—Foreign Key*

The *referential integrity constraint* is a condition that is specified across two relations. During the design of a relational database, the designer may create a relation scheme R that includes the primary key attributes, K, of another relation scheme, say S. In such a situation, the referential integrity constraint specifies the condition that the values that appear under the attributes K in any valid relation under scheme R *must* also appear in the relation under scheme S. The attributes K, in scheme R collectively are referred to as a *foreign key* in scheme R. Unlike the primary key attributes, the foreign key attributes do not have to satisfy the **not null** constraint.

As an example, consider the EMPLOYEES relation scheme and the two additional relation schemes:

```
PROJECTS = (PROJID,PROJNAME,LOCATION)
WORKSIN = (EID,PROJID,HOURS)
```

The PROJECTS relation scheme presents information about different projects, and the WORKSIN relation scheme presents information about which employees work for which projects and how many hours they work. It is clear that the primary key for PROJECTS is the lone attribute PROJID. The primary key for the WORKSIN relation scheme, which represents a relationship between EMPLOYEES and PROJECTS, is the combination of the EMPID and PROJID attributes. We can assume that a single employee can work for multiple projects and that a project certainly can have many employees. The relation scheme WORKSIN includes primary key attributes from the EMPLOYEES and PROJECTS relation schemes. The referential integrity constraint in this situation dictates that if an EMPID value is present in a valid relation under the WORKSIN scheme, then the same value must also be present in the relation under the EMPLOYEES scheme. In a similar manner, a PROJID value in a valid relation under the WORKSIN scheme must also be present in the relation under the PROJECTS scheme.

## Not Null *Constraint*

This constraint specifies the condition that tuple values under certain attributes (specified to be **not null**) cannot be **null**. This condition is almost always imposed on the primary key attributes.[1] Other attributes may also be constrained to be **not null** if the need arises. In the EMPLOYEES relation scheme, the attributes EMPID and ENAME are likely candidates on which the **not null** constraint should be imposed.

1. In Oracle, primary key attributes are automatically constrained to be **not null**.

## 1.3 Tabular View of a Relation

A relation, as defined earlier, can also be informally viewed as a table made up of rows and columns. The columns are labeled with the attribute names of the relation scheme, and the rows correspond to individual tuples of the relation. For example, the sample relation under the **EMPLOYEES** relation scheme can be arranged in a tabular format:

| EMPID | ENAME | ADDRESS | SALARY |
|---|---|---|---|
| 1111 | Jones | 111 Ash St. | 20000 |
| 2222 | Smith | 123 Elm St. | 25000 |
| 3333 | Brown | 234 Oak St. | 30000 |

The four columns are labeled with the attribute names in the relation scheme, and the three rows correspond to the three tuples in the relation. Since the relation scheme and the tuples are defined to be sequences, it is important that the order of the components within a row correspond with the column names.

## 1.4 Sample Databases

Three databases are described in this section. The first represents information that is typically recorded in the grade books of university instructors. The second represents information that is usually maintained in the records of mail-order companies. The third represents information that is ordinarily kept in an investment portfolio tracking system.

### *Grade Book Database*

The grade book database consists of the relations defined in the six schemes shown in Figure 1.1.

- The **CATALOG** relation contains information about course numbers and titles of courses taught by a particular instructor. **CNO** is the primary key for the **CATALOG** relation.
- The **STUDENTS** relation contains information about the students of a particular instructor. The **SID** attribute is the primary key for the **STUDENTS** relation.
- The **COURSES** relation contains information about the various courses that have been taught by a particular instructor. The **TERM** attribute corresponds to the

**Figure 1.1** Grade book database schemes.

```
CATALOG(CNO,CTITLE)
STUDENTS(SID,FNAME,LNAME,MINIT)
COURSES(TERM,LINENO,CNO,A,B,C,D)
COMPONENTS(TERM,LINENO,COMPNAME,MAXPOINTS,WEIGHT)
ENROLLS(SID,TERM,LINENO)
SCORES(SID,TERM,LINENO,COMPNAME,POINTS)
```

term (such as Fall 97 or Spring 98) in which the course was taught; the `LINENO` is a unique section number assigned by the registrar of the university within a term. The combination of `TERM` and `LINENO` is the primary key for this relation. The `CNO` attribute is a foreign key in this relation, as it appears as a primary key in `CATALOG`. `A`, `B`, `C`, and `D` are attributes that represent numerical values that correspond with each letter grade (for example, `A = 90`, `B = 80`, `C = 70`, `D = 60`).

- The `COMPONENTS` relation contains information about the various grading components (such as homework, quizzes, and exams) for a particular course taught by the instructor. For each course taught, identified by the attributes `TERM` and `LINENO`, this relation records the name of the grading component, the maximum points assigned to this component, and the weight of this component relative to the other components. Since each course may have multiple components, the combination of the attributes `TERM`, `LINENO`, and `COMPNAME` forms the primary key. Since the combination of `TERM` and `LINENO` appearing in this relation is a primary key for the `COURSES` relation, it is classified as a foreign key.
- The `ENROLLS` relation records information about which student was enrolled in which course taught by the instructor. The combination of all three attributes (`SID`, `TERM`, and `LINENO`) forms the primary key. There are two foreign keys in this relation: `SID`, referring to the `STUDENTS` relation, and the combination of `TERM` and `LINENO`, referring to the `COURSES` relation.
- The `SCORES` relation records the grading component scores (or points) for each student enrolled in a course. The combination of the attributes `SID`, `TERM`, `LINENO`, and `COMPNAME` forms the primary key for this relation. There are two foreign keys in this relation: the combination of `SID`, `TERM`, and `LINENO`, referring to the `ENROLLS` relation; and the combination of the attributes `TERM`, `LINENO`, and `COMPNAME`, referring to the `COMPONENTS` relation.

A sample from a grade book database is shown in Figure 1.2.

**Figure 1.2** A sample from a grade book database.

*Catalog*

| CNO | CTITLE |
|---|---|
| csc226 | Introduction to Programming I |
| csc227 | Introduction to Programming II |
| csc343 | Assembly Programming |
| csc481 | Automata and Formal Languages |
| csc498 | Introduction to Database Systems |
| csc880 | Deductive Databases and Logic Programming |

*Students*

| SID | FNAME | LNAME | MINIT |
|---|---|---|---|
| 1111 | Nandita | Rajshekhar | K |
| 2222 | Sydney | Corn | A |
| 3333 | Susan | Williams | B |
| 4444 | Naveen | Rajshekhar | B |
| 5555 | Elad | Yam | G |
| 6666 | Lincoln | Herring | F |

*Courses*

| TERM | LINENO | CNO | A | B | C | D |
|---|---|---|---|---|---|---|
| f96 | 1031 | csc226 | 90 | 80 | 65 | 50 |
| f96 | 1032 | csc226 | 90 | 80 | 65 | 50 |
| sp97 | 1031 | csc227 | 90 | 80 | 65 | 50 |

*Components*

| TERM | LINENO | COMPNAME | MAXPOINTS | WEIGHT |
|---|---|---|---|---|
| f96 | 1031 | exam1 | 100 | 30 |
| f96 | 1031 | quizzes | 80 | 20 |
| f96 | 1031 | final | 100 | 50 |
| f96 | 1032 | programs | 400 | 40 |
| f96 | 1032 | midterm | 100 | 20 |
| f96 | 1032 | final | 100 | 40 |
| sp97 | 1031 | paper | 100 | 50 |
| sp97 | 1031 | project | 100 | 50 |

**Figure 1.2** —Continued

*Enrolls*

| SID | TERM | LINENO |
|---|---|---|
| 1111 | f96 | 1031 |
| 2222 | f96 | 1031 |
| 4444 | f96 | 1031 |
| 1111 | f96 | 1032 |
| 2222 | f96 | 1032 |
| 3333 | f96 | 1032 |
| 5555 | sp97 | 1031 |
| 6666 | sp97 | 1031 |

*Scores*

| SID | TERM | LINENO | COMPNAME | POINTS |
|---|---|---|---|---|
| 1111 | f96 | 1031 | exam1 | 90 |
| 1111 | f96 | 1031 | quizzes | 75 |
| 1111 | f96 | 1031 | final | 95 |
| 2222 | f96 | 1031 | exam1 | 70 |
| 2222 | f96 | 1031 | quizzes | 40 |
| 2222 | f96 | 1031 | final | 82 |
| 4444 | f96 | 1031 | exam1 | 83 |
| 4444 | f96 | 1031 | quizzes | 71 |
| 4444 | f96 | 1031 | final | 74 |
| 1111 | f96 | 1032 | programs | 400 |
| 1111 | f96 | 1032 | midterm | 95 |
| 1111 | f96 | 1032 | final | 99 |
| 2222 | f96 | 1032 | programs | 340 |
| 2222 | f96 | 1032 | midterm | 65 |
| 2222 | f96 | 1032 | final | 95 |
| 3333 | f96 | 1032 | programs | 380 |
| 3333 | f96 | 1032 | midterm | 75 |
| 3333 | f96 | 1032 | final | 88 |
| 5555 | sp97 | 1031 | paper | 80 |
| 5555 | sp97 | 1031 | project | 90 |
| 6666 | sp97 | 1031 | paper | 80 |
| 6666 | sp97 | 1031 | project | 85 |

## *Mail-Order Database*

The mail-order database consists of the relations defined in the six schemes shown in Figure 1.3.

**Figure 1.3** Mail-order database schemes.

```
EMPLOYEES(ENO,ENAME,ZIP,HDATE)
PARTS(PNO,PNAME,QOH,PRICE,LEVEL)
CUSTOMERS(CNO,CNAME,STREET,ZIP,PHONE)
ORDERS(ONO,CNO,ENO,RECEIVED,SHIPPED)
ODETAILS(ONO,PNO,QTY)
ZIPCODES(ZIP,CITY)
```

- The `EMPLOYEES` relation contains information about the employees of the company. The `ENO` attribute is the primary key. The `ZIP` attribute is a foreign key referring to the `ZIPCODES` table.
- The `PARTS` relation keeps a record of the inventory of the company. The record for each part includes its number and name as well as the quantity on hand, the unit price, and the reorder level. `PNO` is the primary key for this relation.
- The `CUSTOMERS` relation contains information about the customers of the mail-order company. Each customer is assigned a customer number, `CNO`, which serves as the primary key. The `ZIP` attribute is a foreign key referring to the `ZIPCODES` relation.
- The `ORDERS` relation contains information about the orders placed by customers, the employees who took the orders, and the dates the orders were received and shipped. `ONO` is the primary key. The `CNO` attribute is a foreign key referring to the `CUSTOMERS` relation, and the `ENO` attribute is a foreign key referring to the `EMPLOYEES` table.
- The `ODETAILS` relation contains information about the various parts ordered by the customer within a particular order. The combination of the `ONO` and `PNO` attributes forms the primary key. The `ONO` attribute is a foreign key referring to the `ORDERS` relation, and the `PNO` attribute is a foreign key referring to the `PARTS` relation.
- The `ZIPCODES` relation maintains information about the zip codes for various cities. `ZIP` is the primary key.

  A sample from a mail-order database is shown in Figure 1.4.

**Figure 1.4** A sample from a mail-order database.

*Employees*

| ENO | ENAME | ZIP | HDATE |
|---|---|---|---|
| 1000 | Jones | 67226 | 12-DEC-95 |
| 1001 | Smith | 60606 | 01-JAN-92 |
| 1002 | Brown | 50302 | 01-SEP-94 |

*Parts*

| PNO | PNAME | QOH | PRICE | LEVEL |
|---|---|---|---|---|
| 10506 | Land Before Time I | 200 | 19.99 | 20 |
| 10507 | Land Before Time II | 156 | 19.99 | 20 |
| 10508 | Land Before Time III | 190 | 19.99 | 20 |
| 10509 | Land Before Time IV | 60 | 19.99 | 20 |
| 10601 | Sleeping Beauty | 300 | 24.99 | 20 |
| 10701 | When Harry Met Sally | 120 | 19.99 | 30 |
| 10800 | Dirty Harry | 140 | 14.99 | 30 |
| 10900 | Dr. Zhivago | 100 | 24.99 | 30 |

*Customers*

| CNO | CNAME | STREET | ZIP | PHONE |
|---|---|---|---|---|
| 1111 | Charles | 123 Main St. | 67226 | 316-636-5555 |
| 2222 | Bertram | 237 Ash Ave. | 67226 | 316-689-5555 |
| 3333 | Barbara | 111 Inwood St. | 60606 | 316-111-1234 |

*Orders*

| ONO | CNO | ENO | RECEIVED | SHIPPED |
|---|---|---|---|---|
| 1020 | 1111 | 1000 | 10-DEC-94 | 12-DEC-94 |
| 1021 | 1111 | 1000 | 12-JAN-95 | 15-JAN-95 |
| 1022 | 2222 | 1001 | 13-FEB-95 | 20-FEB-95 |
| 1023 | 3333 | 1000 | 20-JUN-97 | null |

*Odetails*

| ONO | PNO | QTY |
|---|---|---|
| 1020 | 10506 | 1 |
| 1020 | 10507 | 1 |
| 1020 | 10508 | 2 |
| 1020 | 10509 | 3 |
| 1021 | 10601 | 4 |
| 1022 | 10601 | 1 |
| 1022 | 10701 | 1 |
| 1023 | 10800 | 1 |
| 1023 | 10900 | 1 |

*Zip codes*

| ZIP | CITY |
|---|---|
| 67226 | Wichita |
| 60606 | Fort Dodge |
| 50302 | Kansas City |
| 54444 | Columbia |
| 66002 | Liberal |
| 61111 | Fort Hays |

## *Investment Portfolio Database*

The investment portfolio database consists of relations defined in the three schemes shown in Figure 1.5.

**Figure 1.5** Investment portfolio database schemes.

```
MEMBER(MID,PASSWORD,FNAME,LNAME,ADDRESS,EMAIL,BAL)
SECURITY(SYMBOL,CNAME,CURRENT,ASK,BID)
TRANSACTION(MID,SYMBOL,TDATE,TTYPE,QTY,PRICE,COMM,AMOUNT)
```

- The `MEMBER` table contains information about the members of the investment portfolio tracking system. `MID` is the primary key for the `MEMBER` table. The table includes other attributes, such as `PASSWORD`, used to sign in to the application program, and `BAL`, which contains the cash balance in the member's account. The members can buy shares of securities only if they have enough cash in their accounts to cover the cost of the shares.
- The `SECURITY` table contains information about the various securities available for the members to invest in. The attribute `SYMBOL`, the ticker symbol for the security, acts as its primary key. The table includes other attributes, such as `CNAME`, the company name, and `CURRENT`, `ASK`, and `BID`, the price per share of the most recent sale, the current asking price per share, and the current bidding price per share, respectively.
- The `TRANSACTION` table contains entries for every buy or sell transaction executed by a member. The table contains `MID` and `SYMBOL` attributes as foreign keys referring to the `MEMBER` and `SECURITY` tables, respectively. In addition to these, the table contains attributes for transaction date (`TDATE`), transaction type (`TTYPE`), number of shares (`QTY`), price per share of the security (`PRICE`), and commission (`COMM`). The transaction type is either `buy` or `sell`. The table also has a derived attribute, called `AMOUNT`, which is computed from the `QUANTITY`, `PRICE`, and `COMM` attribute values. The `COMM` attribute is assumed to be 1% of the total transaction amount. The `MID`, `SYMBOL`, and `TDATE` attributes combine to form the primary key for the table.

A sample from an investment portfolio database is shown in Figure 1.6.

**Figure 1.6** A sample from an investment portfolio database.

*Member*

| MID | PASSWORD | FNAME | LNAME |
|---|---|---|---|
| 10000 | 1111 | Quigon | Jinn |
| 10001 | 2222 | Obiwan | Kenobi |

*Member (continued)*

| MID | ADDRESS | EMAIL | BAL |
|---|---|---|---|
| 10000 | 12 Star Ave., Moon City, KS | qj@abc.com | 10000 |
| 10001 | 22 Star Ave., Moon City, KS | ok@abc.com | 20000 |

*Security*

| SYMBOL | CNAME | CURRENT | ASK | BID |
|---|---|---|---|---|
| AMZN | Amazon.com | 119.06 | 119.18 | 119.06 |
| EBAY | eBay Inc | 174.00 | 174.25 | 174.00 |
| KLM | KLM Royal Dutch Air | 29.93 | | |
| MSFT | Microsoft Corp | 78.50 | 78.56 | 78.50 |
| ORCL | Oracle Corp | 23.25 | 23.25 | 23.18 |
| SEG | Seagate Corp | 16.82 | 16.82 | 16.52 |

*Transaction*

| MID | SYMBOL | TDATE | TTYPE | QTY | PRICE |
|---|---|---|---|---|---|
| 10000 | ORCL | 20-MAY-99 | buy | 100 | 26.81 |
| 10000 | SEG | 20-MAY-99 | buy | 100 | 32.12 |
| 10000 | ORCL | 09-AUG-99 | buy | 50 | 30.00 |
| 10000 | ORCL | 14-AUG-99 | sell | 20 | 32.00 |

*Transaction (continued)*

| MID | SYMBOL | TDATE | COMM | AMOUNT |
|---|---|---|---|---|
| 10000 | ORCL | 20-MAY-99 | 26.81 | 2707.81 |
| 10000 | SEG | 20-MAY-99 | 32.12 | 3244.12 |
| 10000 | ORCL | 09-AUG-99 | 15.00 | 1515.00 |
| 10000 | ORCL | 14-AUG-99 | 15.00 | 625.00 |

## 1.5 Relational Algebra

*Relational algebra* is a set of algebraic operations that takes as input one (for unary operators) or two (for binary operators) relations and returns a relation as output. Using these operations, we can answer ad hoc queries about the content of any database. A good understanding of relational algebra makes the task of phrasing complex queries in Structured Query Language (SQL) much easier. The relational algebraic operators are briefly introduced here, and then some queries related to the sample databases are answered using these operations.

The relational operators are usually classified into two categories: set-theoretic operations and relation-theoretic operations.

### 1.5.1 Set-Theoretic Operations

The *set-theoretic operations* include *union, difference, intersection,* and *Cartesian product*. These operations are borrowed from mathematical set theory and are applicable in the relational model because relations are nothing but sets of tuples.

The union, difference, and intersection operators are binary operators that operate on two *union-compatible relations*—which means that they have the same number of attributes and that the domains of the corresponding attributes in the two relations are the same. Consider two relations $r$ and $s$ that are union compatible. The set-theoretic operations are defined as follows:

- *Union.* $r \cup s = \{t | t \in r \text{ or } t \in s\}$. In other words, the union of two union-compatible relations contains all the tuples from each of the relations.
- *Difference.* $r - s = \{t | t \in r \text{ and } t \notin s\}$. The difference between two union-compatible relations contains all those tuples in the first relation that are not present in the second relation.
- *Intersection.* $r \cap s = \{t | t \in r \text{ and } t \in s\}$. The intersection of two union-compatible relations contains all the tuples that are contained in both relations.
- *Cartesian product.* The Cartesian product is a binary operator that takes as input two relations ($r$ and $s$ on any scheme) and produces a relation on the scheme that is the concatenation of the relation schemes of the input relations. The tuples in the Cartesian product are constructed by concatenating each tuple in the first input relation with each tuple in the second input relation. Formally, the definition is

  $$r \times s = \{t1.t2 | t1 \in r \text{ and } t2 \in s\}$$

  where $t1.t2$ is the concatenation of tuples $t1$ and $t2$ to form a larger tuple.

Examples of the set-theoretic operations are shown in Figure 1.7.

Since the attribute names in a relation scheme must be unique, the scheme of the Cartesian product of relations $r$ and $s$ in the example contains attribute names prefixed by $r$. and $s$..

**Figure 1.7** Set-theoretic operations.

$r$

| A | B |
|---|---|
| a | b |
| a | c |
| b | d |

$s$

| A | B |
|---|---|
| a | c |
| a | e |

$r \cup s$

| A | B |
|---|---|
| a | b |
| a | c |
| b | d |
| a | e |

$r - s$

| A | B |
|---|---|
| a | b |
| b | d |

$r \cap s$

| A | B |
|---|---|
| a | c |

$r \times s$

| r.A | r.B | s.A | s.B |
|---|---|---|---|
| a | b | a | c |
| a | b | a | e |
| a | c | a | c |
| a | c | a | e |
| b | d | a | c |
| b | d | a | e |

### 1.5.2 Relation-Theoretic Operations

The relation-theoretic operations include *rename*, *select*, *project*, *natural join*, and *division*, among others.

- *Rename*. The rename operator takes as input a relation and returns the same relation as output, but under a different name. This operation is useful and necessary for queries that need to refer to the same relation more than once.

The symbolic notation for the rename operator is $\rho_s(r)$, where $r$ is the input relation and $s$ is the new name.

- *Select.* The select operator acts as a horizontal filter for relations. Given a selection condition, the select operator produces an output relation that consists of only those tuples from the input relation that satisfy the selection condition. Symbolically, the select operator is written as $\sigma_F(r)$, where $F$ is the selection criterion and $r$ is the input relation. Formally, the select operator is defined as follows:

$$\sigma_F(r) = \{t \mid t \in r \text{ and } t \text{ satisfies } F\}$$

- *Project.* The project operator acts as a vertical filter for relations. Given a sublist of attribute names of a relation, the project operator keeps only those values that correspond to the sublist of attribute names and discards other values in tuples. Symbolically, the project operator is written as $\pi_A(r)$, where $A$ is a sublist of the attributes of $r$. Formally, the project operator is defined as follows:

$$\pi_A(r) = \{t[A] \mid t \in r\}$$

where $t[A]$ is a tuple constructed from $t$ by keeping the values that correspond to the attributes in $A$ and discarding other values.

- *Natural join.* The natural join operator takes as input two relations and produces as output a relation whose scheme is the concatenation of the two schemes of the input relations with any duplicate attribute names discarded. A tuple in the first input relation is said to *match* a tuple in the second input relation if both have the same values under the common attributes. The tuples in the natural join are constructed by concatenating each tuple in the first input relation with each *matching* tuple in the second input relation and discarding the values under the common attributes of the second relation. Symbolically, the natural join is written as $r \bowtie s$, where $r$ is a relation on scheme $R$ and $s$ is a relation on scheme $S$. Formally, the natural join operation is defined as follows:

$$r \bowtie s = \{t \mid (\exists u \in r)(\exists v \in s)(t[R] = u \text{ and } t[S] = v)\}$$

- *Division.* The division operator takes as input two relations, called the *dividend relation* ($r$ on scheme $R$) and the *divisor relation* ($s$ on scheme $S$), such that all the attributes in $S$ also appear in $R$ and $s$ is not empty. The output of the division operation is a relation on scheme $R$ with all the attributes common with $S$ discarded. A tuple $t$ is put in the output of the operation if, for all tuples $u$ in $s$, the tuple $tu$ is in $r$, where $tu$ is a tuple constructed from $t$ and $u$ by combining the individual values in these tuples in the proper order to form a tuple in $r$. Symbolically, the division operation is written as $r \div s$ and is defined as follows:

$$r \div s = \{t \mid (\forall u \in s)(tu \in r)\}$$

Examples of the relation-theoretic operations are shown in Figure 1.8.

**Figure 1.8** Relation-theoretic operations.

$r$

| A | C | D |
|---|---|---|
| a | c | d |
| a | e | f |
| a | g | h |
| b | c | d |
| b | g | h |
| c | c | d |
| c | e | f |

$s$

| C | D |
|---|---|
| c | d |
| e | f |

$t$

| B | C | D |
|---|---|---|
| b | c | d |
| b | e | f |

$\sigma_{A='b' \text{ or } C='c'}(r)$

| A | C | D |
|---|---|---|
| a | c | d |
| b | c | d |
| b | g | h |
| c | c | d |

$\pi_A(r)$

| A |
|---|
| a |
| b |
| c |

$r \bowtie t$

| A | C | D | B |
|---|---|---|---|
| a | c | d | b |
| a | e | f | b |
| b | c | d | b |
| c | c | d | b |
| c | e | f | b |

$r \div s$

| A |
|---|
| a |
| c |

Among the relational operators presented so far, there are six basic operators: union, difference, Cartesian product, rename, select, and project. This basic set of operations has the property that none of them can be expressed in terms of the others. The remaining operators presented—namely, intersection, natural join, and division—can be expressed in terms of the basic operators as follows:

- *Intersection.* $r \cap s = r - (r - s)$.

- *Natural join.* $r \bowtie s = \pi_{R \cap S}(\sigma_F(r \times s))$, where $F$ is a selection condition that indicates that the tuple values under the common attributes of $r$ and $s$ are equal.
- *Division.* $r \div s = \pi_{R-S}(r) - \pi_{R-S}((\pi_{R-S}(r) \times s) - r)$.

Even though relation schemes are defined as sequences, they are treated as sets in these equalities for simplicity.

An explanation for the equality for division is in order. First, all candidate tuples for the result are calculated by the expression

$$\pi_{R-S}(r)$$

Second, these candidate tuples are combined with all tuples of $s$ in the expression

$$\pi_{R-S}(r) \times s$$

to give a relation containing all combinations of candidate tuples with all tuples of $s$. Since we are looking for tuples under the scheme $R - S$ that combine with all tuples of $s$ and are also present in $r$, we see that if we subtract $r$ from the previous expression, we will get all the combinations of tuples that are "missing" in $r$. By projecting these tuples on $R - S$, we get all those tuples that should not go to the result in the following expression:

$$\pi_{R-S}((\pi_{R-S}(r) \times s) - r)$$

Finally, we subtract this set from the set of all candidate tuples and obtain the output relation of the division operator.

### 1.5.3 Queries in Relational Algebra

The following is a list of queries related to the three sample databases and the corresponding relational algebraic expressions that compute the answers to the queries. The relational algebraic expressions are broken up into smaller parts and are assigned to temporary variables. One could easily write one whole expression from these individual parts and thereby not require the assignment primitive (:= in the following).

#### *Grade Book Database Queries*

Query 1.1: Get the names of students enrolled in the Assembly Programming class in the f96 term.

$$
\begin{aligned}
t1 &:= \sigma_{CTITLE=\texttt{'Assembly Programming'}}(catalog)\\
t2 &:= \sigma_{TERM=\texttt{'f96'}}(courses)\\
t3 &:= t1 \bowtie t2 \bowtie enrolls \bowtie students\\
result &:= \pi_{FNAME,LNAME,MINIT}(t3)
\end{aligned}
$$

Query 1.2: Get the SID values of students who did not enroll in any class during the f96 term.

$$\pi_{SID}(students) - \pi_{SID}(\sigma_{TERM=\texttt{'f96'}}(enrolls))$$

Query 1.3: Get the SID values of students who have enrolled in csc226 and csc227.

$$
\begin{aligned}
t1 &:= \pi_{SID}(enrolls \bowtie \sigma_{CNO=\texttt{'csc226'}}(courses))\\
t2 &:= \pi_{SID}(enrolls \bowtie \sigma_{CNO=\texttt{'csc227'}}(courses))\\
result &:= t1 \cap t2
\end{aligned}
$$

Query 1.4: Get the SID values of students who have enrolled in csc226 or csc227.

$$
\begin{aligned}
t1 &:= \pi_{SID}(enrolls \bowtie \sigma_{CNO=\texttt{'csc226'}}(courses))\\
t2 &:= \pi_{SID}(enrolls \bowtie \sigma_{CNO=\texttt{'csc227'}}(courses))\\
result &:= t1 \cup t2
\end{aligned}
$$

Query 1.5: Get the SID values of students who have enrolled in *all* the courses in the catalog.

$$\pi_{SID,CNO}(courses \bowtie enrolls) \div \pi_{CNO}(catalog)$$

## *Mail-Order Database Queries*

Query 1.6: Get part names of parts that cost less than \$20.00.

$$\pi_{PNAME}(\sigma_{PRICE<20.00}(parts))$$

Query 1.7: Get pairs of CNO values of customers who have the same zip code.

$$
\begin{aligned}
t1 &:= \rho_{c1}(customers) \times \rho_{c2}(customers)\\
t2 &:= \sigma_{c1.ZIP=c2.ZIP \text{ and } c1.CNO<c2.CNO}(t1)\\
result &:= \pi_{c1.CNO,c2.CNO}(t2)
\end{aligned}
$$

Query 1.8: Get the names of customers who have ordered parts from employees living in Wichita.

$$
\begin{aligned}
t1 &:= \pi_{ENO}(employees \bowtie \sigma_{CITY=\texttt{'Wichita'}}(zip\ codes))\\
result &:= \pi_{CNAME}(customers \bowtie orders \bowtie t1)
\end{aligned}
$$

Query 1.9: Get CNO values of customers who have ordered parts only from employees living in Wichita.

$$t1 := \pi_{ENO}(employees \bowtie \sigma_{CITY \neq \texttt{'Wichita'}}(zip\ codes))$$
$$result := \pi_{CNO}(orders) - \pi_{CNO}(orders \bowtie t1)$$

Query 1.10: Get CNO values of customers who have ordered parts from all employees living in Wichita.

$$t1 := \pi_{ENO}(employees \bowtie \sigma_{CITY = \texttt{'Wichita'}}(zip\ codes))$$
$$result := \pi_{CNO,ENO}(orders) \div t1$$

## *Investment Portfolio Database Queries*

Query 1.11: Get company names of each security whose current price is greater than $100.00.

$$\Pi_{CNAME}(\sigma_{CURRENT>100.00}(security))$$

Query 1.12: Get names of members who have purchased ORCL shares.

$$\Pi_{FNAME,LNAME}(member \bowtie \sigma_{SYMBOL=\texttt{'ORCL'}\ \text{and}\ TTYPE=\texttt{'buy'}}(transaction))$$

Query 1.13: Get names of members who have purchased ORCL shares but not SYBS shares.

$$t1 := \Pi_{MID}(\sigma_{SYMBOL=\texttt{'ORCL'}\ \text{and}\ TTYPE=\texttt{'buy'}}(transaction))$$
$$t2 := \Pi_{MID}(\sigma_{SYMBOL=\texttt{'SYBS'}\ \text{and}\ TTYPE=\texttt{'buy'}}(transaction))$$
$$result := \Pi_{FNAME,LNAME}((t1 - t2) \bowtie member)$$

Query 1.14: Get names of members who have purchased *only* ORCL shares.

$$t1 := \Pi_{MID}(\sigma_{TTYPE=\texttt{'buy'}}(transaction))$$
$$t2 := \Pi_{MID}(\sigma_{SYMBOL<>\texttt{'ORCL'}\ \text{and}\ TTYPE=\texttt{'buy'}}(transaction))$$
$$result := \Pi_{FNAME,LNAME}((t1 - t2) \bowtie member)$$

Query 1.15: Get company names of securities whose shares have been purchased by *all* members.

$$t1 := \Pi_{MID,SYMBOL}(\sigma_{TTYPE=\texttt{'buy'}}(transaction))$$
$$t2 := \Pi_{MID}(member)$$
$$result := \Pi_{CNAME}(security \bowtie (t1 \div t2))$$

# CHAPTER 2

# Oracle SQL

Oracle SQL is a powerful implementation of the SQL-92 standard Structured Query Language, a universal language that can be used to define, query, update, and manage a relational database. This chapter introduces Oracle SQL and its syntax and semantics along with numerous illustrative examples. Topics covered in this chapter include Oracle SQL*Plus, Oracle SQL, the Oracle data dictionary, and Oracle9*i* objects. SQL*Plus is Oracle's interactive interface to the database server. SQL statements can be issued at the `SQL>` prompt, and files containing SQL statements can be executed from within SQL*Plus. Oracle SQL topics discussed in this chapter include creating, dropping, and altering tables; creating and dropping views; querying the database using the `select` statement; and modifying the database using the `insert`, `delete`, and `update` statements. Chapter 2 also introduces Oracle9*i* objects and covers SQL statements to access and manipulate these objects.

## 2.1 Oracle SQL*Plus

Oracle's SQL*Plus program provides a convenient interactive environment with the Oracle database server. The user may type the commands directly at the `SQL>` prompt or have SQL*Plus execute commands residing in operating system files.

### 2.1.1 Entering and Exiting SQL*Plus

To enter the SQL*Plus environment, the `sqlplus` program should be executed in one of the following three ways, where `<userid>` is the Oracle user identification and `<password>` is the associated password:

- `sqlplus <userid>/<password>`
- `sqlplus <userid>`
- `sqlplus`

The Oracle **userid** and **password** are different from the **userid** and **password** required to get access to the operating system. If the **sqlplus** program is invoked with only **<userid>**, the program prompts the user for the password; if it is invoked without any parameters, the program prompts for the **userid** and **password**.

To exit the SQL*Plus environment, the **exit** command must be entered at the **SQL>** prompt.

## 2.1.2 Executing Commands in SQL*Plus

Once the user is within the SQL*Plus environment, the system will usually display the prompt **SQL>** and wait for user commands. The user may enter three kinds of commands:

- SQL statements, to access the database
- PL/SQL blocks, also to access the database
- SQL*Plus commands, for editing and storing SQL statements and PL/SQL blocks, setting options, and formatting query results

SQL statements can be entered at the **SQL>** prompt. A statement may be broken into multiple lines. SQL*Plus displays a line number (starting at 2) after the user presses the **RETURN** key to go to the next line. The SQL statement may be terminated in one of three ways:

- With a semicolon, indicating to SQL*Plus that it should execute the statement immediately.
- With a slash (/) on a line by itself, also indicating to SQL*Plus that it should execute the statement.
- With a blank line, indicating that SQL*Plus should not do anything with the statement. The statement is stored in a buffer and can be executed at a later stage.

The following is a screen capture of an SQL statement executed in SQL*Plus:

```
SQL> select pno,pname,price
  2  from parts;
```

```
       PNO PNAME                               PRICE
---------- ------------------------------ ----------
     10506 Land Before Time I                  19.99
     10507 Land Before Time II                 19.99
     10508 Land Before Time III                19.99
     10509 Land Before Time IV                 19.99
     10601 Sleeping Beauty                     24.99
     10701 When Harry Met Sally                19.99
     10800 Dirty Harry                         14.99
     10900 Dr. Zhivago                         24.99

8 rows selected
```

You can also enter PL/SQL anonymous blocks at the **SQL>** prompt for execution and issue statements such as **create function** and **create procedure** at the **SQL>** prompt to create PL/SQL stored objects. The details of working with PL/SQL within SQL*Plus are given in Chapter 4.

Besides SQL and PL/SQL, users can also enter SQL*Plus commands at the **SQL>** prompt. These commands can manipulate SQL commands and PL/SQL blocks, format and print query results, and set various options for SQL*Plus. SQL*Plus commands must be entered in one line. If the command is long, it may be continued to the next line by typing the hyphen symbol (-) at the end of the line before pressing the **RETURN** key. Here is an example of an SQL*Plus command that formats a column of the SQL query:

```
SQL> column price format -
> $99.99 heading "Sale Price"
SQL> run
  1  select pno,pname,price
  2* from parts

       PNO PNAME                          Sale Price
---------- ------------------------------ ----------
     10506 Land Before Time I                 $19.99
     10507 Land Before Time II                $19.99
     10508 Land Before Time III               $19.99
     10509 Land Before Time IV                $19.99
     10601 Sleeping Beauty                    $24.99
     10701 When Harry Met Sally               $19.99
```

```
10800 Dirty Harry                                $14.99
10900 Dr. Zhivago                                $24.99

8 rows selected
```

The `column` command formats a particular column in the current query (in this case, the column is formatted and given a different name for display purposes). SQL*Plus commands need not be terminated with a semicolon.

The following are a few of the more commonly used SQL*Plus commands:

- `describe`. Lists the column definitions for a database table. The following is an example of the `describe` command:

```
SQL> describe customers
 Name                     Null?    Type
 --------------------- -------- ------------
 CNO                      NOT NULL NUMBER(5)
 CNAME                             VARCHAR2(30)
 STREET                            VARCHAR2(30)
 ZIP                               NUMBER(5)
 PHONE                             CHAR(12)
```

- `execute`. Executes a single PL/SQL statement. The syntax is

```
SQL> execute statement
```

  PL/SQL statements are covered in Chapter 3.

- `help`. Gets online help for SQL*Plus commands. For example,

```
SQL> help column
```

  will list the description of the `column` command. To get a list of all commands, use the following command:

```
SQL> help commands
```

- `host`. Executes a host operating system command without leaving SQL*Plus. For example,

```
SQL> host ls *.sql
```

  will list all the files in the current directory with an `.sql` extension. The exclamation key (`!`) may be used instead of the `host` command to achieve the same effect. If the `host` command is entered without a parameter, an operating system shell is entered. The user may manipulate operating system files or perform any operating system–related activity and return to the SQL*Plus session by logging out of the shell (usually by pressing `CONTROL-D`). This is a particularly useful command when working with a file containing a large collection of statements that are to be executed. You can go back and forth between the operating system shell and SQL*Plus to edit the file and execute the file repeatedly.

- `remark`. Used for comments. Any line beginning with the keyword `remark` or `rem` or two hyphens (`--`) is treated as a comment and is ignored by SQL*Plus.
- `run`. Executes the SQL statement present in the buffer. The `run` command works the same as the slash command, except that it also displays the buffer contents before executing the statement in the buffer.
- `set`. Sets SQL*Plus system variables. Some of the more useful system variables include

```
SQL> set pause on
SQL> set autoCommit on
SQL> set echo on
```

  Setting `pause` to `on` causes SQL*Plus to pause at the beginning of each page. The user must press `RETURN` to see the next page. Setting `autoCommit` to `on` informs Oracle to commit any changes to the database immediately after the SQL statement that has caused the changes is executed. Setting `echo` to `on` causes SQL*Plus to list each of the commands in a file when the file is run with the `start` command. The names of other system variables, along with explanations, can be obtained by using `help` on the `set` command.

- `spool`. Stores the query results in an operating system file. The syntax of the command is

```
SQL> spool filename
```

  To disable spooling to file, use

```
SQL> spool off
```

- `start`. Executes commands stored in an operating system file. This is a useful command and is preferable to entering commands directly on the `SQL>` prompt. If a file called `comm.sql` contains several statements/commands, these can be executed by using the `start` command as follows:

```
SQL> start comm
```

  The file extension `.sql` need not be specified.

Some of the remaining SQL*Plus commands are discussed next.

## 2.1.3 Buffer Manipulation Commands

The most recent command that is entered on the SQL prompt is stored in the SQL*Plus buffer. It is possible to access, change, append to, and save the contents of this buffer. The SQL*Plus buffer editing commands are listed in Figure 2.1. All the editing commands (except for the `list` command) affect only one line, the current line. To make a particular line the current line, simply list that line by typing the line number. The following SQL*Plus session illustrates some of the editing commands:

```
SQL> select cno,canme
  2  from customers
  3  where cno > 2000;
select cno,canme
          *
ERROR at line 1:
ORA-00904: invalid column name
SQL> 1
  1* select cno,canme
SQL> change /can/cna
  1* select cno,cname
```

**Figure 2.1** SQL*Plus buffer editing commands.

| Command | Abbreviation | Explanation |
|---|---|---|
| `append` *text* | `a` *text* | Add *text* to the end of a line. |
| `change` */old/new* | `c` */old/new* | Change *old* to *new* in a line. |
| `change` */text* | `c` */text* | Delete *text* from a line. |
| `clear buffer` | `cl buff` | Delete all lines. |
| `del` | | Delete a line. |
| `get` *file* | | Load contents of file named *file* into buffer. |
| `input` | `i` | Add one or more lines. |
| `input` *text* | `i` *text* | Add a line consisting of *text*. |
| `list` | `l` | List all lines in buffer. |
| `list` *n* | `l` *n* or *n* | List one line and make it the current line. |
| `list *` | `l *` | List the current line. |
| `list last` | `l last` | List the last line. |
| `list` *m n* | `l` *m n* | List lines *m* through *n*. |
| `save` *file* | `sav` *file* | Save contents of buffer to file named *file*. |

```
SQL> list
  1  select cno,cname
  2  from customers
  3* where cno > 2000
SQL> /

       CNO CNAME
---------- ------------------------------
      2222 Bertram
      3333 Barbara

SQL> clear buffer
buffer cleared
SQL> input
  1  select eno,ename
  2  from employees
  3
SQL> /

       ENO ENAME
---------- ------------------------------
      1000 Jones
      1001 Smith
      1002 Brown

SQL> 1
  1* select eno,ename
SQL> append ,zip
  1* select eno,ename,zip

SQL> /

       ENO ENAME                       ZIP
---------- -------------------- ----------
      1000 Jones                     67226
      1001 Smith                     60606
      1002 Brown                     50302
```

The buffer contents can also be edited by using the command

```
SQL> edit
```

The `edit` command invokes a default operating system editor and loads the buffer contents into that editor. After editing, the buffer contents can be saved. Upon exiting the editor, control returns to the SQL*Plus program, which sees the new buffer. The default editor can be changed to `vi` or any other editor by issuing a command like this:

```
SQL> define _editor = vi
```

### 2.1.4 Formatting Query Results

SQL*Plus provides commands to format query results that will produce a finished report.

The `column` command can be used to change the column heading and to reformat column data in a query. The syntax is

```
column <column-name> heading <column-heading>
  format <format-model>
```

Some examples of the `column` command are

```
column sid heading "Student ID" format 99999
column lname heading "Last Name" format A15
column price format $9,99.99
```

When the `order by` clause is used in the query to display the results in some sorted order, the `break` command can be used to create subsets of rows in the result, each of which corresponds to a particular value of the sort column. Space can be added after each subset of rows using the `skip` clause within this command. The `compute` command can be used to display summary information for each of the subsets of rows of the results.

The `ttitle` and `btitle` commands can be used to print titles on the top and bottom of each page.

These query formatting commands are illustrated in the example that follows.[1] The command file creates a report of grades for students in the Fall 1996 term of the course with line number 1031.

```
spool report.dat
clear columns
clear breaks
clear computes
set headsep !
```

1. The online help section for each of these commands provides additional information about them.

```
ttitle 'Student Report!Fall 1996!CSc 226'
btitle 'Report prepared by R. Sunderraman'

column sid heading 'SID' format a5 word_wrapped
column lname heading 'Last Name' format a12 word_wrapped
column fname heading 'First Name' format a10 word_wrapped
column compname heading 'Component' -
       format a10 word_wrapped
column points heading 'Points' format 9990

break on sid skip 2 on lname on fname
compute sum of points on sid

set linesize 79
set pagesize 50
set newpage 0

select E.sid, S.lname, S.fname, C.compname, T.points
from   enrolls E, students S, components C, scores T
where  S.sid = T.sid and
       S.sid = E.sid and
       E.term = C.term and
       E.lineno = C.lineno and
       E.term = T.term and
       E.lineno = T.lineno and
       C.compname = T.compname and
       E.term = 'F96' and
       E.lineno = 1031;
spool off
```

The report generated is shown in Figure 2.2.

### 2.1.5 Screen Capture of an SQL*Plus Session

This section presents a simple way to capture the screen of an SQL*Plus session involving execution of several SQL queries. The following command file containing SQL queries, when executed within SQL*Plus, will capture the SQL*Plus session in the file `capture.dat`:

**Figure 2.2** SQL*Plus report.

```
Fri Mar 20                                     page    1
            Student Report
               Fall 1996
                CSc 226

SID   Last Name    First Name Component  Points
----- ------------ ---------- ---------- ------
1111  RAJSHEKHAR   NANDITA    EXAM1          90
                              QUIZZES        75
                              FINAL          95
***** ************ **********            ------
sum                                         260


2222  CORN         SYDNEY     EXAM1          70
                              QUIZZES        40
                              FINAL          82
***** ************ **********            ------
sum                                         192


4444  HOLMES       ZACK       EXAM1          83
                              QUIZZES        71
                              FINAL          74
***** ************ **********            ------
sum                                         228

        Report prepared by R. Sunderraman
```

```
spool capture.dat
set echo on
-- (1) list cno and cname of customers
select cno,cname
from   agents;
-- (2) List cno and cname of customers
--     living in "Wichita"
```

```
select cno,cname
from   customers,zipcodes
where  customers.zip = zipcodes.zip and
       city = 'Wichita';
set echo off
spool off
exit;
```

## 2.2 Creating, Dropping, and Altering Tables

Oracle SQL provides the **create table**, **drop table**, and **alter table** statements to create and drop tables and to alter their structure. The syntax of these statements is discussed in this section.

Consider the usage of the **create table** and **drop table** statements for the grade book database shown in Figure 2.3. Each **create table** statement has been preceded by a **drop table** statement. This is a practice that many database programmers and administrators follow to drop any previous version, if there is one, of the table being created.

### 2.2.1 drop table

The syntax for the **drop table** statement is quite trivial.[2] The simplest form of this statement is

```
drop table <tablename>;
```

If there are any foreign keys in other tables referring to the primary or candidate keys of the table being dropped, this simple form of the **drop table** statement will cause an error situation, and the table will not be dropped by Oracle.

To force a table drop in cases where the table has other tables referring to its keys, the following version of the **drop table** statement can be used:

```
drop table <tablename> cascade constraints;
```

In this case, Oracle drops all referential integrity constraints that refer to primary and unique keys in the dropped table and then drops the table from the database. Note that the **drop table** statement ends with a semicolon, as does every SQL statement.

2. The following notation is used for describing the syntax of statements in this book: square brackets ([ and ]) enclose optional items, curly brackets ({ and }) enclose items that could be repeated zero or more times, angular brackets (< and >) enclose variable items, and the vertical bar symbol (|) is used to separate options.

**Figure 2.3** Creating tables for the grade book database.

```
drop table catalog cascade constraints;
create table catalog (
  cno       varchar2(7),
  ctitle    varchar2(50),
  primary key (cno));

drop table students cascade constraints;
create table students (
  sid       varchar2(5),
  fname     varchar2(20),
  lname     varchar2(20) not null,
  minit     char,
  primary key (sid));

drop table courses cascade constraints;
create table courses (
  term      varchar2(10),
  lineno    number(4),
  cno       varchar2(7) not null,
  a         number(2) check(a > 0),
  b         number(2) check(b > 0),
  c         number(2) check(c > 0),
  d         number(2) check(d > 0),
  primary key (term,lineno),
  foreign key (cno) references catalog);

drop table components cascade constraints;
create table components (
  term      varchar2(10),
  lineno    number(4) check(lineno >= 1000),
  compname  varchar2(15),
  maxpoints number(4) not null check(maxpoints >= 0),
  weight    number(2) check(weight >= 0),
  primary key (term,lineno,compname),
  foreign key (term,lineno) references courses);
```

**Figure 2.3** —Continued

```
drop table enrolls cascade constraints;
create table enrolls (
  sid       varchar2(5),
  term      varchar2(10),
  lineno    number(4),
  primary key (sid,term,lineno),
  foreign key (sid) references students,
  foreign key (term,lineno) references courses);

drop table scores cascade constraints;
create table scores (
  sid       varchar2(5),
  term      varchar2(10),
  lineno    number(4),
  compname  varchar2(15),
  points    number(4) check(points >= 0),
  primary key (sid,term,lineno,compname),
  foreign key (sid,term,lineno) references enrolls,
  foreign key (term,lineno,compname) references components);
```

## 2.2.2 create table

The **create table** statement has a more complicated syntax:

```
create table <tablename> (col-def, ..., col-def,
                          tab-constr, ..., tab-constr);
```

It begins with the keywords **create table**, followed by the name of the table and then by a list of definitions enclosed within parentheses. The list of definitions consists of two parts: *column definition* and *table constraints*.[3] These individual definitions are separated by commas.

3. Actually, Oracle's **create table** statement provides for several other properties of the table to be defined in the list of definitions—for example, in which tablespace the table should be located, how much space should be allocated, and how space should be allocated when the table grows. These details are left out of the discussion here.

## *Column Definition*

The syntax for a column definition is

```
<column-name> <data-type> [default <expr>] [<column-constraints>]
```

There are four parts to a column definition. The first two, the *column name* and its *data type*, are mandatory, and the remaining two parts, the *default clause* and the *column constraint* clause, are optional. The most commonly used data types are shown in Figure 2.4.

**Figure 2.4** Common Oracle data types.

| Data Type | Description |
|---|---|
| char(n) | Fixed-length character string of length n. Maximum value of n is 255. If (n) is not specified, the default length is 1. If the value stored is a string of a length less than n, the rest of the string is padded to the right by blanks. String constants are specified within single quotes such as 'abc'. |
| varchar2(n) | Variable-length character string having a maximum of n characters. The maximum value of n can be 2000. |
| date | Holds a date field. Usually specified in string format, such as '12-DEC-1997'. |
| number | Integer and real values occupying up to 40 spaces. |
| number(n) | Integer and real values occupying up to n spaces |
| number(n,d) | Real values occupying up to n spaces with d digits after the decimal point. |
| integer | Same as number, but does not allow decimal digits. |
| integer(n) | Same as integer, but occupying n spaces. |

The default clause, if used, specifies the default value needed for the column when a row is inserted without a value for this column. For example, the courses table could have the column named a defined as

```
a number(2) default 90 check(a > 0)
```

indicating that the default value of the column is 90.

If the column being described has a constraint associated with it (such as column value cannot be null, column value is further restricted, or column is a primary, candidate, or foreign key), the constraint could be specified as the last part of the column definition. The syntax for a column constraint is as follows:

```
[constraint <constraint_name>]
  [not] null |
```

```
check (<condition>) |
unique |
primary key |
references <table_name>[(<column_name>)] [on delete cascade]
```

After giving an optional name for the constraint, one of the five possible column constraints is specified. The `not null` constraint may be specified if `null` values are to be prohibited for the column; the `check` constraint can be specified to impose further restrictions on the column values; the `unique` and `primary key` constraints can be specified if the column by itself is a candidate key or a primary key, respectively; and the `references` clause may be used in case the column is a foreign key and it refers to a unique key or primary key in another table. If the column is a foreign key referring to a unique key in another table, the `table_name` must be followed (within parentheses) by the unique key attribute name of the other table. The optional `on delete cascade` clause, if specified, will inform Oracle to automatically delete all the dependent rows when a referenced row (containing a unique or primary key) is deleted.

In the grade book database example, several column constraints have been defined. For example, in the `components` table, the column

```
maxpoints number(4) not null check(maxpoints >= 0)
```

has both the `not null` and the `check` constraints defined, indicating that the column cannot assume a `null` value and that its value must also be greater than or equal to 0. If a particular column is by itself the primary key for the table, the primary key constraint could be specified in the column definition itself. For example, the `cno` column in the `catalog` table could have been defined as

```
cno varchar2(7) primary key
```

If the particular column is a candidate key by itself, the candidate key constraint can be expressed using the `unique` keyword at the end of the column definition. For example, if the `ctitle` column of the `catalog` table were a candidate key, then it could be defined as

```
ctitle varchar2(50) unique
```

If the particular column is a foreign key by itself, the constraint can also be expressed as part of the column definition using the `references` clause. For example, if the `ctitle` column in the `catalog` table were a candidate key and were to be included in the `courses` table under a different name—say, `cname`—then the `cname` column in the `courses` table would be defined as follows:

```
cname varchar2(50) references catalog(ctitle)
```

However, as a common practice, the primary key, candidate key, and foreign key constraints are all expressed as table constraints (discussed next) even if they could be expressed in the column definition.

## *Table Constraints*

After all the columns of the table have been described, any constraints that apply as a whole to the table are described in the table constraints part of the definition list. The three most commonly used table constraints are the primary key, the foreign key, and the candidate key. The syntax for a table constraint is as follows:

```
[constraint <constraint_name>]
  unique (<column> {, <column>}) |
  primary key (<column> {, <column>}) |
  foreign key (<column> {, <column>})
     references <table_name> [(<column> {, <column>})]
       [on delete cascade]
```

Table constraints become necessary if the primary, candidate, or foreign keys consist of more than one attribute.

For example, in the `courses` table definition of the example shown in Figure 2.3, the primary key constraint is defined as

```
primary key (term,lineno)
```

and the foreign key constraint is described as

```
foreign key (cno) references catalog
```

Any candidate key constraints could be expressed as a table constraint using the keyword `unique`.

The SQL code to create the tables for the mail-order database are shown in Figure 2.5. Note that, wherever possible, the primary and foreign key constraints are defined in the column definition itself, unlike in the previous example. This has been done just to be different. It does not matter where you define these constraints. Of course, if the primary, foreign, or candidate keys contain more than one attribute, they have to be defined as table constraints.

The SQL code to create tables for the investment portfolio database is shown in Figure 2.6.

**Figure 2.5** Creating tables for the mail-order database.

```
drop table zipcodes cascade constraints;
create table zipcodes (
  zip      number(5) primary key,
  city     varchar2(30));

drop table employees cascade constraints;
create table employees (
  eno      number(4) primary key,
  ename    varchar2(30),
  zip      number(5) references zipcodes,
  hdate    date);

drop table parts cascade constraints;
create table parts (
  pno      number(5) primary key,
  pname    varchar2(30),
  qoh      integer check(qoh >= 0),
  price    number(6,2) check(price >= 0.0),
  olevel   integer);

drop table customers cascade constraints;
create table customers (
  cno      number(5) primary key,
  cname    varchar2(30),
  street   varchar2(30),
  zip      number(5) references zipcodes,
  phone    char(12));

drop table orders cascade constraints;
create table orders (
  ono      number(5) primary key,
  cno      number(5) references customers,
  eno      number(4) references employees,
  received date,
  shipped  date);
```

**Figure 2.5** —Continued

```
drop table odetails cascade constraints;
create table odetails (
  ono      number(5) references orders,
  pno      number(5) references parts,
  qty      integer check(qty > 0),
  primary key (ono,pno));
```

**Figure 2.6** Creating tables for the investment portfolio database.

```
create table member (
  mid            varchar2 (7),
  password       varchar2 (8) not null,
  fname          varchar2 (15) not null,
  lname          varchar2 (15) not null,
  address        varchar2 (50),
  email          varchar2(30),
  cash_balance   number (10,2) not null,
  primary key (mid)
);

create table security (
  symbol         varchar2 (8),
  cname          varchar2 (30),
  current_price  number (7,3) check (current_price >= 0.0) not null,
  ask_price      number (7,3) check (ask_price >= 0.0),
  bid_price      number (7,3) check (bid_price >= 0.0),
  primary key (symbol)
);

create table transaction (
  mid             varchar2 (7),
  symbol          varchar2 (8),
  trans_date      date,
  trans_type      varchar2 (20) not null,
  quantity        number (7,2) not null,
  price_per_share number (7,3) check (price_per_share >= 0.0)
                  not null,
  commission      number (5,2) check (commission >= 0.0) not null,
  amount          number (8,2) check (amount >= 0.0) not null,
  primary key (mid, symbol, trans_date),
  foreign key (mid) references member,
  foreign key (symbol) references security
);
```

### 2.2.3 `alter table`

Once a table has been created, it is generally not advisable to change its structure. However, if the need does arise, the **`alter table`** statement can be used. The structure of a table can be altered in two ways: by adding a new column and by changing a column's definition.

Adding a column is straightforward. Suppose you want to add two columns—for fax number and customer type (`I` for individual and `B` for business)—to the **`customers`** table in the mail-order database. This can be done as follows:

```
alter table customers add (
  fax   char(12),
  ctype char check(ctype in ('I','B'))
);
```

Changing the definition of a column in a restricted manner can be accomplished with the **`modify`** keyword. Suppose you want to increase the size of the string column **`street`** in the **`customers`** table to `50` from `30`. This can be accomplished as follows:

```
alter table customers modify (
  street     varchar2(50)
);
```

There are some restrictions on how and when the **`alter table`** statement can be used. For example, it is not possible to add a new column with a **`not null`** constraint imposed on it. This is because the table already exists with data, and when you add a new column, that column will contain only **`null`** values until you add data to it. A way around this problem is to define the new column without the **`not null`** constraint; you can then add every row in the table under the new column with some default value and use the **`modify`** option under the **`alter table`** statement to impose the **`not null`** constraint. Other restrictions include decreasing the width of string and number columns, changing the data type, and imposing constraints that do not hold on the current data.

## 2.3 Inserting Rows

This section introduces a simple form of the SQL **`insert`** statement that adds a row to a table in the database. A more general form is discussed in Section 2.6. The syntax of this simple form of insert is

```
insert into <tablename> [(column {, column})]
  values (expression {, expression});
```

The statement starts with the keywords **insert into**, followed by the name of the table into which the row is to be inserted. This is then followed optionally by a list of columns of the table within parentheses, the keyword **values**, and finally a list of values within parentheses. Here are some examples:

```
insert into components values
  ('f96',1031,'exam1',100,30);
insert into courses values
  ('f96',1031,'csc226',90,80,65,50);
insert into courses(term,lineno,cno) values
  ('f96',1037,'csc326');
insert into enrolls(term,lineno,sid) values
  ('f96',1031,'1111');
```

If the column names are not listed, as is the case in the first two of the preceding statements, the values must be listed in the same order in which the columns were defined while creating the table. The third **insert** statement lists only three of the seven columns of the **courses** table and provides values for each of the three columns. The remaining columns are assigned **null** values. In the fourth **insert** statement, all the columns of the **enrolls** table are listed, and their corresponding values are provided. However, note that this is not the order in which the columns were defined while creating the table. An advantage of listing the columns is that you do not have to remember in which order these columns were listed while creating the table. Figures 2.7 and 2.8 list a few of the **insert** statements needed to load two of the sample databases with data.

## 2.4 Querying the Database

Oracle SQL's **select** statement provides a simple and powerful way of expressing ad hoc queries against the database. The **select** statement, when used in conjunction with the variety of functions Oracle provides for string, number, and date manipulations, is able to extract the specified data from the database and present it to the user in an easy-to-read format. In this section, the **select** statement is discussed.

### 2.4.1 Simple select Statement

The simplest form of the **select** statement has the following syntax:

```
select [distinct] <expression> {, <expression>}
from <tablename> [<alias>] {, <tablename> [<alias>]}
[where <search_condition>];
```

**Figure 2.7** Grade book **insert** statements.

```
insert into catalog values
  ('csc226','Introduction to Programming I');

insert into students values
  ('1111','Nandita','Rajshekhar','K');
insert into students values
  ('2222','Sydney','Corn','A');

insert into courses values
  ('f96',1031,'csc226',90,80,65,50);

insert into components values
  ('f96',1031,'exam1',100,30);
insert into components values
  ('f96',1031,'quiz',80,20);
insert into components values
  ('f96',1031,'final',100,50);

insert into enrolls values ('1111','f96',1031);
insert into enrolls values ('2222','f96',1031);

insert into scores values ('1111','f96',1031,'exam1',90);
insert into scores values ('1111','f96',1031,'quiz',75);
insert into scores values ('1111','f96',1031,'final',95);
insert into scores values ('2222','f96',1031,'exam1',70);
insert into scores values ('2222','f96',1031,'quiz',40);
insert into scores values ('2222','f96',1031,'final',82);
```

There are three clauses: `select`, `from`, and `where`. The `where` clause is optional. The `select` clause starts with the `select` keyword, followed by the optional keyword `distinct` and a list of expressions. The `distinct` keyword, if included, would result in duplicates being removed from the result of the query. The expression list normally contains columns of tables being queried. However, it could also contain expressions involving operators on the column values. The nature of these expressions will be clarified by the examples in this section. The `from` clause consists of the keyword `from` followed by a list of table names. Optionally, each table name can be followed

**Figure 2.8** Mail-order **insert** statements.

```
insert into  zipcodes values (67226,'Wichita');

insert into employees values
  (1000,'Jones',67226,'12-DEC-95');

insert into parts values
  (10506,'Land Before Time I',200,19.99,20);
insert into parts values
  (10507,'Land Before Time II',156,19.99,20);
insert into parts values
  (10508,'Land Before Time III',190,19.99,20);
insert into parts values
  (10509,'Land Before Time IV',60,19.99,20);

insert into customers values
  (1111,'Charles','123 Main St.',67226,'316-636-5555');

insert into orders values
  (1020,1111,1000,'10-DEC-94','12-DEC-94');

insert into odetails values (1020,10506,1);
insert into odetails values (1020,10507,1);
insert into odetails values (1020,10508,2);
insert into odetails values (1020,10509,3);
```

by an alias, separated by a space. These aliases can serve the purpose of the renaming operator in relational algebra. The `where` clause consists of the keyword `where` followed by a *search condition*, a Boolean expression involving constants, column names, and appropriate operators. The nature of the search condition will also be clarified by the examples in this section.

The informal semantics (the result set of tuples) of the simple `select` statement is computed as follows: The Cartesian product of the tables mentioned in the `from` clause is taken first. Then the selection criteria mentioned in the `where` clause are applied to the product, which results in a subset of the product. Finally, the columns and expressions mentioned in the **select** clause are projected from this subset to form the result of the query.

Here are some examples of simple queries and their corresponding SQL **select** statements.

Query 2.1: Get **pno** and **pname** values of parts that are priced less than $20.00.

```
select pno,pname
from   parts
where  price < 20.00;
```

This is a simple example involving one table with a simple selection condition based on the column **price** and a projection of two columns, **pno** and **pname**.

Query 2.2: Get all the rows of the **employees** table.

```
select *
from   employees;
```

If all the columns of all the tables mentioned in the **from** clause are to be projected, the * symbol can be used in the **select** clause as shown.

Query 2.3: Get **pno** values of parts for which orders have been placed.

```
select distinct pno
from   odetails;
```

The **distinct** keyword can be used to eliminate duplicate answers, if present. By default, SQL does not eliminate duplicates. In many situations, it should not matter whether duplicates are removed; however, there are situations—for example, when using aggregate operations—where the result of the query depends on whether or not duplicates are removed.

Query 2.4: Get all the details of customers whose names begin with the letter "A".

```
select *
from   customers
where  cname like 'A%';
```

The **like** operator performs pattern matching in string data. A percent sign (%) indicates a match with zero or more spaces or characters, and the underscore sign (_) indicates a match with exactly one space or character. Additional examples of the usage of the **like** operator are:

```
cname like '_ee%'  -- true if the second and
                      third letters of cname
                      are both 'e'.
cname like '%a%a%' -- true if cname contains
                      at least two 'a's.
```

Query 2.5: Get `ono` and `cname` values of customers whose orders have not yet been shipped (i.e., the `shipped` column has a `null` value).

```
select ono,cname
from   orders,customers
where  customers.cno = orders.cno and
       shipped is null;
```

The `is null` predicate tests for `null` values in a particular column. The `is not null` predicate can be used to check to see if a column has a non-`null` value. Using the comparison operators (`=`, `!=`, etc.) with the `null` value can give unpredictable results; hence, it is always advisable to use the `is null` and `is not null` predicates to check for `null` values.

Query 2.6: Get `sid` values of students who have scores between 50 and 70 points in any component of any course in which they have enrolled.

```
select sid
from   scores
where  points between 50 and 70;
```

The `between` predicate used in this example is a short form for the expression `points >= 50 and points <= 70`. There is a corresponding `not between` predicate that is the logical opposite of `between`.

Query 2.7: Get `cname` and `ename` pairs such that the customer with name `cname` has placed an order through the employee with name `ename`.

```
select distinct cname,ename
from   customers,orders,employees
where  customers.cno = orders.cno and
       employees.eno = orders.eno;
```

This is a query involving more than one table. The `where` clause consists of two conditions, referred to as *join conditions*, that relate the data present in the three tables being joined.

Query 2.8: For each `odetail` row, get `ono`, `pno`, `pname`, `qty`, and `price` values along with the total price for this item. The total price is simply the product of unit price and quantity.

```
select x.ono, x.pno, p.pname, x.qty,
       p.price, (x.qty * p.price) total
from   odetails x, parts p
where  x.pno = p.pno
```

This query illustrates aliases used in the **from** clause and arithmetic expressions and naming a new column in the **select** clause. If the last expression in the **select** clause did not have the column name **total**, by default the column would be labeled by the text of the expression. Note that the aliases in the **from** clause in this example are not necessary. Since the only common column between the `parts` and `odetails` tables is `pno`, any references to it in the query must be preceded by the table name of the alias, such as `x.pno`. The prefixes on all other references are not necessary, even though they are shown in the example.

Query 2.9: Get all pairs of `cno` values for customers based in the same zip code.

```
select c1.cno, c2.cno
from   customers c1, customers c2
where  c1.zip = c2.zip and c1.cno < c2.cno;
```

The aliases used in this query are necessary because there is a reference to two different rows of the same table. The `c1.cno < c2.cno` condition is used to eliminate any redundant answers.

Query 2.10: Get `pno` values for parts that have been ordered by at least two different customers.

```
select distinct y1.pno
from   orders x1, orders x2, odetails y1, odetails y2
where  y1.pno = y2.pno and y1.ono = x1.ono and
       y2.ono = x2.ono and x1.cno < x2.cno
```

Notice the extensive use of aliases in this example. The `x1.cno < x2.cno` condition is used to eliminate any redundant answers.

### 2.4.2 Sub-Selects

The search criteria in the **where** clause may itself contain a **select** statement. Such a **select** statement within the search criteria is referred to as a *sub-select*, and the whole structure is often referred to as a *nested select statement*. SQL supports several built-in predicates that can be used to test the sub-selects for certain conditions. These built-in predicates are `in` and `not in`, the quantified comparisons $\theta$`any` and $\theta$`all`, and `exists` and `not exists`.

## *Predicates* `in` *and* `not in`

The general forms of the `in` and `not in` predicates are:

```
expr in (sub-select)
expr in (value {, value})
expr not in (sub-select)
expr not in (value {, value})
```

Here are some example queries that use the `in` and `not in` predicates.

Query 2.11: Get `cname` values of customers who have placed orders with employees living in Fort Dodge. The following `select` statement gets the `eno` values of employees from Fort Dodge:

```
select eno
from   employees,zipcodes
where  employees.zip = zipcodes.zip and
       city = 'Fort Dodge';
```

The following nested `select` statement, which contains the previous `select` statement in its `where` clause using the `in` predicate, returns the answers to the query:

```
select distinct cname
from   orders,customers
where  orders.cno = customers.cno and
       eno in (select eno
               from   employees,zipcodes
               where  employees.zip = zipcodes.zip
                      and city = 'Fort Dodge');
```

Query 2.12: Get `cname` values of customers living in Fort Dodge or Liberal.

```
select cname
from   customers,zipcodes
where  customers.zip = zipcodes.zip and
       city in ('Fort Dodge','Liberal');
```

In this example, the `in` predicate is used with a fixed set of values.

Query 2.13: Get `cno` and `cname` values of customers who have placed an order for *Dirty Harry* or *Dr. Zhivago*.

```
select cno,cname
from   customers
where  cno in
        (select cno
         from   orders
         where  ono in
                 (select ono
                  from   odetails
                  where  pno in
                          (select pno
                           from   parts
                           where  pname in
                                ('Dirty Harry',
                                 'Dr. Zhivago'))));
```

This is a deeply nested SQL `select` statement with several occurrences of the `in` predicate.

Query 2.14: Get `cname` values of customers who have ordered a product with `pno` = 10506.

```
select cname
from   customers
where  10506 in
          (select pno
           from   orders,odetails
           where  orders.ono = odetails.pno and
                  orders.cno = customers.cno);
```

This is a nested `select` statement, but with a difference. The inner `select` (i.e., the sub-select) statement refers to data that are defined in the outer `select` statement. The condition `orders.cno = customers.cno` in the sub-select refers to the `cno` value in the `customers` table in the outer `select`. Inner `select`s can refer to values in outer `select`s; however, the outer `select`s cannot refer to values within the scope of inner `select`s. This scoping rule is analogous to scoping rules for variables in block-structured programming languages. Nested `select` statements in SQL in which the inner `select` refers to data in the outer `select` are sometimes referred to as *correlated select statements.*

## *Quantified Comparison Predicates*

The general forms of the quantified comparison predicates are

```
expr <any  (sub-select)
expr <=any (sub-select)
expr =any  (sub-select)
expr <>any (sub-select)
expr >any  (sub-select)
expr >=any (sub-select)

expr <all  (sub-select)
expr <=all (sub-select)
expr =all  (sub-select)
expr <>all (sub-select)
expr >all  (sub-select)
expr >=all (sub-select)
```

There are two groups of quantified comparisons: `all-comparisons`, in which the comparisons are made with all the values in the sub-select statement, and `any-comparisons`, in which the comparison succeeds if it matches any one value in the sub-select. For example, the predicate

```
expr >any (sub-select)
```

is true if the value of the expression is greater than any one value in the sub-select, and the predicate

```
expr >all (sub-select)
```

is true if the value of the expression is greater than all values in the sub-select. The sub-select must result in a set of atomic values (single column); otherwise, the comparison will not make sense.

If the sub-select is guaranteed to return exactly one value, the `all` and `any` quantification to this comparison may be dropped and the query will check for the one-on-one comparison between the expression and the value returned in the sub-select.

Here are some examples using the quantified comparison predicates.

Query 2.15: Get `pname` values of parts with the lowest price.

```
select pname
from   parts
where  price <=all (select price
                    from   parts);
```

The inner **select** statement in this example returns a set of values corresponding to the prices of the parts. If the price of the part under consideration in the outer **select** statement is less than or equal to all the values returned by the inner **select**, then the part being selected in the outer **select** statement costs the least.

Query 2.16: Get `cname` values of customers who have ordered parts from any one employee based in Wichita or Liberal.

```
select cname
from   customers,orders
where  customers.cno = orders.cno and
       eno in
          (select eno
           from   employees,zipcodes
           where  employees.zip = zipcodes.zip and
                  city in ('Wichita','Liberal'));
```

The inner **select** statement returns the **eno** values of all employees located in Wichita or Liberal. The outer **select** then checks to see if the customer under consideration has placed an order with any one of these employees, using the **in** predicate. Note that the **=any** predicate has the same meaning as the **in** predicate and hence could be used interchangeably. However, for readability purposes, the **in** predicate is more commonly used.

Query 2.17: Get `pname` values of parts that cost less than the least-expensive *Land Before Time* part.

```
select pname
from   parts
where  price <all
          (select  price
           from    parts
           where  pname like 'Land Before Time%');
```

## *Predicates* exists *and* not exists

The general forms of the `exists` and `not exists` predicates are:

```
exists (sub-select)
not exists (sub-select)
```

The `exists` predicate is true if the sub-select results in a nonempty set of values, and it is false otherwise. Similarly, the `not exists` predicate is true if the sub-select results in an empty set of values, and it is false otherwise. Some examples using the `exists` and `not exists` predicates follow.

Query 2.18: Get `cname` values of customers who have placed at least one order through the employee with `eno = 1000`.

```
select cname
from   customers
where  exists
         (select 'a'
          from   orders
          where  orders.cno = customers.cno and
                 eno = 1000);
```

This is a correlated query in which the inner `select` statement returns a list of rows from the `orders` table representing all orders taken by employee 1000 and placed by the customer under consideration in the outer `select`. If this set is nonempty, it means that the customer under consideration in the outer `select` has indeed placed an order with employee 1000, and the name of the customer is projected in the final result. Note that it does not matter which columns are projected in the inner `select` statement; the `exists` clause simply checks if any tuple results from the inner `select`. For efficiency purposes, it is best to include some literal, such as `'a'`, in the select list of such expressions.

Query 2.19: Get `cname` values of customers who have not placed any orders through the employee with `eno = 1000`.

```
select cname
from   customers
where  not exists
         (select 'a'
          from   orders x
          where  orders.cno = customers.cno and
                 eno = 1000);
```

This query is similar to the previous one, except that the **not exists** predicate is used.

Query 2.20: Get cno values of customers who have placed an order for both parts, pno = 10506 and pno = 10507, within the same order.

```
select cno
from   orders
where  exists (select 'a'
               from   odetails
               where  odetails.ono = orders.ono and
                      odetails.pno = 10506) and
       exists (select 'a'
               from   odetails
               where  odetails.ono = orders.ono and
                      odetails.pno = 10507);
```

This query has two sub-selects. The first returns rows from **odetails** for the order under consideration in the outer **select**, such that the part being ordered is 10506. The second sub-select does the same for part 10507. Since the row under consideration in the outer **select** is the same for both sub-selects, the query is answered correctly.

It does appear that there are many ways a particular query could be phrased in SQL. Consider the following query: *Get the names of cities of customers who have placed an order through the employee with* eno = 1000. Here are five different SQL **select** statements that answer this query:

```
select distinct city
from   customers,zipcodes
where  customers.zip = zipcodes.zip and
       cno in (select cno
               from   orders
               where  eno = 1000);

select distinct city
from   customers,zipcodes
where  customers.zip = zipcodes.zip and
       cno =any (select cno
                 from   orders
                 where  eno = 1000);
```

```
select distinct city
from   customers,zipcodes
where  customers.zip = zipcodes.zip and
       exists (select *
               from   orders
               where  orders.cno = customers.cno and
                      eno = 1000);

select distinct city
from   customers c, orders o, zipcodes z
where  c.zip = z.zip and
       c.cno = o.cno and
       o.eno = 1000;

select distinct city
from   customers,zipcodes
where  customers.zip = zipcodes.zip and
       1000 in (select eno
                from   orders
                where  orders.cno = customers.cno);
```

There are probably a few more SQL **select** statements for this query.

### 2.4.3 Union

Oracle SQL provides for a **union** operator that computes the union of two sub-queries, each of which is expressed as a sub-select. There are two forms:

```
(sub-select) union (sub-select)
(sub-select) union all (sub-select)
```

The **union** operator eliminates duplicates, whereas the **union all** operator keeps duplicates, if there are any. A simple example follows.

Query 2.21: Get cities in which customers or employees are located.

```
select city
from   customers,zipcodes
where  customers.zip = zipcodes.zip
union
select city
from   employees,zipcodes
where  employees.zip = zipcodes.zip
```

The following will not eliminate duplicates:

```
select city
from   customers,zipcodes
where  customers.zip = zipcodes.zip
union  all
select city
from   employees,zipcodes
where  employees.zip = zipcodes.zip
```

### 2.4.4 Forall Queries

Recall that the division operator of relational algebra was best suited to answer a particular type of query, which we shall refer to as a *forall query*. Unfortunately, SQL does not provide a straightforward equivalent of the division operator. However, such queries can be expressed in SQL by using the `not exists` predicate and rephrasing the query into an equivalent form using double negation. This technique is illustrated by the following two examples.

Query 2.22: Get `cno` values of customers who have placed orders with `ALL` employees from Wichita.

This query can be rephrased as follows:

*Get* `cno` *values of customers such that (the set of employees from Wichita with whom the customer has* `NOT` *placed an order) is* `EMPTY`.

Notice the double negation used in this rephrased query.[4] Instead of searching for the connections between customers and employees that are present in the `orders` table, this rephrased query would seek the "missing" connections between customers and employees. If missing connections do not exist, it reports the customer in the answer. The SQL version follows:

```
select c.cno
from   customers c
where  not exists
          (select *
           from employees e, zipcodes z
           where e.city = 'Wichita' and
                 e.zip = c.zip and
                 not exists (select *
```

4. Although the word `NOT` is used only once, the word `EMPTY` contains the second negation.

```
                              from orders x
                              where x.cno = c.cno and
                                    x.eno = e.eno));
```

Query 2.23: Get pno values of parts that have been ordered by ALL customers from Wichita. The rephrased form is as follows:

> Get pno values of parts such that (the set of customers from Wichita who have NOT ordered this part) is EMPTY.

The SQL select statement for this query is

```
select pno
from   parts p
where  not exists
         (select cno
          from   customers c, zipcodes z
          where  c.zip = z.zip and
                 z.city = 'Wichita' and
                 not exists
                   (select *
                    from orders o, odetails od
                    where  o.ono = od.ono and
                           od.pno = p.pno and
                           o.cno = c.cno));
```

This query has a structure similar to the previous one, with three levels of nesting.

## 2.4.5 Aggregate Functions

Oracle SQL supports five aggregate functions: **count**, **sum**, **avg**, **max**, and **min**. Figure 2.9 summarizes the characteristics of each. These functions are normally used in the **select** clause of the **select** statement, although they can sometimes be used in the conditions in the **where** clause or the **having** clause. An important point to note when using aggregate functions is that all **null** values are discarded before these functions are evaluated. The aggregate functions are illustrated by the following queries.

Query 2.24: Get total quantity of part 10601 that has been ordered.

```
select sum(qty) TOTAL
from   odetails
where  pno = 10601;
```

**Figure 2.9** Aggregate functions.

| Name | Argument Type | Result Type | Description |
|---|---|---|---|
| count | Any (can be *) | Numeric | Count of occurrences |
| sum | Numeric | Numeric | Sum of arguments |
| avg | Numeric | Numeric | Average of arguments |
| max | Char or numeric | Same as argument | Maximum value |
| min | Char or numeric | Same as argument | Minimum value |

This is a straightforward usage of the aggregate function `sum`.

Query 2.25: Get the total sales in dollars on all orders.

```
select sum(price*qty) TOTAL_SALES
from   orders,odetails,parts
where  orders.ono = odetails.ono and
       odetails.pno = parts.pno;
```

The `sum` aggregate function has been applied to the computed column `price*qty`, and the column has been named as `TOTAL_SALES`.

Query 2.26: Get the total number of customers.

```
select count(cno) NUM_CUSTOMERS
from   customers;
```

An alternate solution to this query is

```
select count(*)
from   customers;
```

These two `select` statements give the same result, because `cno` is a key for the `customers` table.

Query 2.27: Get the number of cities in which customers are based.

```
select count(distinct city)
from   customers, zipcodes
where  customers.zip = zipcodes.zip;
```

If the keyword `distinct` is not used, you will get an incorrect result, as there could be more than one customer in the same city.

Query 2.28: Get `pname` values of parts that cost more than the average cost of all parts.

```
select pname
from   parts
where  price > (select avg(price)
                from   parts);
```

The sub-select statement in this query is guaranteed to return a single value; hence, the use of the comparison in the **where** clause is correct.

Query 2.29: Get **pname** values of parts ordered by at least two different customers.

```
select p.pname
from   parts p
where  2 <= (select count(distinct cno)
             from   orders,odetails
             where  orders.ono = odetails.ono and
                    pno = p.pno);
```

This is a correlated nested **select** statement. Notice the **distinct** keyword used in the sub-select. Without this, an incorrect answer will be generated if a customer orders the same part more than once.

## 2.4.6 The group by and having Clauses

So far, the aggregate functions have been applied to the whole table or a subset of the table satisfying the **where** clause. But there are many situations where the aggregate functions need to be applied to groups of rows based on certain column values rather than the whole table. SQL's **select** statement provides the **group by** and **having** clauses to address this situation.

The **group by** clause is used to form groups of rows of a resulting table based on column values. When the **group by** clause is used, all aggregate operations are computed on the individual groups, not on the entire table. The **having** clause is used to eliminate certain groups from further consideration. The syntax of the **select** statement with these two clauses is

```
select [distinct] <expression> {, <expression>}
from <tablename> [<alias>] {, <tablename> [<alias>]}
[where <search_condition>];
[group by <column> {, <column>}]
[having <condition>]
```

The **group by** clause follows the **where** clause and has a list of column names (at least one) after the keywords **group by**. The rows of the resulting table are partitioned into groups of rows, each group having the same value under the columns listed in the **group by** clause. The table contains a single row of summary information for each group. The **having** clause, if used, follows the **group by** clause; it has a condition that is used to keep some groups and eliminate others from further consideration. If the **having** clause is omitted, Oracle returns summary rows for each group. Some examples follow.

Query 2.30: For each part, get pno and pname values along with total sales in dollars.

```
select   parts.pno,pname,sum(qty*price) TOTAL_SALES
from     odetails,parts
where    odetails.pno = parts.pno
group by parts.pno,pname;
```

It is important to note that the **where** clause is evaluated first, before any groups are formed. Since only one summary row is returned for each group, any column that may result in more than one value for a group is not allowed in the **select** clause.

Query 2.31: Get employee name, employee number, part name, and part number, together with the total quantity each employee supplies of that part to customers with cno values 1111 or 2222.

```
select   e.eno, e.ename, p.pno, p.pname, sum(qty)
from     orders x, parts p, employees a,
         odetails od
where    x.ono = od.ono and x.eno = e.eno and
         od.pno = p.pno and x.cno in (1111, 2222)
group by e.eno, e.ename, p.pno, p.pname;
```

The orders, along with other pertinent information, are grouped according to eno, ename, pno, and pname values, and then the sum of the quantities for each group is calculated. The **where** clause condition is applied first, in order to consider only the two customers in question before groups are formed and aggregates are calculated.

Query 2.32: For each part, get pno and pname values along with total sales in dollars, but only when the total sales exceed $1000.

```
select   parts.pno,pname,sum(qty*price) TOTAL_SALES
from     odetails,parts
where    odetails.pno = parts.pno
group by parts.pno,pname
having   sum(qty*price) > 1000;
```

This is essentially the same as Query 2.30. The **having** clause eliminates any groups for which the total dollar sales are less than or equal to $1000.

Query 2.33: Get **pno** and **pname** values of parts ordered by at least two different customers.

```
select parts.pno,parts.pname
from   orders,odetails,parts
where  orders.ono = odetails.ono and
       odetails.pno = parts.pno
group by parts.pno,parts.pname
having   count(distinct cno) >= 2;
```

In this query, the parts ordered by customers are grouped by **pno** and **pname**, and any group with two or more distinct **cno** values produces a row in the result.

### 2.4.7 The Full `select` Statement

Oracle SQL's full **select** statement is summarized in this section. The **order by** clause, which allows the result of the **select** statement to be sorted in ascending or descending order based on column values, is introduced.

The general form of a sub-select statement is

```
select [distinct] <expression> {, <expression>}
from <tablename> [<alias>] {, <tablename> [<alias>]}
[where <search_condition>];
[group by <column> {, <column>}]
[having <condition>]
```

and the general form of SQL's **select** statement is

```
<sub-select>
{union [all] <sub-select>}
[order by result_column [asc|desc]
          {, result_column [asc|desc]}]
```

The **order by** clause comes at the end and is used to sort the result of a query based on column values. The conceptual order of evaluation of a **select** statement is as follows:

1. The product of all tables in the **from** clause is formed.
2. The **where** clause is then evaluated to eliminate rows that do not satisfy the `search_condition`.

3. The rows are grouped using the columns in the **group by** clause.
4. Groups that do not satisfy the **condition** in the **having** clause are eliminated.
5. The expressions in the **select** clause target list are evaluated.
6. If the **distinct** keyword is present in the **select** clause, duplicate rows are now eliminated.
7. The **union** is taken after each sub-select is evaluated.
8. The resulting rows are sorted according to the columns specified in the **order by** clause.

Note that this is only the conceptual order; the actual sequence of steps taken by Oracle may be different and may have several additional steps for optimization.

## 2.4.8 String, Number, and Date Functions

Oracle provides strong support for the **string**, **number**, and **date** data types. A variety of functions are available to manipulate these data types and to convert from one data type to another. Details of these functions, along with numerous examples, are presented here.

### *Conversion Functions*

Oracle provides functions that can convert data from one data type into another. The three commonly used data-conversion functions are **to_char**, **to_number**, and **to_date**.

- The **to_char** function converts a **number** or a **date** into a character string. For example,

  ```
  to_char(1234) equals '1234'
  ```

  The details of converting a **date** into a character string are covered when discussing date functions.

- The **to_number** function converts a character string into a **number**. Of course, for this conversion to be valid, the character string should contain only digits and other symbols that make up **numbers**. For example,

  ```
  to_number('1234') equals 1234
  ```

- The to_date function converts a have **number** or a character string into a **date**. The details of this function are presented when discussing date functions later in this chapter.

Actually, Oracle performs some of these conversions automatically. Any **number** or **date** value is automatically converted to a **string**—i.e., you can use string functions on **numbers** and **dates**. Any character string data that contain only characters that can be used in **numbers** are also automatically converted to **numbers**, and you can use numeric functions on such string data. A character string of the form 'DD-MON-YY' is automatically converted into a **date**, and date functions can be used on such string data.

Oracle provides two other functions related to data conversion, called **translate** and **decode**. The syntax of the **translate** function is

```
translate(string,from,to)
```

where **string** is the input string to be transformed, and **from** and **to** are character strings used in the transformation process. Each character that appears in **string** and also in **from** is transformed into the corresponding character (i.e., in the same position as in **from**) in **to**. If there is no corresponding character in **to**, the character is omitted from the result. For example,

```
translate('abcdef','abcd','1234') equals '1234ef'
translate('abcdef','cde','12') equals 'ab12f'
```

The **decode** function has the following syntax:

```
decode(value,if1,then1,if2,then2,...,ifN,thenN,else)
```

where **value** is the value to be tested, and the rest of the inputs are used to produce the output. The output of the function is **then1** if **value** is equal to **if1**, and so on. If the **value** is none of the **if** values, then the **else** value is the output of the function. For example, the **select** statement

```
select decode(city,'Witchita','Wichita',
                   'Whichita','Wichita',city) CITY
from   zipcodes;
```

could be used to correct the many incorrect spellings of Wichita.

## *String Functions*

Oracle SQL provides a host of string functions that allow the user to manipulate strings and character data. These are summarized here:

- *Concatenation* (||). Two or more strings can be concatenated using the || operator. For example, the concatenation of the **fname** and **lname** with a comma in the middle is denoted as

```
fname || ', ' || lname
```

- `lpad(string,length,['chars'])`. The `lpad` function pads the input `string` to the left with the `chars` until the length of the string reaches `length`. If the `chars` input is not provided, then the padding is done with spaces. For example,

  ```
  lpad('ha',5,'a') equals 'aaaha'
  lpad('ha',5,'ab') equals 'abaha'
  lpad('ha',5) equals '   ha'
  ```

- `rpad(string,length,['chars'])`. `rpad` is similar to `lpad`, except that the padding occurs to the right of the string. For example,

  ```
  rpad('Jones',10,'.') equals 'Jones.....'
  rpad('Jones',10,'xy') equals 'Jonesxyxyx'
  rpad('Jones',10) equals 'Jones     '
  ```

- `ltrim(string,['chars'])`. The `ltrim` function removes from the left of `string` any character that appears in `chars` until it finds one that is not in `chars`. For example,

  ```
  ltrim('abracadabra','abc') equals 'racadabra'
  ltrim('    abra') equals 'abra'
  ```

  If `chars` is not provided as input, the space character is trimmed from the left.

- `rtrim(string,['chars'])`. `rtrim` is similar to `ltrim`, except that the trimming occurs to the right of the string. For example,

  ```
  rtrim('abracadabra','abc') equals 'abracadabr'
  rtrim('abra       ') equals 'abra'
  ```

- `lower(string)`. Converts all the characters of the `string` input to lowercase. For example,

  ```
  lower('ToNY') equals 'tony'
  ```

- `upper(string)`. Converts all the characters of the `string` input to uppercase. For example,

  ```
  upper('ToNY') equals 'TONY'
  ```

- `initcap(string)`. Converts the first character of the `string` input to uppercase. For example,

  ```
  initcap('tony') equals 'Tony'
  ```

- `length(string)`. Returns the length of the `string` input.

- `substr(string,start,[n])`. Returns the substring of `string` starting at position `start` and of length `n`. If `n` is not provided, the substring ends at the end of `string`. For example,

  ```
  substr('abracadabra',1,5) equals 'abrac'
  substr('abracadabra',4) equals 'acadabra'
  ```

- `instr(string,'chars'[,start [,n]])`. The `instr` function searches the `string` input for `chars` starting from position `start` for the `n`th occurrence and returns the position (returns `0` if not found). If `start` is not provided, the string is searched from the beginning; if `n` is not provided, the string is searched for the first occurrence. For example,

  ```
  instr('Johnny Miller','Mill') equals 8
  instr('abracadabra','bra',1,2) equals 9
  ```

Here are some examples of the usage of the string functions in SQL's `select` statement.

1. The SQL `select` statement

   ```
   select fname || ', ' || lname NAME
   from   students;
   ```

   produces the following output:

   ```
   NAME
   -----------------------------------------
   Nandita, Rajshekhar
   Sydney, Corn
   Susan, Williams
   Naveen, Rajshekhar
   Elad, Yam
   Lincoln, Herring

   6 rows selected
   ```

2. The SQL `select` statement

   ```
   select sid,
          decode(substr(term,1,2),
                 'sp','spring'||substr(term,length(term)-1),
                 'su','summer'||substr(term,length(term)-1),
                 'wi','winter'||substr(term,length(term)-1),
                      'fall'  ||substr(term,length(term)-1))
   ```

```
            term,
            lineno
from    enrolls;
```

produces the following output:

```
SID   TERM                 LINENO
----- ---------------- ----------
1111  fall96                 1031
2222  fall96                 1031
4444  fall96                 1031
1111  fall96                 1032
2222  fall96                 1032
3333  fall96                 1032
5555  spring97               1031
6666  spring97               1031

8 rows selected
```

3. The SQL `select` statement

```
select rpad(upper(cname),20,'.') CUSTOMER, phone
from   customers;
```

produces the following output:

```
CUSTOMER             PHONE
-------------------- ------------
CHARLES............. 316-636-5555
BERTRAM............. 316-689-5555
BARBARA............. 316-111-1234
```

4. The SQL `select` statement

```
select pno,pname
from   parts
where  instr(pname,'Time') > 0 or
       instr(pname,'Harry') > 0;
```

produces the following output:

```
       PNO PNAME
---------- ------------------------------
     10506 Land Before Time I
     10507 Land Before Time II
     10508 Land Before Time III
     10509 Land Before Time IV
     10701 When Harry Met Sally
     10800 Dirty Harry

6 rows selected
```

### *Numeric Functions*

Oracle SQL provides numerous functions that manipulate numbers. Among them are addition (+), subtraction (-), multiplication (*), division (/), absolute value (`abs`), ceiling (`ceil`), floor (`floor`), modulus (`mod`), power (`power`), and square root (`sqrt`). These functions can be used in the `select` clause or in the condition of the `where` clause. These are single-valued functions—i.e., the inputs are single values. Numeric functions that operate on a set of values are `min`, `max`, `sum`, and `avg`, which have been discussed in the context of aggregate functions. There are two list-valued functions—i.e., functions that operate on a list of values. These are `least` and `greatest`. Examples of all these numeric functions are shown in the following `select` statements:

1. The `select` statement

```
select qoh,olevel,qoh+olevel PLUS,
       qoh-olevel SUBT, qoh*olevel MULT,
       qoh/olevel DIVD
from   parts;
```

produces the following output:

```
  QOH OLEVEL PLUS SUBT MULT       DIVD
----- ------ ---- ---- ---- ----------
  200     20  220  180 4000         10
  156     20  176  136 3120        7.8
  190     20  210  170 3800        9.5
   60     20   80   40 1200          3
  300     20  320  280 6000         15
  120     30  150   90 3600          4
```

```
140       30  170   110 4200 4.66666667
100       30  130    70 3000 3.33333333

8 rows selected
```

2. The **select** statement

```
select qoh,olevel,qoh/olevel DIVD,
       ceil(qoh/olevel) CEILING,
       floor(qoh/olevel) FLOOR
from   parts;
```

produces the following output:

```
  QOH  OLEVEL       DIVD CEILING FLOOR
----- ------- ---------- ------- -----
  200      20         10      10    10
  156      20        7.8       8     7
  190      20        9.5      10     9
   60      20          3       3     3
  300      20         15      15    15
  120      30          4       4     4
  140      30 4.66666667       5     4
  100      30 3.33333333       4     3

8 rows selected
```

3. The **select** statement

```
select qoh,olevel,mod(qoh,olevel) MOD,
       power(olevel,3) POWER,sqrt(qoh) SQRT
from   parts;
```

produces the following output:

```
  QOH  OLEVEL  MOD  POWER       SQRT
----- ------- ---- ------ ----------
  200      20    0   8000 14.1421356
  156      20   16   8000  12.489996
  190      20   10   8000 13.7840488
   60      20    0   8000 7.74596669
  300      20    0   8000 17.3205081
  120      30    0  27000 10.9544512
```

```
 140       30   20  27000 11.8321596
 100       30   10  27000         10

8 rows selected
```

4. The `select` statement

```
select qoh,olevel,least(qoh,8*olevel) LEAST,
       greatest(qoh,8*olevel) GREATEST
from   parts;
```

produces the following output:

```
  QOH OLEVEL LEAST GREATEST
----- ------ ----- --------
  200     20   160      200
  156     20   156      160
  190     20   160      190
   60     20    60      160
  300     20   160      300
  120     30   120      240
  140     30   140      240
  100     30   100      240

8 rows selected
```

## *Date Functions*

Oracle provides the **date** data type to model time and date and a powerful set of operators to format and manipulate such data. Internally, the **date** data are stored in a special format that includes date (day, month, and year) as well as time (hours, minutes, and seconds).[5] However, the user sees the date in an external form, which, as a default, is a string of the form `'DD-MON-YY'`.

Some of the commonly used date functions are **sysdate**, **next_day**, **add_months**, **last_day**, **months_between**, **least**, **greatest**, **round**, and **trunc**. In addition to these functions, there are two other conversion functions, which were introduced earlier: **to_date** and **to_char**. Moreover, you can overload the addition (+) and subtraction (-) operators with dates. A brief description of these functions follows:

---

5. The **date** value is stored in seven bytes, one each for century, year, month, day, hours, minutes, and seconds.

- `+, -`. You can add (or subtract) a number to (or from) a date to get a new date. The number is in days. You can also subtract two dates to find the number of days between them.
- `sysdate`. This function takes no input and returns the current date and time.
- `next_day(d,day)`. This function takes as input a date `d` and a string `day` that represents a day of the week, and it returns as output the next date after `d` whose day of the week is the same as `day`.
- `add_months(d,count)`. This function takes a date `d` and a number `count` as input and returns a new date that is `count` months after `d`.
- `last_day(d)`. This function takes as input a date `d` and returns the date corresponding to the last day of the month in which `d` belongs.
- `months_between(d2,d1)`. Given two dates `d2` and `d1`, this function returns the number of months between `d1` and `d2` (`d2 - d1`).
- `least(d1,d2,...,dn)`. Given a list of dates, this function returns the earliest date.
- `greatest(d1,d2,...,dn)`. Given a list of dates, this function returns the latest date.
- `trunc(d)`. Given a date `d`, this function returns the same date but with the time reset to `12:00 AM midnight`.
- `round(d)`. Given a date `d`, this function returns the same date with the time reset to `12:00 AM midnight` if `d` is before noon or rounds the date up to the next day (again `12:00 AM midnight`) if `d` is after noon.
- `to_char(d,format)`. Given a date `d` and a `format` as a string, this function returns a character-string equivalent of the date based on the `format`. The contents of the `format` are summarized in Figure 2.10.
- `to_date(s,format)`. Given a string `s` and a `format`, this function returns a date corresponding to the string `s` based on `format`.

The date functions are illustrated by the following SQL `select` statements. (Notice the use of a system table called `dual`, which is a dummy table consisting of one column and one row.)

1. The SQL `select` statement

```
select hdate,sysdate,hdate+2,hdate-2,sysdate-hdate
from   employees;
```

**Figure 2.10** Date formats.

| Format | Description | Example |
|---|---|---|
| MM | Month number | 7 |
| MON | Three-letter abbreviation of month | JAN |
| MONTH | Fully spelled-out month | JANUARY |
| D | Number of days in the week | 3 |
| DD | Number of days in the month | 16 |
| DDD | Number of days in the year | 234 |
| DY | Three-letter abbreviation of day of week | WED |
| DAY | Fully spelled-out day of week | WEDNESDAY |
| Y | Last digit of year | 8 |
| YY | Last two digits of year | 98 |
| YYY | Last three digits of year | 998 |
| YYYY | Full four-digit year | 1998 |
| HH12 | Hours of the day (1 to 12) | 10 |
| HH24 | Hours of the day (0 to 23) | 17 |
| MI | Minutes of hour | 34 |
| SS | Seconds of minute | 35 |
| AM | Displays AM or PM depending on time | AM |

produces the following output:

```
HDATE     SYSDATE   HDATE+2   HDATE-2   SYSDATE-HDATE
--------- --------- --------- --------- -------------
12-DEC-95 12-JAN-98 14-DEC-95 10-DEC-95     762.51772
01-JAN-92 12-JAN-98 03-JAN-92 30-DEC-91    2203.51772
01-SEP-94 12-JAN-98 03-SEP-94 30-AUG-94    1229.51772
```

2. The SQL **select** statement

```
select months_between('02-JAN-96','02-MAY-95')
from   dual;
```

produces the following output:

```
MONTHS_BETWEEN('02-JAN-96','02-MAY-95')
---------------------------------------
                                      8
```

3. The SQL **select** statement

```
select hdate, to_char(hdate,'DAY') DAY,
       next_day(hdate,'MONDAY'),last_day(hdate),
       add_months(hdate,3)
from   employees;
```

produces the following output:

```
HDATE     DAY       NEXT_DAY( LAST_DAY( ADD_MONTH
--------- --------- --------- --------- ---------
12-DEC-95 TUESDAY   18-DEC-95 31-DEC-95 12-MAR-96
01-JAN-92 WEDNESDAY 06-JAN-92 31-JAN-92 01-APR-92
01-SEP-94 THURSDAY  05-SEP-94 30-SEP-94 01-DEC-94
```

4. The SQL **select** statement

```
select received,shipped,least(received+4,shipped),
       greatest(received+4,shipped)
from   orders;
```

produces the following output:

```
RECEIVED  SHIPPED   LEAST(REC GREATEST(
--------- --------- --------- ---------
10-DEC-94 12-DEC-94 12-DEC-94 14-DEC-94
12-JAN-95 15-JAN-95 15-JAN-95 16-JAN-95
13-FEB-95 20-FEB-95 17-FEB-95 20-FEB-95
20-JUN-97
```

5. The SQL **select** statement

```
select to_char(sysdate,'DD-MON-YY, HH:MI:SS')
       SYSDATE, trunc(sysdate),round(sysdate)
from   dual;
```

produces the following output:

```
SYSDATE              TRUNC(SYS ROUND(SYS
-------------------  --------- ---------
12-JAN-98, 12:37:03  12-JAN-98 13-JAN-98
```

6. The SQL **select** statement

```
select to_date('12 JANUARY 1997','DD MONTH YYYY')+5
from   dual;
```

produces the following output:

```
TO_DATE('
---------
17-JAN-97
```

Here are some queries that involve dates.

Query 2.34: Get **ename** values of employees who placed an order that was received in one month and shipped in a different month.

```
select ename
from   employees
where  eno in
         (select eno
          from   orders
          where  to_char(received,'MM') !=
                 to_char(shipped,'MM'));
```

The dates are converted into numeric months using the **to_char** function and then compared.

Query 2.35: Get **ono** values of orders that were shipped within two days of their receipt.

```
select ono
from   orders
where  (shipped - received) <= 2;
```

Use date subtraction to figure out if the difference in dates is less than or equal to 2.

Query 2.36: Get **ename** values of employees who placed an order within the first week of their hire date.

```
select ename
from   employees
where  eno in
         (select eno
          from   orders
          where  (received - hdate) < 7);
```

Use date subtraction here also.

Query 2.37: Get the name of the employee who was hired on the earliest date.

```
select ename
from   employees
where  hdate = (select min(hdate)
                from   employees);
```

The `min` aggregate function is used on the date column to find the earliest date.

## 2.5 Views

A *view* is a table that is derived from other views and the base tables that are created using the `create table` statement. Views depend on other tables and views to exist. Views can be used in queries just as if they were ordinary or base tables. However, they are dynamic in nature—i.e., their contents change automatically when the base tables and views on which their definitions are based change. Views are created in Oracle using the `create view` statement and are dropped from the database using the `drop view` statement.

### 2.5.1 `create view`

The syntax of the `create view` statement is

```
create view <viewname> as <select-statement>;
```

The statement starts with the keywords `create view`, followed by the name of the view and the keyword `as`, and is terminated by a `select` statement. The `select` statement is a query whose result is a table that is assigned to the view. The query results can vary from time to time depending on the database contents, thereby giving the views a dynamic nature. An example of a view definition is

```
create view employee_sales as
  select   employees.eno,ename,sum(price*qty) SALES
  from     employees,orders,odetails,parts
  where    employees.eno = orders.eno and
           orders.ono = odetails.ono and
           odetails.pno = parts.pno
  group by employees.eno,ename;
```

This view creates a derived table that has three columns: `eno`, `ename`, and `SALES`. This table records the number and names of employees along with their total sales.

As another interesting example of views, consider the portfolio of a member in the investment portfolio database. The portfolio can be computed from the transaction entries for that member. The shares currently owned by the member are computed by first partitioning the **transaction** table into two parts: **buy_transaction** and **sell_transaction**. Then, the number of shares of a company currently owned by the member is the difference between the number of shares bought and the number of shares sold for that particular company. The current portfolio of members is found in the SQL view **portfolio** shown in Figure 2.11.

**Figure 2.11** Creating views for the investment portfolio database.

```
create view buy_transaction as
  select mid, symbol, sum(quantity) total
  from   transaction
  where  trans_type = 'buy'
  group  by mid, symbol;

create view sell_transaction as
  select mid, symbol, sum(quantity) total
  from   transaction
  where  trans_type = 'sell'
  group  by mid, symbol;

create view portfolio as
  (select b.mid, b.symbol, (b.total - s.total) quantity
   from   buy_transaction b, sell_transaction s
   where  b.mid = s.mid and
          b.symbol = s.symbol and
          (b.total - s.total) > 0)
  union
  (select b.mid, b.symbol, b.total  quantity
   from   buy_transaction b
   where  not exists (
              select *
              from   sell_transaction s
              where  b.mid = s.mid and
                     b.symbol = s.symbol));
```

## 2.5.2 drop view

The **drop view** statement has a simple syntax:

```
drop view <viewname>;
```

where the name of the view follows the keywords **drop view**.

# 2.6 Modifying the Database

Oracle SQL provides three statements (**insert**, **update**, and **delete**) to modify the contents of the database. The syntax and use of these statements are discussed in this section.

## 2.6.1 insert

The **insert** statement has one of the following two forms:

```
insert into <tablename> [(column {, column})]
values (expression {, expression})

insert into <tablename> [(column {, column})]
<select-statement>
```

The first form was discussed in an earlier section. The second form allows you to insert rows that are a result of the **<select-statement>**. Here is an example of the second form of the **insert** statement.

Example 2.6.1 Assume that the **parts** table has grown too large and you have decided to partition it into three smaller tables (horizontal partitions) based on the **price** column. Let the names of these three tables be **cheap_parts**, **soso_parts**, and **expensive_parts**. Assume that these three tables have been created in the database. The following **insert** statements will accomplish the task of loading these tables with data from the **parts** table:

```
insert into cheap_parts
  select *
  from   parts
  where  price <= 20.00;

insert into soso_parts
  select *
  from   parts
  where  price between 20.00 and 50.00;

insert into expensive_parts
  select *
  from   parts
  where  price > 50.00;
```

## 2.6.2 update

The **update** statement has the following syntax:

```
update <tablename> [alias]
set    <column> = <expression>
       {, <column> = <expression>}
[where <search_condition>]
```

It has three clauses: the **update** clause, which contains the name of the table to be updated along with an optional alias; the **set** clause, which has one or more assignments that assign an expression to a column; and an optional **where** clause, which can restrict the rows to be updated. If the **where** clause is missing, all rows of the table are updated. Some examples of the **update** statement follow.

Example 2.6.2 The **update** statement

```
update parts
set    qoh = qoh + 100
where  qoh < 5*olevel;
```

increases by 100 the **qoh** values of those rows of the **parts** table that have a **qoh** value less than 5 times the **olevel** value.

The **update** statement

```
update parts
set    qoh = (select max(qoh)
              from   parts)
where  qoh < 100;
```

sets the **qoh** value of those parts whose current **qoh** value is less than 100 to the maximum **qoh** value present in the table. Notice the use of a **select** statement as an expression in the **set** clause.

The **update** statement

```
update parts
set    qoh = 2*qoh
where  3 <= (select sum(qty)
             from   odetails
             where  odetails.pno = parts.pno);
```

doubles the **qoh** values of those parts that have been ordered in quantities of 3 or more. Notice the sub-select in the **where** clause.

### 2.6.3 delete

The delete statement has the following syntax:

```
delete from <tablename> [alias]
[where <search_condition>]
```

It has two clauses: the delete from clause, which is followed by a table name and an optional alias, and the where clause, which is followed by a search condition. The where clause, if used, restricts the rows to be deleted. It is important to note that if the where clause is missing, all the rows in the table are deleted. Some examples of the delete statement follow:

Example 2.6.3 The delete statement

```
delete from customers;
```

deletes all rows in the customers table.

The delete statement

```
delete from customers
where  zip in (select zip
               from   zipcodes
               where city = 'Fort Hays');
```

deletes all customers who live in Fort Hays.

The delete statement

```
delete from employees
where  eno in (select   eno
               from     orders,odetails,parts
               where    orders.ono = odetails.ono and
                        odetails.pno = parts.pno
               group by eno
               having   sum(price*qty) < 200);
```

deletes all employees who have orders totaling less than $200. Notice the sub-select statement in the where clause.

### 2.6.4 commit and rollback

The changes made to the database using the insert, delete, and update statements can be reversed if necessary. Oracle SQL provides two statements: commit and rollback. The changes made to the database can be made permanent by using the **commit** statement. The changes made to the database since the last commit can be reversed by using the **rollback** statement. Some actions can force a commit even without the user issuing the **commit** statement. When the user exits an SQL session, the system automatically commits all the changes. Other statements that result in an automatic commit include **create table**, **drop table**, and **alter table**.

## 2.7 Sequences

A *sequence* is an object that consists of an integer value initialized to a particular value at its definition time. Oracle creates the next value in the sequence each time a request is made for the next value. This mechanism is particularly useful when assigning unique key values to columns. The syntax of the **create sequence** statement is

```
create sequence <seq-name>
  [increment by integer]
  [start with integer]
  [maxvalue integer | nomaxvalue]
  [minvalue integer | nominvalue]
  [cycle|nocycle]
```

where **<seq-name>** is the name given to the sequence. The default increment value is 1. However, by providing a positive integer in the **increment by** clause, you can define the sequence as an increasing sequence with an increment value other than 1. In a similar manner, a decreasing sequence can be obtained by providing a negative integer in the **increment by** clause. By using the **start with** clause, you can start the sequence at any integer. The default start value for an increasing sequence is **minvalue**, and that for a decreasing sequence is **maxvalue**. **minvalue**, the lowest value the sequence will generate, has a default of 1. **maxvalue** is the highest integer the sequence will generate. If you specify the **cycle** clause, the integers will be recycled if the **minvalue** or **maxvalue** is specified. An example of a sequence definition is

```
create sequence custseq start with 1000;
```

which creates a sequence that starts with the value 1000 and is incremented by 1 each time a new value is requested.

The sequences are accessed by the two functions **nextval** and **currval**. The **nextval** function is basically a request to the system to generate the next value in the sequence. The **currval** function returns the current value of the sequence. This function cannot be invoked before the first **nextval** function is called. A sample usage of the **nextval** function is

```
insert into customers
  values(custseq.nextval,'Jones','123 Main St.',
         67226,'111-111-1111');
```

## 2.8 Oracle Data Dictionary

The Oracle data dictionary stores all information about the objects of the database. This includes the names and structures of all tables, constraints, indexes, views, synonyms, sequences, triggers, procedures, functions, and packages. The data dictionary is stored in specially created system tables. This section will focus on the most commonly used data dictionary tables. The tables that constitute the data dictionary are all accessible via the system view **dictionary** or its synonym **dict**. This is the starting point for any exploration of the data dictionary.

### 2.8.1 The user_catalog Table

The **user_catalog** table contains information about the tables and views defined by a particular user. The schema for this table is

```
user_catalog(table_name,table_type);
```

This table can also be referred to by its public synonym, **cat**. The following SQL **select** statement lists all the tables and views defined by the current user:

```
select *
from   cat;
```

### 2.8.2 The user_objects Table

The **user_objects** table contains information about all objects defined by the current user. In addition to the information available under **user_cat**, you can find out views, functions and procedures, indexes, synonyms, triggers, and so forth. defined by the current user. The schema for this table is

```
user_objects(object_name,object_id, object_type,
             created, last_ddl_time, timestamp,
             status)
```

Here, created is a date column indicating the time that the object was created, last_ddl_time is a date column indicating the time that the object was affected by a Data Definition Language (DDL) statement, timestamp is the same as created except in character string form, and the status column indicates a valid or invalid object.

### 2.8.3 The user_tables Table

If you want more information about the user table than just its name, you can use the dictionary table user_tables. In addition to the name of the table, you can obtain here space-related information and statistical information about the table. To get the names of all of its columns, use the describe user_tables command at the SQL> prompt. This table can also be accessed via its public synonym, tabs.

### 2.8.4 The user_tab_columns Table

Information specific to the columns of tables is listed in the dictionary table user_tab_columns. In addition to the name of the table to which the column belongs and the column name, definition-related information and statistical information are kept in this table. The detailed column names of this table can be obtained by using the describe command. This table can also be accessed via its public synonym, cols.

### 2.8.5 The user_views Table

Information about user views is kept in the table user_views. The schema of this table is

```
user_views(view_name,text_length,text)
```

where text_length is the length in characters of the base query on which the view is based and text is the actual text of the base query.

## 2.9 Oracle9*i* Object Features

A gentle introduction to Oracle9*i*'s object-oriented features is presented in this section. Oracle9*i* is referred to as an Object-Relational Database Management System, as it supports the purely relational view (as in Oracle 7), the object-relational view in which the user designs the database using the relational model but incorporates several object-oriented features and concepts into the design, and the purely object-oriented view in which the user designs the database based solely on an object-oriented approach. Topics introduced in this section are abstract data types, collection objects such as varying arrays and nested relations, and querying and updating object-relational tables. The mail-order database is used to illustrate the various concepts. The design of the mail-order database, of course, is modified to show one possible object-relational design.

### 2.9.1 The `create type` Statement

The `create type` statement in Oracle9*i* is versatile and can be used to create an object type, a named varying array (`VARRAY`), or a nested table type.

The simplest form[6] of the `create type` statement to create an object type has the following syntax:

```
create type [schema.]type_name as object (
  attribute_name  datatype
  [, attribute_name  datatype]...
  | [ member {procedure_specification | function_specification}
    [, member {procedure_specification |
              function_specification}]... ]
  | [ pragma restrict_references (method_name, constraints)
    [, pragma restrict_references (method_name,
       constraints)]... ]  );
```

After naming the object type, one or more attributes must be included in the type definition. The data types of these attributes can be any Oracle data type, including another object type. After the attributes are defined, member functions or procedures can be specified. Note that only the specifications of the member functions or procedures are included in the type definition. The implementations of these functions or procedures are done separately, in the `create type body` statement to be discussed in Section 3.11. Finally, one or more `pragma`s or compiler directives may be included. These impose certain restrictions on the functions or procedures, such as restricting the function or procedure from updating the database state (`WNDS: Write No Database State`), restricting the function or procedure from querying the database (`RNDS: Read No Database State`), and so on.

6. For the detailed syntax, please consult the Oracle9*i* online documentation.

An object type is essentially an abstract data type that is capable of storing both variables and methods that operate on the variables. As an example, consider the **address** attribute used in the mail-order database. Assume that this attribute is present in both the **customers** and **employees** tables. A good way to model this situation is to create an object type called **address_type** and include attributes of this type in the **customers** and **employees** tables. The **create type** statement necessary to accomplish this is

```
create type address_type as object (
  street varchar2(30),
  city   varchar2(30),
  state  varchar2(20),
  zip    number(5)
);
```

This creates a new object type, called **address_type**, and also creates default methods to construct objects of this type and to access data members of objects of this type. User-defined methods, discussed later, can also be included.

## 2.9.2 The Varying Array Collection Type

Oracle9*i* supports two kinds of collection object types: varying arrays and nested tables. Varying arrays allow the possibility of storing multiple values for an attribute within a row. While defining the type, the maximum number of values that will be allowed must be specified.

The general syntax of the **create type** statement to create a varying array is

```
create type type_name AS VARRAY (limit) OF datatype;
```

where **type_name** is the name given to the type, **limit** is the maximum number of values allowed in the varying array, and **datatype** can be any Oracle9*i* basic type or an object type.

For example, consider the fact that customers and employees may have more than one phone number. A varying array type can be created for phone numbers, and attributes of the varying array type can then be included in the **customers** and **employees** tables. The **create type** statement to define the varying array for phone numbers is

```
create type phones_varray_type as varray(3) of char(12);
```

In this case, a varying array type called **phones_varray_type** is created with a maximum of three phone numbers. Each phone number is defined to be of type `char(12)`. In general, varying arrays of any basic Oracle data type or even other abstract types can be created.

Proceeding further with the design of the mail-order database, a `person_type` object type is created as follows:

```
create type person_type as object (
  name      varchar2(30),
  address   address_type,
  phones    phones_varray_type
);
```

This type includes the name, address, and phone numbers of the person. Notice the use of the object type, `address_type`, defined earlier.

Now the `employees` and `customers` tables can be defined using the `create table` statement as usual. However, this time, the newly created object types are used to define various attributes of these tables. The `create table` statements follow:

```
create table o_employees (
  eno       number(4) not null primary key,
  person    person_type,
  hdate     date
);

create table o_customers (
  cno       number(5) not null primary key,
  person    person_type
);
```

Notice that the tables have been renamed with the `o_` prefix, so as not to cause confusion with the tables defined in the mail-order database. Both of these tables include an attribute called `person`, which is of type `person_type`. The `person_type` object type includes an address object type and a varying array of phone numbers. The `parts` table is left unchanged from the earlier version. The `create table` statement to create it is

```
create table o_parts(
  pno       number(5) not null primary key,
  pname     varchar2(30),
  qoh       integer check(qoh >= 0),
  price     number(6,2) check(price >= 0.0),
  olevel    integer;
);
```

## 2.9.3 Inserting Rows

Once the object-relational tables have been created, rows can be inserted with the **insert into** SQL statement. The syntax for inserting values into columns associated with object types uses the object type constructors that go by the same names as the object types themselves. The following **insert** statements illustrate the syntax for inserting values into the **o_employees** table:

```
insert into o_employees values
  (1000,
   person_type(
     'Jones',
     address_type('123 Main St','Wichita','KS',67226),
     phones_varray_type('316-555-1212',null,null)),
   '12-DEC-95');

insert into o_employees values
  (1001,
   person_type(
     'Smith',
     address_type('101 Elm St','Fort Dodge','KS',60606),
     phones_varray_type('316-555-2121','316-555-2323',null)),
   '01-JAN-92');

insert into o_employees values
  (1002,
   person_type(
     'Brown',
     address_type('100 Elm St','Kansas City','KS',50302),
     phones_varray_type('780-555-1111',null,null)),
   '01-SEP-94');

insert into o_employees values
  (1003,
   person_type(
     'Green',
     null,
     phones_varray_type('316-666-1212',null,null)),
   '12-OCT-95');
```

Notice the nested syntax for the **insert** statement. Also notice how the constructor methods for the various object types at the different levels of the nesting are employed with appropriate arguments to create the object instances for column values. The **null** specification for the missing phone numbers in the varying arrays is not necessary. If it is not specified, the values are undefined. Also note that the last employee has a **null** value for the **address_type** attribute.

A similar set of **insert into** statements for the **o_customers** table follows:

```
insert into o_customers values
  (1111,
   person_type(
     'Charles',
     address_type('123 Main St','Wichita','KS',67226),
     phones_varray_type('316-636-5555',null,null)));

insert into o_customers values
  (2222,
   person_type(
     'Bertram',
     address_type('237 Ash Ave','Wichita','KS',67226),
     phones_varray_type('316-689-5555','316-689-5556',null)));

insert into o_customers values
  (3333,
   person_type(
     'Barbara',
     address_type('111 Inwood St','Fort Dodge','KS',60606),
     phones_varray_type('316-111-1234','316-111-1235',null)));
```

### 2.9.4 User-Defined Methods

An object type typically includes several attributes or variables and methods that operate on the variables. When an object type is created, Oracle automatically creates methods to construct and access objects of that type. In addition to these methods, the user may specify other methods for an object type. The user-defined methods are created by specifying the method prototype in the **create type** statement and by completing the method implementation in the **create type body** statement.

Consider the order details information in the mail-order database containing the line item details for a particular order. The following **create type** statement creates an object type called **odetails_type** containing two attributes, **pno** and **qty**, along with a method, called **cost**, which computes the cost of this line item in the order:

```
create type odetails_type as object (
  pno      number(5),
  qty      integer,
  member function cost return number,
  pragma restrict_references(cost,WNDS)
);
```

The two lines that define the method **cost** for this object type are

```
member function cost return number,
pragma restrict_references(cost,WNDS)
```

The first line specifies the member function prototype. In this case, the method has no parameters, but in general, one could specify certain parameters. The body of this method, which should be specified in the **create type body** statement, is presented in Section 3.11. The method could potentially modify the database state if it wishes, which is neither desirable nor allowed if this method is to be used in an SQL query. Therefore, a **pragma** statement must be specified to restrict the method from updating the database state (**WNDS: Write No Database State**). Other available restrictions are: **RNDS: Read No Database State** (no queries allowed), **WNPS: Write No Package State** (no values of package variables are modified), and **RNPS: Read No Package State** (no package variables are referenced).

## 2.9.5 Nested Tables

The second type of collection object supported by Oracle9*i* is the nested table. In contrast to varying arrays, which have a fixed maximum number of entries, nested tables can support an unlimited number of entries per row. As the name suggests, nested tables are tables within tables. The general syntax of the **create type** statement to create a nested table is

```
create type type_name as table of datatype;
```

where **type_name** is the name given to the nested table and **datatype** is any valid Oracle9*i* basic data type or an object type.

In the mail-order database example, a table object type consisting of many **odetails_type** objects can be defined as follows:

```
create type odetails_ntable_type as
  table of odetails_type;
```

An attribute of this type can then be included in another object type, called `o_order_type`, which corresponds to the orders in the mail-order database. This way, the order details for a particular order are logically associated with the order information itself, rather than in a separate table, as was the case in the relational design of the mail-order database. The `o_order_type` object type includes all the information that was included in the `orders` table in the earlier design of the mail-order database. It also includes a nested table for order details and a user-defined method, called `total_cost`, which computes and returns the total cost for the entire order. The object type definition is

```
create type o_order_type as object (
  ono       number(5),
  odetails odetails_ntable_type,
  cno       number(5),
  eno       number(4),
  received date,
  shipped  date,
  member function total_cost return number,
  pragma restrict_references(total_cost,WNDS)
);
```

The method implementation for `total_cost` is presented in Section 3.11.

### 2.9.6 Object Tables

In Oracle9*i*, it is possible to create tables made up of objects instead of rows. Once an object type has been defined, a table of that object type can be created using a variation of the `create table` statement that is illustrated in the following example. Consider the `o_order_type` object type. A table, called `o_orders`, can be created using the following statement:

```
create table o_orders of o_order_type (
  primary key (ono)
)
nested table odetails store as odetails_tab;
```

This table consists of objects of type `o_order_type`. The primary key constraint is included here. Notice the `of` keyword used in this statement. Object tables offer considerable flexibility, in that one can define a single object type and then create as many tables as required from that object type template. Constraints such as primary keys are applicable at the table level. The syntax for accessing attributes of object rows in an object table is the same as if the attributes were defined at the table level. Examples of queries that access the object rows are presented later. The clause

```
nested table odetails store as odetails_tab;
```

that appears at the end of the preceding **create table** statement specifies that the nested table attribute **odetails** is to be stored externally under the user-chosen name **odetails_tab**. Unlike varying arrays, which are stored in-line by Oracle9*i*, nested tables are stored externally, and the clause naming the external table is required for any table that includes a nested table.

## 2.9.7 Inserting Rows into Nested Tables

Inserting rows into a table containing a nested table is done in a similar manner as with varying arrays. The object type constructors are invoked, and individual rows of the nested table are specified in a comma-separated manner. The following **insert into** statements insert four orders into the **o_orders** table:

```
insert into o_orders values
  (1020,
   odetails_ntable_type(odetails_type(10506,1),
                        odetails_type(10507,1),
                        odetails_type(10508,2),
                        odetails_type(10509,3)),
   1111,1000,'10-DEC-94','12-DEC-94');

insert into o_orders values
  (1021,
   odetails_ntable_type(odetails_type(10601,4)),
   1111,1000,'12-JAN-95','15-JAN-95');

insert into o_orders values
  (1022,
   odetails_ntable_type(odetails_type(10601,1),
                        odetails_type(10701,1)),
   2222,1001,'13-FEB-95','20-FEB-95');

insert into o_orders values
  (1023,
```

```
odetails_ntable_type(odetails_type(10800,1),
                     odetails_type(10900,1)),
3333,1000,'20-JUN-97',null);
```

Since the `o_orders` table is a table of objects, the preceding inserts should have technically invoked the object constructor for `o_order_type` as follows:

```
insert into o_orders values
  (o_order_type(1025,
     odetails_ntable_type(odetails_type(10601,1),
                          odetails_type(10701,1)),
     2222,1001,'13-FEB-95','20-FEB-95'));
```

However, Oracle9*i* allows the object tables to be viewed as relational tables and allows both types of `insert` statements (with and without invoking the object constructor). This feature makes it easy to migrate from the purely relational approach to the object-relational approach.

### 2.9.8 Querying and Accessing Data

Querying object-relational tables is accomplished using the SQL `select` statement. To access the nested attributes, the dot notation is used. For example, consider the following query:

```
-- Get the names and street addresses for employees
-- hired after 01-JAN-93
select e.person.name, e.person.address.street
from   o_employees e
where  e.hdate > '01-JAN-93';
```

Here, the query refers to the innermost basic attributes in the complex object structure using the dot notation. The expression

```
e.person.address.street
```

refers to the `street` attribute defined within the `address` attribute, which is defined within the `person` attribute of the `o_employees` table. Notice the use of table aliases in this query. Table aliases are required when table definitions are based on object types.

The next query performs a join of the two tables `o_employees` and `o_customers`, based on the `zip` attribute that lies deep in the object structure.

```
-- Get the names of employees and customers who
-- live in the same zip code
select e.person.name EMPLOYEE, c.person.name CUSTOMER
from   o_employees e, o_customers c
where  e.person.address.zip = c.person.address.zip;
```

## *Querying Collection Objects*

It is not possible to query a varying array in SQL; however, one can access the varying array in PL/SQL using procedural notation. This will be covered in Section 3.11. However, querying nested tables is possible with the SQL `select` statement. Consider the query: Get `pno` and `qty` values of parts ordered in order with `ono = 1020` with `qty > 1`. Our first attempt might be to write something like this:

```
select nt.pno, nt.qty
from   (select o.odetails    -- WRONG!!
        from   o_orders o
        where  o.ono = 1020)
where  nt.qty > 1;
```

The conceptual problem with this is that the result of any `select` operation on a table is a table. Hence, the result of the nested `select` above is a table within a table! For logical consistency, Oracle provides the `THE` operator, which essentially *flattens* the nested table. It is also necessary to give an alias to the flattened table a name, so that it can be referenced in the outer `select` statement. So, the correct SQL query is

```
select nt.pno, nt.qty
from   THE(select o.odetails
           from   o_orders o
           where  o.ono = 1020) nt
where  nt.qty > 1;
```

This query accesses the nested table column `odetails` in the `o_orders` table. The nested table can be placed in the `from` clause of the SQL `select` query, provided that it appears in the select list of a nested `select` statement and the nested `select` statement is enclosed as an argument to the special `THE` operator that flattens the nested table. Notice the use of the `where` clause both in the nested table and in the main table, implying that it is possible to restrict rows within the nested table object as well as within the main table in the same query. The aliasing of the tables in the query is also required.

Another point to note with respect to the previous query is that it is incorrect to specify a nested `select` statement that may result in more than one nested table, as in the following variant of that query:

```
select nt.pno, nt.qty
from   THE(select o.odetails     -- WRONG!!
           from   o_orders o
           where  o.ono > 1020) nt
where  nt.qty > 1;
```

Here, the nested `select` may result in more than one nested table; hence, an error message will be generated.

The next query invokes the user-defined method `cost` to compute the line item cost of each item in a particular order:

```
-- Get pno, qty, and line item cost values for parts
-- ordered in order number 1020 with qty > 1
select nt.pno, nt.qty, nt.cost()
from   THE(select o.odetails
           from   o_orders o
           where  o.ono = 1020) nt
where  nt.qty > 1;
```

To obtain the total cost for a particular order, the following query sums the line item costs:

```
-- Get the total cost of items in order number 1020
select sum(nt.cost())
from THE(select o.odetails
         from   o_orders o
         where  o.ono = 1020) nt;
```

The previous query can also be solved by invoking the method called `total_cost` on the row objects of the `o_orders` table as follows:

```
-- Get the total cost of items in order number 1020
select o.total_cost()
from   o_orders o
where  o.ono = 1020;
```

The `THE` operator can also be used to perform inserts directly into a nested table. For example, the following statement inserts a new line item in the nested table for the order number 1020:

```
insert into THE(select o.odetails
                from   o_orders o
                where ono = 1020)
values  (10800,5);
```

### Updates and Deletes

Updates and deletes to object-relational tables are done in a similar manner to purely relational tables, using the **update** and **delete** statements. Attributes are accessed in a similar manner as in the queries.

The following **update** statement changes the street address for a particular customer:

```
update o_customers c
set    c.person.address.street = '111 New Street'
where  c.cno = 1111;
```

and the following **delete** statement deletes a particular customer row:

```
delete from o_customers c
where  c.person.address.street like '111%';
```

## Exercises

2.1 To get interesting answers to queries in subsequent exercises, populate the mail-order database, using SQL **insert** statements, with at least 30 customers, 10 employees, 5 zip codes, and 50 parts. Also insert around 100 orders (an average of about 3 per customer), with each order containing an average of 2 parts.

2.2 Populate the grade book database, using SQL **insert** statements, with at least 50 rows in the **students** table, 10 rows in the **catalog** table, 12 rows in the **courses** table, 40 rows in the **components** table (resulting in an average of between three and four components per course), 120 rows in the **enrolls** table (resulting in an average of about 10 students in each course), and the appropriate number of rows in the **scores** table to complete the database.

2.3 Consider the following relations of the mail-order database:

```
EMPLOYEES(ENO,ENAME,ZIP,HDATE)
PARTS(PNO,PNAME,QOH,PRICE,LEVEL)
CUSTOMERS(CNO,CNAME,STREET,ZIP,PHONE)
ORDERS(ONO,CNO,ENO,RECEIVED,SHIPPED)
```

```
ODETAILS(ONO,PNO,QTY)
ZIPCODES(ZIP,CITY)
```

Write SQL expressions that answer the following queries:

(a) Get the names of parts that cost less than $20.00.

(b) Get the names and cities of employees who have taken orders for parts costing more than $50.00.

(c) Get the pairs of customer number values of customers having the same zip code.

(d) Get the names of customers who have ordered parts from employees living in Wichita.

(e) Get the names of customers who have ordered parts *only* from employees living in Wichita.

(f) Get the names of customers who have ordered *all* parts costing less than $20.00.

(g) Get the names of employees along with their total sales for the year 1995.

(h) Get the numbers and names of employees who have never made a sale to a customer living in the same zip code as the employee.

(i) Get the names of customers who have placed the highest number of orders.

(j) Get the names of customers who have placed the most expensive orders.

(k) Get the names of parts that have been ordered the most (in terms of quantity ordered, not number of orders).

(l) Get the names of parts along with the number of orders they appear in, sorted in decreasing order of the number of orders.

(m) Get the average waiting time for all orders in number of days. The waiting time for an order is defined as the difference between the shipped date and the received date. *Note:* The dates should be truncated to `12:00 AM` so that the difference is always a whole number of days.

(n) Get the names of customers who had to wait the longest for their orders to be shipped.

(o) For all orders greater than $100.00, get the order number and the waiting time for the order.

2.4 Consider the following relations of the grade book database:

```
CATALOG(CNO,CTITLE)
STUDENTS(SID,FNAME,LNAME,MINIT)
COURSES(TERM,LINENO,CNO,A,B,C,D)
COMPONENTS(TERM,LINENO,COMPNAME,MAXPOINTS,WEIGHT)
```

```
ENROLLS(SID,TERM,LINENO)
SCORES(SID,TERM,LINENO,COMPNAME,POINTS)
```

Write SQL expressions that answer the following queries:

(a) Get the names of students enrolled in the Automata class in the Fall 1996 term.

(b) Get the course numbers and titles of courses in which Timothy Thomas has enrolled.

(c) Get the **SID** values of students who did not enroll in any class during the Fall 1996 term.

(d) Get the **SID** values of students who have enrolled in CSc226 and CSc227.

(e) Get the **SID** values of students who have enrolled in CSc226 or CSc227.

(f) Get the **SID** values of students who have enrolled in *all* the courses in the catalog.

(g) Get the names of students who have enrolled in the highest number of courses.

(h) Get the names of students who have enrolled in the lowest number of courses (the student must have enrolled in at least one course).

(i) Get the names of students who have not enrolled in any course.

(j) Get the titles of courses that have had enrollments of five or fewer students.

(k) Get the terms, line numbers, course numbers, and course titles of courses, along with their total enrollments.

(l) Get the terms, line numbers, and course titles of courses with the highest enrollments.

(m) Get the terms, line numbers, and course titles of courses that have enrollments greater than or equal to the average enrollment in all courses.

(n) Get the student IDs of students, the terms and line numbers of courses they have enrolled in, the component names of the courses, the student scores in the components of the courses, and the weighted average of the component scores.

(o) Given a term and line number of a course (for example, w98 and 1585), get the student IDs, last names, and first names of students enrolled in the class along with each student's course average rounded off to the nearest integer. The course average is the sum of the weighted averages of the individual component scores.

2.5 Consider the following relations of the investment portfolio database:

```
MEMBER(MID,PASSWORD,FNAME,LNAME,ADDRESS,EMAIL,CASH_BALANCE)
SECURITY(SYMBOL,CNAME,CURRENT_PRICE,ASK_PRICE,BID_PRICE)
TRANSACTION(MID,SYMBOL,TRANS_DATE,TRANS_TYPE,QUANTITY,
            PRICE_PER_SHARE,COMMISSION,AMOUNT)
```

(a) Get company names of securities whose current prices are greater than $100.00.

(b) Get names of members who have purchased ORCL shares.

(c) Get names of members who have purchased ORCL shares but *not* SYBS shares.

(d) Get names of members who have purchased *only* ORCL shares.

(e) Get company names of securities whose shares have been purchased by *all* members.

(f) Get names of members who have purchased shares from *all* of the companies that the member with `mid = 11000` has purchased shares from.

(g) Get names of members who have purchased shares *only* from a subset of the companies that the member with `mid = 11000` has purchased shares from.

(h) Get names of members who have purchased shares from *exactly* the same companies that the member with `mid = 11000` has purchased shares from.

2.6 For the mail-order database, write SQL expressions to perform the following updates to the database:

(a) Decrease by 15 percent the prices of all parts that cost less than $20.00.

(b) Update all the `null`-valued shipped dates of orders to the current date.

(c) Decrease by $10.00 the prices of parts that cost more than the average price of all parts.

(d) Transfer all the orders belonging to the employee with `eno = 1000` to the employee with `eno = 1001`.

(e) Delete all the orders for customers living in Wichita.

(f) Delete all the orders for employees with the minimum sales.

2.7 For the grade book database, write SQL expressions to perform the following updates to the database:

(a) Update all the `null`-valued scores to zeros.

(b) Delete the component `QUIZ2` from the `components` table.

(c) Drop the student with `sid = 1234` from the Fall 1997 course with `lineno = 1111`.

(d) Enroll all students in the Fall 1997 course with `lineno = 1111` into the Fall 1997 course with `lineno = 1112`.

(e) Give all students in the Fall 1997 course with `lineno = 1111` 10 extra points in the `EXAM1` component.

(f) Delete all the courses from the `courses` table that have enrollments of fewer than five students.

2.8 For the investment portfolio database, write SQL expressions to perform the following updates to the database:

(a) Delete the member with `mid = 11000` from the database. Make sure that all the transactions for this member are archived in a backup table with the same structure as the **transaction** table. These transactions then must be deleted from the **transaction** table.

(b) Insert a **buy** transaction for the member with `mid = 10000` for 100 shares of ORCL at the present bid price. Assume a commission of 1% and that the transaction takes place at the same time as the insert. The member's cash balance should be updated appropriately.

(c) Insert a **sell** transaction for the member with `mid = 10000` for 250 shares of SYBS at the present ask price. Assume a commission of 1% and that the transaction takes place at the same time as the insert. The member's cash balance should be updated appropriately.

(d) Make necessary updates to reflect a stock split of 2:1 for ORCL. The stock split implies the doubling of the number of shares currently owned by each member and halving the current price of the security. The ask and bid prices should be reset to **null**.

(e) Make necessary updates to the database to reflect the merger of two companies: Mindspring Enterprises, Inc. (symbol: MSPG) and EarthLink Network, Inc. (symbol: ELNK). The merger agreement indicates that the new company will trade under the ELNK symbol and be called EarthSpring Enterprises, Inc. Also, each shareholder of MSPG will receive one share of the new company's stock for each MSPG share he or she owns, and each shareholder of ELNK will receive 1.5 shares for each ELNK share he or she owns. The current price for the new company should be the current price of MSPG. The ask and bid prices should be set to **null**.

# CHAPTER 3

# PL/SQL

This chapter introduces PL/SQL, its syntax and semantics, through several illustrative examples. Topics covered include data types and variables, program control statements, program structure constructs (such as blocks, procedures, functions, and packages), database access using cursors, exception handling, triggers, stored procedures and functions, and two built-in packages: `dbms_output`, useful for debugging purposes, and `dbms_sql`, useful for dynamic SQL. PL/SQL access to Oracle9*i* objects is introduced at the end.

## 3.1 What Is PL/SQL?

PL/SQL is Oracle's procedural extension to SQL. It supplements SQL with several high-level programming language features such as block structure, variables, constants and types, the assignment statement, conditional statements, loops, customized error handling, and structured data. Since PL/SQL is seamlessly integrated with Oracle's SQL implementation, many of the data types in PL/SQL are compatible with those of the database columns. In addition, almost any SQL statement can be used in a PL/SQL program without any special preprocessing, unlike embedded SQL. In this sense, PL/SQL can be considered a superset of SQL. The one exception is SQL's data definition statements, such as `create table`. These are not allowed in PL/SQL, because PL/SQL code is compiled and it cannot refer to objects that do not yet exist at compile time. You can work around this restriction by using the dynamic SQL package `dbms_sql`, which allows for the data definition statements to be created dynamically at run time and then executed.

**Figure 3.1** PL/SQL scalar data types.

| Category | Data Type | Description |
|---|---|---|
| Numeric | `binary_integer` | Integer in the range $-2^{31} - 1$ to $2^{31} - 1$. |
| | `natural` | Integer in the range 0 to $2^{31}$ |
| | `positive` | Integer in the range 1 to $2^{31}$ |
| | `number(p,s)` | Same as Oracle SQL's **number**, where **p** is the precision and **s** is the scale |
| Character | `char(n)` | Fixed-length character string of length **n** |
| | `varchar2(n)` | Variable-length character string of maximum length **n** |
| Boolean | `boolean` | Boolean data type **(true, false)** |
| Date-Time | `date` | Same as Oracle SQL's **date** |

An interesting feature of PL/SQL is that it allows the user to store compiled code in the database, thereby allowing any number of applications to access and share the same functions and procedures. These applications can be running as Web applications under the Web Application Server or as form applications under the Developer/2000 environment. PL/SQL can also be used to implement program logic embedded within client-side applications, such as those found in Oracle Forms triggers. Oracle's SQL*Plus environment also allows the execution of PL/SQL code, which makes it more than just an SQL interpreter.

## 3.2 Data Types and Variables

PL/SQL supports a variety of data types. Since it is closely tied to Oracle SQL, many of these data types are compatible with Oracle SQL's data types, which can be classified into two categories: *scalar* and *composite*. The scalar data types include all of the Oracle SQL data types and a few new ones, such as **binary_integer** and **boolean**. The scalar data types are summarized in Figure 3.1.

Variables[1] are declared in PL/SQL using the syntax

```
<variable-name> <datatype> [not null][:= <initial-value>];
```

and constants are declared as follows:

1. PL/SQL identifiers are formed in the usual manner; they start with a letter and contain letters, digits, and underscore characters. They are not case sensitive.

```
<constant-name> constant <datatype> := <value>;
```

Example 3.2.1 Some examples of variable and constant declarations are shown in Figure 3.2.

**Figure 3.2** Variable and constant declarations.

```
i binary_integer;
cno number(5) not null := 1111;
cname varchar2(30);
commission real(5,2) := 12.5;
maxcolumns constant integer(2) := 30;
hired_date date;
done boolean;
```

Any variable that is declared to be **`not null`** must be initialized in its declaration. All variables that are not defined to be **`not null`** are initialized to have the value `null`.

An important point to note here is that PL/SQL allows only one variable to be declared at a time. For example, the following would be invalid in PL/SQL:

```
a, b, c number;
```

Variables can also be declared to have *anchored* data types—i.e., data types that are determined by looking up another object's data type. This other object could be a column in the database, thereby providing the ability to match the data types of PL/SQL variables with the data types of columns defined in the database. The anchored declarations have the syntax

```
<variable-name> <object>%type [not null][:= <initial-value>];
```

where `<object>` is another previously declared PL/SQL variable or a database column.

Example 3.2.2 Some examples of anchored declarations are shown in Figure 3.3.

**Figure 3.3** Anchored variable declarations.

```
cnum customers.cno%type;
cname customers.cname%type;
commission real(5,2) := 12.5;
x commission%type;
```

There are at least two advantages to variables with anchored data types. First, these variables are synchronized with the database columns. The database columns may change their data types, and the PL/SQL program will remain compatible. Second, variables declared within the PL/SQL program are normalized—i.e., changing one data type does not affect how the corresponding anchored variables will be used. Of course, in both cases, the changes in data types have to be minor—i.e., changes in widths, precisions, or scales only. An important point to note is that anchored data types are evaluated at compile time. Therefore, if any changes are made to the data types of variables that affect other types, the program must be recompiled before these changes are reflected in their anchored variables.

PL/SQL provides two composite data types, *tables* and *records*, which are discussed in separate sections later in this chapter.

Comments in PL/SQL are expressed using one of two notations:

- *Single-line comments.* Any characters that follow two dashes (`--`) in a line are treated as comments by PL/SQL.
- *Block comments.* Any characters that come after the two-character sequence `/*` and before the two-character sequence `*/` are treated as comments by PL/SQL.

## 3.3 Program Control Statements

Like any other high-level programming language, PL/SQL provides for the **null** statement, assignment statement, conditional statements, and loops. These statements are introduced in this section.

### 3.3.1 `null` Statement

The syntax of the **null** statement is

```
null;
```

and it performs no action. This statement is sometimes useful to improve readability of the program.

### 3.3.2 Assignment Statement

The assignment statement has the syntax

```
<variable> := <expression>;
```

where the expression on the right side is compatible with the data type of the variable on the left side of the assignment.

Example 3.3.1 Some examples of the assignment statement are given in Figure 3.4.

**Figure 3.4** Assignment statements.

```
i := i + 1;
cname := 'Jones';
sales := price * qty;
```

## 3.3.3 Conditional Statements

There are three varieties of the conditional statement in PL/SQL:

```
if-then
if-then-else
if-then-elsif
```

These are discussed next.

### if-then

The syntax of the `if-then` statement in PL/SQL is

```
if <condition> then
  <statement-list>;
end if;
```

where `<condition>` is any Boolean expression. This statement ends with the keywords `end if`. Note the space character between the `end` and `if` keywords. The statements between these keywords are executed if the `condition` evaluates to `true`. Otherwise, these statements are skipped. In either case, control passes to the statement following the `if-then` statement.

Example 3.3.2 An example of the use of the `if-then` statement is shown in Figure 3.5.[2] The `put_line` procedure within the `dbms_output` package takes as input a `number`, `string`, or `date` value and sends it to the standard output. In this

2. This and many subsequent examples use the built-in package `dbms_output` and several of its procedures. Some of the built-in packages, including `dbms_output`, are discussed in Section 3.9.

**Figure 3.5** `if-then` statement.

```
if (cnum > 1000) and (cnum < 9000) then
  i := i + 1;
  dbms_output.put_line('Customer ' || cnum);
end if;
```

example, a **string** value is sent in to the **put_line** procedure. The || operator is the PL/SQL concatenation operation, the same operator used in Oracle SQL.

## if-then-else

The syntax of the **if-then-else** statement in PL/SQL is

```
if <condition> then
  <statement-list-1>;
else
  <statement-list-2>;
end if;
```

where **<condition>** is any Boolean expression. This statement also ends with the keywords **end if**. The statements between the **then** and **else** keywords are executed if the **condition** evaluates to **true**; the statements between the **else** and **end if** keywords are executed if the **condition** evaluates to **false** or **null**. In either case, control passes to the statement following the **if-then-else** statement.

Example 3.3.3 An example of the use of the **if-then-else** statement is shown in Figure 3.6.

**Figure 3.6** `if-then-else` statement.

```
if (cnum > 1000) and (cnum < 9000) then
  i := i + 1;
  dbms_output.put_line('Valid Customer ' || cnum);
else
  j := j + 1;
  dbms_output.put_line('Invalid Customer ' || cnum);
end if;
```

### `if-then-elsif`

The **`if-then-elsif`** variety of the conditional statement is used when one has to deal with multiple and mutually exclusive conditions. The syntax is as follows:

```
if <condition-1> then
    <statement-list-1>;
  elsif <condition-2> then
    <statement-list-2>;
  .
  .
  .
  elsif <condition-n> then
    <statement-list-n>;
  else
    <statement-list-n+1>
end if;
```

The conditions are evaluated from the beginning. The group of statements associated with the first condition that evaluates to **`true`** is executed, and control passes to the statement following this statement. If all the conditions evaluate to **`false`** or **`null`**, then the statements associated with the **`else`** clause are executed. The **`else`** clause is optional.

Example 3.3.4 An example of the **`if-then-elsif`** statement is given in Figure 3.7.

**Figure 3.7** `if-then-elsif` statement.

```
if (score > 90) then
    na := na + 1;
  elsif (score > 80) then
    nb := nb + 1;
  elsif (score > 70) then
    nc := nc + 1;
  elsif (score > 60) then
    nd := nd + 1;
  else
    nf := nf + 1;
end if;
```

## 3.3.4 Loops

There are three kinds of loop control structures available in PL/SQL: **loop**, **for loop**, and **while loop**. These loops are discussed here.

### loop

The basic **loop** statement has the following syntax:

```
loop
  <statement-list>;
end loop;
```

This loop repeatedly executes the statement list until it finds an **exit** statement.

Example 3.3.5 An example of the **loop** statement is given in Figure 3.8.

**Figure 3.8** loop statement.

```
loop
  i := i + 1;
  if i > 10 then
    exit;
  end if;
  sum := sum + i;
end loop;
```

If the **exit** statement is placed in a conditional statement within the loop body, the statements in the body of the loop are executed a certain number of times and control is transferred to the next statement following the loop when the condition is met. The **if-then** statement in the earlier example could have been replaced by the following equivalent **exit-when** statement:

```
exit when i > 10;
```

The basic loop has the potential for not terminating at all. If the **exit** statement is never encountered within the body of the loop, the loop will never terminate.

### for loop

If the number of times the loop body is to be executed is known, the **for loop** statement can be used. The syntax of the **for loop** statement is

```
for <loop-counter> in [reverse] <lower>..<upper> loop
  <statements>;
end loop;
```

where `<loop-counter>` is the loop control variable that is implicitly declared by PL/SQL. It should not be declared in the program. The lower and upper bounds for the loop control variable are specified in `<lower>` and `<upper>`, respectively. These must be integer expressions. The `reverse` keyword is optional; if it is not used, the loop starts with the loop control variable set at the lower bound, each time incrementing (by 1) the loop counter variable until it reaches the upper bound. If the `reverse` keyword is used, the loop control variable starts at the upper bound and each time is decremented (by 1) until it reaches the lower bound. In either case, if the lower bound is greater than the upper bound, the loop body is skipped. PL/SQL does not provide the `steps` feature in its `for loop` statement, which would allow the increment or decrement of the loop control variable to be done by a number other than 1.

Example 3.3.6 A couple of examples of the `for loop` statement are shown in Figure 3.9. The first `for loop` executes 10 times, with `i` starting at `1` and terminating at `10`. Since the loop control variable is automatically declared by PL/SQL in the `for loop`, its scope is the `for loop`, and it is not available outside of the loop. Therefore, it would be incorrect to use the value of the loop control variable after the loop has terminated. The second `for loop` executes 5 times, with `i` starting at `5` and terminating at `1`.

## while loop

The `while loop` statement has the syntax

**Figure 3.9** `for loop` statement.

```
for i in 1..10 loop
  dbms_output.put_line('i = ' || i);
  sum := sum + i;
end loop;

for i in reverse 1..5 loop
  dbms_output.put_line('i = ' || i);
  sum := sum + 2*i;
end loop;
```

```
while <condition> loop
  <statement-list>
end loop;
```

and it continues to execute the statements in its body as long as the condition remains **true**. The loop terminates when the condition evaluates to **false** or **null**. The **exit** statement may also be used to exit the loop.

Example 3.3.7 An example of the **while loop** statement is given in Figure 3.10. This program fragment that involves the **while loop** computes the sum of the powers of 2 that do not exceed 1000.

**Figure 3.10** while loop statement.

```
i := 1;
sum := 0;
while (i < 1000) loop
  sum := sum + i;
  i := 2 * i;
end loop;
```

## 3.4 Program Structure

PL/SQL, like many high-level languages, groups its statements into units called *blocks*. Blocks can be unnamed (*anonymous blocks*) or named (*subprograms*). The subprograms can be either functions or procedures, just as in any high-level programming language. PL/SQL further allows the possibility of grouping related functions, procedures, and data types into *packages*. These features of PL/SQL are discussed in this section.

### 3.4.1 Anonymous Blocks

An anonymous block has the following structure:

```
declare
  -- Declaration Section
  -- Data, subprogram declarations
```

```
begin
  -- Executable Section
  null; -- Program statements

exception
  -- Exception Section
  -- Exception handlers
  when others then
     null; -- Default handler

end;
```

There are three parts to an anonymous block: (1) the declaration section, (2) the executable section, and (3) the exception section. The declaration section begins with the keyword **declare** and ends with the keyword **begin**. The declaration section consists of type, constant, variable, exception, and cursor declarations. At the end, subprograms, if there are any, are declared.

Example 3.4.1 An example of an anonymous block is shown in Figure 3.11. This block gets all the rows from the **customers** table and prints the names of the customers on the screen. It does use several features of PL/SQL, such as PL/SQL tables and cursors, that will be covered later in this chapter.

Anonymous blocks can be executed within the SQL*Plus environment, like SQL statements. Normally, the anonymous block is placed in a file, and the file is executed within SQL*Plus.

Example 3.4.2 A sample run of the anonymous block is shown in Figure 3.12. It is assumed that the anonymous block is placed in the file **p2.sql**.

### 3.4.2 Procedures and Functions

Procedures are declared using the following syntax:

```
procedure <proc-name>
     [(<parameter>, ... , <parameter>)] is
  [<declarations>]
begin
  executable section;
[exception
  exception handlers;]
end;
```

**Figure 3.11** Anonymous block.

```
declare
  type customers_table is table  of customers%rowtype
       index by binary_integer;

  c_table customers_table;
  cursor c is select cno,cname,street,zip,phone
              from  customers;
  c_rec c%rowtype;
  i binary_integer;
begin
  i := 1;
  for c_rec in c loop
    exit when c%notfound;
    c_table(i) := c_rec;
    i := i + 1;
  end loop;
  for i in 1..c_table.count loop
    dbms_output.put_line(
      'c_table(' || i || ').cname = ' || c_table(i).cname);
  end loop;
end;
/
```

**Figure 3.12** Execution script for an anonymous block.

```
SQL> start p2
c_table(1).cname = Charles
c_table(2).cname = Bertram
c_table(3).cname = Barbara

PL/SQL procedure successfully completed.

SQL> exit
```

where

- <proc-name> is the name given to the procedure.
- <parameter> is a parameter with the following syntax:[3]

```
<variable-name> [in | out | in out] <datatype>
```

  The `in`, `out`, and `in out` parameter types are for input, output, and input/output parameters, respectively.
- <declarations> is the declaration of local variables, constants, and so on.
- After the executable section, the procedure may end with an optional exception section, as with anonymous blocks.

Example 3.4.3 The anonymous block shown next contains a procedure that accepts as input a customer number and returns the name, phone, and city values for that customer. If such a customer is not found, `status` is returned as `false`; otherwise, `status` is returned as `true`.

```
DECLARE
  cnum customers.cno%type;
  ccname customers.cname%type;
  cphone customers.phone%type;
  ccity zipcodes.city%type;
  status boolean;

  procedure get_cust_details(
      cust_no     in  customers.cno%type,
      cust_name   out customers.cname%type,
      cust_phone  out customers.phone%type,
      cust_city   out zipcodes.city%type,
      status      out boolean) is
  begin
    select cname,phone,city
    into   cust_name,cust_phone,cust_city
    from   customers,zipcodes
    where  customers.zip = zipcodes.zip and
           customers.cno = cust_no;
    status := true;
```

3. The data type of the parameter cannot be constrained—i.e., it is illegal to specify the data type as `char(20)` or `varchar2(40)`; these must be specified simply as `char` or `varchar2`.

```
    exception
      when no_data_found then
        status := false;
  end;
begin
  cnum := 1111;
  get_cust_details(cnum,ccname,cphone,ccity,status);
  if (status) then
    dbms_output.put_line(cnum   || '  ' || ccname || '  ' ||
                         cphone || '  ' || ccity);
  else
    dbms_output.put_line('Customer ' || cnum       ||
                         ' not found');
  end if;
  cnum := 5555;
  get_cust_details(cnum,ccname,cphone,ccity,status);
  if (status) then
    dbms_output.put_line(cnum   || '  ' || ccname || '  ' ||
                         cphone || '  ' || ccity);
  else
    dbms_output.put_line('Customer ' || cnum       ||
                         ' not found');
  end if;
end;
/
```

The following is a session capture of the run under SQL*Plus (assuming that the previous block is stored in a file called `p3.sql`):

```
SQL> start p3
1111  Charles  316-636-5555  Wichita
Customer 5555 not found

PL/SQL procedure successfully completed.

SQL>
```

Functions are declared using the following syntax:

```
function <function-name>
     [(<parameter>, ... , <parameter>)]
   return <datatype> is
```

```
  [<declarations>]
begin
  executable section;
[exception
  exception handlers;]
end;
```

The syntax is almost identical to that of a procedure declaration, except that the function declaration requires the **return** keyword followed by a data type.

Example 3.4.4 The following anonymous block contains a function declaration. Given an employee number, the function computes and returns the total sales for that employee.

```
declare
  enum customers.cno%type;
  total number(10,2);
  status boolean;

  function total_emp_sales(emp_no in  employees.eno%type)
    return number is
  sales number;
  begin
    select sum(price*qty)
    into   sales
    from   orders,odetails,parts
    where  orders.eno = emp_no and
           orders.ono = odetails.ono and
           odetails.pno = parts.pno;
    return (sales);
  end;

begin
  enum := 1000;
  total := total_emp_sales(enum);
  dbms_output.put_line('Total sales for employee ' ||
                       enum   || ' is ' || total);
end;
/
```

The following is a screen capture of the run under SQL*Plus (assuming that the previous block is stored in a file called `p4.sql`):

```
SQL> start p4
Total sales for employee 1000 is 279.87

PL/SQL procedure successfully completed.

SQL>
```

### 3.4.3 Stored Procedures and Functions

The procedures and functions discussed so far were part of an anonymous block and were called from within the executable section of the anonymous block. However, it is possible to store the procedure or function definition in the database and have it invoked from various environments that have access to the database. This feature in PL/SQL is very attractive, as it allows for sharing of PL/SQL code by different applications running at different places. The `create procedure` and `create function` statements are used to create the stored procedures and functions. Their syntax is

```
create [or replace] procedure <proc-name>
  [(<parameter-list>)] as
  <declarations>
begin
  <executable-section>
  [exception
    <exception-section>]
end;

create [or replace] function <func-name>
  [(<parameter-list>)] return <datatype> as
  <declarations>
begin
  <executable-section>
  [exception
    <exception-section>]
end;
```

The syntax is almost identical to declaring procedures or functions within anonymous blocks, except for the `create` keyword at the beginning and the use of the `as` keyword instead of the `is` keyword.

Example 3.4.5 The following stored function takes as input a customer number and returns the city in which the customer lives:

```
create or replace function get_city(cnum in customers.cno%type)
      return zipcodes.city%type as
  ccity zipcodes.city%type;
begin
  select city
  into   ccity
  from   customers,zipcodes
  where  cno = cnum and
         customers.zip = zipcodes.zip;
  return (ccity);
end;
/
```

A stored procedure or a function can be invoked from various environments, including an SQL statement, another stored procedure or function, an anonymous block or a procedure or function defined within it, an embedded SQL program, a database trigger, and Oracle tools such as Developer/2000 Forms. There are some restrictions when a stored function is invoked from within an SQL statement—for example, that there should be no **out** parameters, the function should be applicable to a row in the table, and the return data type should be compatible with an SQL data type.

Example 3.4.6 The following is a call made to the stored function **get_city** in an SQL query:

```
SQL> select cno,cname,get_city(cno)
  2  from customers;

   CNO CNAME    GET_CITY(CNO)
 ----- -------- -------------
  1111 Charles  Wichita

  2222 Bertram  Wichita

  3333 Barbara  Fort Dodge
SQL>
```

### 3.4.4 Packages

A *package* is a group of related PL/SQL objects (variables, constants, types, and cursors), procedures, and functions that is stored in the database. A package definition consists of two parts: the package *specification* and the package *body*. The package specification is the interface that is used by other programs to make a call to the functions and procedures stored in the database as part of the package or to use certain types or cursors defined in the package. The package body contains the actual code and any other implementation-dependent details for the functions and procedures of the package. It may also contain some private objects not visible to the user of the package. The concept of a package is similar to that of an object in an object-oriented language. An advantage of creating packages in this manner is that the package body can change without affecting any programs that are accessing the package.

The syntax for creating a package specification is

```
create [or replace] package <package-name> as
  <PL/SQL declarations>;
end;
```

where `<PL/SQL declarations>` is any set of variable, type, constant, procedure, or function declarations. The procedure and function declarations consist only of the name, parameter list, and function return type. They do not contain the actual code, since this has to be specified in the package body. The syntax to create a package body is

```
create [or replace] package body <package-name> as
  <PL/SQL declarations>;
[begin
  <initialization-code>
 end;]
end;
```

where the `<PL/SQL declarations>` now contain the code for the functions and procedures defined in the specification. At the end of the body, you can specify an initialization code fragment that initializes variables and other features of the package.

Example 3.4.7 The next code fragment defines a package called **process_orders**, containing three procedures:

- **add_order**. This procedure takes as input an order number, customer number, employee number, and received date and tries to insert a new row in the **orders** table. If the received date is **null**, the current date is used. The shipped date is left as **null**. If any errors occur, an entry is made in the **orders_errors** table, which is assumed to have three columns: (1) transaction date, (2) order number, and (3) message column.

- **add_order_details**. This procedure receives as input an order number, part number, and quantity and attempts to add a row corresponding to the input in the **odetails** table. If the quantity on hand for the part is less than what is ordered, an error message is sent to the **odetails_errors** table, which consists of four columns: (1) transaction date, (2) order number, (3) part number, and (4) message column. Otherwise, the part is sold by subtracting the quantity ordered from the quantity on hand for this part. A check is also made for the reorder level. If the updated quantity for the part is below the reorder level, a message is sent to the **restock** table, which consists of two columns: the transaction date and the part number of the part to be reordered.
- **ship_order**. This procedure takes as input an order number and a shipped date and tries to update the **shipped** value for the order. If the shipped date is **null**, the current date is used. If any errors occur, a message is left in the **orders_errors** table.

```
-- PACKAGE PROCESS_ORDERS SPECS ---

create or replace package process_orders as
  procedure add_order_details
    (onum      in odetails.ono%type,
     pnum      in odetails.pno%type,
     quantity  in odetails.qty%type);
  procedure add_order
    (onum in orders.ono%type,
     cnum in orders.cno%type,
     enum in orders.eno%type,
     receive in date);
  procedure ship_order
    (onum in orders.ono%type,
     ship in date);
end;
/
show errors
```

```
-- PACKAGE PROCESS_ORDERS BODY ---

create or replace package body process_orders as

  procedure add_order_details
    (onum      in odetails.ono%type,
     pnum      in odetails.pno%type,
     quantity  in odetails.qty%type) is
  cur_q parts.qoh%type;
  lev parts.olevel%type;
  begin
    select qoh,olevel
    into   cur_q,lev
    from   parts
    where  pno = pnum;
    if (cur_q > quantity) then
      update parts
      set qoh = qoh - quantity
      where pno = pnum;
      if (cur_q - quantity) < lev then
        insert into restock
          values (sysdate,pnum);
      end if;
      insert into odetails
        values (onum,pnum,quantity);
    else
      insert into odetails_errors
        values(sysdate,onum,pnum,'Do not have enough to sell');
    end if;
  exception
    when others then
      rollback work;
      insert into odetails_errors
        values(sysdate,onum,pnum,'error inserting order detail');
  end;

  procedure add_order
    (onum in orders.ono%type,
     cnum in orders.cno%type,
```

```
     enum in orders.eno%type,
     receive in date) is
  begin
    if (receive is null) then
      insert into orders
        values (onum,cnum,enum,sysdate,null);
    else
      insert into orders
        values (onum,cnum,enum,receive,null);
    end if;
  exception
    when others then
      rollback work;
      insert into orders_errors
        values(sysdate,onum,'error inserting order');
  end;

  procedure ship_order
    (onum in orders.ono%type,
     ship in date) is
  begin
    if (ship is null) then
      update orders
      set    shipped = sysdate
      where  ono = onum;
    else
      update orders
      set    shipped = ship
      where  ono = onum;
    end if;
  exception
    when others then
      rollback work;
      insert into orders_errors
        values(sysdate,onum,'error updating shipped date');
  end;
end;
/
show errors
```

As an exercise, execute the following commands against the mail-order database in SQL*Plus:

```
SQL> execute process_orders.add_order
        (2000,1111,1000,null);
SQL> execute process_orders.add_order_details
        (2000,10509,50);
SQL> execute process_orders.add_order_details
        (2000,10701,200);
SQL> execute process_orders.ship_order
        (2000,'29-JAN-98');
SQL> execute process_orders.add_order
        (2001,1234,1000,null)
SQL> execute process_orders.add_order_details
        (2000,10999,5);
```

Now take a look at the `restock`, `orders_errors`, and `odetails_errors` tables.

## 3.5 Triggers

An SQL *trigger* is a mechanism that automatically executes a specified PL/SQL block (referred to as the *triggered action*) when a *triggering event* occurs on a table. The triggering event may be one of `insert`, `delete`, or `update`. The trigger is associated with a database table and is *fired* when the triggering event takes place on the table.

Triggers are created in Oracle using the `create trigger` statement, whose syntax is

```
create [or replace] trigger trigger-name
{before | after}
{delete | insert | update [of column [, column] ...]}
[or
{delete | insert | update [of column [, column] ...]}
] ...
ON table-name
[ [referencing { old [as] <old> [new [as] <new>]
               | new [as] <new> [old [as] <old>] } ]
 for each row
 [when (condition)] ]
pl/sql_block
```

where the following assumptions can be made:

- The optional `or replace` is used to change the definition of an existing trigger without first dropping it.
- `trigger-name` is the name of the trigger to be created.
- `before` indicates that Oracle fires the trigger before executing the triggering statement, and `after` indicates that Oracle fires the trigger after executing the triggering statement.
- `delete` indicates that the triggering event is a `delete` statement.
- `insert` indicates that the triggering event is an `insert` statement.
- `update...of` indicates that the triggering event is an `update` statement involving the columns mentioned.
- `table-name` is the name of the table on which the trigger is defined.
- `referencing` specifies correlation names that can be used to refer to the old and new values of the row components that are being affected by the trigger.
- `for each row` designates the trigger to be a row trigger—i.e., the trigger is fired once for each row that is affected by the triggering event and meets the optional trigger constraint defined in the `when` clause. If this clause is omitted, the trigger is a statement trigger—i.e., the trigger is fired only once, when the triggering event is met, if the optional trigger constraint is met.
- `when` specifies the trigger restriction. The trigger restriction contains an SQL condition that must be satisfied for the trigger to be fired.
- `pl/sql_block` is the PL/SQL block that Oracle executes as the trigger action.

Example 3.5.1 The trigger that follows is executed when a row is inserted into the `odetails` table. The trigger checks to see if the quantity ordered is more than the quantity on hand. If it is, an error message is generated, and the row is not inserted. Otherwise, the trigger updates the quantity on hand for the part and checks to see if it has fallen below the reorder level. If it has, it sends a row to the `restock` table indicating that the part needs to be reordered.

```
create or replace trigger insert_odetails
before insert on odetails
for each row
declare my_qoh parts.qoh%type;
        my_olevel parts.olevel%type;
        out_of_stock exception;
begin
```

```
  select qoh, olevel
  into   my_qoh, my_olevel
  from   parts
  where  parts.pno = :new.pno;

  if (:new.qty < my_qoh) then
    update parts
    set    qoh = qoh - :new.qty
    where  parts.pno = :new.pno;
    if ((my_qoh - :new.qty) < my_olevel) then
       update parts
       set    qoh = olevel * 5
       where  parts.pno = :new.pno;
       insert into restock values (sysdate,:new.pno);
    end if;
  else
    raise out_of_stock;
 end if;
exception
  when out_of_stock then
-- error number between -20000 and -20999
    raise_application_error(-20001,'cannot add this odetails row');
end;
/
```

Assume that the following anonymous block (stored in the file **trig2test.sql**) is executed to create a new order:

```
declare
  quantity_ordered_too_big exception;
  pragma exception_init(quantity_ordered_too_big,-20001);
begin
  process_orders.add_order(2000,1111,1000,null);
  insert into odetails values(2000,10900,10);
  dbms_output.put_line('Added row to odetails table');
  insert into odetails values(2000,10506,1500);
exception
  when quantity_ordered_too_big then
    dbms_output.put_line('Could not add part to order');
    dbms_output.put_line(sqlerrm);
end;
/
```

The following SQL*Plus session illustrates the use of the trigger. The part numbers, quantity on hand, and reorder levels before the block executes are

```
SQL> select pno,qoh,olevel
  2  from parts
  3  where pno in (10900,10506);

       PNO        QOH     OLEVEL
---------- ---------- ----------
     10506        200         20
     10900         90         30
```

The execution of the **trig2test** block is shown next:

```
SQL> start trig2test
Added row to odetails table
Could not add part to order
ORA-20001: CANNOT ADD THIS ODETAILS ROW
ORA-06512: at "BOOK.INSERT_ODETAILS",
line 27
ORA-04088: error during execution of trigger
'BOOK.INSERT_ODETAILS'

PL/SQL procedure successfully completed.
```

Notice that the first **odetails** row was added successfully but did result in an entry being added to the **restock** table, as the **qoh** value went below the reorder level. The second row is not added to the **odetails** table, since the quantity ordered is greater than the quantity on hand. The trigger raises an **application error** and sends it back to the anonymous block that caused the trigger to fire. The anonymous block then processes this exception and exits gracefully. The **restock** table and the relevant columns of the **parts** table, after the trigger is executed, are

```
SQL> select * from restock;

TDATE            PNO
--------- ----------
14-APR-98      10900

SQL> select pno,qoh,olevel
  2  from parts
  3  where pno in (10900,10506);
```

```
       PNO        QOH     OLEVEL
---------- ---------- ----------
     10506        200         20
     10900        150         30
```

Notice that the quantity-on-hand value for the 10900 part has been reset to 5 times the olevel value by the trigger.

The raise_application_error procedure is a useful way to communicate application-specific errors from the server side (usually a database trigger) to the client-side application (in this case, the anonymous block). The anonymous block in this example is executed in the server side itself, but the block running on the client side can easily be envisioned.

Example 3.5.2 The trigger that follows is defined on the **parts** table and is triggered when the **price** column is updated. Each time someone updates the price of a particular part, the trigger makes an entry in a log file of this update along with the **userid** of the person performing the update and the date of the update. The log file is created using

```
create table parts_log (
  pno             number(5),
  username        char(8),
  update_date     date,
  old_price       number(6,2),
  new_price       number(6,2));
```

The trigger is defined as

```
create or replace trigger update_price_of_parts
after update of price on parts
for each row
begin
 insert into parts_log
 values (:old.pno,user,sysdate,:old.price,:new.price);
end;
/
show errors
```

The following SQL*Plus session illustrates the use of this trigger:

```
SQL> update parts set price = 55.00 where pno = 10900;


1 row updated.
```

```
SQL> select * from parts_log;

       PNO USERNAME UPDATE_DA  OLD_PRICE  NEW_PRICE
---------- -------- --------- ---------- ----------
     10900 BOOK     26-JAN-98      24.99         55

SQL>
```

## 3.6 Database Access Using Cursors

As was mentioned earlier, almost any SQL statement can be used in a PL/SQL program. However, when the result of an SQL query (**select** statement) consists of more than one row, the simple **select into** statement cannot be used. To handle this situation, PL/SQL provides *cursors*. A PL/SQL cursor, allows the program to fetch and process information from the database into the PL/SQL program, one row at a time. The cursors used for processing a query resulting in more than one row are called *explicit cursors*. These are in contrast to *implicit cursors*, which are automatically defined by PL/SQL for the **select into** statements, which result in one or fewer rows, and for the **insert**, **delete**, and **update** operations. The programmer need not be aware of the implicit cursors, as they are automatically created and used by PL/SQL.

Cursors can also have parameters. Such cursors are referred to as *parameterized cursors*. Having parameters makes cursors more flexible, and several similar queries can be coded into one cursor definition using the parameter mechanism.

A relatively new feature in PL/SQL is that of a *cursor variable*. In contrast to explicit cursors, which require a **select** statement to be specified in their declaration, cursor variables provide a pointer or reference to the cursor work area and thereby increase the flexibility of the use of cursors.

### 3.6.1 Explicit Cursors

The syntax for declaring a PL/SQL explicit cursor without parameters is

```
cursor <cname> [return <return-spec>] is
    <select-statement>;
```

where

- `<cname>` is the name given to the cursor.
- `<select-statement>` is the SQL `select` statement associated with the cursor.

The optional `return` clause specifies the row structure that is to be returned by the cursor. The `return` clause is usually specified so that the compiler can verify the usage of this cursor at various points in the program. Otherwise, there is a possibility of a run-time error if the cursor is not used properly. Here are some examples of cursor declarations:

```
cursor c1 return customers%rowtype is
  select * from customers;
cursor c2 is
  select pno,pname,price*markdown sale_price
  from   parts;
```

Cursor `c1` uses the `return` clause, which is consistent with the select list of the `select` statement in the SQL query associated with the cursor. Cursor `c2` uses a PL/SQL variable, `markdown`, in the `select` statement associated with the cursor.

The cursor definition may involve PL/SQL variables. PL/SQL easily resolves the name conflicts. However, it is important to note that if a cursor definition has a PL/SQL variable with the same name as that of a database column that is relevant to the cursor, the database column name gets precedence and all occurrences of the name are treated as the database column, not the PL/SQL variable. For this reason, it is always advisable to have a naming convention for PL/SQL variables that differentiates them from database column names.

The `return` clause is also useful when cursors are defined in a PL/SQL package. This clause can be used in the package specification, and the actual SQL query that is associated with the cursor can be specified in the package body, as the following example illustrates:

```
package ppp is
  type cur_rec_type is record
   (pno   parts.pno%type,
    pname parts.pname%type,
    sale_price parts.price%type);

  cursor c2 return cur_rec_type;
  .
  .
  .
end ppp;
```

```
package body ppp is

  cursor c2 return cur_rec_type is
    select pno,pname,price*markdown sale_price
    from   parts;
  .
  .
  .
end ppp;
```

Once a cursor has been declared, it can be processed using the **open**, **fetch**, and **close** statements. The syntax for these statements is

```
open <cname>;
fetch <cname> into <Record-or-VariableList>;
close <cname>;
```

The record or the variable list into which the cursor rows are to be fetched must be compatible with the cursor row type. Otherwise, a run-time error can occur. It is always good programming practice to (1) open cursors only when they are going to be used and not much earlier and (2) close all cursors as soon as they are processed and not wait until later. By adhering to these practices, memory is used optimally.

To obtain information about a particular cursor that is being processed, *cursor attributes* can be used. There are four such attributes:

- `%found`. This attribute returns **true** if a record was successfully fetched from the cursor; otherwise, it returns **false**.
- `%notfound`. This attribute returns **true** if a record was not successfully fetched from the cursor; otherwise, it returns **false**.
- `%rowcount`. This attribute returns the number of records fetched from the cursor at the time it is used.
- `%isopen`. This cursor returns **true** if the cursor is open; otherwise, it returns **false**.

The following example illustrates the use of the cursor statements and attributes:

```
declare
  cursor c1 is
    select cno,cname,city
    from   customers,zipcodes
    where  customers.zip = zipcodes.zip;
  c1_rec c1%rowtype;
begin
```

```
    if not c1%isopen then
      open c1;
    end if;
    fetch c1 into c1_rec;
    while c1%found loop
      dbms_output.put_line('Row Number ' || c1%rowcount || '> ' ||
                           c1_rec.cno || '  ' || c1_rec.cname  ||
                          '  ' || c1_rec.city);
      fetch c1 into c1_rec;
    end loop;
    close c1;
  end;
  /
```

## *Cursor* `for loop`

PL/SQL provides a variation of the **for loop** to be used with cursors. This loop is very useful in situations in which all rows of the cursor are to be processed. The syntax is

```
for <record_index> in <cname> loop
  <loop-body>;
end loop;
```

where

- **<record_index>** is a record variable that is implicitly declared by PL/SQL. The scope of this record variable is the **for loop**, and it cannot be accessed outside the **for loop**. The structure of the record is the same as that of a row of the cursor.
- **<cname>** is the cursor that is to be processed.

Within the body of this loop, the individual fields of the records can be accessed in the usual way. The loop terminates automatically when all rows of the cursor have been fetched. There is no need to **open**, **fetch**, or **close** the cursor, and there is no need to declare the record into which the cursor rows are to be fetched. The previous example is modified with a cursor **for loop** in the following:

```
declare
  cursor c1 is
    select cno,cname,city
    from   customers,zipcodes
    where  customers.zip = zipcodes.zip;
begin
```

```
  for c1_rec in c1 loop
    dbms_output.put_line('Row Number ' || c1%rowcount || '> ' ||
                         c1_rec.cno || '  ' || c1_rec.cname  ||
                        '  ' || c1_rec.city);
  end loop;
end;
/
```

Notice the economy of code when the cursor `for loop` is used.

An explicit cursor may also be "implicitly" defined within a cursor `for loop` as follows:

```
for i in (select * from employees) loop
  .
  .
  .
end loop;
```

Here, the cursor is not even declared in the `declare` section. In this case, there is no need to `declare`, `open`, `fetch`, or `close` the cursor.

## 3.6.2 Parameterized Cursors

PL/SQL allows for cursors to take input parameters. This feature makes the cursors more flexible. The syntax for declaring a PL/SQL explicit cursor with parameters is

```
cursor <cname>  (<parameter-list>)
  [return <return-spec>]
  is <select-statement>;
```

The parameters are specified immediately after the cursor name, as a list within parentheses. Here is an example of cursors with parameters:

```
cursor c3(city_in in zipcodes.city%type) is
  select orders.eno,ename,sum(qty*price) Sales
  from   employees,orders,odetails,parts,zipcodes
  where  employees.eno = orders.eno and
         orders.ono = odetails.ono and
         odetails.pno = parts.pno and
         employees.zip = zipcodes.zip and
         zipcodes.city = city_in
  group by orders.eno,ename;
```

Cursor `c3` involves a parameter `city_in`, which is used in the SQL `select` statement associated with the cursor. Given a city, this cursor returns the sales totals for every employee from that city. The `open` statement for such cursors will have the actual argument for the parameters, as follows:

```
open c3('Wichita');
```

If a cursor loop is used to process this cursor, it will be done as follows:

```
for c3_rec in c3('Wichita') loop
  .
  .
  .
end loop;
```

## 3.6.3 select for update

PL/SQL cursors can also be used to perform updates (`update` and `delete`) on the database. The cursor, when used for this purpose, should be declared using the `for update` clause, as follows:

```
cursor <cname> is
  <select-statement> for update;
```

The `select` statement should involve only one database table, as it does not make much sense to perform an update on a row generated from more than one table. Once the cursor is declared in this manner, the following statements can be used to perform a delete of a row or a modification to the row:

```
update <table-name>
set    <set-clause>
where current of <cname>;

delete from <table-name>
where current of <cname>;
```

It is important to note that these two statements can be used only after the cursor is opened and a particular row has been fetched. Here is a simple example that uses the cursor mechanism to update part prices. In the following anonymous block, the price of every part whose quantity-on-hand value is more than 175 is set to 80% of its old price:

```
declare
  cursor c1 is
    select * from parts
    for update;
  c1_rec c1%rowtype;
```

```
begin
  for c1_rec in c1 loop
    if (c1_rec.qoh > 175) then
      update parts set price = 0.8 * price
      where current of c1;
    end if;
  end loop;
end;
/
```

### 3.6.4 Cursor Variables

In contrast to explicit cursors, cursor variables are not required to have the SQL **select** statement associated with them at the time of their declaration. Different SQL **select** statements can be associated with cursor variables at different times in the program, and these cursor variables can be passed as parameters to other program modules. In a sense, cursor variables are similar to PL/SQL variables, and explicit cursors are similar to PL/SQL constants. This results in the possibility of the cursor being opened in one procedure, possibly a few rows being fetched in that procedure, and the rest of the processing happening in another procedure.

To declare a cursor variable, first a type declaration must be made and then the variable must be declared. The syntax is

```
type <cursor-var-type-name> is ref cursor
  [return <return-type>];
```

The optional **return** clause is used to constrain the type of **select** statement that will be associated with the cursor at a later time. If the **return** clause is missing, any **select** statement can be associated with the cursor. Cursor variables that are declared with the **return** clause are sometimes referred to as *constrained cursor variables*.

Cursor variables are opened using the following syntax:

```
open <cname> for <select-statement>;
```

This is the time when an SQL query is associated with a cursor variable. If the cursor variable is a constrained variable, the return type of the variable must be consistent with the select list used in the query in the **open** statement. Otherwise, a **rowtype_mismatch** exception will be generated by the system. Of course, if the cursor is not constrained, the **open** statement should succeed. The **select** statement must be explicitly stated; it should not be a value of a string variable. In this sense, the cursor variables are not a substitute for dynamic SQL (the **dbms_sql** package).

Once opened, a cursor variable is used in the same manner as explicit cursors. The **fetch** and **close** statements use the same syntax that is used for explicit cursors. All the cursor attributes are also available on cursor variables.

The following example illustrates the use of cursor variables. The procedure described here displays the table whose name is an input parameter. The table name must be one of the six tables of the mail-order database: **customers**, **employees**, **orders**, **odetails**, **parts**, or **zipcodes**. A cursor variable is declared, with its return type not stated in the declaration. Then, based on the table name, the appropriate **select** statement is used to open the cursor. The cursor is then processed.

```
create or replace procedure display_table
      (tname IN varchar2) as
  type cur_type is ref cursor;

  invalid_table_error exception;
  c1 cur_type;
  emp_rec  employees%rowtype;
  cust_rec customers%rowtype;
  zip_rec  zipcodes%rowtype;
  ord_rec  orders%rowtype;
  od_rec   odetails%rowtype;
  part_rec parts%rowtype;

begin
  if upper(tname) = 'CUSTOMERS' then
    open c1 for select * from customers;
  elsif upper(tname) = 'EMPLOYEES' then
    open c1 for select * from employees;
  elsif upper(tname) = 'ORDERS' then
    open c1 for select * from orders;
  elsif upper(tname) = 'ODETAILS' then
    open c1 for select * from odetails;
  elsif upper(tname) = 'PARTS' then
    open c1 for select * from parts;
  elsif upper(tname) = 'ZIPCODES' then
    open c1 for select * from zipcodes;
  else
    raise invalid_table_error;
  end if;
```

```
loop
  if upper(tname) = 'CUSTOMERS' then
    fetch c1 into cust_rec;
    exit when c1%notfound;
    dbms_output.put_line(cust_rec.cno || ' ' ||
                         cust_rec.cname || ' ' ||
                         cust_rec.street || ' ' ||
                         cust_rec.zip || ' ' ||
                         cust_rec.phone);
  elsif upper(tname) = 'EMPLOYEES' then
    fetch c1 into emp_rec;
    exit when c1%notfound;
    dbms_output.put_line(emp_rec.eno || ' ' ||
                         emp_rec.ename || ' ' ||
                         emp_rec.zip || ' ' ||
                         emp_rec.hdate);
  elsif upper(tname) = 'PARTS' then
    fetch c1 into part_rec;
    exit when c1%notfound;
    dbms_output.put_line(part_rec.pno || ' ' ||
                         part_rec.pname || ' ' ||
                         part_rec.qoh || ' ' ||
                         part_rec.price || ' ' ||
                         part_rec.olevel);
  elsif upper(tname) = 'ZIPCODES' then
    fetch c1 into zip_rec;
    exit when c1%notfound;
    dbms_output.put_line(zip_rec.zip || ' ' ||
                         zip_rec.city);
  elsif upper(tname) = 'ORDERS' then
    fetch c1 into ord_rec;
    exit when c1%notfound;
    dbms_output.put_line(ord_rec.ono || ' ' ||
                         ord_rec.cno || ' ' ||
                         ord_rec.eno || ' ' ||
                         ord_rec.received || ' ' ||
                         ord_rec.shipped);
  elsif upper(tname) = 'ODETAILS' then
    fetch c1 into od_rec;
    exit when c1%notfound;
```

```
            dbms_output.put_line(od_rec.ono || ' ' ||
                                 od_rec.pno || ' ' ||
                                 od_rec.qty);
        end if;
      end loop;
      close c1;

      exception
        when invalid_table_error then
          dbms_output.put_line('not a valid table name');
    end;
    /
```

The following is a sample SQL*Plus session to illustrate the preceding example:

```
SQL> execute display_table('customers');
1111 Charles 123 Main St. 67226 316-636-5555
2222 Bertram 237 Ash Ave. 67226 316-689-5555
3333 Barbara 111 Inwood St. 60606 316-111-1234

PL/SQL procedure successfully completed.

SQL> execute display_table('abcd');
not a valid table name

PL/SQL procedure successfully completed.
```

## 3.7 Records

A PL/SQL *record* is a composite data structure, similar to a record structure in a high-level programming language. PL/SQL records can be table based, cursor based, or programmer defined.

### 3.7.1 Table-Based Records

A record whose structure is the same as that of a row in a database table is called a *table-based record*, a structure that is useful in situations in which the application program is reading (or writing) rows from (to) database tables. The syntax to declare table-based records is

```
<record-var-name> <table-name>%rowtype;
```

where <record-var-name> is the variable name and <table-name> is the name of the table whose row structure is being used in the record definition. A possible usage of table-based records is as follows:

```
declare
  customer_rec customers%rowtype;
begin
  select *
  into   customer_rec
  from   customers
  where  cno = '1111';
  if (customer_rec.phone is null) then
    dbms_output.put_line('Phone number is absent');
  else
    dbms_output.put_line('Phone number is '|| customer_rec.phone);
  end if;
end;
```

The individual fields of the record variable are accessed in the usual way, using the dot notation. The previous anonymous block retrieves the row corresponding to a customer into a record variable and then checks for the phone number in that row.

### 3.7.2 Cursor-Based Records

A record whose structure is based on the select list of a cursor is called a *cursor-based* record. If the select list involves an expression other than a column name, an alias must be present; otherwise, PL/SQL would have no way of naming the corresponding field in the cursor-based record. The syntax to define a cursor-based record is

```
<record-var-name> <cursor-name>%rowtype;
```

where <record-var-name> is the variable name and <cursor-name> is the name of the cursor upon which the record is based. A possible usage of cursor-based records is

```
declare
  cursor c1 is
    select orders.eno employee_no,
           ename employee_name,
           sum(price*qty) total_sales
    from   employees,orders,odetails,parts
    where  employees.eno = orders.eno and
```

```
              orders.ono = odetails.ono and
              odetails.pno = parts.pno
       group by orders.eno, ename;

     emp_sales_rec c1%rowtype;

   begin
     open c1;
     loop
       fetch c1 into emp_sales_rec;
       exit when c1%notfound;
       dbms_output.put_line(emp_sales_rec.employee_no || '   ' ||
                            emp_sales_rec.employee_name || '   ' ||
                            emp_sales_rec.total_sales);
     end loop;
     close c1;
   end;
   /
```

The preceding example declares a cursor-based record and then processes the cursor using the record. Notice the aliases used in the select list of the cursor and the same names used for the fields of the record.

## 3.7.3 Programmer-Defined Records

Programmer-defined records are similar to records in high-level programming languages. A `type` declaration is needed before record variables can be declared. The general syntax for the record type declaration is

```
type <type-name> is record
 (<field1> <datatype1>,
  <field2> <datatype2>,
  .
  .
  .
  <fieldN> <datatypeN>);
```

where `<type-name>` is the name given to the record type, `<fieldI>` is the name of the `I`th field of the record, and `<datatypeI>` is the corresponding data type for the field. The data type can be almost any data type available in PL/SQL. An example follows:

```
declare
  type my_rec_type is record
    (number integer,
     name varchar2(20));
```

```
  r1 my_rec_type;
  r2 my_rec_type;
begin
  r1.number := 111;
  r1.name := 'jones';
  r2 := r1;
  dbms_output.put_line('Number = ' || r2.number ||
                       '  Name = ' || r2.name);
end
```

This example illustrates how a programmer-defined record is declared and used in an assignment statement.

## 3.8 PL/SQL Tables

PL/SQL tables are similar to database tables, except that they always consist of just one column indexed by binary integers. These tables have no bound and grow dynamically, much like database tables. They can also be likened to single-dimension arrays in high-level languages. They are also *sparse*—i.e., the rows that are defined in the PL/SQL table may not be sequential. The fact that PL/SQL tables are sparse leads to an interesting conclusion—namely, that the rows of a database table that has a single primary key attribute of type integer can be stored in the PL/SQL table indexed by the key value, thereby providing for direct access to these rows, much like a hash table.

The syntax for declaring a PL/SQL table type is

```
type <table-type-name> is table of <datatype>
  index by binary_integer;
```

where `<table-type-name>` is the name given to the table type and `<datatype>` is the data type of the elements of the table. This data type can include any scalar data type as well as any record data type whose fields are scalar. The data type cannot be another PL/SQL table type. The `%rowtype` and `%type` attributes can be used in specifying the data type of the elements of the PL/SQL table.

PL/SQL provides a set of operations that can be applied to PL/SQL tables to get information about the table as well as to delete rows from the table. These operations are summarized next, along with sample usages. (The operations are invoked using the dot notation, somewhat similar to invoking methods in an object-oriented language.)

- `count`. This operation returns the number of elements in the PL/SQL table.

```
n := the_table.count;
```

- **delete**. This operation deletes the specified row or all the rows between the specified indexes from a PL/SQL table. The following invocation of the **delete** operation deletes the forty-third row in **the_table**:

  ```
  the_table.delete(43);
  ```

  The following invocation deletes all the rows between and including the indexes −10 and 25:

  ```
  the_table.delete(-10,25);
  ```

- **exists**. This operation returns **true** if there exists a row in the specified index; otherwise, it returns **false**.

  ```
  if the_table.exists(3) then
    ...
  ```

- **first**. This operation returns the lowest-valued index in the PL/SQL table containing an element. If the PL/SQL table is empty, **null** is returned.

  ```
  i := the_table.first;
  ```

- **last**. This operation returns the highest-valued index in the PL/SQL table containing an element. If the PL/SQL table is empty, **null** is returned.

  ```
  i := the_table.last;
  ```

- **next**. Given an index in a PL/SQL table, this operation returns the next-higher–valued index where an element exists. If such an element does not exist, **null** is returned.

  ```
  i := the_table.next(5)
  ```

- **prior**. Given an index in a PL/SQL table, this operation returns the next-lower–valued index where an element exists. If such an element does not exist, **null** is returned.

  ```
  i := the_table.prior(5)
  ```

A detailed example follows. The anonymous block retrieves information from the Oracle data dictionary table **user_tab_columns** and prints the relational schemes of tables whose names start with the letter “Z”. The information is first retrieved into a PL/SQL table and then processed.

```
declare
  type dd_rec_type is record (
    table_name varchar2(30),
    column_name varchar2(30),
    data_type  varchar2(9));
  type dd_table_type is table of dd_rec_type
```

```
       index by binary_integer;
  dd_table dd_table_type;
  dd_rec dd_rec_type;
  cursor c1 is
     select table_name,column_name,data_type
     from   user_tab_columns
     where  table_name like 'Z%'
     order  by table_name,column_name;
  i binary_integer;
  prev varchar2(30);
  newentry boolean;

begin
  i := 0;
  open c1;
  loop
    fetch c1 into dd_rec;
    exit when c1%notfound;
    i := i + 1;
    dd_table(i) := dd_rec;
  end loop;
  close c1;
  dbms_output.put_line('Tables Starting with "Z"');
  dbms_output.put_line('-----------------------');
  prev := '';
  newentry := false;
  for i in 1 .. dd_table.count loop
    if (i = 1) then
      dbms_output.put(dd_table(i).table_name || '(');
      prev := dd_table(i).table_name;
    elsif (prev != dd_table(i).table_name) then
      dbms_output.put_line(');');
      dbms_output.put(dd_table(i).table_name || '(');
      prev := dd_table(i).table_name;
      newentry := false;
    end if;
    if (newentry) then
      dbms_output.put(', ');
    end if;
    newentry := true;
    dbms_output.put(dd_table(i).column_name || ':');
    dbms_output.put(dd_table(i).data_type);
```

```
  end loop;
  dbms_output.put_line(');');
end;
/
```

The following is a sample run of the anonymous block in SQL*Plus, assuming that the block resides in the file `p10.sql`:

```
SQL> start p10
Tables Starting with "Z"
------------------------
ZIPCODES(CITY:VARCHAR2, ZIP:NUMBER);
ZZZ(COL1:NUMBER, COL2:NUMBER, COL3:VARCHAR2);

PL/SQL procedure successfully completed.

SQL>
```

## 3.9 Built-in Packages

PL/SQL provides several built-in packages. This section discusses two very useful packages: `dbms_output`, which is used for debugging purposes, and `dbms_sql`, which is used for executing dynamic SQL and PL/SQL statements.

### 3.9.1 The dbms_output Package

The `dbms_output` package allows the user to display information to the session's output device (usually the screen) as the PL/SQL program executes. The `put_line` procedure belonging to the `dbms_output` package has already been used many times in this chapter. This and the remaining procedures that constitute the `dbms_output` package are described here.

The `dbms_output` package works with a buffer into which information can be written using the `put`, `put_line`, and `new_line` procedures. This information can subsequently be retrieved using the `get_line` and `get_lines` procedures. Besides these procedures to write to and read from the buffer, two additional procedures, `disable` and `enable`, are provided. These procedures, which disable and enable the buffering process, are discussed in detail next.

- `disable`. This procedure disables all calls to the `dbms_output` package, except the `enable` procedure. The statement has the following syntax:

```
dbms_output.disable;
```

An alternative way to disable the calls to the package is to issue the following command in SQL*Plus:

```
SQL> set serveroutput off
```

- `enable`. This procedure enables all calls to the `dbms_output` package. It takes as input an optional buffer size. The call is made as follows:

  ```
  dbms_output.enable(1000000);
  ```

  This call will initialize the buffer size to `1000000`. If the buffer size is not provided, as in

  ```
  dbms_output.enable;
  ```

  the default buffer size is `2000`. The package can also be enabled from SQL*Plus as follows:

  ```
  SQL> set serveroutput on size 1000000
  ```

  or

  ```
  SQL> set serveroutput on
  ```

- `new_line`. This procedure inserts an end-of-line marker in the buffer. The syntax is

  ```
  dbms_output.new_line;
  ```

- `put`. This procedure puts information into the buffer. The input to the procedure can be of type `varchar2`, `number`, or `date`. Examples are

  ```
  dbms_output.put(emp_rec.eno);
  dbms_output.put(emp_rec.hdate);
  dbms_output.put(emp_rec.ename);
  ```

- `put_line`. This procedure is the same as `put`, except that an end-of-line marker is also placed in the buffer.

- `get_line`. This procedure retrieves one line of information from the buffer. Even though the `put` and `put_line` procedures can put into the buffer information that is of the `numeric`, `string`, or `date` type, the `get_line` procedure retrieves this information in character string form. The procedure has the following specification:

  ```
  procedure get_line(line out varchar2,
                     status out integer);
  ```

The maximum size of the line is 255. The **status** output indicates whether an error has occurred. Upon successful retrieval of a line from the buffer, **status** is set to 0; otherwise, it is set to 1.

- **get_lines**. This procedure retrieves a specified number of lines from the buffer and returns them in a PL/SQL table of string type. The specification is as follows:

```
type string255_table is table of varchar2(255)
     index by binary_integer;
procedure get_lines(lines out string255_table,
                    nlines in out integer);
```

  The **nlines** parameter is the number of lines to be retrieved and also serves as the number of lines actually retrieved.

## 3.9.2 The dbms_sql Package

The **dbms_sql** package provides the ability to execute dynamically created SQL statements in PL/SQL. These statements are created as a character string and are sent to Oracle for syntax checking. After they are verified to be syntactically correct, they are sent for execution. The processing required is different for nonquery data manipulation statements such as **insert**, **delete**, and **update**; for Data Definition Language (DDL) statements such as **create table** and **alter table**; and for query statements. The details are discussed here.

### *Executing Nonquery Statements*

The steps involved in executing an **insert**, **delete**, or **update** statement are as follows:

1. *Open the cursor*. All database processing takes place using cursors in PL/SQL. For static PL/SQL, the cursor processing was either implicitly done by PL/SQL or explicitly done by the programmer, as discussed in Section 3.6. Dynamic SQL statements must also be processed using cursors; hence, the first step is to open a cursor. This is done using the following function call:

```
handle := dbms_sql.open_cursor;
```

   The **open_cursor** function takes no input and returns an integer cursor ID as output. This cursor ID must be used in subsequent references to the cursor. More than one SQL statement can be executed sequentially within the same cursor, or the same statement can be executed multiple times within the cursor.

2. *Parse the statement*. The next step is to *parse* the SQL statement. The SQL statement is stored in a string variable and is sent to the Oracle server for syntax checking. The `parse` procedure has the specification

```
procedure parse(handle in integer,
                stmt in varchar2,
                language in integer);
```

where `handle` is the cursor ID that is returned by the `open_cursor` call, `stmt` is the string variable containing the SQL statement (without the terminating semicolon), and `language` is one of the following constants:

- `DBMS_SQL.V6` for Oracle Version 6
- `DBMS_SQL.V7` for Oracle Version 7
- `DBMS_SQL.NATIVE` for the database to which the program is connected.

If the SQL statement is not syntactically correct, an exception is raised.

3. *Bind any input variables*. After opening the cursor and parsing the statement, any placeholders in the SQL statement need to be bound to actual PL/SQL variables or constants. This is done with `bind_variable`, an overloaded procedure having the specifications

```
procedure bind_variable(handle in integer,
                        name in varchar2,
                        value in number);
procedure bind_variable(handle in integer,
                        name in varchar2,
                        value in varchar2);
procedure bind_variable(handle in integer,
                        name in varchar2,
                        value in date);
procedure bind_variable_char(handle in integer,
                             name in varchar2,
                             value in char);
```

where `handle` is the cursor ID, `name` is the placeholder name in the dynamic SQL statement, and `value` is the PL/SQL constant or variable to be bound to the placeholder. Examples of usage are

```
dbms_sql.bind_variable(handle,':n',10);
dbms_sql.bind_variable(handle,':n',enum);
dbms_sql.bind_variable(handle,':c','jones');
dbms_sql.bind_variable(handle,':c',ename);
dbms_sql.bind_variable(handle,':d',hdate);
```

It is good practice to precede the placeholder names with colons, as shown in the preceding examples.

4. *Execute the statement*. After the statement is parsed and any placeholders are assigned values, the statement is ready to be executed. The function **execute** is used for this purpose, as follows:

   ```
   nrows := dbms_sql.execute(handle);
   ```

   **handle** is the cursor ID, and the function returns the number of rows processed.

5. *Close the cursor*. The final step is to close the cursor and release any resources used in the process. This is done as follows:

   ```
   dbms_sql.close_cursor(handle);
   ```

   An example of executing a dynamic **update** statement is

```
declare
  handle integer;
  stmt varchar2(256);
  discount parts.price%type := 0.8;
  part_number parts.pno%type := 10506;
  nrows integer;
begin

  stmt := 'update parts set price = price * :fract' ||
          ' where pno = :pnum';

  handle := dbms_sql.open_cursor;
  dbms_sql.parse(handle,stmt,DBMS_SQL.V7);
  dbms_sql.bind_variable(handle,':fract',discount);
  dbms_sql.bind_variable(handle,':pnum',part_number);
  nrows := dbms_sql.execute(handle);
  dbms_output.put_line('number of rows updated = ' || nrows);
  dbms_sql.close_cursor(handle);

  exception
    when others then
      dbms_sql.close_cursor(handle);
end;
/
```

The steps involved in executing a DDL statement such as **drop table** or **create table** are essentially the same as for **insert**, **delete**, or **update**, except that the two steps **bind-variable** and **execute** are not necessary. This is because placeholders are not allowed in dynamic DDL statements and the **execute** takes place at the time the statement is parsed. An example follows:

```
declare
  handle integer;
  stmt1 varchar2(256);
  stmt2 varchar2(256);
begin
  stmt1 := 'drop table zzz';
  stmt2 := 'create table zzz (col1 integer,' ||
           ' col2 number(4), col3 varchar2(30))';
  handle := dbms_sql.open_cursor;
  dbms_sql.parse(handle,stmt1,DBMS_SQL.V7);
  dbms_output.put_line('Table ZZZ dropped');
  dbms_sql.parse(handle,stmt2,DBMS_SQL.V7);
  dbms_output.put_line('Table ZZZ created');
  dbms_sql.close_cursor(handle);
  exception
    when others then
      dbms_sql.close_cursor(handle);
end;
/
```

## *Executing Queries*

The steps involved in executing a dynamic query are more complicated. Additional steps to define output variables, fetch the rows, and return results to PL/SQL variables are needed. The sequence of steps required to process a dynamic query is as follows:

1. *Open the cursor*. Same as before.
2. *Parse the statement*. Same as before. Note that the **select** statement should not have the **into** clause because the results are processed differently in dynamic SQL.
3. *Bind any input variables*. Same as before.
4. *Define the output variables*. The output variables into which the results of the query are to be returned must be defined using the **define_column** procedure. The process is similar to binding input variables to placeholders, except that the select list items are identified by positions (1, 2, 3, etc.), not by names. The specification of the **define_column** is overloaded as follows:

```
procedure define_column(handle in integer,
                        position in integer,
                        column in number);
procedure define_column(handle in integer,
                        position in integer,
                        column in varchar2,
                        col_size in integer);
procedure define_column(handle in integer,
                        position in integer,
                        column in date,
                        col_size in integer);
procedure define_column_char(handle in integer,
                        position in integer,
                        column in char,
                        col_size in integer);
```

where **handle** is the cursor ID, **position** is the position of the select list item that is being defined, **column** is the PL/SQL variable of appropriate type, and **col_size**, which is required, is the maximum size, in bytes, of the output data. Examples of its usage are

```
dbms_sql.define_column(handle,1,ccno);
dbms_sql.define_column(handle,2,ccname,30);
dbms_sql.define_column(handle,3,ccstreet,30);
dbms_sql.define_column(handle,4,ccdate,9);
```

5. *Execute the query*. Same as before.
6. *Fetch the rows*. The rows of the result of the query are fetched into a buffer using the **fetch_rows** function, as follows:

   ```
   if dbms_sql.fetch_rows(handle) = 0 then
         exit;
   else
     .
     .
     .
   ```

   The function returns the number of rows in the results of the query.
7. *Return the results to PL/SQL variables*. After **fetch_rows** is called, a call to the **column_value** procedure retrieves the values into PL/SQL variables. Typically, the same variable that was bound in the **define_column** call is used here. This procedure is also overloaded and has the specification

```
procedure column_value(handle in integer,
                       position in integer,
                       value out number);
procedure column_value(handle in integer,
                       position in integer,
                       value out varchar2);
procedure column_value(handle in integer,
                       position in integer,
                       value out date);
procedure column_value(handle in integer,
                       position in integer,
                       value out char);
```

where **handle** is the cursor ID, **position** is the position in the select list of the query, and **value** is the output variable for this select list item. Each of these functions has a fourth optional output parameter, called **error**, which returns any numeric error codes, and an optional fifth parameter, called **actual_length**, which returns the original length of the column value (before any possible truncation). Examples of **column_value** usage are

```
dbms_sql.column_value(handle,1,ccno);
dbms_sql.column_value(handle,2,ccname);
dbms_sql.column_value(handle,3,ccstreet);
dbms_sql.column_value(handle,4,ccdate);
```

8. *Close the cursor*. Same as before.

An example containing dynamic queries follows. A package called **dsql** is defined. It contains two procedures:

- **get_columns**. This procedure takes as input **startch**, a character, and returns information about all the columns of any database table in the database whose name starts with **startch**. The information is returned in a PL/SQL table of records with three fields: table name, column name, and data type. The number of elements in the PL/SQL table is also returned. The query is based on the data dictionary table **user_tab_columns**.
- **get_query_results**. This procedure takes the following as input:
  - **query_string**, which has as its value an SQL **select** statement.
  - **ncols**, the number of select list items in the SQL **select** statement.
  - **column_types**, a PL/SQL table that contains the data types of each of the select list items.

The procedure then executes the query and returns the results in the output parameter **result**, along with the number of rows in the result in the variable **nrows**. The **result** output parameter is a PL/SQL table of strings. The individual columns in a row of the result of the query are concatenated into a long string with the bar character (|) between two values.

```
-- p20.sql
create or replace package dsql as
  type dd_rec_type is record (
    table_name varchar2(30),
    column_name varchar2(30),
    data_type  varchar2(9));
  type dd_table_type is table of dd_rec_type
       index by binary_integer;
  type string1024_table is table of varchar2(1024)
       index by binary_integer;
  type string9_table is table of varchar2(9)
       index by binary_integer;
  type number_table is table of number
       index by binary_integer;

procedure get_columns(startch in char,
                      dd_table out dd_table_type,
                      n out number);

procedure get_query_results(query_string in varchar2,
                            ncols in number,
                            column_types in string9_table,
                            result out string1024_table,
                            nrows out number);

end dsql;
/
show errors

create or replace package body dsql as

procedure get_columns(startch in char,
                      dd_table out dd_table_type,
                      n out number) as
```

```
handle integer;
dbms_return integer;
tablename varchar(30);
colname varchar(30);
datatype varchar(9);
counter integer := 0;

begin

  handle := dbms_sql.open_cursor;
  dbms_sql.parse(handle,
    'select distinct table_name,column_name,data_type ' ||
    'from   user_tab_columns '                           ||
    'where  table_name like '''                          ||
    startch                                              ||
    '%'''                                                ||
    'order by table_name,column_name', DBMS_SQL.V7);

  dbms_sql.define_column(handle, 1, tablename, 30);
  dbms_sql.define_column(handle, 2, colname, 30);
  dbms_sql.define_column(handle, 3, datatype, 9);

  dbms_return := dbms_sql.execute(handle);

  counter := 0;
  loop
    if dbms_sql.fetch_rows(handle) = 0 then
      exit;
    else
      dbms_sql.column_value(handle, 1, tablename);
      dbms_sql.column_value(handle, 2, colname);
      dbms_sql.column_value(handle, 3, datatype);

      counter := counter + 1;
      dd_table(counter).table_name := tablename;
      dd_table(counter).column_name := colname;
      dd_table(counter).data_type := datatype;
    end if;
  end loop;
  n := counter;
```

```
  dbms_sql.close_cursor(handle);

exception
  when others then
    dbms_sql.close_cursor(handle);
    n := -1;
end get_columns;

procedure get_query_results(query_string in varchar2,
                            ncols in number,
                            column_types in string9_table,
                            result out string1024_table,
                            nrows out number) as

y1 string1024_table;
y2 number_table;
counter integer;
i integer;
handle integer;
dbms_return integer;
temp string1024_table;

begin

  for i in 1 .. ncols loop
    y1(i) := '';
    y2(i) := 0;
  end loop;

  counter := 0;
  handle := dbms_sql.open_cursor;
  dbms_sql.parse(handle,query_string,DBMS_SQL.V7);

  for i in 1 .. ncols loop
    if ((column_types(i) = 'VARCHAR2') or
        (column_types(i) = 'CHAR')) then
      dbms_sql.define_column(handle, i, y1(i) , 300);
    else
      dbms_sql.define_column(handle, i, y2(i));
    end if;
```

```
  end loop;

  dbms_return := dbms_sql.execute(handle);

  loop
     if dbms_sql.fetch_rows(handle) = 0 then
       exit;
     else
       for i in 1 .. ncols loop
         if ((column_types(i) = 'VARCHAR2') or
             (column_types(i) = 'CHAR')) then
           dbms_sql.column_value(handle, i, y1(i));
         else
           dbms_sql.column_value(handle, i, y2(i));
         end if;
       end loop;
       counter := counter + 1;
       temp(counter) := '';

       for i in 1 .. ncols loop
         if ((column_types(i) = 'VARCHAR2') or
             (column_types(i) = 'CHAR')) then
           temp(counter) := temp(counter) || rtrim(y1(i)) || '|';
         else
           temp(counter) := temp(counter) || trim(y2(i)) || '|';
         end if;
       end loop;
   end if;
  end loop;

  nrows := counter;
  result := temp;
  dbms_sql.close_cursor(handle);

  exception
    when others then
      dbms_sql.close_cursor(handle);
      nrows := -1;
end get_query_results;
end dsql;
```

```
/
show errors
```

The following package, called **dsql_driver**, contains two procedures to drive the two procedures in the **dsql** package:

```
-- p21.sql
create or replace package dsql_driver as
procedure drive_get_columns(startch in char);
procedure drive_get_query_results(
    query_string in varchar2,
    ncols in number,
    column_types in dsql.string9_table);
end dsql_driver;
/

create or replace package body dsql_driver as
procedure drive_get_columns(startch in char) as
  dd_table dsql.dd_table_type;
  i binary_integer;
  n number;
  prev varchar2(30);
  newentry boolean;
begin
  dsql.get_columns(startch,dd_table,n);
  dbms_output.put_line('N =  ' || n);

  dbms_output.put_line('Tables Starting with ' || startch);
  dbms_output.put_line('------------------------');
  prev := '';
  newentry := false;
  for i in 1 .. dd_table.count loop
    if (i = 1) then
      dbms_output.put(dd_table(i).table_name || '(');
      prev := dd_table(i).table_name;
    elsif (prev != dd_table(i).table_name) then
      dbms_output.put_line(');');
      dbms_output.put(dd_table(i).table_name || '(');
      prev := dd_table(i).table_name;
      newentry := false;
    end if;
```

```
      if (newentry) then
        dbms_output.put(', ');
      end if;
      newentry := true;
      dbms_output.put(dd_table(i).column_name || ':');
      dbms_output.put(dd_table(i).data_type);
    end loop;
    dbms_output.put_line(');');
  end;

  procedure drive_get_query_results
      (query_string in varchar2,
       ncols in number,
       column_types in dsql.string9_table) as
  result dsql.string1024_table;
  nrows number;
  i binary_integer;

  begin
    dsql.get_query_results(query_string,ncols,column_types,
                           result,nrows);
    for i in 1 .. nrows loop
      dbms_output.put_line(result(i));
    end loop;
  end;

  end dsql_driver;
  /
  show errors
```

The following anonymous PL/SQL block calls the driver procedure for the `get_query_results` procedure:

```
-- p22.sql
declare
 query_string varchar2(256);
 ncols number;
 column_types dsql.string9_table;
begin
  query_string := 'select cno,cname,city ' ||
                  'from customers,zipcodes ' ||
```

```
                  'where customers.zip = zipcodes.zip';
  ncols := 3;
  column_types(1) := 'NUMBER';
  column_types(2) := 'VARCHAR2';
  column_types(3) := 'VARCHAR2';

  dsql_driver.drive_get_query_results(query_string,
                                      ncols,
                                      column_types);
end;
/

SQL> execute dsql_driver.drive_get_columns('Z');
N =  2
Tables Starting with Z
------------------------
ZIPCODES(CITY:VARCHAR2, ZIP:NUMBER);

PL/SQL procedure successfully completed.

SQL> start p22
1111|Charles|Wichita|
2222|Bertram|Wichita|
3333|Barbara|Fort Dodge|

PL/SQL procedure successfully completed.

SQL>
```

## 3.10 Error Handling

PL/SQL implements run-time error handling via *exceptions* and *exception handlers*. Exceptions can be associated with Oracle system errors or with application program errors. When an error occurs during the execution of a PL/SQL program, an exception is *raised*. Immediately, program control is transferred to the exception section of the block in which the exception was raised. If such a section exists, and if there is code present to handle the exception, the exception is handled and the program returns to the environment that called the block in which the error occurred. Otherwise, program control is passed on to the enclosing block's exception handler, if there is one.

Exceptions can be of two types: *system exceptions* and *user-defined exceptions*. System exceptions are raised automatically by PL/SQL, and they correspond to errors in PL/SQL or Oracle database processing. Some commonly occurring system exceptions have been given names by PL/SQL:

- `CURSOR_ALREADY_OPENED` (SQLCODE $= -6511$). Attempt to open cursor that is already open.
- `DUP_VAL_ON_INDEX` (SQLCODE $= -1$). Attempt to store duplicate value in a unique index column.
- `INVALID_CURSOR` (SQLCODE $= -1001$). Attempt to use a cursor that does not exist or is not open.
- `INVALID_NUMBER` (SQLCODE $= -1722$). Attempt to convert a `string` into a `number` using the `to_number` function failed.
- `LOGIN_DENIED` (SQLCODE $= -1017$). Invalid user name or password when attempting to connect to database.
- `NO_DATA_FOUND` (SQLCODE $= +100$). Attempt to access uninitialized row in a PL/SQL table or `select into` resulted in no row.
- `TOO_MANY_ROWS` (SQLCODE $= -1422$). `select into` resulted in more than one row.
- `VALUE_ERROR` (SQLCODE $= -6502$). Error during conversion of data.
- `ZERO_DIVIDE` (SQLCODE $= -1476$). Divide by zero error.

System errors that have not been given names can be handled using the `when others` clause in the exception section. It is useful to print the values of the variables `sqlcode` and `sqlerrm` to see the error code and the error message associated with the error. These variables are available to any PL/SQL program, as they are declared in the `standard` package of PL/SQL.

The exception section of a PL/SQL block contains code to handle the exceptions. The syntax is

```
when <exception-name> then
  <Error-Handling-Code>;
```

where the name of the exception is mentioned after the `when` keyword. If the name is not known, `others` can be used to trap the exception. Any number of these

**when** clauses can be used. If the error-handling code is the same for more than one exception, the **when** clauses can be combined by placing an **or** between the exception names.

User-defined exceptions are also treated in a similar manner, except that the user has to define the exception first and then raise the exception at the appropriate point in the program. User-defined exceptions are declared using the syntax

```
<exception-name> exception;
```

and are raised using the syntax

```
raise <exception-name>;
```

An example illustrating some of the previous concepts follows:

```
create or replace procedure insert_odetails
  (onum in integer, pnum in integer, qty in integer) as

  invalid_quantity exception;
begin
  if (qty <= 0) then
    raise invalid_quantity;
  end if;

  insert into odetails values (onum,pnum,qty);

  exception
    when dup_val_on_index then
      dbms_output.put_line('primary key violation');
      dbms_output.put_line(sqlcode || '--' || sqlerrm);

    when invalid_quantity then
      dbms_output.put_line('Quantity is invalid');

    when others then
      dbms_output.put_line('other error');
      dbms_output.put_line(sqlcode || '--' || sqlerrm);
end;
/
```

The preceding stored procedure tries to insert a row in the **odetails** table. If the quantity value is negative or zero, a user-defined exception is raised. If a primary key violation takes place, the system exception `DUP_VAL_ON_INDEX` is raised. If a foreign key violation takes place, the **when others** clause executes and an appropriate error message is displayed. The following is a screen capture of an SQL*Plus session illustrating the various possibilities:

```
SQL> select * from odetails;

       ONO        PNO        QTY
---------- ---------- ----------
      1020      10506          1
      1020      10507          1
      1020      10508          2
      1020      10509          3
      1021      10601          4
      1022      10601          1
      1022      10701          1
      1023      10800          1
      1023      10900          1
      2000      10900        140

10 rows selected

SQL> execute insert_odetails(1234,1111,-5);
Quantity is invalid

PL/SQL procedure successfully completed.

SQL> execute insert_odetails(2000,10900,10);
primary key violation
-1--ORA-00001: unique constraint (BOOK.SYS_C0068915)
violated

PL/SQL procedure successfully completed.

SQL> execute insert_odetails(2000,11001,10);
other error
100--ORA-01403: no data found
ORA-01403: no data found
ORA-06512: at
```

```
"book.insert_odetails", line 5
ORA-04088: error during execution of trigger
'book.insert_odetails'

PL/SQL procedure successfully completed.
SQL>
```

## 3.11 PL/SQL Access to Oracle9*i* Objects

Object-oriented features of Oracle9*i*'s PL/SQL language are briefly introduced in this section. Object variables can be declared and used in PL/SQL based on object types defined in the database. The structure of the objects can be easily traversed using the dot notation, objects can be modified, and, if needed, the database can be updated using the modified objects. Examples of object type method implementations are presented in this section. Accessing varying arrays in PL/SQL and manipulating/ querying of nested tables are also presented.

### 3.11.1 Declaring and Initializing Objects

PL/SQL object variables are declared in the same manner as ordinary variables, by following the variable name with the object type name. The variables may be given an initial value at the time of declaration using the object type constructors. For example, the following declaration declares a `person_type` object variable `p` and initializes it:

```
p person_type := person_type('aaa',
    address_type('sss','ccc','sss',11111),
    phones_varray_type(null,null,null));
```

The variable, once initialized, can be used in other PL/SQL statements, and its attributes can be accessed using the dot notation. The following PL/SQL anonymous block creates a `person_type` object, initializes it, updates its attributes, and calls a procedure to display the object:

```
declare
  p person_type := person_type('aaa',
   address_type('sss','ccc','sss',11111),
   phones_varray_type(null,null,null));
  procedure display_person(p in person_type) is
```

```
    begin
      if (p is not null) then
        dbms_output.put_line('Name: ' || p.name);
        dbms_output.put_line('Street: ' || p.address.street);
        dbms_output.put_line('City: ' || p.address.city);
        dbms_output.put_line('State: ' || p.address.state);
        dbms_output.put_line('Zip: ' || p.address.zip);
        if (p.phones(1) is not null) then
          dbms_output.put_line('Phone 1: ' || p.phones(1));
        end if;
        if (p.phones(2) is not null) then
          dbms_output.put_line('Phone 2: ' || p.phones(2));
        end if;
        if (p.phones(3) is not null) then
          dbms_output.put_line('Phone 3: ' || p.phones(3));
        end if;
      end if;
    end;
  begin
    p.name := 'D. Maul';
    p.address.street := '123 Kenobi St.';
    p.address.city := 'Death Star';
    p.address.state := 'Tattoine';
    p.address.zip := '66666';
    p.phones(1) := '111-1234';
    p.phones(2) := '111-1235';
    p.phones(3) := null;
    display_person(p);
  end;
  /
  show errors
```

Notice the use of the `is null` predicate on both the object variable and its attribute. Object variables that are not initialized are assigned the `null` reference.

### 3.11.2 Object Type Method Implementation

Methods associated with object types are specified in PL/SQL. Recall the two methods, `cost` and `total_cost`, specified in the object type declarations for `odetails_type` and `o_order_type` (respectively) in Chapter 2. The `create type` `body` statement is used to specify the implementation of methods for object types. The PL/SQL code for the two methods is shown below:

```
create or replace type body odetails_type as
member function cost return number is
  p parts.price%type;
begin
  select price into p from parts where pno = self.pno;
  return p * self.qty;
end;
end;
/
show errors

create or replace type body o_order_type as
  member function total_cost return number is
    i          integer;
    item       odetails_type;
    total      number := 0;
    item_cost  number;
  begin
    for i in 1..self.odetails.count  loop
      item := self.odetails(i);
      item_cost := item.cost();
      total := total + item_cost ;
    end loop;
    return total;
  end;
end;
/
show errors
```

Notice the use of the `self` keyword, which allows the method to refer to the attributes of the object on which the method is applied. Nested tables in the database can be treated as PL/SQL tables when accessed within PL/SQL. Hence, the syntax for accessing an individual item within the nested table `odetails` is `self.odetails(i)`. Also notice the call to `cost()` in the `total_cost` method where the individual line item costs are summed up to produce the total cost of an order.

## 3.11.3 Accessing Database Objects in PL/SQL

Database objects and object tables can be accessed within PL/SQL with ease. Several examples are presented here.

Example 3.11.1 The following PL/SQL anonymous block queries the `o_employees` table and displays employee details. It employs a standard PL/SQL cursor and uses the dot notation to access the attributes within the object structure.

```
declare
  p person_type;
  enum o_employees.eno%type;
  cursor c is
    select eno,person from o_employees;

begin
  open c;
  loop
    fetch c into enum, p;
    exit when c%notfound;
    dbms_output.put('ENO: ' || enum);
    dbms_output.put('   ENAME: ' || p.name);
    dbms_output.put_line('   ZIP: ' || p.address.zip);
  end loop;
  close c;
end;
/
show errors
```

Example 3.11.2 The following PL/SQL anonymous block queries the nested table `odetails` within the `o_orders` table and prints all the line item details for order 1020:

```
declare
  onum o_orders.ono%type;
  cursor c is
    select nt.pno, nt.qty
    from   THE(select o.odetails
               from   o_orders o
               where  o.ono = onum) nt;

  pnum parts.pno%type;
```

```
  qty number;

begin
  onum := 1020;

  open c;
  loop
    fetch c into pnum,qtty;
    exit when c%notfound;
    dbms_output.put_line('PNO = ' || pnum || '  QTY = ' || qtty);
   end loop;
end;
/
show errors
```

Notice the **THE** operator that is applied to the nested table to flatten its rows for access in the outer query.

Example 3.11.3 The following PL/SQL anonymous block contains a function that takes an employee number and returns the total sales for that employee. This function queries the `o_orders` table using a PL/SQL cursor. Since the `o_orders` table is an object table, it has no column names, so it is not possible to select any named columns from this table. To access the row objects, one must use the `value` operator, which takes the table alias as input and returns the row object.

```
declare
  enum o_employees.eno%type;
  total number(10,2);

  function total_emp_sales(emp_no in employees.eno%type)
    return number is
  sales number := 0.0;
  cursor c is
    select value(o)
    from   o_orders o
    where  o.eno = emp_no;
  od o_order_type;
```

```
  begin
    open c;
    loop
      fetch c into od;
      exit when c%notfound;
      sales := sales + od.total_cost();
    end loop;
    return (sales);
  end;

begin
  enum := 1001;
  total := total_emp_sales(enum);
  dbms_output.put_line('Total sales for employee ' ||
                       enum   || ' is ' || total);
end;
/
show errors
```

Notice the call to the method **total_cost**, which computes the total sales value for a particular order. The total sales for each order are summed up to produce the total sales for the employee. The anonymous PL/SQL block invokes the function **total_emp_sales** and displays the total sales for employee 1001.

### 3.11.4 Accessing Varying Arrays in PL/SQL

Recall that it is not possible to query and access varying array attributes of objects in SQL. PL/SQL provides an easy way to access varying arrays by allowing varying array objects in the database to be read into PL/SQL variables. The following PL/SQL anonymous block reads the **phones** varying array for employee 1002 and displays the results:

```
declare
  enum o_employees.eno%type;
  phs o_employees.person.phones%type;
begin
  enum := 1002;

  select e.person.phones
  into   phs
```

```
  from   o_employees e
  where  e.eno = enum;

  for i in 1..3 loop
    if (phs(i) is not null) then
      dbms_output.put_line('Phone for employee ' ||
                           enum   || ' is ' || phs(i));
    end if;
  end loop;
end;
/
show errors
```

If the varying arrays are to be updated, the updates can be done in PL/SQL and the varying arrays can then be stored back in the database. The following PL/SQL anonymous block illustrates the addition of a new phone number for employee 1002:

```
declare
  enum o_employees.eno%type;
  phs o_employees.person.phones%type;
begin
  enum := 1002;

  select e.person.phones
  into   phs
  from   o_employees e
  where  e.eno = enum;

  phs(2) := '999-999-0000';

  update o_employees e
  set    e.person.phones = phs
  where  e.eno = enum;
end;
/
show errors
```

Note that it is not possible to access the elements within the varying array directly in an SQL query or `update` statement. Instead, the varying array must be retrieved into a PL/SQL variable, updated, and then written back to the database.

## 3.11.5 Built-in Methods for Collection Objects

All of the PL/SQL table operators presented in Section 3.8 are also applicable to varying array and nested table objects. In addition to these, the following two additional methods are applicable to collection objects:

- The **extend** method adds elements at the end of a nested table. This method has three variations:

```
extend      : adds a null element at the end
extend(n)   : adds n null elements at the end
extend(n,i) : adds n copies of element i at the end
```

  The **extend** method should not be applied to a varying array, since its size is fixed. However, applying **extend** to a varying array is legal, and it does not change the varying array.

- The **trim** method deletes elements at the end of a nested table. This method has two variations:

```
trim    : deletes the last element
trim(n) : deletes the last n elements
```

These built-in methods can be used only in the procedural PL/SQL code and not in SQL. An example of the **count** method is shown in the following anonymous PL/SQL block, which queries the **o_employees** table and prints the employee numbers and the number of phone number entries for each employee:

```
declare
  cursor c is
    select e.eno, e.person.phones
    from   o_employees e;
  enum o_employees.eno%type;
  phs  o_employees.person.phones%type;
begin
  open c;
  loop
    fetch c into enum, phs;
    exit when c%notfound;
    dbms_output.put_line('Employee ' ||
        enum || ' has ' ||
        phs.count || ' phone numbers');
  end loop;
```

```
  close c;
end;
/
show errors
```

# Exercises

## *Mail-Order Database Problems*

3.1 Write a PL/SQL procedure that finds the five employees with the highest sales figures in terms of dollars and prints their numbers and names along with the total sales for each.

3.2 Write a PL/SQL procedure that performs an update of a zip code value. It takes the old and new values of the zip code and changes all occurrences of the old value to the new throughout the database.

3.3 Assume that the `odetails` table has an additional column, called `cost`, whose value is the product of the quantity and price of the part being ordered. Also assume that the `orders` table has an additional column, called `order_cost`, whose value is the sum of the `cost` values for each part in the order. Write a PL/SQL procedure that processes an update to the `price` value of a part. The procedure takes the part number and new price as input and performs an update to the `price` column of the `parts` table along with appropriate changes to the `cost` and `order_cost` values.

3.4 Write a PL/SQL procedure that takes as input two parameters: (1) `conditions`, a PL/SQL table containing several selection conditions as strings, and (2) `nconds`, which contains the number of conditions in `conditions`. The procedure then computes the query

```
select customers.cno,cname,employees.eno,ename
from customers,orders,employees
where customers.cno = orders.cno and
      employees.eno = orders.eno and
      C;
```

where `C` is the conjunction of the conditions in the input parameter. Some examples of the input conditions are:

```
customers.zip = 60606
customers.zip = employees.zip
cname like 'C%'
```

The results of the query are sent to the standard output. Write a PL/SQL anonymous block to test this procedure.

## *Grade Book Database Problems*

3.5 Write a PL/SQL procedure that takes as input the term, line number, and component name for a particular course and processes the student scores for this course. The scores are assumed to be in a temporary table called **temp_scores** with two columns: **sid** and **points**. The procedure should add each of the scores mentioned in the temporary table into the **scores** table. If the term, line number, or component name is invalid, the procedure should simply return. If the student ID is invalid or the score is outside the range of allowed values, the procedure should send an error message to the standard output and continue processing the remaining scores. Write a PL/SQL anonymous block to test this procedure.

3.6 Write a PL/SQL procedure that takes as input the term and line number for a particular course and processes updates to the student scores for this course. The updates to the scores are assumed to be in a temporary table called **temp_updates** with three columns: **compname**, **sid**, and **change**. The **change** column is a positive or negative number indicating the change to be made to the current score. If the term or line number of the course is invalid, the procedure should simply return. Otherwise, the procedure should process each of the updates. If the component name of the student ID is invalid or if the updated score is outside the range of allowed values, the procedure should send an error message to the standard output and continue processing the remaining updates. Write a PL/SQL anonymous block to test this procedure.

3.7 Write a PL/SQL procedure that finds the student with the highest overall average in every course. In case there is more than one student tied for the highest average, the procedure should return all of the students. The results should be returned in a PL/SQL table of records, where each record has the fields term, line number, course title, student ID, student name, and overall average. Also, write an anonymous PL/SQL block that makes a call to the procedure and prints the results to the standard output.

3.8 Write a trigger that fires when a row is deleted from the **enrolls** table. The trigger should record the dropped student's scores in a temporary table, called **deleted_scores**, and cascade the deletes to ensure that the referential integrity constraints are maintained.

3.9 Write a PL/SQL procedure that finds the course numbers, titles, terms, line numbers, and total enrollments for the courses with the 10 highest enrollments. The procedure should send the results to the standard output.

3.10 Write a PL/SQL stored procedure that takes the name of a database table as input and prints the number of columns and rows in that table to the standard output.

## *Investment Portfolio Database Problems*

3.11 Write a PL/SQL stored procedure that takes as input a security symbol and produces a ratings list for that security symbol in the following format:

```
                          MY PORTFOLIO

Symbol Shares    Current  Market     Purchase     Gain    %Gain
                   PPS    Value        Price
-------------------------------------------------------------
ORCL    100.00    23.25   2325.00    2708.06   -383.06   -14.14
SEG     100.00    30.00   3000.00    3244.62   -244.62    -7.53
-------------------------------------------------------------
  Security Value:         5325.00    5952.68   -627.68   -10.54
  Cash Balance:          94047.33
  Account Value:         99372.33
-------------------------------------------------------------
```

3.12 Write a PL/SQL stored procedure that produces a listing of the five top-rated securities based on the consensus mean.

3.13 Write a PL/SQL stored procedure to produce a portfolio view for a member. The procedure should take as input the member ID and produce a report in the following format:

```
Symbol: ORCL
Company: Oracle Corporation
Ratings:  Strong Buy  (rating = 1) : *****
          Buy         (rating = 2) : **
          Hold        (rating = 3) : **
          Sell        (rating = 4) :
          Strong Sell (rating = 5) :
          Consensus:        1.67
```

The number of stars after each rating is the number of analysts rating the security with that particular rating. The consensus mean is the weighted mean of the ratings.

## *Mail-Order Database Problems (Object Version)*

3.14 Write a PL/SQL stored procedure that produces an invoice report for a particular order. The order number is an input parameter to this procedure. The report is to be sent to display. The format of the report should be

```
Customer: Bertram          Customer Number: 2222
Street  : 237 Ash Ave.
City    : Wichita
ZIP     : 67226
Phone   : 316-689-5555
--------------------------------------------------------------
Order No: 1022
Taken By: Smith (1001)
Received On: 13-FEB-95
Shipped  On: 20-FEB-95

Part No.              Part Name      Quan.   Price     Ext
-------------------------------------------------------------
   10601          Sleeping Beauty      1     24.99     24.99
   10701     When Harry Met Sally      1     19.99     19.99
-------------------------------------------------------------
                                TOTAL:                 44.98
-------------------------------------------------------------
```

3.15 Write a PL/SQL stored procedure that prints all customer information to display. The format of the output is as follows:

```
CNO   CNAME        STREET           ZIP    PHONES
------------------------------------------------------
1111  Charles      123 Main St.     67226  316-636-5555
                                           316-666-1234
2222  Bertram      237 Ash Ave.     67226  316-689-5556
                                           316-666-1233
                                           316-666-1235
3333  Barbara      111 Inwood St.   60606  316-111-1234
------------------------------------------------------
```

3.16 Write a PL/SQL stored procedure that computes and prints the names of the employees with the five highest sales totals. The output should contain the sales totals and should be sorted in decreasing order of sales total.

3.17 Write a PL/SQL anonymous block that prompts the user for an area code and prints the names and addresses of all customers who have at least one phone number with that particular area code.

3.18 Write a PL/SQL anonymous block that prompts the user for a part number and prints the order number of all orders in which the particular part was ordered, along with the quantity. At the end, it should print a total quantity of the part ordered in all orders.

# CHAPTER 4

# Web Programming with PL/SQL

The proliferation of the Internet over the past decade or so has created a new genre of application software commonly referred to as *Web applications*. These Web applications are accessed by ordinary users from their computers' Web browsers, and user requests are sent off to remote Web servers for processing. The communication between the Web browser (sometimes referred to as the client) and the Web server follows the HyperText Transfer Protocol (HTTP). The Web servers in turn dispatch these requests to other programs on the server for processing. In many instances, these applications are accessing databases hosted on the server. The Web application software can be broken down into the following categories:

- *Presentation logic*. This part consists of the graphical user interface (GUI) that is responsible for accepting input data and requests from the user and displaying the results of the requests.
- *Business logic*. This part consists of code that validates data obtained from the user. This code makes sure that the data are valid and, if so, sends the data to the database for updates.
- *Data access logic*. This part consists of code that connects to the database and performs the necessary updates or queries.

A *three-tier system* is one that has its presentation, business logic, and data access components logically separated. Web applications are perfect for the three-tier architecture, as the presentation layer is always separate with the use of HyperText Markup Language (HTML), and the business and data access layers can easily be divided up like a traditional client-server application.

Oracle9*i* provides several methodologies to program Web applications that access an Oracle database. One such methodology is to use PL/SQL as the programming language to implement the three layers of the Web application. This chapter introduces Web application development in PL/SQL. Oracle9*i* provides **`mod_plsql`**, an Apache module extension written by Oracle that allows for dynamic HTML code to be generated from Oracle PL/SQL code. Using PL/SQL stored procedures and packages, programmers can create sophisticated Web applications that interface seamlessly with an Oracle9*i* database. Dynamic HTML pages can be created with the use of the PL/SQL Web Toolkit, a powerful collection of packages for dynamic HTML creation. Web applications developed with **`mod_plsql`** allow the programmer to generate dynamic HTML pages that may contain data obtained from the Oracle9*i* database. They also allow for data to be collected from a user interacting with a Web page, using HTML forms, and then stored into the database.

The PL/SQL Web Toolkit is a collection of built-in packages that contain procedures to produce the various HTML elements of a Web page. The **`htp`** and **`htf`** packages in the toolkit contain procedures to generate the basic HTML elements that constitute an HTML document. Other packages are available for performing more specific tasks, such as dynamic SQL, cookie management, and pattern matching.

This chapter begins with a brief introduction to HTTP, the protocol of the World Wide Web. It then introduces concepts and techniques required to program Web-based applications using PL/SQL. A grade book Web application that accesses the grade book database is used to illustrate various programming techniques. A summary of the PL/SQL Web Toolkit is provided, and some of the more useful procedures in this toolkit are illustrated with examples.

PL/SQL Server Pages (PSP) is introduced toward the end of the chapter. PSP pages are essentially HTML pages with embedded PL/SQL code. They are compiled into the database as regular PL/SQL procedures, which can then be invoked from a Web browser. The PSP approach is a complementary mechanism to writing PL/SQL stored procedures to program Web applications. PSP can be used to generate Web pages that contain mostly presentation aspects.

## 4.1 HTTP

HTTP is the protocol of the World Wide Web. It was created to enable Web servers and Web clients (typically Web browsers) to communicate with each other. It is a relatively simple yet powerful application-layer protocol that allows servers and clients on the Internet to interact seamlessly. The protocol involves two types of messages: *requests* that emanate from the client directed toward a server and *responses* that are generated from the server back to the client. The protocol is defined in such a way that the server need not and does not remember previous requests (e.g., earlier requests from the same client). Each request is treated independently by the server, resulting in a *stateless* protocol (i.e., the server does not remember the context or state in which requests are made).

## 4.1.1 Resources and URLs

Web clients request *resources* that may be simple static files or dynamic files generated as output of programs. Resources may also include binary data representing images or sound or even streaming data such as live audio or video. Resources are uniquely identified using *Uniform Resource Locaters* (URLs). An example of a URL is

```
http://tinman.cs.gsu.edu:7777/raj/index.html
```

Here the resource is a file called **index.html** located under the directory called **raj** (**/raj/index.html** is referred to as the *local path* of the resource). The host computer where this resource is located is specified as **tinman.cs.gsu.edu**, and **7777** is the port number on which the Web server is listening for requests. The protocol being used is **http**. If the port number is not specified, by default the HTTP Web server listens on port 80.

## 4.1.2 Format of HTTP Messages

The HTTP message format consists of:

- An initial line (different for request and response messages)
- Zero or more header lines (each containing a header-value pair)
- A blank line
- An optional message body that may contain any number of lines of text, query data, query results, or even binary data

### *Initial Request Line*

The initial request line consists of three parts: a *method* name, the *local path* of the requested resource, and the *version* of HTTP being used. Three of the most commonly used methods are `GET`, `POST`, and `HEAD`.

The `GET` method is the simplest and most frequently used. It simply requests a resource identified by the local path specified in the initial request line. An example of the `GET` method request line is

```
GET /users/cscabcx/public_html/index.html HTTP/1.0
```

Here, the request uses the HTTP 1.0 protocol to obtain a static file identified by the local path /users/cscabcx/public_html/index.html.

Another example of a GET method request line is

```
GET /cgi-bin/cscabcx/getQuote?symbol=ORCL HTTP/1.0
```

Here, the request uses the HTTP 1.0 protocol to invoke a program called getQuote residing in the local path /cgi-bin/cscabcx/getQuote. The request also sends to the program a parameter called symbol with the value ORCL. This request will most likely result in a dynamic HTML page that is generated by the getQuote program.

The POST method is a more complicated method of sending a request, wherein the client sends (posts) input data to be processed by a program (somewhat similar to the second of the preceding GET examples). However, with a POST request, an unlimited amount of input data may be sent. This input data are packaged within the body of the request message, as shown in the following POST request example:

```
POST /cgi-bin/cscabcx/processGrades HTTP/1.0
Some headers
Sid=111111111&examScore=98&Sid=222222222&examScore=95
```

The processGrades program on the server side is responsible for reading the posted input data and processing it. The program then generates a response—for example, a dynamic HTML page containing a message that the data was processed.

The HEAD method is just like the GET method, except that it asks the server to return response headers only, not the actual resource. No message body is returned in this case. This method checks the properties of a resource without downloading the actual resource itself, thereby saving bandwidth. For example, the HEAD method can be used to retrieve the last-modified date for a particular resource, and the client can then compare this date with the date of its most recently saved version of the resource, to determine whether to request the resource from the server.

### *Initial Response Line*

The initial response line, also called the *status line*, has three parts separated by spaces: the HTTP version, a response status code, and a reason phrase (in English) that describes the status code. Two common examples of initial response lines are:

```
HTTP/1.0 200 OK
HTTP/1.0 404 Not Found
```

Status codes are three-digit numbers. The numbers 100-199 are used for informational messages, 200-299 are used to indicate success of some kind, 300-399 are used to redirect clients to another URL, 400-499 are used for indicating errors on the client's part, and 500-599 are used to indicate errors on the server's part. The most common codes are 200 OK, 404 Not Found, and 500 Server Error.

### Headers

Header lines provide information about the request or response or about the object being sent in the message body. Headers are specified with the format `Header-name: value`, ending with `CR-LF`.

Header names are not case sensitive, but the values may be. Typical headers that go with requests are

```
From: tinman.cs.gsu.edu
User-Agent: Mozilla/1.0
Content-Length: 64
```

The `From` header tells the source of the request, the `User-Agent` header indicates the client browser program name, and the `Content-Length` header indicates the length in bytes of the message body.

Typical headers that go with responses are

```
Server: Apache/1.3.26
Last-Modified: Fri, 13 Sep 2002 18:29:06 GMT
Content-Type: text/html
```

The `Server` header indicates the name of the Web server program, the `Last-Modified` header indicates the latest time the resource was modified, and the `Content-Type` header indicates the MIME type of the data in the body.

### Message Body

Requests may contain a message body if they are sending form data to the server, and responses almost always contain a message body containing the requested resource.

### A Sample HTTP Exchange

The following is a sample HTTP exchange between a client requesting the resource

```
http://tinman.cs.gsu.edu/~raj/hello.html
```

and a server that responds to this request. The client sends the following request:

```
GET /~raj/hello.html HTTP/1.0
From: Kenny@a.b.edu
User-Agent: Mozilla/1.0
[blank line here followed by no body]
```

and the server responds

```
HTTP/1.0 200 OK
Date: Fri, 13 Sep 2002 18:29:06 GMT
Content-Type: text/html
Content-Length: 80
```

```
<html>
<head><title>Hello</title></head>
<body>
<b>Hello</b>
</body>
</html>
```

## 4.2 A Simple Example

To produce a dynamic HTML page from a PL/SQL procedure, you must use the built-in packages of the PL/SQL Web Toolkit. One of the commonly used packages in this toolkit is the HyperText Procedures (**htp**) package. The **htp** package contains a large collection of procedures that produce the basic elements of HTML. The smallest sequence of statements in any procedure that produces a dynamic HTML page is

```
http.htmlOpen;       -- produces <HTML>
htp.headOpen;        -- produces <HEAD>
htp.title('title');  -- produces <TITLE>title</TITLE>
htp.headClose;       -- produces </HEAD>
htp.bodyOpen;        -- produces <BODY>
.
.
.
htp.bodyClose;       -- produces </BODY>
htp.htmlClose;       -- produces </HTML>
```

To produce a line of text in the HTML document, the **htp.print** procedure is used. It is overloaded in its input parameter and has the following syntax:

```
procedure htp.print(cbuf IN VARCHAR2);
procedure htp.print(cbuf IN DATE);
procedure htp.print(cbuf IN NUMBER);
```

The input can be a string, **date**, or **number**. The procedure prints the input to the HTML document. The **date** and **number** values are converted to the default string format before printing.

Example 4.2.1 The following procedure makes use of the **htp** package of the PL/SQL Web Toolkit to produce a simple dynamic HTML page. It makes a call to the **sysdate** function to print the date and day of the week in the document.

```
create or replace procedure simple as
begin
   htp.htmlOpen;
```

```
    htp.headOpen;
    htp.title('Simple Example');
    htp.headClose;
    htp.bodyOpen;
    htp.line;
    htp.header(1,'Simple Example');
    htp.line;
    htp.paragraph;
    -- Print SQL variable sysdate
    htp.print('Today''s date is:  ' ||
              to_char(sysdate, 'DD/MM/YYYY'));
    htp.br;
    htp.print('Today''s day  is:  ' ||
              to_char(sysdate, 'DAY'));
    htp.paragraph;
    htp.print('Ordinary <em>tags</em> can be ' ||
              'used in the strings that we send.');
    -- Print SQL variable USER
    htp.print('Your Oracle USERID is ' || USER);
    htp.line;
    htp.address('Raj Sunderraman');
    htp.bodyClose;
    htp.htmlClose;
end;
/
show errors
```

The preceding procedure must be compiled (in SQL*Plus) before it can be invoked within a Web browser. A typical URL to invoke this procedure is

```
http://tinman.cs.gsu.edu:7777/pls/book/simple
```

In this URL, `http://tinman.cs.gsu.edu:7777` contains the host name and port on which the Oracle HTTP Listener is running. The second part of this URL, `/pls/book/`, is the virtual path for the particular Database Access Descriptor (DAD) created by the database administrator. The last part of the URL, `simple`, is the PL/SQL procedure that is to be executed. If there were parameters to the procedure, they would have to be specified. The details of specifying parameters are discussed in Section 4.4. Once the procedure is executed, it generates a dynamic HTML document, whose HTML source is

```
<HTML>
<HEAD>
```

```
<TITLE>Simple Example</TITLE>
</HEAD>
<BODY>
<HR>
<H1>Simple Example</H1>
<HR>
<P>
Today's date is:  04/02/1998
<BR>
Today's day is:  WEDNESDAY
<P>
Ordinary <em>tags</em> can be used in the strings
that we send.
Your Oracle USERID is BOOK.
<HR>
<ADDRESS>Raj Sunderraman</ADDRESS>
<HR>
</BODY>
</HTML>
```

The Web page created by the `simple` procedure is shown in Figure 4.1.

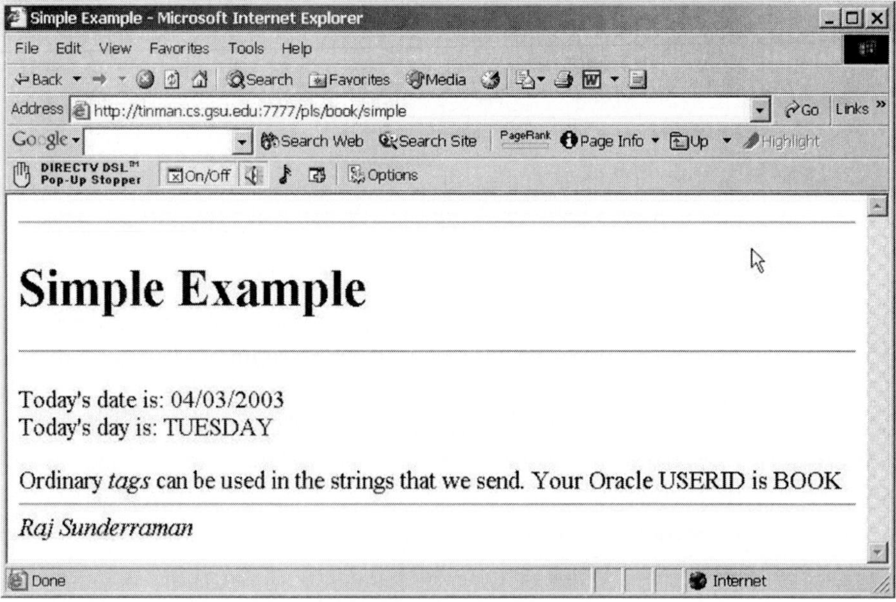


**Figure 4.1** Web page produced by the `simple` procedure.

## 4.3 Printing HTML Tables

To print an HTML table from within a PL/SQL procedure, the following **htp** procedures must be invoked in sequence:

1. **htp.tableOpen**. This procedure must be invoked first. It produces HTML code that describes the properties of the table.
2. **htp.tableRowOpen**. This procedure must be invoked once for each row in the table. It produces the <TR> tag.
3. **htp.tableHeader**. This procedure is used to produce the HTML code for the individual cells within a row of the table (used for column headings).
4. **htp.tableData**. This procedure is used to produce the HTML code for the individual cells within a row of the table (used for regular columns).
5. **htp.tableRowClose**. This procedure must be called for each row, after all the column values have been processed. It produces the </TR> tag.
6. **htp.tableClose**. This procedure must be called at the end. It produces the </table> tag.

The following code fragment illustrates the use of the preceding procedures:

```
cursor c1 is
   select   *
   from     catalog;

htp.tableOpen(cattributes => 'border=2 width=60%' );
htp.tableRowOpen;
htp.tableHeader('Course Number');
htp.tableHeader('Course Title');
htp.tableRowClose;
for cat_rec in c1 loop
   htp.tableRowOpen;
   htp.tableData(cat_rec.cno);
   htp.tableData(cat_rec.ctitle);
   htp.tableRowClose;
end loop;
htp.tableClose;
```

This code fragment displays the contents of the **catalog** database table of the grade book database. It uses the HTML table format. The rows of the HTML table are created dynamically by processing a PL/SQL cursor.

## 4.4 Passing Parameters

A PL/SQL procedure that is invoked via the `mod_plsql` Apache module from a Web browser can be passed parameters using one of two methods: the `GET` method or the `POST` method.

In the `GET` method, the parameters are passed directly in the URL itself. At the end of the URL for the procedure, the following is included:

```
?par1=val1&par2=val1&...&parN=valN
```

Here, `par1`, . . . , `parN` are parameter names and `val1`, . . . , `valN` are their corresponding values.

Example 4.4.1 Consider the following procedure that takes as input two parameters: `str` and `num`:

```
create or replace procedure pl1(
         str in varchar2, num in number) as
-- Parameter str will be printed num times.
begin
   htp.htmlOpen;
   htp.headOpen;
   htp.title('Parameters');
   htp.headClose;
   htp.bodyOpen;
   htp.line;
   htp.header(1,'Parameter Passing');
   htp.line;
   for i in 1..num loop
      htp.print(i || '. ' || str);
      htp.br;
   end loop;
   htp.line;
   htp.bodyClose;
   htp.htmlClose;
end;
/
show errors
```

This procedure produces an HTML page in which the `str` parameter is printed `num` times. It is invoked using the URL

```
http://host:port/pls/book/pl1?str=Hello&num=4
```

The procedure, when executed, produces the following HTML source:

```
<HTML>
<HEAD>
<TITLE>Parameters</TITLE>
</HEAD>
<BODY>
<HR>
<H1>Parameter Passing</H1>
<HR>
1. Hello
<BR>
2. Hello
<BR>
3. Hello
<BR>
4. Hello
<BR>
<HR>
</BODY>
</HTML>
```

In the POST method, parameters are sent to standard input, and the mod_plsql module takes care of delivering these parameters to the appropriate procedure. The POST method is typically used when the procedure is the target of an HTML form. HTML form processing is discussed later in this chapter.

### 4.4.1 Flexible Parameter Passing

In certain situations, one does not know the number and names of the parameters being sent to a PL/SQL procedure for processing. The mod_plsql module provides a flexible mechanism to send and receive parameters in such situations. The names of parameters and their corresponding values can be received into PL/SQL arrays (OWA.vc_arr) by invoking the procedure with a "!" symbol preceding the procedure name in the URL. For example, the following URL:

```
http://host:7777/pls/book/!flexParameters?a=1&b=1&a=5&c=9
```

would invoke the following PL/SQL procedure with four parameters: num_entries (contains number of name-value pairs received), name_array (contains names of parameters starting at index 1), value_array (contains corresponding values of parameters starting at index 1), and **reserved** (an array variable that is reserved for future use and is currently not used).

The following procedure, **flexParameters**, simply prints the name-value pairs it receives. In this sample invocation, **num-entries** is 4, **name_array** is (a,b,a,c), and **value_array** is (1,1,5,9).

```
create or replace procedure flexParameters(
   num_entries  IN NUMBER,
   name_array   IN OWA.vc_arr,
   value_array  IN OWA.vc_arr,
   reserved     IN OWA.vc_arr) AS
   ct      INTEGER;
BEGIN
   htp.htmlopen;
   htp.headopen;
   htp.title('Dynamic Parameters');
   htp.headclose;
   htp.bodyopen;
   htp.header(1, 'Dynamic Parameters');
   for ct in 1..num_entries loop
      htp.print(name_array(ct)||'='||value_array(ct));
      htp.br;
      htp.br;
   end loop;
   htp.bodyClose;
   htp.htmlClose;
Exception
   when others then
      htp.print('Error in flexParameters');
end flexParameters;
/
show errors
```

## 4.5 Processing HTML Forms

An HTML form is used to accept input from the user via GUI elements such as text-entry fields, checkboxes, radio buttons, selection lists, and so on. This user input is usually submitted to a server program for processing. The HTML page containing the HTML form may either be a static document or be produced dynamically by a program (useful if it contains information that may change).

If the HTML form page has dynamic data, the application developer needs to write two procedures: one to create the dynamic HTML page containing the form and the other to process the user input obtained from the HTML form generated by the first procedure. The second procedure receives a number of input parameters from the HTML form, and it is important to name these input parameters with the same names that were chosen for the GUI elements in the HTML form.

The following `htp` procedures are used in creating the form page of the dynamic HTML document:

- `htp.formOpen`. This procedure must be called at the beginning. Its syntax is

  ```
  htp.formOpen(curl in varchar2,
               cmethod in varchar2 default 'POST',
               ctarget in varchar2,
               cenctype in varchar2 default null,
               cattributes in varchar2 default null);
  ```

  The only required parameter is `curl`, which specifies the URL of the PL/SQL procedure that receives and processes the form input. The `formOpen` procedure call generates the following HTML tag:

  ```
  <FORM ACTION="curl" METHOD="cmethod"
     TARGET="ctarget" ENCTYPE="cenctype" cattributes>
  ```

- `htp.formSubmit`. This procedure creates a button element in the form that, when clicked, causes the form to be submitted for processing. The syntax is

  ```
  htp.formSubmit(cname in varchar2 default null,
                 cvalue in varchar2 default 'Submit',
                 cattributes in varchar2 default null);
  ```

  All three parameters are optional. However, if the `cname` and `cvalue` parameters are specified, then the `cname/cvalue` pair is included in the submitted data. This feature can be used in situations in which the form has more than one submit button. The procedure that receives form data will examine the value of the `cname` parameter and then take action based on its value. The procedure call generates the following tag:

  ```
  <INPUT TYPE="submit" NAME="cname"
         VALUE="cvalue" cattributes>
  ```

- `htp.formReset`. This procedure creates a `reset` button that, when selected, resets all the form fields to their initial values. The syntax is

  ```
  htp.formReset(cvalue in varchar2 default 'Reset'
                cattributes in varchar2 default null);
  ```

When executed, the procedure generates this tag:

```
<INPUT TYPE="reset" VALUE="cvalue" cattributes>
```

- `htp.formClose`. This procedure must be called at the end, after all form elements have been defined. Its syntax is

  ```
  htp.formClose;
  ```

  When executed, it produces the `</FORM>` tag.

HTML forms can have the following types of elements (each element's corresponding `htp` procedure is listed in parentheses):

- Single-line input text fields (`htp.formText`).
- Single-line input password fields (`htp.formPassword`).
- Checkboxes (`htp.formCheckbox`).
- Radio buttons (`htp.formRadio`).
- Submit buttons (`htp.formSubmit`).
- Text areas (`htp.formTextarea`).
- Selects (`htp.formSelectOpen`, `htp.formSelectOption`, `htp.formSelectClose`). Allows the user to choose one or more items from a set of alternatives described by textual labels. These are usually rendered as a pull-down or pop-up menu or a fixed-size list.

Many of these form elements are used and explained in the several examples that follow. A detailed explanation of the `htp` procedures to create these form elements can be found in the online documentation that accompanies Oracle9*i*.

Example 4.5.1 The following set of procedures (`get_access`, `start_session`, `teacher_menu`) and functions (`check_access`) implements a simple user authentication scheme for a teacher to access the grade book system.

```
create or replace procedure get_access as
-- This procedure displays a Web page with an HTML form
-- containing text fields for userid and password.
-- When submitted, the form invokes procedure start_session.
begin
   htp.htmlOpen;
   htp.headOpen;
   htp.title('Get password');
   htp.header(1, 'Grade Book Access Page');
```

```
   htp.headClose;
   htp.bodyOpen;
   -- Start an HTML form; specify start_session procedure
   -- as ACTION parameter.
   htp.formOpen(owa_util.get_owa_service_path ||
                'start_session');
   htp.nl;
   htp.nl;
   htp.print('Today is ' ||
            to_char(sysdate, 'Day') || '  ' ||
            to_char(sysdate, 'Dd / Mon / YYYY HH:MI AM'));
   htp.nl;
   htp.nl;

   -- Add two text fields for userid and password
   -- formatted within an HTML table.
   htp.tableOpen;
   htp.tableRowOpen;
   htp.tableData(htf.strong('USER ID: '));
   htp.tableData(htf.formText('usid', 20, 50));
   htp.tableRowClose;
   htp.tableRowOpen;
   htp.tableData(htf.strong('PASSWORD: '));
   htp.tableData(htf.formPassword('passwd', 20, 50));
   htp.tableRowClose;
   htp.tableClose;

   -- Add form submit button.
   htp.formSubmit(NULL, ' Proceed ');
   htp.formReset;
   htp.formClose;
   htp.bodyClose;
   htp.htmlClose;
Exception
   when others then
      htp.print('error in get_access');
end get_access;
/
show errors
```

The get_access procedure produces an HTML page that contains an HTML form. The form contains two text fields (to accept the user ID and password for a user), a submit button, and a reset button. When submitted, the form invokes the second procedure, called start_session, with two parameters named usid and passwd. The start_session procedure is described later.

It is worthy to note the following for the previous procedure:

- The formOpen statement makes use of the utility procedure owa_util.get_owa_service_path to dynamically determine the fixed part of the URL, which is the prefix to the PL/SQL procedure call. This allows for portable PL/SQL code.
- A function variant of the formText procedure is invoked in

  ```
  htp.tableData(htf.formText('usid', 20, 50));
  ```

  This is necessary in this context because the HTML code being generated for the text field is to be embedded within the HTML table cell. The htf package is a mirror of the htp package, with functions returning HTML code rather than procedures printing HTML code.

The Web page created by the get_access procedure is shown in Figure 4.2.

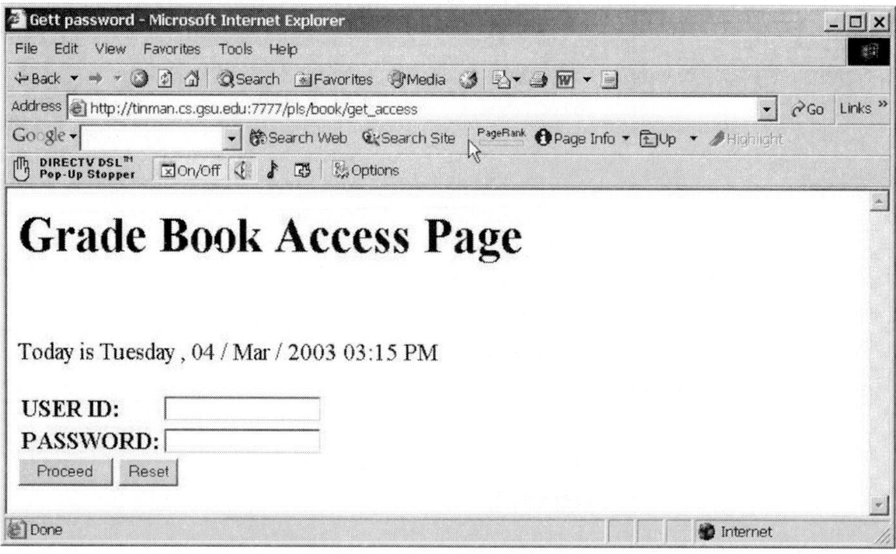


**Figure 4.2** Grade book access page (produced by get_access).

Upon submission of the HTML form from the initial grade book access page, the **start_session** procedure is invoked with two parameters: **usid** and **passwd**. The PL/SQL code for **start_session** is

```
procedure start_session(usid in varchar2   DEFAULT NULL,
                        passwd in varchar2 DEFAULT NULL) AS
-- This procedure receives user ID and password values from
-- get_access, authenticates the values with the values in
-- the database, and calls the teacher_menu procedure to
-- display the main menu for teachers.
   user_buffer    varchar2(15);
   passwd_buffer  varchar2(15);
   time_buffer    date;
   auth_buffer    varchar2(15);
   random_num     varchar2(10);
   access_buffer  varchar2(30);
   bad_passwd     exception;

begin
   -- Obtain database values corresponding to user.
   select A.userid, A.password, A.lastAccess, A.authority
   into   user_buffer, passwd_buffer, time_buffer,
          auth_buffer
   from   users A
   where  upper(A.userid)=upper(start_session.usid);

   -- If passwords do not match, raise exception.
   if start_session.passwd != passwd_buffer then
      raise bad_passwd;
   end if;

-- If passwords match, generate random string and
-- update u_access and lastAccess values in database.
random_num := to_char(sysdate, 'SSSSS');
access_buffer := user_buffer || ',' || random_num;
update users
set u_access = access_buffer,
    lastAccess = sysdate
where users.userid=user_buffer;
commit;
```

```
-- Invoke procedure to display teacher menu.
teacher_menu(access_buffer);

Exception
   when bad_passwd then
      htp.print('Bad password ');
   when no_data_found then
      htp.print('Invalid user');
   when others then
      htp.print('Error in start_session');
end start_session;
```

This procedure first consults a database table called **users**, which contains information about all authorized users of the grade book application program. The **users** table has the following definition:

```
create table users (
   userid     varchar2(15),
   password   varchar2(15),
   lastaccess date,
   u_access   varchar(30),
   authority  varchar2(15)
);
```

The **userid** and **password** columns contain the user IDs and passwords of the users. The **lastaccess** column records the time of last access for each user. The **u_access** column is initially set to **null**. As soon as a particular user is authorized to access the grade book application, this entry is recorded. It contains the user ID, followed by a comma, followed by a random string generated at the time of access. This column value is passed along to every other PL/SQL procedure, and each of them verifies the value of the **authority** column based on this random string. The **authority** column can have one of two values: **Teacher** or **Student**. The grade book application allows these two types of users. A different menu of choices for each category of users is presented by the system. The **start_session** procedure, after verifying that the user ID and password are correct, generates the **u_access** column value and stores it. It then invokes the appropriate menu of choices for the user.

The Web page created by the **start_session** procedure via a call to the **teacher_menu** procedure is shown in Figure 4.3. The **teacher_menu** procedure is quite straightforward:

```
procedure teacher_menu(u_access in varchar2 default NULL,
                       userid in varchar2 default NULL) as
```

```
-- This procedure displays the main menu for teachers.
   access_check varchar2(30);
   no_access    exception;
begin
   if (u_access is NULL) then
      raise no_access;
   end if;

   -- Call check_user function, which returns the authority
   -- value for the given u_access value.
   access_check := check_access(u_access);

   -- If return value is not Teacher, deny access to menu.
   if  (access_check != 'Teacher') then
      raise no_access;
   end if;

   -- Publish Web page with teacher menu.
   htp.htmlOpen;
   htp.headOpen;
   htp.htitle('Teacher Menu');
   htp.headClose;
   htp.bodyOpen;
   -- Open HTML form and specify ACTION parameter.
   htp.formOpen(owa_util.get_owa_service_path ||
            'process_teacher_option');

   -- Send u_access and userid as hidden parameters.
   htp.formHidden('u_access', u_access);
   htp.formHidden('userid', userid);
   -- Create menu option buttons.
   htp.formSubmit('opt', 'Add Catalog Entry'); htp.br;
   htp.formSubmit('opt', 'Add Course Entry'); htp.br;
   htp.formSubmit('opt', 'Select a Course'); htp.br;
   htp.formSubmit('opt', 'Search Userid-Password'); htp.br;
   htp.formSubmit('opt', 'Change Password'); htp.br;
   htp.formSubmit('opt', 'Logout'); htp.br;
   htp.formClose;
   htp.bodyClose;
   htp.htmlClose;
```

```
Exception
   when no_access then
        htp.print('No Access to Gradebook');
   when others then
      htp.print('Error in teacher_menu');
      htp.br;
      htp.print(SQLERRM); -- Useful for debugging purposes.
end teacher_menu;
```

After verifying that the `u_access` value received in this procedure is indeed that of a `Teacher` (this is done by the `check_access` function call), this procedure simply publishes an HTML form with several submit buttons, one for each of the menu options.

The `check_access` procedure that follows simply queries the users table for the authority value associated with the given `u_access` value:

```
function check_access(u_access in varchar2 default NULL)
return varchar2 as
-- This function takes as input the u_access value and
-- queries the database for the corresponding authority
-- value. The function returns the authority value if it
-- is found. Otherwise, it returns the string '0'.
   return_value varchar2(30);
   auth_buffer  varchar2(20);
   no_access    exception;

begin
   if u_access is null
      then raise no_access;
   end if;
   select authority into auth_buffer
   from   users U
   where  U.u_access = check_access.u_access;
   return_value := auth_buffer;

   return(return_value);
   Exception
      when no_data_found then return('0');
      when no_access then return ('0');
      when others then
         htp.print('error in check_access');
end check_access;
```

## 4.6 Multivalued Parameters

Sometimes it is necessary to pass multiple values for the same HTML form element parameter. For example, in an HTML select list that allows the user to select more than one value, the select list parameter may contain more than one value. Likewise, with HTML checkboxes, the user may be able to check more than one box. The way to handle this situation is to use the `ident_arr` data type found in the `owa_util` package. The `mod_plsql` module automatically passes the multiple values in the `ident_arr` parameter, which is similar to a PL/SQL table. It is good practice to send a dummy value as the first entry in this array, to handle any errors that may arise if the user does not select any item in the select list or checkboxes.

Multivalued parameters are used in the grade book system to facilitate the entering of scores for a particular grading component by a teacher. The sequence of steps taken by a teacher to enter scores follows:

1. The teacher chooses the Select a Course option in the Teacher Menu of Figure 4.3. This request is processed by the `process_teacher_option` and `select_course` procedures. The resulting Web page contains a pull-down list of courses along with a teacher submenu consisting of the options:
   - Add Students to Course
   - Add Component to Course
   - Add Student Score

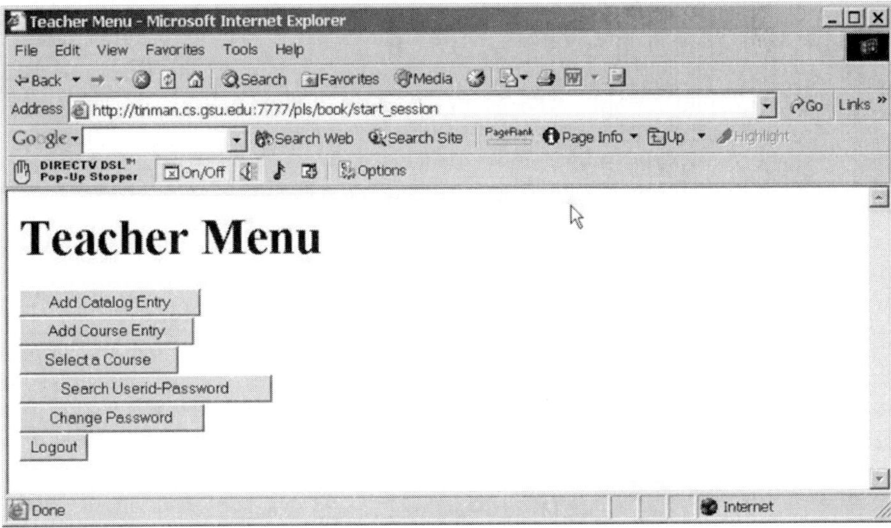


**Figure 4.3** Teacher options page (produced by `start_session`).

- Modify Student Score
- Drop Student from Course
- Print Course Report

2. The teacher selects the appropriate course in the pull-down list of courses and chooses the Add Student Score option in the teacher submenu. This request is processed by the `process_teacher_sub_option` and `add_scores` procedures. The resulting Web page contains a pull-down list of grading components for the course along with a submit button.
3. The teacher chooses the grading component from the pull-down list for which he or she wishes to enter the scores and submits the request. This request is processed by the `process_scores` procedure. The resulting Web page contains a list of student names enrolled in the course along with a text box next to the name for the score. The Web page also contains a submit button labeled Enter the scores.
4. The teacher enters the scores for each of the students and submits the request for processing by procedure `insert_scores`.

Multivalued parameters are used in steps 3 and 4 of the above sequence. The rest of the section discusses the various procedures and Web pages used in steps 1 to 4.

## 4.6.1 Procedure `process_teacher_option`

The `process_teacher_option` procedure receives the `opt` parameter from the user along with `user_access` and `userid`. It simply examines the value of the input parameter `opt` and calls the appropriate procedure (in this case, `select_course`).

```
create or replace procedure process_teacher_option(
   opt in varchar2 default null,
   u_access in varchar2 default null,
   userid in varchar2 default null) as
-- This procedure takes as input the opt parameter
-- and, based on its value, calls the appropriate procedure.
begin
   if (opt = 'Add Catalog Entry') then
      add_all.create_catalog(u_access);
   elsif (opt = 'Add Student') then
      add_all.create_student(u_access);
   elsif (opt = 'Add Course Entry') then
      add_all.create_course(u_access);
```

```
   if (opt = 'Select a Course') then
      select_course(u_access, userid);
   elsif (opt = 'Change Password') then
      user_access.change_password(u_access);
   elsif (opt = 'Logout') then
      user_access.logout(u_access);
   end if;
end;
```

### 4.6.2 Procedure `select_course`

The `select_course` procedure first performs the usual check on the `u_access` value. After that, it queries the `courses` table to obtain all the courses and presents them in a select list followed by a submenu of options. The term, course number, and line number values are encoded and sent to the next procedure as the value of the select list parameter named `tcl`. For example, `(f96,csc226,1031)` is a possible value for the parameter `tcl` that encodes the Fall 96 offering of CSc226 with line number 1031.

```
create or replace procedure select_course(
   u_access in varchar2 default NULL,
   userid in varchar2 default NULL) as
-- This procedure produces an HTML form containing a
-- pull-down list of courses (course number, term, and
-- line no values) available along with a submenu of
-- teacher options.
   access_check    varchar2(30);
   no_access       exception;
   cursor c1 is
      select courses.term,cno,courses.lineno
      from   courses;
begin
   -- Perform u_access check.
   if (u_access = NULL) then
      raise no_access;
   end if;
   access_check := check_access(u_access);
   if (access_check != 'Teacher') then
      raise no_access;
   end if;
   -- Publish HTML page containing teacher submenu.
```

```
   htp.htmlOpen;
   htp.headOpen;
   htp.title('Select Course');
   htp.header(1,'Select Course ');
   htp.headClose;
   htp.bodyOpen;
   htp.FormOpen(owa_util.get_owa_service_path ||
                'process_teacher_sub_option');
   htp.nl;
   -- Put a pull-down list of courses.
   htp.formSelectOpen('tcl', 'Select Course: ');
   for c1_rec in c1 loop
      -- Encode term, cno, and lineno values as a string.
      htp.formSelectOption('(' ||c1_rec.term||','||
                           c1_rec.cno||','||
                           c1_rec.lineno || ')');
   end loop;
   htp.formSelectClose;
   htp.br; htp.br;
   -- Submit hidden parameters u_access and userid
   htp.formHidden('u_access', u_access);
   htp.formHidden('userid', userid);
   -- Display teacher submenu.
   htp.formSubmit('opt', 'Add Students to Course');
   htp.br;
   htp.formSubmit('opt', 'Add Component to Course');
   htp.br;
   htp.formSubmit('opt', 'Add Student Score');
   htp.br;
   htp.formSubmit('opt', 'Modify Student Score');
   htp.br;
   htp.formSubmit('opt', 'Drop Student from Course');
   htp.br;
   htp.formClose;
   htp.bodyClose;
   htp.htmlClose;
Exception
   when no_access then
      htp.print('You are not logged on');
   when others then
      htp.print('Error in select_course');
end select_course;
```

The HTML page rendered by the `select_course` procedure is shown in Figure 4.4.

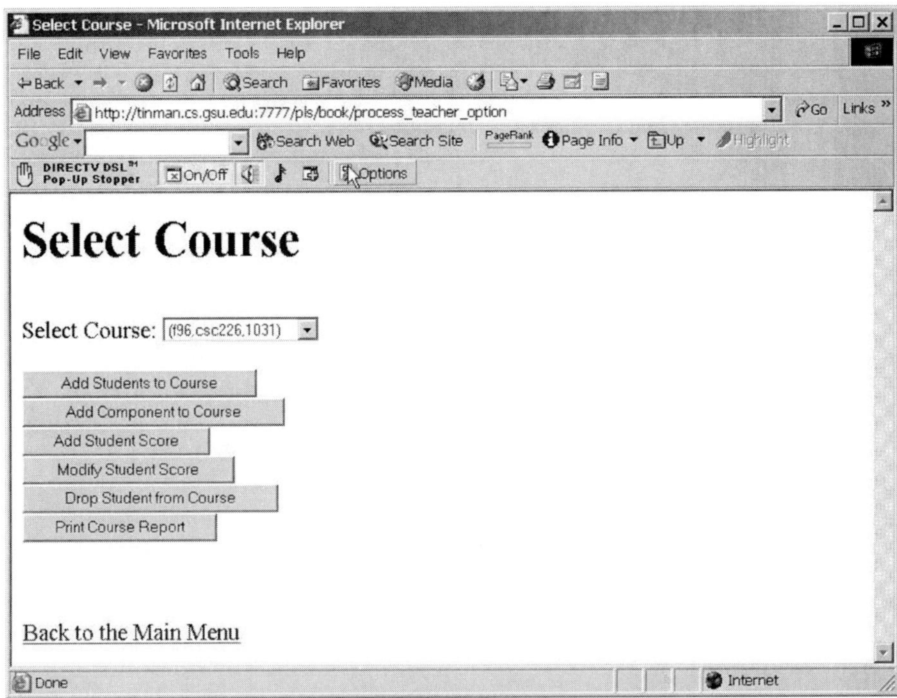


**Figure 4.4** Teacher submenu (displayed by `select_course` procedure).

## 4.6.3 Procedure `process_teacher_sub_option`

When the user chooses a course and submits the Add Student Score option in the teacher submenu page, control is sent to the `process_teacher_sub_option` procedure shown next, which simply examines the value of the `opt` parameter and calls the necessary procedure (in this case, the `add_scores` procedure). It also needs to decipher the `tcl` parameter value to extract the term, course number, and line number values.

```
create or replace procedure
process_teacher_sub_option(u_access in varchar2,
                           userid in varchar2,
                           opt in varchar2,
                           tcl in varchar2) as
```

```
-- This procedure examines the opt parameter value and
-- makes a call to the appropriate procedure.
   access_check varchar2(30);
   no_access    exception;
   p1 integer;
   p2 integer;
   term_in courses.term%type;
   lnum courses.lineno%type;
   cnum courses.cno%type;

begin
   -- Perform u_access check.
   if (u_access = NULL) then
      raise no_access;
   end if;
   access_check := check_access(u_access);
   if (access_check != 'Teacher') then
      raise no_access;
   end if;
   -- Extract term, cno, and lineno values from variable tcl.
   p1 := instr(tcl,',',1,2)+1;
   p2 := instr(tcl,')',1,1)-1;
   term_in := substr(tcl,2,instr(tcl,',',1)-2);
   lnum := to_number(substr(tcl,p1,p2-p1+1));
   cnum := substr(tcl,instr(tcl,',',1,1)+1,
                     p1-instr(tcl,',',1,1)-2);
   -- Call appropriate procedure.
   if (opt = 'Add Students to Course') then
      add_enrolled_students(u_access, term_in, lnum, cnum);
   elsif (opt = 'Add Component to Course') then
      add_course_components(u_access, term_in, lnum, cnum);
   if (opt = 'Add Student Score') then
      add_scores(u_access, userid, term_in, lnum, cnum);
   elsif (opt = 'Modify Student Score') then
      modify_student_score(u_access, term_in, lnum, cnum);
elsif (opt = 'Drop Student from Course') then
      drop_enrolled_student(u_access, term_in, lnum, cnum);
elsif (opt = 'Print Course Report') then
      display_report(u_access, term_in, lnum, cnum);
   end if;
```

```
Exception
  when no_access then
     htp.print('You are not logged on');
  when others then
     htp.print('error in process_teacher_option');
end process_teacher_sub_option;
```

### 4.6.4 Procedure add_scores

The add_scores procedure shown next displays a pull-down list of course components for the particular course (identified by the term and line number) for which the scores are to be added. The user chooses the component for which the scores are to be added and submits the form.

```
procedure add_scores(
   u_access in varchar2 default NULL,
   term_in in varchar2 default NULL,
   lnum in number default NULL,
   cnum in varchar2 default NULL) as
-- This procedure publishes an HTML form containing a
-- pull-down list of course grading components. The user
-- will choose one of these to add scores to.
   access_check       varchar2(30);
   no_access       exception;

   cursor c1 is
      select term, lineno, compname
      from   components
      where  term = term_in and lineno = lnum;
begin
   -- Perform u_access check
   if (u_access = NULL) then
      raise no_access;
   end if;

   access_check := user_access.check_access(u_access);
   if (access_check != 'Teacher') then
      raise no_access;
   end if;
```

```
   -- Publish HTML page with pull-down list of grading
   -- components
    htp.htmlOpen;
    htp.headOpen;
    htp.title('Selecting Component');
    htp.header(1,'Selecting Component');
    htp.headClose;
    htp.bodyOpen;
    htp.formOpen(owa_util.get_owa_service_path ||
                 'add_all.process_scores');
    htp.nl;

    htp.formSelectOpen('comp',
                       'Choose the course component: ');
    -- Process SQL cursor to get grading component names
    for crec in c1 loop
       htp.formSelectOption(crec.compname);
    end loop;
    htp.formSelectClose;
    -- Send some hidden parameters
    htp.formHidden('term_in', term_in);
    htp.formHidden('cnum', cnum);
    htp.formHidden('lnum', lnum);
    htp.formHidden('u_access', u_access);

    htp.formSubmit;
    htp.formClose;
    htp.bodyClose;
    htp.htmlClose;
Exception
    when no_access then
       htp.print('You are not logged on');
    when others then
       htp.print('Something is wrong in add_scores');
end add_scores;
```

As can be seen in the code, the procedure makes an SQL query to obtain the grading components for the given course and uses the answers to form a select list element in an HTML form. It also prepares several hidden fields that are required by subsequent procedures.

The Web page created by the `add_scores` procedure is shown in Figure 4.5.

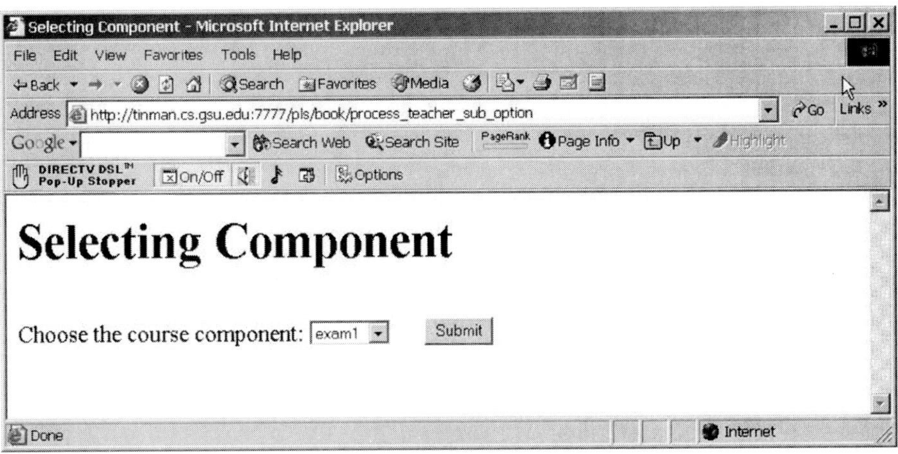


**Figure 4.5** Web page created by `add_scores` procedure.

## 4.6.5 Procedure process_scores

Once the teacher selects the course component for which scores are to be entered, control is passed on to the `process_scores` procedure shown here:

```
procedure process_scores (
   u_access in varchar2 default NULL,
   term_in in varchar2 default NULL,
   lnum in integer default NULL,
   comp in varchar2 default NULL,
   cnum in varchar2 default NULL) as
-- This procedure produces an HTML form containing
-- a list of students in the class along with a list of
-- text box fields in which the user can enter the scores.
   access_check    varchar2(30);
   no_access       exception;

   cursor c1 is
      select distinct B.lname, B.fname,
             A.sid, A.term, A.lineno
      from   enrolls A, students B
      where  (A.term = term_in) and
             (A.lineno = lnum) and
             (A.sid = B.sid);
begin
```

```
-- Perform u_access check
if (u_access = NULL) then
   raise no_access;
end if;

access_check := user_access.check_access(u_access);
if (access_check != 'Teacher') then
   raise no_access;
end if;
-- Publish HTML page
htp.htmlOpen;
htp.headOpen;
htp.title('Entering Scores');
htp.header(1,'Entering Scores for ' || cnum ||
             ',' || lnum || ',' || term_in);
htp.headClose;
htp.bodyOpen;
htp.formOpen(owa_util.get_owa_service_path ||
          'insert_all.insert_scores');
-- Send hidden parameters
htp.formHidden('u_access', u_access);
htp.formHidden('term_in', term_in);
htp.formHidden('lnum', lnum);
htp.formHidden('comp', comp);
-- Send dummy values for two multivalued parameters
htp.formHidden('score_arr', '000');
htp.formHidden('ids', '0000');

htp.print('Component: ');
htp.print(comp);
htp.nl;
htp.nl;
htp.tableOpen;
-- This loops over the list of students
for crec in c1 loop
   htp.tableRowopen;
   -- Print student name
   htp.tableData(htf.strong(crec.lname||', '
                           || crec.fname));
   -- Print text box next to student name
   htp.tableData(htf.formText('score_arr', 3, 3));
```

```
        -- Send hidden field for student ID
        htp.formHidden('ids', crec.sid);
        htp.tableRowClose;
      end loop;
      htp.tableClose;
      htp.formSubmit(NULL,'Enter the scores');
      htp.formclose;
      htp.bodyClose;
      htp.htmlClose;
    Exception
      when no_access then
        htp.print('You are not logged on');
      when others then
        htp.print('Something is wrong in process_scores');
    end process_scores;
```

This procedure displays a form containing the names of all students enrolled in the course and a form text field, called **scrarr**, next to each student name. This is an example of a parameter that will take multiple values. Notice that the form contains a hidden dummy value as the first entry. This is introduced as a programming trick to ensure that at least one value is present when this form is submitted. The form also contains a hidden field (**ids**) that is also a multivalued parameter.

The Web page created by the **process_scores** procedure is shown in Figure 4.6.

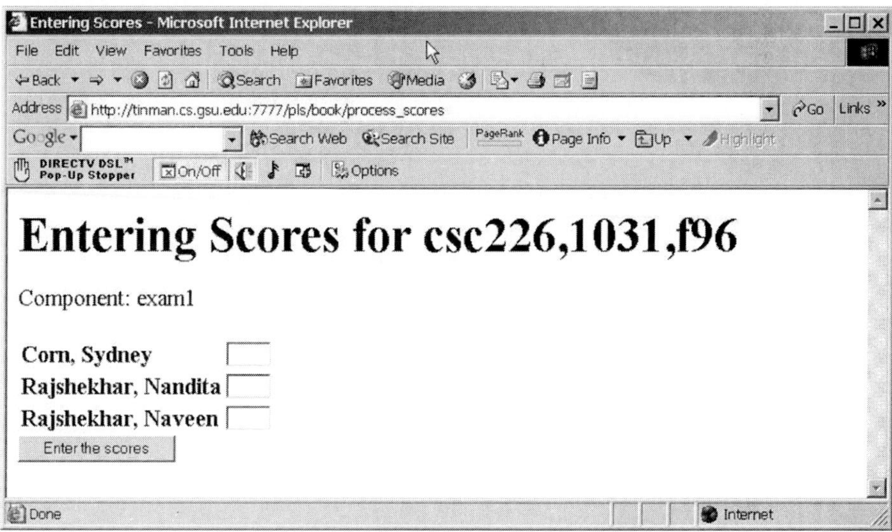


**Figure 4.6** Web page created by the **process_scores** procedure.

## 4.6.6 Procedure insert_scores

Once the user enters the scores for the students for the particular course component and submits the form for processing, a call is made to the **insert_scores** procedure shown here:

```
procedure insert_scores(u_access in varchar2 default NULL,
            term_in in varchar2 default NULL,
            lnum in number default NULL,
            comp in varchar2 default NULL,
            score_arr in owa_util.ident_arr,
            ids in owa_util.ident_arr) as
-- This procedure receives the scores for each student
-- for a particular grading component of the course and
-- enters them into the database table scores.
   access_check    varchar2(30);
   no_access       exception;
   counter         integer;

begin
   -- Perform u_access check
   if (u_access = NULL) then
      raise no_access;
   end if;

   access_check := user_access.check_access(u_access);
   if (access_check != 'Teacher') then
      raise no_access;
   end if;
   -- Publish HTML page
   htp.htmlOpen;
   htp.headOpen;
   htp.title('Inserting Scores');
   htp.headClose;
   htp.bodyOpen;
   htp.nl;
   -- Start at index 2 (because index 1 contains dummy)
   counter := 2;
   loop
      insert into scores(sid, term, lineno,
                         compname, points)
```

```
         values(ids(counter), term_in, lnum,
                    comp, score_arr(counter));
         counter := counter+1;
      end  loop;
      commit;

      EXCEPTION
         when no_access then
            htp.print('You are not logged on');
            htp.bodyClose;
            htp.htmlClose;
         when no_data_found then
            if (counter = 2) then
               htp.print('No DATA');
               htp.bodyClose;
               htp.htmlClose;
            else
               htp.print('Inserted scores successfully');
               htp.bodyClose;
               htp.htmlClose;
            end if;
         when others then
            htp.print('Other Error');
            htp.bodyClose;
            htp.htmlClose;
   end insert_scores;
```

This procedure accepts the multivalued parameters **ids** and **scrarr**, along with other parameters, and proceeds to insert the rows into the **scores** table. Notice that the first entry is skipped, as it contains a dummy value.

## 4.7 PL/SQL Web Toolkit

The PL/SQL Web Toolkit consists of the following packages:

- **htp**. A hypertext procedure generates a line in an HTML document that contains the HTML tag that corresponds to its name. For instance, the **htp.line** procedure generates the <HR> tag. The **htp** procedures are grouped into the following categories:
  - *Print procedures*. **p**, **print**, **prn**, **prints**, **ps**

- *Head-related tags.* `title`, `base`, `isindex`, `linkRel`, `linkRev`, `meta`
- *General body tags.* `line`, `hr`, `nl`, `br`, `header`, `anchor`, `anchor2`, `mailto`, `img`, `img2`, `para`, `paragraph`, `address`, `comment`, `preOpen`, `preClose`, `blockquoteOpen`, `blockquoteClose`, `base`, `area`, `mapOpen`, `mapClose`, `bgsound`, `div`, `listingOpen`, `listingClose`, `nobr`, `wbr`, `center`, `centerOpen`, `centerClose`, `dfn`, `big`, `small`, `sub`, `sup`, `basefont`, `fontOpen`, `fontClose`, `plaintext`, `s`, `strike`
- *List tags.* `listHeader`, `listItem`, `ulistOpen`, `ulistClose`, `olistOpen`, `olistClose`, `dlistOpen`, `dlistClose`, `dlistTerm`, `dlistDef`, `menulistOpen`, `menulistClose`, `dirlistOpen`, `dirlistClose`
- *Character format tags.* `cite`, `code`, `emphasis`, `em`, `keyboard`, `kbd`, `sample`, `strong`, `variable`
- *Physical format tags.* `bold`, `italic`, `teletype`
- *Form tags.* `formOpen`, `formClose`, `formCheckBox`, `formHidden`, `formImage`, `formPassword`, `formRadio`, `formSubmit`, `formReset`, `formText`, `formSelectOpen`, `formSelectOption`, `formSelectClose`, `formTextarea`, `formTextareaOpen`, `formTextareaClose`, `formTextarea2`, `formTextareaOpen2`
- *Table tags.* `tableOpen`, `tableRowOpen`, `tableHeader`, `tableData`, `tableCaption`, `tableRowClose`, `tableClose`

- `htf`. A hypertext function returns the HTML tag that corresponds to its name. However, it is not sufficient to call an `htf` function on its own, because the HTML tag is not passed to the `mod_plsql` module. The output of an `htf` function must be passed to `htp.print` in order to actually be part of an HTML document. Every HyperText Function (`htf`) has a corresponding HyperText Procedure (`htp`) with the same name, parameters, and function. `htf` functions are generally used only when you need to nest calls.
- `OWA_UTIL`. This is a collection of useful utility procedures and functions. It is divided into the following areas:
  - `OWA_UTIL` HTML Utilities. The purposes of these range from printing signature tags on HTML pages to retrieving the values of CGI environment variables and performing URL redirects.
  - `OWA_UTIL` Dynamic SQL Utilities. These enable the user to produce Web pages with dynamically generated SQL code.
  - `OWA_UTIL` Date Utilites. These make it easier to properly handle dates, which are simple strings in HTML but are properly treated as a data type by the Oracle RDBMS.

- `OWA_OPT_LOCK`. The procedures in this package enable the user to impose optimistic locking strategies, to prevent lost updates.
- `OWA_PATTERN`. This is a set of procedures and functions the user can use to perform string matching and substitution with rich regular expression functionality.
- `OWA_TEXT`. This is a set of procedures, functions, and data types used by `OWA_PATTERN` for manipulating large data strings. They are externalized, so you can use them directly if you wish.
- `OWA_IMAGE`. This is a set of data types and functions for manipulating HTML image maps.
- `OWA_COOKIES`. This is a set of data types, procedures, and functions for manipulating HTML cookies.

The details of these packages can be found in the online documentation that comes with Oracle9*i*. Many of the procedures and functions have been used in the earlier examples in this chapter.

The table printing and dynamic SQL utilities of the `OWA_UTIL` package are discussed next.

## 4.7.1 Table Printing Utility

The `tablePrint` function in the `OWA_UTIL` package is used to print database tables in a Web page. This function enables programmers to print Oracle tables as either preformatted or HTML tables, depending on the Web browser capabilities. The syntax is as follows:

```
owa_util.tablePrint(
   ctable in varchar2
   cattributes in varchar2 DEFAULT NULL
   ntable_type in integer DEFAULT HTML_TABLE
   ccolumns in varchar2 DEFAULT '*'
   cclauses in varchar2 DEFAULT NULL
   ccol_aliases in varchar2 DEFAULT NULL
   nrow_min in number DEFAULT 0
   nrow_max in number DEFAULT NULL);
```

where `ctable` is the name of the table to be printed, `cattributes` is an HTML table attribute, `ntable_type` is either `owa_util.html_table` or `owa_util.pre_table`, `ccolumns` is a comma-separated list of columns to be printed, `cclauses` is a selection condition, `ccol_aliases` is a list of aliases for the columns, and `nrow_min` and nrow_max are the minimum and maximum numbers of rows to be printed. The function returns true or false to indicate whether there are more rows available beyond the nrow_max requested.

Example 4.7.1 The following package contains procedures that illustrate the use of the tablePrint function:

```
create or replace package was_tprint as
   procedure tprint1;
   procedure tprint2;
   procedure tprint3;
end was_tprint;
/
show errors;
create or replace package body was_tprint as

procedure tprint1 as
   ignore boolean;
begin
   ignore := owa_util.tablePrint
      ('courses', 'BORDER', OWA_UTIL.PRE_TABLE,
       'cno, lineno',
       'where term=''F96'' order by lineno',
       'Course Number, Line Number');
end;

procedure tprint2 as
   ignore boolean;
begin
   ignore := owa_util.tablePrint
      ('courses', 'BORDER', OWA_UTIL.HTML_TABLE,
       'cno, lineno',
       'where term=''F96'' order by lineno',
       'Course Number, Line Number');
end;

procedure tprint3 as
   ignore boolean;
begin
   ignore := owa_util.tablePrint
      ('courses', 'BORDER', OWA_UTIL.HTML_TABLE);
end;
end was_tprint;
```

The preceding package has three procedures that print the courses table in several forms. The first procedure, tprint1, prints the cno and lineno columns for all courses in the F96 term as an HTML preformatted table; the second procedure, tprint2, prints the same as an HTML table. The third procedure, tprint3, prints the entire courses table as an HTML table.

## 4.7.2 Dynamic SQL

The bind_variables function in the OWA_UTIL package prepares an SQL query (binding any variables to it) and stores the output in an opened cursor. The integer returned by the function is a unique identifier for that cursor. The syntax is as follows:

```
owa_util.bind_variables(
   theQuery,
   bv1Name, bv1Value,
 .
 .
 .
   bv25Name, bv25Value, bv25Name);
```

Here, theQuery is a string variable containing an SQL query, possibly with bind variables, and the remaining parameters are the bind variable names and their values (there is a maximum limit of 25 such pairs).

The results of the query can be printed using the cellsprint procedure

```
owa_util.cellsprint(
   p_theCursor in integer
   p_max_rows in number DEFAULT 100
   p_format_numbers in varchar2 DEFAULT NULL);
```

This procedure generates an HTML table from the output of an SQL query. SQL atomic data items are mapped to HTML cells, and SQL rows are mapped to HTML rows. The code to begin and end the HTML table must be written separately. The p_theCursor parameter contains the output of a call made to the bind_variables procedure.

Example 4.7.2 The following package illustrates the use of the dynamic SQL utilities discussed earlier. The dsql1 procedure brings up a Web page with a pull-down list of courses. The user may select one of the courses, and upon submission of the form the second procedure, dsql2, prints the students enrolled in the particular course. The query to obtain the enrolled students is assigned to a string variable and has three bind variables.

```
create or replace package was_dsql as
   procedure dsql1;
   procedure dsql2(tcl in varchar2);
end was_dsql;

create or replace package body was_dsql as
procedure dsql1 as
-- This procedure displays a pull-down list of courses
   cursor c1 is
      select cno,term,lineno
      from   courses;
begin
   htp.htmlOpen;
   htp.headOpen;
   htp.title('Select Course');
   htp.header(1,'Display Enrolled Students');
   htp.headClose;
   htp.bodyOpen;
   htp.FormOpen(owa_util.get_owa_service_path ||
             'was_dsql.dsql2');
   htp.nl;
   htp.formSelectOpen('tcl','Select Course: ');
   -- Encode term, cno, and lineno as a string
   for c1_rec in c1 loop
      htp.formSelectOption('(' ||c1_rec.term||','||
                           c1_rec.cno||','||
                           c1_rec.lineno || ')');
   end loop;
   htp.formSelectClose;
   htp.formSubmit(null,'Display Enrolled Students');
   htp.formClose;
   htp.bodyClose;
   htp.htmlClose;
end dsql1;

procedure dsql2(tcl in varchar2)
-- This procedure decodes the tcl value and extracts
-- term, cno, and lineno values and displays a list
-- of students enrolled in this course.
as
```

```
   query varchar2(1024);
   cursor_id integer;
   p1 integer;
   p2 integer;
   trm  courses.term%type;
   cnum courses.cno%type;
   lnum courses.lineno%type;
begin
   -- Decode term, cno, and lineno values
   p1 := instr(tcl,',',1,2)+1;
   p2 := instr(tcl,')',1,1)-1;
   trm := substr(tcl,2,instr(tcl,',',1)-2);
   lnum := to_number(substr(tcl,p1,p2-p1+1));
   cnum := substr(tcl,instr(tcl,',',1,1)+1,
                   p1-instr(tcl,',',1,1)-2);
   htp.htmlOpen;
   htp.headOpen;
   htp.title('Dynamic SQL Utilities');
   htp.headClose;
   htp.bodyOpen;
   htp.line;
   htp.header(1,'Students enrolled in');
   htp.print(cnum); htp.br;
   htp.print(trm); htp.br;
   htp.print(lnum); htp.br;
   htp.line;
   -- Construct query string with placeholders for
   -- cno, term, and lineno values
   query :=
      'select students.sid,fname,lname ' ||
      'from enrolls,courses,students ' ||
      'where enrolls.lineno = courses.lineno and ' ||
      '      enrolls.term = courses.term and ' ||
      '      students.sid = enrolls.sid and ' ||
      '      cno = :cc and ' ||
      '      courses.term = :tt and ' ||
      '      courses.lineno = :ll';
   -- Invoke utility to prepare cursor value for query
   cursor_id :=
      owa_util.bind_variables(query,
```

```
            'cc',cnum,'tt',trm,'ll',lnum);
      -- Print open table tag
      htp.tableOpen(cborder => 'BORDER=1');
      -- Invoke utility to generate table row tags
      owa_util.cellsprint(cursor_id);
      -- Print close table tag
      htp.tableClose;
      htp.bodyClose;
      htp.htmlClose;
   end dsql2;
   end was_dsql;
```

Notice that explicit statements are written to open and close the HTML table, as the **cellsprint** procedure generates only the code for the rows of the HTML table.

## 4.8 PL/SQL Server Pages (PSP)

The PL/SQL Web Toolkit provides a convenient and efficient mechanism for generating dynamic Web pages containing data from an Oracle9*i* database. One potential drawback with this approach is that it is quite cumbersome to generate HTML code line-by-line via procedure/function calls, especially when the code corresponds to static content. Oracle9*i* provides a complementary methodology, called PL/SQL Server Pages (PSP), that relieves some of the tedium involved in generating HTML code using the PL/SQL Web Toolkit. PSP allows Web developers to embed PL/SQL code within HTML pages, so they can leave the HTML design to script-friendly HTML authoring tools and their users. Dynamic Web page content is generated using the PL/SQL code within HTML pages (now called *PSP pages*) on the server side. This is certainly more convenient than generating HTML code from PL/SQL using the Web Toolkit, especially for complex and presentation-rich HTML pages.

PSP pages are handled via the Oracle PL/SQL Web gateway (**mod_plsql**) attached to the Oracle Web server. PSP pages are basically loaded to the database as Oracle PL/SQL procedures, then called in the same way other Web Toolkit–based PL/SQL procedures are called. Therefore, mixing PL/SQL procedures with Web Toolkit calls and PSP pages in the same Web application is possible. This actually presents a flexible solution. If the Web pages to be generated include more HTML code than PL/SQL code, it is easier to develop them using PSP. On the other hand, if the Web pages include more PL/SQL code than HTML code to be generated, standard PL/SQL procedures should be developed and HTML should be generated from PL/SQL code using the Web Toolkit packages.

Example 4.8.1 Consider the grade book application introduced earlier in this chapter. The first procedure in the application is the **get_access** procedure. It includes mostly **htp** calls to generate HTML elements including forms, tables, and input fields. Therefore, it makes sense to implement this page using an HTML authoring tool and then later embed PL/SQL code to generate the dynamic content. Following is the PSP page for get_access (get_access.psp):

```
<%@ page  language="PL/SQL" %>
<%@ plsql procedure="get_access" %>
<%!
   /**
      get_access.psp
      Overview: This is the first PSP page in the grade book
      application. It allows users to log in to the system.
   **/
%>
<HTML>
<HEAD>
<TITLE>Get password</TITLE>
<H1>Grade Book Access Page</H1>
</HEAD>
<BODY>
<FORM ACTION="<%=owa_util.get_owa_service_path%>start_session"
METHOD="POST">
<BR>
<BR>
Today is <%=to_char(sysdate, 'Day')%>,
         <%=to_char(sysdate, 'Dd / Mon / YYYY HH:MI AM')%>
<BR>
<BR>
<TABLE>
<TR>
<TD><STRONG>USER ID: </STRONG></TD>
<TD><INPUT TYPE="text" NAME="usid" SIZE="20"
           MAXLENGTH="50"></TD>
</TR>
<TR>
<TD><STRONG>PASSWORD: </STRONG></TD>
<TD><INPUT TYPE="password" NAME="passwd" SIZE="20"
           MAXLENGTH="50"></TD>
```

```
</TR>
</TABLE>
<INPUT TYPE="submit" VALUE="Proceed">
<INPUT TYPE="reset"  VALUE="Reset">
</FORM>
</BODY>
</HTML>
```

As seen in the script, PL/SQL code is embedded in the page within `<%` and `%>` tags. A PSP page starts with the following two directives:

```
<%@ page  language="PL/SQL" %>
<%@ plsql procedure="get_access" %>
```

The first directive indicates that the scripting language for this HTML page is PL/SQL. The second line indicates that this page will be loaded to the database as a `get_access` procedure. This line is optional; if it is omitted, the file name of the PSP page will be used as the stored procedure name. Comments are included as in HTML pages.

A utility program called `loadpsp` is used to load the PSP pages into the Oracle9*i* database. Following is the command that needs to be executed to load the `get_access.psp` page to the database:

```
loadpsp -replace -user scott/tiger get_access.psp
```

The `-replace` option tells the database to replace an existing procedure with the same name, and the `-user` option allows the PSP page to be loaded into a particular database schema.

Once loaded, the `get_access` procedure is accessed using the following URL:

```
http://host:port/pls/book/get_access
```

## 4.8.1 Parameter Passing in PSP

The `get_access` procedure calls the `start_session` procedure, which first checks the user login information and then calls the `teacher_menu` procedure to display the menu. No HTML is generated within the `start_session` procedure. Therefore, it is better to leave `start_session` as-is in the form of a PL/SQL procedure. The `teacher_menu` procedure, on the other hand, generates a lot of HTML code, so it is better to use the following PSP page to generate it:

```
<%@ page  language="PL/SQL" %>
<%@ plsql procedure="teacher_menu" %>
```

```
<%@ plsql parameter="u_access" type="varchar2"
    default="null" %>
<%@ plsql parameter="userid"   type="varchar2"
    default="null" %>

<%!
   /**
      Program: teacher_menu.psp
      Overview: Display the teacher menu.
   **/
%>
<HTML>
<HEAD>
<TITLE>Teacher Menu</TITLE><H1>Teacher Menu</H1>
</HEAD>
<BODY>

<%
   if check_access(u_access) = 'Teacher' then
%>

<FORM ACTION=
"<%=owa_util.get_owa_service_path%>process_teacher_option"
METHOD="POST">
<INPUT TYPE="hidden" NAME="u_access" VALUE=<%=u_access%>
<INPUT TYPE="hidden" NAME="userid"   VALUE=<%=userid%>
<INPUT TYPE="submit" NAME="opt" VALUE="AddCatalogEntry">
<BR>
<INPUT TYPE="submit" NAME="opt" VALUE="AddCourseEntry">
<BR>
<INPUT TYPE="submit" NAME="opt" VALUE="SelectACourse">
<BR>
<INPUT TYPE="submit" NAME="opt" VALUE="SearchUserid">
<BR>
<INPUT TYPE="submit" NAME="opt" VALUE="ChangePassword">
<BR>
<INPUT TYPE="submit" NAME="opt" VALUE="Logout">
<BR>
</FORM>
<% else %>
```

```
  No access to grade book by this user!
<% end if; %>
</BODY>
</HTML>
```

The teacher_menu script takes two input parameters, u_access and userid. In PSP pages, procedure parameters are defined using the directive

```
<% plsql parameter= "param name" type = "param type"
  default = "default value" %>
```

In teacher_menu.psp, the following lines of code define these two parameters:

```
<%@ plsql parameter="u_access" type="varchar2"
    default="null" %>
<%@ plsql parameter="userid"   type="varchar2"
    default="null" %>
```

The type and default parameters are optional. If the type is not specified, the character string type is taken as the default.

Other PL/SQL statements in PSP pages are included using the following syntax:

```
<% PL/SQL statement;
  [ PL/SQL statement; ] ... %>
```

Expressions are included using the following syntax:

```
<%= PL/SQL expression %>
```

In teacher_menu.psp, the following lines include two expressions:

```
<INPUT TYPE="hidden" NAME="u_access" VALUE=<%=u_access%> >
<INPUT TYPE="hidden" NAME="userid"   VALUE=<%=userid%> >
```

These expressions access the values of the PL/SQL variables u_access and userid (procedure parameters, in this case). The values are included in the HTML page generated as values of the hidden input variables (u_access and userid) that will be sent to the procedure being called to process the menu option chosen by the user.

The PSP expression <%=owa_util.get_owa_service_path%> in the previous two examples generates the URL prefix for the accessed page. The procedure name, along with any parameters, is appended to this URL prefix to specify the ACTION parameter of the form tag.

## 4.8.2 Other PSP Syntax

As shown in the `teacher_menu` example, PL/SQL `IF-THEN-ELSE` blocks can be used to write conditional HTML and script fragments. The syntax is

```
<% IF-condition THEN %>
   [HTML code]
<% ELSE %>
   [HTML code]
<% end if; %>
```

To include other HTML or PSP files in a script, one can use

```
<%@ include file="path name" %>
```

PL/SQL declarations are specified using

```
<%! PL/SQL declaration;
   [ PL/SQL declaration; ] ... %>
```

PL/SQL code is included as

```
<% PL/SQL statement;
   [ PL/SQL statement; ] ... %>
```

This section ends with several examples of SQL query cursors processed within a PSP script.

Example 4.8.2 The following PSP script displays the contents of the `catalog` table in the grade book database using the `tableprint` utility:

```
<%@ page language="PL/SQL" %>
<%@ plsql procedure="show_catalog" %>
<HTML>
<HEAD><TITLE>Display Contents of Catalog
Table</TITLE></HEAD>
<BODY>
<%
declare
dummy boolean;
begin
dummy := owa_util.tableprint('catalog','border');
end;
%>
</BODY>
</HTML>
```

The PL/SQL code containing the call to the `tableprint` utility is embedded within the HTML code.

Example 4.8.3 The following script is a variation of the previous script illustrating the use of a cursor `for` loop to display courses with the string "Database" within their titles:

```
<%@ page language="PL/SQL" %>
<%@ plsql procedure="show_catalog2" %>
<HTML>
<HEAD><TITLE>Database Courses</TITLE></HEAD>
<BODY>
<P><h3>Database Courses in Catalog</h3>
<UL>
<% for crs in (select * from catalog where ctitle like
    '%Database%') loop %>
<LI> <B><%= crs.cno %> <%= crs.ctitle %></B>
<% end loop; %>
</UL>
</BODY>
</HTML>
```

Example 4.8.4 The following script displays the `parts` table from the mail-order database. It takes as one parameter a minimum price value. It then displays all parts that cost more than this minimum price using a different-colored font from the font used for those parts that cost less than or the same as the minimum price.

```
<%@ page language="PL/SQL" %>
<%@ plsql procedure="show_parts" %>
<%@ plsql parameter="mprice" type="NUMBER" default="100" %>
<%! color varchar2(7); %>

<HTML>
<HEAD><TITLE>Show Parts</TITLE></HEAD>
<BODY>
<P>Part Listing with different colored display for parts
   greater than <%= mprice %>.
<TABLE BORDER>
<TR>
<TH>PNO</TH>
<TH>Part Name</TH>
```

```
<TH>Price</TH>
</TR>
<%
for p in (select * from parts order by price desc) loop
   if p.price > mprice then
      color := '#CCFFFF';
   else
      color := '#CCCCCC';
   end if;
%>
<TR BGCOLOR="<%= color %>">
<TD><%= p.pno %></TD>
<TD><%= p.pname %></TD>
<TD><%= p.price %></TD>
</TR>
<% end loop; %>
</TABLE>
</BODY>
</HTML>
```

A PL/SQL variable called **color** is declared within this script and is assigned a color value depending on the price of each part.

## Exercises

4.1 Write PL/SQL programs or PSP scripts that enable order processing in the mail-order database system. The initial Web page should allow employees to sign in using their employee numbers. Upon validating the employee number, a second Web page containing a pull-down list of customer numbers, 10 text fields (each containing two text boxes, one for part number and the other for quantity), and a submit button should be displayed. Upon choosing a customer number and entering up to 10 parts in the order, the employee will submit the order for processing. A PL/SQL procedure should process the order request and handle any error situations appropriately. A success or failure message should be displayed by this procedure.

4.2 Consider the grade book database. Write a PL/SQL procedure or a PSP script that accepts term and line number values from an HTML form and produces a final grade report for the specified class. The format of this report should be as follows:

*CSc 4710 Database Systems, F01, 1220*

| SID | LNAME | FNAME | MT (400/40) | FINAL (500/60) | AVG | GRADE |
|---|---|---|---|---|---|---|
| 9002 | Blake | Gary | 360 | 490 | 94.8 | A |
| 9000 | Jones | Tony | 300 | 300 | 66.0 | D |
| 9001 | Smith | Charlie | 380 | 400 | 86.0 | B |

4.3 Consider the following database schema that catalogs the popular Yu-Gi-Oh trading cards:

```
create table yugiohcards (
   cardCode      char(8) primary key,
   series        char(4),
   cardName      varchar2(50),
   attribute     varchar2(50),
   cardType      varchar2(20),
   attackPoints  number(5),
   defensePoints number(5),
   elementType   char(20),
   rarity        varchar2(20),
   description   varchar2(256),
   numStars      number(2)
);
```

Each row in this table describes a trading card. Each card has numerous characteristics, such as **`rarity`** (Secret Rare, Ultra Rare, Super Rare, Rare, and Common) and **`cardType`** (Fiend, Dragon, Spellcaster, Warrior, Pyro, Thunder, Magic, Trap, etc). Develop a search engine using the PL/SQL Web Toolkit or PSP scripts to search cards from this database. The search page should contain the following HTML form elements:

- Select lists for the following columns: **`series`**, **`cardType`**, **`attribute`**, and **`rarity`**
- Text box fields for the `cardName` and `description` columns
- Text box fields preceded by pull-down lists with three labels (<=, =, >=) for the `attackPoints`, `defensePoints`, and `numStars` columns
- A submit button labeled Find Cards

The initial search page is produced by a PL/SQL procedure, since it has dynamic content (the values within select lists and pull-down lists). The user may choose one or more values from a select list, choose one value from a pull-down list, enter some text or numbers in text boxes, and submit the search request. A second PL/SQL procedure should take these values as input and create an SQL **select** statement to query the database and return rows that match the search criteria in tabular form.

4.4 Implement a bookmarks management system in PL/SQL or PSP scripts. An individual's bookmarks are organized under categories and subcategories. The bookmark data are stored in a table with the following schema:

```
create table bookmarks (
   category varchar2(30),
   subcategory varchar2(30),
   bookmarkTitle varchar2(100),
   bookmarkURL varchar2(100)
);
```

It is possible for a bookmark to be listed without a category (i.e., for the category and subcategory to be **null**) or listed within a category but not under a subcategory (i.e., just the subcategory value is **null**). It is impossible for the category value to be **null** and the subcategory value to be non-**null**.

The initial Web page should list all the major categories and any bookmarks without categories as hyperlinks. When the user clicks a category, a new page listing as hyperlinks all the subcategories within that category and any bookmarks within the category without subcategories should be displayed. When the user clicks a subcategory, a new page listing as hyperlinks all the bookmarks within that subcategory should be displayed. Of course, clicking a bookmark hyperlink in any page should take the user to the URL specified by the bookmark.

Finally, a hyperlink for adding bookmarks should be placed at the top of each page. When this hyperlink is invoked, a separate Web page with pull-down lists of existing categories and subcategories and text boxes for category, subcategory, bookmark title, and bookmark URL should be displayed. The user may either choose an existing category/subcategory or enter a new category or subcategory, then provide the title and URL for the bookmark. This information, when submitted, should be processed and entered into the database. Appropriate error processing should be undertaken.

4.5 Write PL/SQL procedures or PSP scripts to implement the Student menu in the online grade book system. The students should be able to:

- Register themselves
- Sign in
- View all their grades for a particular course in tabular format

- View their standing for a particular component in the form of a graph, as follows:

```
98 *
97 ** YOUR SCORE
96 *
89 **
84 *
76 *
```

The stars next to the scores represent students getting that particular score.

The scores are arranged in descending order, as can be seen in the example.

# CHAPTER 5

# Oracle JDBC

Oracle supports the JDBC API by providing drivers that work with the Oracle database server. JDBC consists of Java classes that make database access from a Java environment easy and powerful. In this chapter, the JDBC API is introduced. Packed with examples, this chapter shows how to connect to the Oracle database, issue SQL statements, and process results. Invoking Oracle stored procedures and obtaining metadata via the JDBC classes are also discussed.

## 5.1 What Is JDBC?

JDBC[1] is an Application Programming Interface (API) that enables database access in Java. It consists of a set of classes and interfaces written in Java that allows the programmer to send SQL statements to a database server for execution and, in the case of an SQL query, to retrieve query results.

Writing database applications in Java using JDBC has at least two advantages: (1) portability across database servers and (2) portability across hardware architectures. The portability across database servers is a consequence of the JDBC API. Various database vendors (Oracle, Sybase, and Informix, to name a few) provide JDBC drivers, which are basically implementations of the JDBC API for their database engines. The JDBC drivers take care of the server dependencies, and the applications written in Java using JDBC are independent of the database server. The portability

1. JDBC is a trademark name and not an acronym. However, it is thought of as Java Database Connectivity.

across hardware platforms is a result of the Java language. Hence, the combination of Java and JDBC to develop database applications is an ideal match, as it is possible for the applications to be written once and run anywhere.

## 5.2 A Simple JDBC Program

A simple Java program that accesses an Oracle database using JDBC is shown here:

```
import java.sql.*;
import java.io.*;
class simple {
  public static void main (String args [])
      throws SQLException, IOException {

    try {
      Class.forName ("oracle.jdbc.driver.OracleDriver");
    } catch (ClassNotFoundException e) {
        System.out.println ("Could not load the driver");
      }
    String user, pass;
    user = readEntry("userid  : ");
    pass = readEntry("password: ");
    Connection conn = DriverManager.getConnection(
                "jdbc:oracle:oci8:"+user+"/"+pass);

    Statement stmt = conn.createStatement ();

    ResultSet rset = stmt.executeQuery
           ("select eno,ename,zip,hdate from employees");
    while (rset.next ()) {
      System.out.println(rset.getString(1) + "   " +
                         rset.getString(2) + "   " +
                         rset.getString(3) + "   " +
                         rset.getString(4));
    }
    stmt.close();
    conn.close();
  }
```

```
    //readEntry function -- to read input string
    static String readEntry(String prompt) {
      try {
        StringBuffer buffer = new StringBuffer();
        System.out.print(prompt);
        System.out.flush();
        int c = System.in.read();
        while(c != '\n' && c != -1) {
          buffer.append((char)c);
          c = System.in.read();
        }
        return buffer.toString().trim();
      } catch (IOException e) {
        return "";
        }
    }
}
```

The preceding program executes the SQL query

```
select eno,ename,zip,hdate
from   employees;
```

and prints the results of the query to the standard output. The **readEntry** function prints the prompt to the standard output and reads a string and returns it. This function is used throughout the chapter.

## 5.3 Developing JDBC Applications

The following basic steps are involved in developing JDBC applications:

1. Import the JDBC classes (`java.sql.*`).
2. Load the JDBC drivers.
3. Connect to the database.
4. Interact with the database using JDBC.
5. Disconnect from the database.

## 5.3.1 Loading the JDBC Drivers

A Java program can load several JDBC drivers at any time. This allows for the possibility of the program interacting with more than one database running on possibly different servers. The syntax to load Oracle JDBC drivers[2] is

```
Class.forName("oracle.jdbc.driver.OracleDriver")
```

## 5.3.2 Connecting to the Database

A connection to the database is established via the `DriverManager` class. The `DriverManager` class provides a basic service for managing a set of JDBC drivers. Once the JDBC drivers are loaded, the `getConnection` method can be applied to the `DriverManager` class as follows:

```
Connection conn = DriverManager.getConnection(url);
```

where `url` is of the form

```
jdbc:oracle:drivertype:user/password@database
```

The `drivertype` is `oci7`, `oci8`, or `thin`, depending on the version of Oracle OCI being used; `thin` is used in an applet. The `@database` phrase is optional, because there is a default database associated with the installation. If it is specified, it must be one of the following:

- An SQL*Net name-value pair
- (For JDBC OCI) An entry in the `tnsnames.ora` file
- (For JDBC Thin) A string of the form `host:port:sid`

When `getConnection` is called, the `DriverManager` will attempt to locate a suitable driver from among those loaded at initialization and those loaded explicitly using the same `classloader` as the current `applet` or application. After it finds a suitable driver, it returns a `Connection` object. Once the connection is established, all the interactions with the database are then performed via this `Connection` object.

---

2. Use `oracle.jdbc.dnlddriver.OracleDriver` for the driver name when the Java code corresponds to an applet.

### 5.3.3 The `Connection` Object

A `Connection` represents a session with a specific database. All SQL statements are executed and results are returned within the context of a `Connection`. A single Java application can have any number of `Connections` with a single database or multiple databases.

A `Connection`'s database is able to provide information describing its tables, its supported SQL grammar, its stored procedures, its capabilities, and so on. This information is obtained with the `getMetaData` method.

An important point to note is that, by default, the `Connection` object automatically commits changes after executing each statement. If autocommit has been disabled, an explicit commit must be done or database changes will not be saved. Another point to note is that the `Connection` class is an interface. Hence, `Connection` objects cannot be created explicitly; they can be created only by using the `getConnection` method on the `DriverManager` class.

Once a `Connection` is established, the `Connection` object is used to send SQL statements to the database server. JDBC provides three classes for sending SQL statements to the database server:

- `Statement`. Used for SQL statements without parameters.
- `PreparedStatement`. Used in situations in which the same statement, with possibly different parameters, is to be executed multiple times. The `PreparedStatement` normally contains a precompiled SQL statement. It has the potential to be more efficient than the `Statement` object, as it is precompiled and stored for future use.
- `CallableStatement`. Used for executing stored procedures.

The `Connection` class has three methods to create instances of these classes:

- `createStatement`. SQL statements without parameters are normally executed using `Statement` objects. The `createStatement` method has the following specification:

  ```
  public abstract Statement createStatement()
    throws SQLException
  ```

  When invoked on a `Connection` object, the `createStatement` method returns a new `Statement` object. If the same SQL statement is to be executed many times, it is more efficient to use an instance of the class `PreparedStatement`, described next.

- `prepareStatement`. An SQL statement with or without `IN` parameters can be precompiled and stored in a `PreparedStatement` object. This object can then be used to efficiently execute this statement multiple times. The `prepareStatement` method has the specification

```
public abstract PreparedStatement
   prepareStatement(String sql) throws SQLException
```

where `sql` is an SQL statement that may contain one or more `'?' IN` parameter placeholders. The method, when invoked on a `Connection` object, returns a new `PreparedStatement` object containing the precompiled statement.

- `prepareCall`. An SQL stored procedure call is handled by creating a `CallableStatement` for it. The `CallableStatement` provides methods for setting up its `IN` and `OUT` parameters and methods for executing it. The `prepareCall` method, when invoked on a `Connection` object, returns a `CallableStatement` and has the specification

```
public abstract CallableStatement
  prepareCall(String sql) throws SQLException
```

where `sql` is an SQL statement that may contain one or more `'?'` parameter placeholders. Typically this statement is a JDBC function call escape string.

Examples of these three methods are given in subsequent sections. There are some other useful methods in the `Connection` class:

- `close`. In some cases, it is desirable to immediately release a `Connection` object's database and JDBC resources, instead of waiting for them to be automatically released; the `close` method provides this immediate release. Its specification is

```
public abstract void close() throws SQLException
```

Note that a `Connection` object is automatically closed when it is garbage-collected.

- `setAutoCommit`. If a connection is in autocommit mode, then all its SQL statements will be executed and committed as individual transactions. Otherwise, its SQL statements are grouped into transactions that are terminated by either `commit` or `rollback`. By default, new connections are in autocommit mode. The commit occurs when the statement completes or the next execute occurs, whichever comes first. In the case of statements returning a `ResultSet`, the statement completes when the last row of the `ResultSet` has been retrieved or the `ResultSet` has been closed. The `setAutoCommit` method sets or resets the autocommit mode and has the following specification:

```
public abstract void setAutoCommit
        (boolean autoCommit) throws SQLException
```

where `autoCommit` should be set to `true` to enable autocommit and to `false` to disable autocommit.

- `commit`. This method should be used only if the autocommit mode is set to `false`. `commit` makes all changes made since the previous commit/rollback permanent and releases any database locks currently held by the `Connection`. It has the following specification:

```
public abstract void commit() throws SQLException
```

- `rollback`. This method drops all changes made since the previous commit/rollback and releases any database locks currently held by the `Connection`. It has the following specification:

```
public abstract void rollback() throws SQLException
```

  This method should also be used only when the autocommit mode is set to `false`.

- `getMetaData`. A `Connection`'s database is able to provide information describing its tables, its supported SQL grammar, its stored procedures, its capabilities, and so on. This information is made available through a `DatabaseMetaData` object. It can be obtained using the `getMetaData` method, which has the following specification:

```
public abstract DatabaseMetaData getMetaData()
  throws SQLException
```

  The `DatabaseMetaData` object is discussed in Section 5.7.

## 5.4 Nonquery SQL Statements

To execute a nonquery SQL statement from a Java program using JDBC, one of the following three statement objects must be used:

- `Statement`
- `PreparedStatement`
- `CallableStatement`

This section describes how these three classes are used to execute SQL DDL or nonquery statements.

## 5.4.1 Using the Statement Object

The Statement class is used for executing SQL statements without parameters. The SQL statement can be a DDL statement (such as create table), a nonquery statement (such as insert, delete, or update), or an SQL query (select statement). The mechanism to handle an SQL select statement is explained in Section 5.5.

The createStatement method of the Connection class is used to instantiate a Statement object. The syntax for doing so is

```
Statement s = conn.createStatement();
```

where conn is a previously created Connection object. You can create as many Statement objects as you wish in a Java program. In most normal cases,[3] it is sufficient to create just one instance of the Statement object.

Once the Statement object has been created, its executeUpdate method can be invoked to execute a nonquery SQL statement. Its specification is

```
public abstract int executeUpdate(String sql)
  throws SQLException
```

where sql is a string variable containing the nonquery SQL statement. This method returns either the row count for insert, update, or delete or 0 for SQL DDL statements that return nothing.

Example 5.4.1 The following function performs an insert into the catalog table of the grade book database:

```
void add_catalog(Connection conn)
  throws SQLException, IOException {

  Statement stmt = conn.createStatement();

  String cnum   = readEntry("Course Number: ");
  String ctitle = readEntry("Course Title : ");
  String query = "insert into catalog values (" +
          "'" + cnum + "','" + ctitle + "')";
  try {
    int nrows = stmt.executeUpdate(query);
  } catch (SQLException e) {
      System.out.println("Error Adding Catalog Entry");
```

3. There are situations, such as performing multiple queries at the same time, when more than one instance of this class would have to be created.

```
        while (e != null) {
          System.out.println("Message:"+e.getMessage());
          e = e.getNextException();
        }
        return;
      }
    stmt.close();
    System.out.println("Added Catalog Entry");
  }
```

The preceding function receives an open **Connection** object as input. It first reads from standard input the course number and course title, then creates a **String** object, called **query**, which contains as its value the **insert** statement,[4] then creates a **Statement** object, and finally invokes the **executeUpdate** method on the **Statement** object with the SQL statement in **query**. The error checking is explained in Section 5.8. The **try-catch** mechanism of Java is used extensively to trap any errors that are encountered.

Example 5.4.2 The following function creates a table from within a Java program using JDBC:

```
void create_table(Connection conn)
  throws SQLException, IOException {
  String query =  "create table deleted_scores (" +
           "sid       varchar2(5) not null," +
           "term      varchar2(10) not null," +
           "lineno    number(4) not null," +
           "compname  varchar2(15) not null," +
           "points    number(4) check(points >= 0))";

  Statement stmt = conn.createStatement ();
  try {
    stmt.executeUpdate(query);
  } catch (SQLException e) {
      System.out.println("Could not create table");
      while (e != null) {
        System.out.println("Message:"+e.getMessage());
        e = e.getNextException();
      }
```

4. An important point to note is that the statement is not terminated with the traditional semicolon.

```
      return;
    }
  System.out.println("Table created");
  stmt.close();
}
```

This is a similar example, except that the SQL statement that is sent to the database server for execution is a DDL statement.

Example 5.4.3 The following function deletes a student row from the **enrolls** table of the grade book database:

```
void drop_student(Connection conn,
                  String term_in, String ls)
    throws SQLException, IOException {

  String id = readEntry("Student ID to drop: ");
  String query0 = "insert into deleted_scores " +
    "select * from scores where sid = '" + id +
    "' and term = '" + term_in + "' and lineno = " + ls;
  String query1 = "delete scores where sid = '" + id +
    "' and term = '" + term_in + "' and lineno = " + ls;
  String query2 = "delete enrolls where sid = '" + id +
    "' and term = '" + term_in + "' and lineno = " + ls;

  conn.setAutoCommit(false);
  Statement stmt = conn.createStatement ();
  int nrows;
  try {
    nrows = stmt.executeUpdate(query0);
    nrows = stmt.executeUpdate(query1);
    nrows = stmt.executeUpdate(query2);
  } catch (SQLException e) {
      System.out.println("Could not drop student");
      while (e != null) {
        System.out.println("Message: "+e.getMessage());
        e = e.getNextException();
      }
      conn.rollback();
      return;
    }
```

```
    System.out.println("Dropped student");
    conn.commit();
    conn.setAutoCommit(true);
    stmt.close();
}
```

This function first disables the autocommit mode for the `Connection`. It then copies the rows from the `scores` tables that correspond to the student being dropped into a backup table called `deleted_scores`. After that, to maintain the referential integrity constraint, it deletes all the rows in the `scores` table before deleting the student row from the `enrolls` table.

## 5.4.2 Using the `PreparedStatement` Object

The `PreparedStatement` object is used in situations in which the same SQL statement, with possibly different parameters, has to be executed a number of times. The `PreparedStatement` class is derived from the `Statement` class discussed earlier. Unlike the `Statement` object, a `PreparedStatement` object is created with an SQL statement. As a result, the `PreparedStatement` object contains not just an SQL statement, but an SQL statement that is precompiled. This results in efficient execution of the statement, especially if it has to be executed repeatedly.

Usually, the `PreparedStatement` object is used with SQL statements that have parameters. This has the advantage that the same statement can be supplied with different values at different times and be executed efficiently each time, without recompilation.

The `prepareStatement` method of the `Connection` class is used to create an instance of the `PreparedStatement` class. It has the syntax

```
public abstract PreparedStatement
  prepareStatement(String sql) throws SQLException
```

where `sql` is an SQL statement that may contain one or more `'?'` `IN` parameter placeholders. It returns a new `PreparedStatement` object containing the precompiled statement. An SQL statement with or without `IN` parameters can be precompiled and stored in a `PreparedStatement` object. This object can then be used to efficiently execute this statement multiple times.

Once the statement is prepared, its parameters must be set before it can be executed. The input parameters for a `PreparedStatement` object are set using the `setXXX` method, where `XXX` is a Java primitive type. The syntax for the `setString` method is

```
public abstract void setString
  (int parameterIndex,
   String x) throws SQLException
```

where **parameterIndex** is the index of the parameter (starting at 1), and **x** is the value to be assigned to the parameter. This method sets a parameter to a Java **String** value. The driver converts this to an Oracle SQL **VARCHAR** when it sends it to the database. The other **setXXX** methods are similar.

After providing the input parameters for the **PreparedStatement** object, it can be executed using the **executeUpdate** or **executeQuery** method.

Example 5.4.4 The following function executes a sequence of **inserts** into the **students** table of the grade book database:

```
void add_students(Connection conn)
    throws SQLException, IOException {

  String id, ln, fn, mi;
  PreparedStatement stmt = conn.prepareStatement(
    "insert into students values (?, ?, ?, ?)"  );
  do {
    id = readEntry("ID (0 to stop): ");
    if (id.equals("0"))
      break;
    ln = readEntry("Last  Name     : ");
    fn = readEntry("First Name     : ");
    mi = readEntry("Middle Initial: ");
    try {
      stmt.setString(1,id);
      stmt.setString(2,fn);
      stmt.setString(3,ln);
      stmt.setString(4,mi);
      stmt.executeUpdate();
    } catch (SQLException e) {
      System.out.println("Error adding student");
    }
  } while (true);
  stmt.close();
}
```

The function repeatedly reads information about new students and inserts it into the **students** table. The loop stops when the user enters an ID of **0**. Since the same statement with different values for the columns is to be executed many times, the `PreparedStatement` object is used.

### 5.4.3 Using the `CallableStatement` Object

The `CallableStatement` object is used to execute PL/SQL stored procedures and anonymous blocks. The call to the stored procedure or function or anonymous PL/SQL block is written in an escape syntax in one of the following forms:

```
{call procedure_name(?, ?, ..., ?)}
{? = call function_name(?, ?, ..., ?)}
("begin proc (:1, :2, ..., :n); end;")
("begin :1 := func(:1,:2, ..., :n); end;")
("anonymous-block")
```

The first two forms are recommended for portability purposes, and the last three are Oracle specific. The `anonymous-block` may contain any number of parameter placeholders, as in the other forms.

The `CallableStatement` class is derived from `PreparedStatement`, thereby inheriting many of its methods. A `CallableStatement` object is instantiated by calling the `prepareCall` method on a JDBC `Connection` object whose specification is

```
public abstract CallableStatement
   prepareCall(String sql) throws SQLException
```

where `sql` is an SQL statement that may contain one or more `'?'` parameter placeholders.

The `CallableStatement` class provides methods for setting up its `IN` and `OUT` parameters and methods for executing PL/SQL stored procedures and anonymous blocks. The `IN` parameters are set in the same manner as in the case of `PreparedStatement`, using the `setXXX` methods. The `java.sql.Types` type for each of the `OUT` parameters must be registered before the `CallableStatement` object can be executed. This is done using

```
public abstract void
  registerOutParameter(int parameterIndex,
                        int sType) throws SQLException
```

where

- `parameterIndex` is the index of the parameter (the first parameter is 1, the second is 2, etc.).
- `sType` is the SQL type code defined by `java.sql.Types`.

For parameters of type NUMERIC or DECIMAL, the following version of registerOutParameter that accepts a scale value must be used:

```
public abstract void
  registerOutParameter(int parameterIndex,
                       int sType,
                       int scale) throws SQLException
```

In this situation

- parameterIndex is the same as before.
- sType is a NUMERIC or DECIMAL constant found in java.sql.Types.
- scale is a value greater than or equal to zero representing the desired number of digits to the right of the decimal point.

The OUT parameters are read using the getXXX method provided by the CallableStatement class. It is important to note that when reading the value of an OUT parameter, the getXXX method whose Java type XXX corresponds to the parameter's registered SQL type must be used.

Example 5.4.5 The following example makes calls to the stored procedures add_orders and add_order_details of the process_orders package discussed in Chapter 3:

```
import java.sql.*;
import java.io.*;
class call3 {
  public static void main (String args [])
      throws SQLException, IOException {
    try {
      Class.forName ("oracle.jdbc.driver.OracleDriver");
    } catch (ClassNotFoundException e) {
        System.out.println ("Could not load the driver");
      }
    String user, pass;
    user = readEntry("userid  : ");
    pass = readEntry("password: ");
    Connection conn = DriverManager.getConnection
      ("jdbc:oracle:oci8:"+user+"/"+pass);

    int enum = readNumber("Enter the employee number: ");
    int cnum = readNumber("Enter the customer number: ");
```

```
  int onum = readNumber("Enter the order    number: ");
  CallableStatement stmt = conn.prepareCall
    ("{call process_orders.add_order(?,?,?,?)}");
  stmt.setInt(1,onum);
  stmt.setInt(2,cnum);
  stmt.setInt(3,enum);
  stmt.setNull(4,Types.DATE);
  conn.setAutoCommit(false);
  try {
    stmt.executeUpdate();
  } catch (SQLException e) {
      System.out.println("Could not add order");
      conn.rollback();
      return;
    }
  stmt = conn.prepareCall
    ("{call process_orders.add_order_details(?,?,?)}");
  do {
    int pnum = readNumber("Enter the part number (0 to stop): ");
    if (pnum == 0)
      break;
    int qty = readNumber("Enter the quantity    : ");
    stmt.setInt(1,onum);
    stmt.setInt(2,pnum);
    stmt.setInt(3,qty);
    try {
      stmt.executeUpdate();
    } catch (SQLException e) {
        System.out.println("Could not add odetail");
      }
  } while (true);
conn.commit();
conn.setAutoCommit(true);
stmt.close();
conn.close();
}
//readNumber function -- to read input number
static int readNumber(String prompt)
      throws IOException {
   String snum;
```

```
        int num = 0;
        boolean numok;
        do {
          snum = readEntry(prompt);
          try {
            num = Integer.parseInt(snum);
            numok = true;
          } catch (NumberFormatException e) {
              numok = false;
              System.out.println("Invalid number; enter again");
            }
        } while (!numok);
        return num;
      }
    }
```

The program reads the information about a new order from the standard input and makes a call to the `add_order` stored procedure using a `CallableStatement` object. It then repeatedly reads the order details information and makes a call to the `add_order_details` stored procedure. Note that both stored procedures called have only input parameters. Also note the use of the `setNull` method to set the value of an `IN` parameter to `null`.

Example 5.4.6 The following program makes a call to a stored function, `get_city`, which takes as input a customer number and returns the city for the customer:

```
import java.sql.*;
import java.io.*;
class call1 {
  public static void main (String args [])
      throws SQLException, IOException {
    try {
      Class.forName ("oracle.jdbc.driver.OracleDriver");
    } catch (ClassNotFoundException e) {
        System.out.println ("Could not load the driver");
      }
    String user, pass;
    user = readEntry("userid  : ");
    pass = readEntry("password: ");
    Connection conn = DriverManager.getConnection
      ("jdbc:oracle:oci8:"+user+"/"+pass);
```

```
    String cnum = readEntry(
      "Enter the customer number to find city: ");
    CallableStatement stmt =
      conn.prepareCall ("{? = call get_city (?)}");
    stmt.setString(2,cnum);
    stmt.registerOutParameter(1,Types.VARCHAR);
    stmt.execute();
    String city = stmt.getString(1);
    if (stmt.wasNull())
      System.out.println("Customer's city = Null");
    else
      System.out.println("Customer's city = "+stmt.getString(1));
    stmt.close();
    conn.close();
  }
}
```

Note the `registerOutParameter` method invocation for the return value of the function. Also note the use of the `wasNull` method of the `Statement` object to check to see whether the last value retrieved using a `getXXX` method was `null`.

## 5.5 Executing SQL Queries

An SQL query can be executed using any of the three statement objects: `Statement`, `PreparedStatement`, or `CallableStatement`. The `executeQuery` method must be used to execute the query. Its syntax when used on a `Statement` object is

```
public abstract ResultSet
  executeQuery(String sql) throws SQLException
```

and when used on the `PreparedStatement` and `CallableStatement` objects is

```
public abstract ResultSet
  executeQuery() throws SQLException
```

where `sql` is an SQL `select` statement. This method executes an SQL statement that returns a single `ResultSet` object. The `ResultSet` class is discussed next.

## 5.5.1 The ResultSet Class

The ResultSet class provides access to a table of data generated by executing a query. The table rows are retrieved in sequence, and within a row the column values can be accessed in any order. A ResultSet object maintains a cursor pointing to its current row of data. Initially the cursor is positioned before the first row. The next method moves the cursor to the next row. Therefore, it is important to use the next method before any of the rows are retrieved.

To retrieve the current row's column values, the getXXX methods are used, where XXX is a Java type. The column values can be retrieved either by using the index number of the column or by using the name of the column. In general, using the column index will be more efficient. Columns are numbered from 1. For the getXXX methods, the JDBC driver attempts to convert the underlying data to the specified Java type and returns a suitable Java value. See the online JDBC documentation for allowable mappings from SQL types to Java types with the ResultSet.getXXX methods.

Column names used as input to getXXX methods are case insensitive. When performing a getXXX using a column name, if several columns have the same name, the value of the first matching column will be returned. The column name option is designed to be used when column names are used in the SQL query.

A ResultSet is automatically closed by the Statement that generated it when that Statement is closed or re-executed or when it is used to retrieve the next result from a sequence of multiple results. This is important to note in situations in which more than one ResultSet is worked with at the same time. Since only one ResultSet is active for a Statement object, two or more Statement objects will become necessary in such situations.

## 5.5.2 ResultSet Methods

The methods provided for the ResultSet class are summarized here:

- next. This method moves the cursor to the next row in the ResultSet. It has the following specification:

  ```
  public abstract boolean next() throws SQLException
  ```

  A ResultSet's cursor is initially positioned before its first row. The first call to next makes the first row the current row; any subsequent call moves the cursor to the next row. next returns true if the next row is defined; otherwise, it returns false.

- close. This method explicitly closes a ResultSet and releases any JDBC resources. It has the following specification:

```
public abstract void close() throws SQLException
```

Note that a `ResultSet` is automatically closed by the `Statement` that generated it when that `Statement` is closed or re-executed or when it is used to retrieve the next result from a sequence of multiple results. A `ResultSet` is also automatically closed when it is garbage-collected.

- `wasNull`. This method is used to check whether the previous column value read was `null`. It has the following specification:

```
public abstract boolean wasNull() throws SQLException
```

A column may have the value of SQL `null`; `wasNull` returns `true` if the last column read had this special value and `false` otherwise. Note that a call to `getXXX` on a column to try to read its value must be made prior to the call to `wasNull`.

- `getString`. This is one of many `getXXX` methods used to retrieve the column values of the current row in a `ResultSet`. It has two versions. The first is

```
public abstract String getString(int columnIndex)
  throws SQLException
```

which takes a `columnIndex` as input (value of 1 or more) and returns the column value for that index as a Java `String` object. The second is

```
public abstract String getString(String columnName)
  throws SQLException
```

which takes the `columnName` as input and returns the column value as a Java `String`. In both cases, if the value is SQL `null`, the result is Java `null`.

- `getMetaData`. This method is used to obtain information about the `ResultSet` other than the rows. It has the following specification:

```
public abstract ResultSetMetaData getMetaData()
  throws SQLException
```

The number, types, and properties of the columns of a `ResultSet` are provided by this method. The metadata of a `ResultSet` are discussed later in this chapter.

- `findColumn`. This method returns the index of a column given its name. It has the following specification:

```
public abstract int findColumn(String columnName)
  throws SQLException
```

### 5.5.3 An SQL Query Example

Consider the grade book database and the problem of printing a class report (Figure 5.1) that contains a listing of all students along with their scores for each component and their course average and final grade.

**Figure 5.1** Class report (grade book database).

```
SID  LNAME   FNAME     EXAM1(400/40)  FINAL(500/60)  AVG GRADE
9002 Blake   Gary      360            490            94.8   A
9000 Jones   Tony      300            300            66.0   D
9001 Smith   Charlie   380            400            86.0   B
```

The following function (**print_report**) generates this report. It takes as input an open **Connection** to the database and the term and line number for the course for which the report is to be printed.

```
void print_report(Connection conn,
                  String term_in, String ls)
    throws SQLException, IOException {

  String query0 = "select a, b, c, d from courses " +
    "where term = '" + term_in + "' and lineno = " + ls;

  String query1 = "select compname, maxpoints, weight " +
    "from components where term = '" + term_in +
    "' and lineno = " + ls;

  String query2 = "select E.sid, S.lname, S.fname " +
    "from enrolls E, students S " +
    "where S.sid = E.sid and " +
    "E.term = '" + term_in + "' and " +
    "E.lineno = " + ls + " order by lname, fname";

  String query3 = "select points " + "from scores " +
     "where term = '" +  term_in + "' and " +
     "lineno = " + ls + " and " +
     "sid = ? and " +    // substitute ? by sid
     "compname = ?";  // substitute ? by compname
```

```
double total;
int scaleA, scaleB, scaleC, scaleD;
// Read the grade cut-off points from courses
Statement stmt = conn.createStatement ();
ResultSet rset0;
try {
  rset0 = stmt.executeQuery(query0);
} catch (SQLException e) {
    System.out.println("Problem reading scales");
    while (e != null) {
      System.out.println("Message:"+e.getMessage());
      e = e.getNextException();
    }
    return;
  }
rset0.next();
scaleA = rset0.getInt(1);
scaleB = rset0.getInt(2);
scaleC = rset0.getInt(3);
scaleD = rset0.getInt(4);

System.out.print("SID  LNAME       FNAME     ");
// Read the component information into arrays
ResultSet rset1;
try {
  rset1 = stmt.executeQuery(query1);
} catch (SQLException e) {
    System.out.println("Problem reading components");
    while (e != null) {
      System.out.println("Message:"+e.getMessage());
      e = e.getNextException();
    }
    return;
  }
String comp_names[] = new String[20];
double comp_maxpoints[] = new double[20];
double comp_weight[] = new double[20];
int ncomps=0;
```

```
while (rset1.next()) {
  System.out.print(rset1.getString(1)+"("+
                   rset1.getString(2)+"/"+
                   rset1.getString(3)+")  ");
  comp_names[ncomps] = rset1.getString(1);
  comp_maxpoints[ncomps] = rset1.getDouble(2);
  comp_weight[ncomps] = rset1.getDouble(3);
  ncomps++;
}

System.out.println("AVG    GRADE");
// Read the students enrolled in the class.
// For each student and for each grade component,
// read the score, print and keep total.
ResultSet rset2;
try {
  rset2 = stmt.executeQuery(query2);
} catch (SQLException e) {
    System.out.println("Problem reading students");
    while (e != null) {
      System.out.println("Message:"+e.getMessage());
      e = e.getNextException();
    }
    return;
  }

PreparedStatement stmt2 =
  conn.prepareStatement(query3);
while (rset2.next()) {
  total = 0.0;
  System.out.print(rset2.getString(1)+" ");
  System.out.print(rset2.getString(2));
  for (int k=0;k < (12-rset2.getString(2).length()); k++)
    System.out.print(" ");
  System.out.print(rset2.getString(3));
  for (int k=0;k < (12-rset2.getString(3).length()); k++)
    System.out.print(" ");
  for (int i=0; i < ncomps; i++) {
    stmt2.setString(1,rset2.getString(1));
    stmt2.setString(2,comp_names[i]);
```

```
        ResultSet rset3;
        try {
          rset3 = stmt2.executeQuery();
        } catch (SQLException e) {
            System.out.println("Problem reading scores");
            while (e != null) {
              System.out.println("Message:"+e.getMessage());
              e = e.getNextException();
            }
            return;
          }
        try {
          rset3.next();
        } catch (SQLException e) {
            System.out.println("No entry for " +
              rset2.getString(3) + " in " + comp_names[i]);
            while (e != null) {
              System.out.println("Message:"+e.getMessage());
              e = e.getNextException();
            }
            continue;
          }
        total = total + ((rset3.getDouble(1)/comp_maxpoints[i])*
                  comp_weight[i]);
        System.out.print(rset3.getString(1));
      }

      // Print the total and grade
      Double tot = new Double(total);
      for (int k2=0;k2 < (6-tot.toString().length()); k2++)
        System.out.print(" ");
      System.out.print(total + "      ");
      if (total >= scaleA) System.out.println("A");
      else if (total >= scaleB) System.out.println("B");
      else if (total >= scaleC) System.out.println("C");
      else if (total >= scaleD) System.out.println("D");
      else System.out.println("F");
   }
   stmt.close();
  }
```

The procedure performs the following steps:

- Executes `query0` to obtain the cut-off points for the grades. This is a simple query with no parameters and is executed by using a `Statement` object.
- Executes `query1` to obtain the information about the grade components for the course. This information is printed to the report and is also stored in Java arrays for later use.
- Executes `query2` to get the students enrolled in the course.
- For each student in the result set of `query2` and for each component for the course, using nested loops, executes `query3` to obtain the score. After obtaining the score, prints it to the report and updates the total for the student. Since `query3` is to be executed many times, a `PreparedStatement` object is used. At the end of the inner loop, prints the student's average and grade.

### 5.5.4 ResultSet Metadata

The `ResultSetMetaData` class provides the ability to find out about the types and properties of columns in a `ResultSet` object. This is a very useful feature, especially when the query being executed is not known at compile time, as is the case with dynamic SQL.

The `ResultSetMetaData` object can be created by invoking the `getMetaData` method on a `ResultSet` object, as follows:

```
ResultSetMetaData rsetmd = rset.getMetaData();
```

where `rset` is a previously defined `ResultSet` object. The `rsetmd` object now contains all the metadata information about the `ResultSet rset`. The metadata information can be extracted using one of these `ResultSetMetaData` methods:

- `getColumnCount`. This method returns the number of columns in the `ResultSet`. Its specification is

  ```
  public abstract int getColumnCount()
   throws SQLException
  ```

- `isNullable`. This method checks to see if a particular column can have a `null` value. It has the specification

  ```
  public abstract int isNullable(int column)
   throws SQLException
  ```

where `column` is the column index. The return value is one of the following integer constants defined in this class: `columnNoNulls`, `columnNullable`, or `columnNullableUnknown`.

- `getColumnDisplaySize`. This method returns the column's normal maximum width. It has the specification

  ```
  public abstract int getColumnDisplaySize(int column)
   throws SQLException
  ```

  where `column` is the column index.

- `getColumnLabel`. This method returns the suggested column title for use in printouts and displays. It has the specification

  ```
  public abstract String getColumnLabel(int column)
   throws SQLException
  ```

  where `column` is the column index.

- `getColumnName`. This method returns the column name for a given column index. It has the specification

  ```
  public abstract String getColumnName(int column)
   throws SQLException
  ```

  where `column` is the column index.

- `getPrecision`. This method returns a column's number of decimal digits. It has the specification

  ```
  public abstract int getPrecision(int column)
   throws SQLException
  ```

  where `column` is the column index.

- `getScale`. This method returns a column's number of decimal digits to the right of the decimal point. It has the specification

  ```
  public abstract int getScale(int column)
    throws SQLException
  ```

  where `column` is the column index.

- `getTableName`. This method returns the name of the table for the given column. If not applicable, it returns the empty string object. It has the specification

  ```
  public abstract String getTableName(int column)
    throws SQLException
  ```

where `column` is the column index.

- `getColumnType`. This method returns the column's SQL type. See `java.sql.Types` for a list of SQL types. This method has the specification

```
public abstract int getColumnType(int column)
  throws SQLException
```

where `column` is the column index.

- `getColumnTypeName`. This method returns the column's data-source-specific type name. It has the specification

```
public abstract String getColumnTypeName(int column)
  throws SQLException
```

where `column` is the column index.

Example 5.5.1 The following is a Java program that interprets SQL queries and prints the results. The user may enter the SQL `select` statement at the `SQL>` prompt on one or more lines. (The `SQL>` prompt is echoed after each carriage return.) The query must be terminated with a semicolon. The display showing the results of the query is similar to the SQL*Plus display. Several `ResultSetMetaData` methods are invoked to display the results. The user may exit the program by typing `exit` and a semicolon.

```
import java.sql.*;
import java.io.*;
class meta3 {
public static void main (String args [])
    throws SQLException, IOException {

  try {
    Class.forName ("oracle.jdbc.driver.OracleDriver");
  } catch (ClassNotFoundException e) {
      System.out.println ("Could not load the driver");
    }

  String user, pass;
  user = readEntry("userid  : ");
  pass = readEntry("password: ");
  Connection conn = DriverManager.getConnection(
     "jdbc:oracle:oci8:"+user+"/"+pass);
```

```
System.out.println("Welcome to the SQL Interpreter\n");
System.out.print("SQL> ");
Statement stmt = conn.createStatement ();
do {
  String query = readQuery();
  if (query .equals("exit"))
    break;
  ResultSet rset;
  try {
    rset = stmt.executeQuery(query);
  } catch (SQLException e) {
      System.out.println("Not well formed query");
      continue;
    }
  ResultSetMetaData rsetmd = rset.getMetaData();
  int nCols;
  nCols = rsetmd.getColumnCount();
  for (int i = 1; i <= nCols; i++) {
    System.out.print(rsetmd.getColumnName(i));
    int colSize = rsetmd.getColumnDisplaySize(i);
    for (int k=0;
         k < colSize-rsetmd.getColumnName(i).length();
         k++)
      System.out.print(" ");
  }
  System.out.println("");
  while (rset.next ()) {
    for (int i = 1; i <= nCols; i++) {
      String val = rset.getString(i);
      if (rset.wasNull())
        System.out.print("null");
      else
        System.out.print(rset.getString(i));
      int colSize;
      if (rset.wasNull()) colSize = 4;
      else colSize = rsetmd.getColumnDisplaySize(i);
      if (rset.wasNull()) {
        for (int k=0; k < colSize-4; k++)
          System.out.print(" ");
```

```
          }
          else {
            for (int k=0;
                 k < colSize-rset.getString(i).length();
                 k++)
              System.out.print(" ");
          }
        }
        System.out.println("");
      }
    } while (true);
    stmt.close();
    conn.close();
    System.out.println("Thank you for using the SQL"+
                       " Interpreter\n");
  }
  //readQuery function
  static String readQuery() {
     try {
       StringBuffer buffer = new StringBuffer();
       System.out.flush();
       int c = System.in.read();
       while(c != ';' && c != -1) {
          if (c != '\n')
            buffer.append((char)c);
          else {
            buffer.append(" ");
            System.out.print("SQL> ");
            System.out.flush();
          }
          c = System.in.read();
        }
        return buffer.toString().trim();
      } catch (IOException e) {
        return "";
        }
    }
  }
```

*Note:* `null` values are checked before printing them using the `wasNull` method. The following is a screen capture of a session with the previous program:

```
[/home/book/jdbc][3:40pm] java meta3
userid  : book
password: book
Welcome to the SQL Interpreter

SQL> select cno,cname
SQL> from customers;
CNO                   CNAME
1111                  Charles
2222                  Bertram
3333                  Barbara
9999                  Johnny
SQL> select cno,cname,city
SQL> from customers,zipcodes
SQL> where customers.zip = zipcodes.zip;
CNO              CNAME                CITY
1111             Charles              Wichita
2222             Bertram              Wichita
3333             Barbara              Fort Dodge
9999             Johnny               null
SQL> select cno,zip
SQL> from customers;
CNO                   ZIP
1111                  67226
2222                  67226
3333                  60606
9999                  99999
SQL> select cno,city
SQL> from customers;
Not well formed query
SQL> exit;
Thank you for using the SQL Interpreter

[/home/book/jdbc][3:41pm]
```

## 5.5.5 The Oracle REF CURSOR Type

The Oracle JDBC driver supports bind variables of type `REF CURSOR`, a reference to a cursor that is represented by a JDBC `ResultSet`. Using the `getCursor` method of the `CallableStatement` object, you can convert a `REF CURSOR` value returned by a PL/SQL procedure/function into a JDBC `ResultSet`. You must import classes from the `oracle.jdbc.driver` package to work with `REF CURSOR` values.

Example 5.5.2 The following is a PL/SQL package specification containing one function, called `get_courses`, which takes as input a `term` value and returns a reference to a cursor that contains the line number, course number, and course title for all courses taught in a given term:

```
create or replace package refcursor_jdbc as
  type refcurtype is ref cursor;
  function get_courses (term_in varchar2)
           return refcurtype;
end refcursor_jdbc;
/
show errors
create or replace package body refcursor_jdbc as
  function get_courses (term_in varchar2)
           return refcurtype as
    rc refcurtype;
  begin
   open rc for
     select lineno, courses.cno, ctitle
     from   courses, catalog
     where  courses.cno = catalog.cno and
            courses.term = term_in;
   return rc;
  end;
end refcursor_jdbc;
/
show errors
```

Once this package has been defined in the Oracle database, it can be accessed within a JDBC program. The following is a Java program that reads the value of `term` from standard input and makes a call to the `get_courses` function. It then processes the results and prints the courses on the screen.

```
import java.sql.*;
import java.io.*;
import oracle.jdbc.driver.*;

class refcur {
  public static void main (String args [])
       throws SQLException, ClassNotFoundException {

    try {
      Class.forName ("oracle.jdbc.driver.OracleDriver");
    } catch (ClassNotFoundException e) {
        System.out.println ("Could not load the driver");
      }

    String user, pass;
    user = readEntry("userid  : ");
    pass = readEntry("password: ");
    Connection conn = DriverManager.getConnection
       ("jdbc:oracle:oci8:"+user+"/"+pass);

    String term_in = readEntry("Enter Term: ");

    CallableStatement cstmt = conn.prepareCall
        ("{ ? = call refcursor_jdbc.get_courses (?)}");

    cstmt.registerOutParameter (1, OracleTypes.CURSOR);
    cstmt.setString (2, term_in);
    cstmt.execute ();
    ResultSet rset = (ResultSet)cstmt.getObject(1);
    System.out.println("Courses offered during " +
                       term_in + " are:");
    while (rset.next ()) {
      System.out.print(rset.getString(1) + "  ");
      System.out.print(rset.getString(2) + "  ");
      System.out.println(rset.getString(3));
    }
    cstmt.close();
    conn.close();
  }
}
```

Notice the statement

```
cstmt.registerOutParameter (1, OracleTypes.CURSOR);
```

which registers the data type of the return value of the function to be `OracleTypes.CURSOR`. Also notice the use of the `getObject` method to obtain the result set corresponding to the cursor reference. The following is the screen capture of a sample run of the preceding program:

```
[~book/jdbc][12:41pm] java refcur
userid  : book
password: book
Enter Term: F96
Courses offered during F96 are:
1031  CSC226  INTRODUCTION TO PROGRAMMING I
1032  CSC226  INTRODUCTION TO PROGRAMMING I
[~book/jdbc][12:42pm]
```

## 5.5.6 Processing Multiple `ResultSets`

An example of executing an anonymous PL/SQL block that contains several `REF CURSOR` values is shown here. This results in multiple `ResultSet` objects that need to be processed sequentially.

Example 5.5.3 An anonymous PL/SQL block that contains three cursor references is executed from within a Java program. The program reads in a customer number and executes the anonymous PL/SQL block. The first cursor reference contains a cursor that returns the total number of orders for the particular customer, the second cursor reference contains a cursor that returns the order number and received date for orders for the given customer, and the third cursor reference contains a cursor for the order details for each order for the given customer. Once this PL/SQL block is executed, the three result sets are retrieved in sequence and processed. The Java program follows:

```
import oracle.jdbc.driver.*;
import java.sql.*;
import java.io.*;

class call2 {
 public static void main (String args [])
     throws SQLException, IOException {
```

```
try {
  Class.forName ("oracle.jdbc.driver.OracleDriver");
 } catch (ClassNotFoundException e) {
     System.out.println ("Could not load the driver");
   }

String user, pass;
user = readEntry("userid  : ");
pass = readEntry("password: ");
Connection conn = DriverManager.getConnection
   ("jdbc:oracle:oci8:"+user+"/"+pass);

String cnum = readEntry("Enter customer number: ");
CallableStatement cstmt;
ResultSet rset;

cstmt = conn.prepareCall
 ("begin " +
  "open ? for select count(*) from orders " +
    "where cno = ?;" +
  "open ? for select ono,received from orders " +
    "where cno = ?;" +
  "open ? for select orders.ono,parts.pno,pname,qty " +
    "from orders,odetails,parts where " +
    "orders.ono = odetails.ono and " +
    "odetails.pno = parts.pno " +
    "and cno = ?;" +  "end;");

cstmt.setString(2,cnum);
cstmt.setString(4,cnum);
cstmt.setString(6,cnum);
cstmt.registerOutParameter (1, OracleTypes.CURSOR);
cstmt.registerOutParameter (3, OracleTypes.CURSOR);
cstmt.registerOutParameter (5, OracleTypes.CURSOR);
cstmt.execute ();

rset = ((OracleCallableStatement)cstmt).getCursor(1);
while (rset.next ()) {
  System.out.println ("Customer has " +
                   rset.getString(1) + " orders");
```

```
    }
    System.out.println("The orders are:");
    rset = ((OracleCallableStatement)cstmt).getCursor(3);
    while (rset.next ()) {
      System.out.print("Order Number " +rset.getString(1));
      System.out.println(":Received on " +rset.getDate(2).toString());
    }
    System.out.println("The order details are:");
    System.out.println("ONO   PNO    PNAME    QUANTITY");
    rset = ((OracleCallableStatement)cstmt).getCursor(5);
    ResultSetMetaData rsetmd = rset.getMetaData();
    while (rset.next ()) {
      System.out.print(rset.getString(1));
      System.out.print(" " + rset.getString(2));
      System.out.print(" " + rset.getString(3));
      for (int k=0;
           k<(rsetmd.getColumnDisplaySize(3)-
              rset.getString(3).length()); k++)
        System.out.print(" ");
      System.out.println(" " + rset.getString(4));
    }
    cstmt.close();
    conn.close();
  }
}
```

Note the use of the statement

```
rset = ((OracleCallableStatement)cstmt).getCursor(1);
```

The `getCursor` method is not available for a `CallableStatement` object (hence the cast). The following is a screen capture of a sample run of the preceding program:

```
[~book/jdbc][12:10pm] java call2
userid  : book
password: book
Enter the customer number: 1111
Customer has 5 orders
The orders are:
Order Number 1020:Received on 1994-12-10
Order Number 1021:Received on 1995-01-12
Order Number 2000:Received on 1998-01-26
```

```
Order Number 3005:Received on 1998-02-19
Order Number 3000:Received on 1998-02-19
The order details are:
ONO   PNO    PNAME                       QUANTITY
1020 10506 Land Before Time I                1
1020 10507 Land Before Time II               1
1020 10508 Land Before Time III              2
1020 10509 Land Before Time IV               3
1021 10601 Sleeping Beauty                   4
3000 10506 Land Before Time I               20
2000 10900 Dr. Zhivago                     140
3000 10507 Land Before Time II              20
3005 10506 Land Before Time I               10
3005 10507 Land Before Time II              10
[~book/jdbc][12:10pm]
```

## 5.6 Grade Book Application

An application developed for the grade book database is introduced here. It is a terminal-based application having the following main menu:

```
        Main Menu

(1) Add Catalog
(2) Add Course
(3) Add Students
(4) Select Course
(q) Quit
```

The user options at the main menu level are as follows:

- `Add Catalog`. Requests information about new catalog entry and adds an entry to the `catalog` table.
- `Add Course`. Requests information about new courses and adds an entry to the `course` table.
- `Add Students`. Repeatedly requests information about new students and adds entries to the `students` table. The processing is stopped when the user types in 0 for `sid`.

- `Select Course`. This option asks for the term and then lists all the courses taught in that term, asks the user to select a particular course (line number), and displays the following submenu:

```
            SELECT COURSE SUBMENU

    (1) Add Students to Course
    (2) Add Course Components
    (3) Add Student Scores
    (4) Modify Student Score
    (5) Drop Student from Course
    (6) Print Course Report
    (q) Quit
```

These submenu options are valid for a given course offering:

- `Add Enrolls`. Repeatedly requests `sid` values and inserts into `enrolls` table.
- `Add Course Components`. Requests information about a component and inserts into `components` table.
- `Add Scores`. First lists all the components for the course and asks the user to choose one, then displays each student's name and requests the student's score for the selected component. These scores are inserted into the `scores` table.
- `Modify Scores`. Requests `sid` and `compname` values, then displays old score and requests new score. Finally, performs an update in the `scores` table.
- `Delete Enrolls`. Requests `sid` value and then deletes row from `enrolls` table.
- `Report`. Generates a course report.

Many of the functions required to implement this application have already been discussed. Some of the remaining functions are discussed next.

### 5.6.1 Function select_course

The following is the `select_course` function, which asks the user for the term and displays all the courses taught in that term. The user is then asked to select one of these courses for manipulation. A submenu is shown for the selected course, and various options are processed. The function takes as input an open `Connection` to the database.

```
void select_course(Connection conn)
 throws SQLException, IOException {

 String query1 = "select distinct lineno," +
   "courses.cno,ctitle from courses,catalog " +
   "where courses.cno = catalog.cno and term = '";
 String query;
 String term_in = readEntry("Term: ");
 query = query1 + term_in + "'";

 Statement stmt = conn.createStatement ();
 ResultSet rset = stmt.executeQuery(query);
 System.out.println("");
 while (rset.next ()) {
   System.out.println(rset.getString(1) + "    " +
                      rset.getString(2) + "    " +
                      rset.getString(3));
 }
 System.out.println("");
 String ls = readEntry("Select a course: ");

 grade2 g2 = new grade2();
 boolean done;
 char ch,ch1;

 done = false;
 do {
   g2.print_menu();
   System.out.print("Type in your option:");
   System.out.flush();
   ch = (char) System.in.read();
   ch1 = (char) System.in.read();
   switch (ch) {
    case '1': g2.add_enrolls(conn,term_in,ls);
              break;
    case '2': g2.add_course_component(conn,term_in,ls);
              break;
    case '3': g2.add_scores(conn,term_in,ls);
              break;
```

```
          case '4': g2.modify_score(conn,term_in,ls);
                    break;
          case '5': g2.drop_student(conn,term_in,ls);
                    break;
          case '6': g2.print_report(conn,term_in,ls);
                    break;
          case 'q': done = true;
                    break;
          default : System.out.println("Invalid option");
        }
      } while (!done);
    }
```

The query to find the courses taught in a particular term is formed and executed. The results are displayed for the user to select a course. The user enters the line number of the course, and a submenu is shown. The submenu and other functions dealing with it are defined in the `grade2` class.

### 5.6.2 Function add_enrolls

The `add_enrolls` function repeatedly requests the student ID from the user for a particular course and adds it to the `enrolls` table. The user may stop the loop by providing a value of `0` for the ID. This function takes as input an open `Connection` and the term and line number for the course for which the students are to be enrolled. The function is

```
void add_enrolls(Connection conn, String term_in,
                 String ls) throws IOException,
                                   SQLException {
 String id;
 PreparedStatement stmt = conn.prepareStatement(
   "insert into enrolls values " +
   "(?,'" + term_in + "','"+ls+")"  );
 do {
   id = readEntry("Student Id (0 to stop): ");
   if (id.equals("0"))
     break;
   try {
     stmt.setString(1,id);
```

```
      stmt.executeUpdate();
    } catch (SQLException e) {
      System.out.println("Error adding student.");
      while (e != null) {
       System.out.println("Message:"+e.getMessage());
       e = e.getNextException();
      }
    }
  } while (true);
  stmt.close();
}
```

A PreparedStatement object is used to speed up the execution of the insert statement.

### 5.6.3 Function add_scores

The add_scores function shown next takes as input an open Connection and the term and line number for the course for which the scores are to be added:

```
void add_scores(Connection conn,
                String term_in, String ls)
  throws SQLException, IOException {

  String query1 = "select distinct compname " +
    "from   courses,components " +
    "where  courses.term = components.term and " +
    " courses.lineno = components.lineno and " +
    " courses.term = '" + term_in + "'" + " and " +
    " courses.lineno = " + ls;

  Statement stmt1 = conn.createStatement ();
  ResultSet rset1 = stmt1.executeQuery(query1);
  System.out.println("");
  while (rset1.next ()) {
    System.out.println(rset1.getString(1));
  }
  System.out.println("");
  String cname = readEntry("Enter a component name: ");
```

```
  String query2 =
    "select distinct students.sid, lname, fname " +
    "from   enrolls,students " +
    "where  enrolls.sid = students.sid and " +
    " enrolls.term = '" + term_in + "'" + " and" +
    " enrolls.lineno = " + ls +
    " order by lname, fname";

  ResultSet rset2 = stmt1.executeQuery(query2);
  System.out.println("");

  PreparedStatement stmt2 = conn.prepareStatement(
    "insert into scores values (?,'"+
     term_in + "'," + ls + ",'" + cname + "', ?)");

  while (rset2.next ()) {
    String pts = readEntry(cname + " Score for " +
      rset2.getString(1) + ": " + rset2.getString(2) +
      ", " + rset2.getString(3) + ": ");
    try {
      stmt2.setString(1,rset2.getString(1));
      stmt2.setString(2,pts);
      stmt2.executeUpdate();
    } catch (SQLException e) {
        System.out.println("Score was not added!");
        while (e != null) {
          System.out.println("Message:"+e.getMessage());
          e = e.getNextException();
        }
      }
  }
  stmt1.close();
  stmt2.close();
}
```

This function performs the following steps:

- Executes **query1** to get the component names, then displays the component names so that the user can choose one. The **Statement** object is used for this query.

- Executes **query2** to get the students enrolled in the course. The **Statement** object is also used for this query.
- For each student enrolled in the course, prompts the user with the student ID and name and requests the score for the chosen component.
- Using a **PreparedStatement** object, inserts the score in the **scores** table.

## 5.6.4 Function modify_score

The **modify_score** function takes as input an open **Connection** to the database and the line number and term for the course in which the student's score is to be modified. The function asks the user for the student ID and the component name for which the score is to be modified. It then displays the old score and requests the new one. Finally, it performs an **update** statement in the **scores** table. The function is

```
void modify_score(Connection conn, String term_in,
   String ls) throws SQLException, IOException {

 String id    = readEntry("Student's ID  : ");
 String cname = readEntry("Component Name: ");
 String query1 = "select points from scores " +
   "where sid = '" + id + "' and term = '" + term_in +
   "' and lineno = " + ls + " and compname = '" +
   cname + "'";

 Statement stmt = conn.createStatement ();
 ResultSet rset;
 try {
   rset = stmt.executeQuery(query1);
 } catch (SQLException e) {
     System.out.println("Error");
     while (e != null) {
       System.out.println("Message:"+e.getMessage());
       e = e.getNextException();
     }
     return;
   }
 System.out.println("");
```

```
  if ( rset.next () ) {
    System.out.println("Old Score = " +rset.getString(1));
    String ns = readEntry("Enter New Score: ");
    String query2 = "update scores set points = " + ns +
      " where sid = '" + id + "' and compname = '" +
      cname + "' and term = '" + term_in +
      "' and lineno = " + ls ;
    try {
      stmt.executeUpdate(query2);
    } catch (SQLException e) {
        System.out.println("Could not modify score");
        while (e != null) {
          System.out.println("Message:"+e.getMessage());
          e = e.getNextException();
        }
        return;
      }
    System.out.println("Modified score successfully");
  }
  else
    System.out.println("Score not found");
  stmt.close();
}
```

## 5.7 Database Metadata

To obtain information about the database as a whole, the `DatabaseMetaData` interface is used in JDBC. A `DatabaseMetaData` object is created by invoking the `getMetaData` method on a `Connection` object, as follows:

```
DatabaseMetaData dmd = conn.getMetaData();
```

where `conn` is a previously created `Connection` object. The literally hundreds of methods that come with the `DatabaseMetaData` class retrieve all kinds of information about the database system to which a `Connection` is made. Many of these methods return the results in a `ResultSet` object.

Some of these methods take arguments that are `String` patterns. These arguments all have names such as `xxxPattern`. Within a pattern `String`, `"%"` means match any substring of zero or more characters, and `"_"` means match any one character. Only metadata entries matching the search pattern are returned. If a search pattern argument is set to a **null ref**, it means that argument's criteria should be dropped from the search.

An `SQLException` will be thrown if a driver does not support a metadata method. In the case of methods that return a `ResultSet`, either a `ResultSet` (which may be empty) is returned or an `SQLException` is thrown.

A few of the `DatabaseMetaData` methods are illustrated in the following Java program:

```
import java.sql.*;
import java.io.*;

class meta2 {
  public static void main (String args [])
      throws SQLException, IOException {

    try {
      Class.forName ("oracle.jdbc.driver.OracleDriver");
    } catch (ClassNotFoundException e) {
        System.out.println ("Could not load the driver");
      }
    String user, pass;
    user = readEntry("userid  : ");
    pass = readEntry("password: ");
    Connection conn = DriverManager.getConnection(
      "jdbc:oracle:oci8:"+user+"/"+pass);

    DatabaseMetaData dmd = conn.getMetaData();

    System.out.println("Database Product Name = " +
           dmd.getDatabaseProductName());
    System.out.println("JDBC Driver Name = " +
           dmd.getDriverName());
    System.out.println("Tables starting with C " +
                      "in schema BOOK are:");
    ResultSet rset = dmd.getTables(null,"BOOK","C%",null);
    while (rset.next()) {
      System.out.println(rset.getString(3));
        // print table name
    }
    int n = dmd.getMaxColumnsInTable();
```

```
        System.out.println("Maximum number of columns " +
                           "allowed in a table = " + n);

        conn.close();
    }
}
```

A session capture of a run of the previous program follows:

```
[~book/jdbc][11:44am] java meta2
userid  : book
password: book
Database Product Name = Oracle
JDBC Driver Name = Oracle JDBC driver
Tables starting with C in schema BOOK are:
CUSTSEQ
CATALOG
COMPONENTS
COURSES
CUSTOMERS
Maximum number of columns allowed in a table = 254
```

## 5.8 Errors and Warnings

The JDBC API provides three classes to deal with errors, warnings, and data truncations that take place during database access: `SQLException`, `SQLWarning`, and `DataTruncation`.

### 5.8.1 The SQLException Class

The `SQLException` class provides information about errors while accessing the database. It is derived from the more general class, `java.lang.Exception`. An `SQLException` object contains the following:

- The error message as a `String` object. The message can be retrieved by using the inherited `getMessage` method.
- The `SQLState` string identifying the exception according to the X/Open SQL specification. The `SQLState` can be retrieved using the `getSQLState` method.

- An error code that is specific to the vendor. This value can be retrieved using the `getErrorCode` method.
- A link to the next `SQLException` object, in case there is more than one error. The next `SQLException` can be retrieved using the `getNextException` method.

The `SQLException` object is typically used within a `try-catch` construct, as follows:

```
try {
  some JDBC statement to access the database;
} catch (SQLException e) {
    System.out.println("SQL Exception caught!");
    while (e != null) {
      System.out.println("Error Message = " +e.getMessage());
      System.out.println("SQL State = " +e.getSQLState());
      System.out.println("Error Code  = " +e.getErrorCode());
      e = e.getNextException();
    }
  }
```

## 5.8.2 The SQLWarning Class

The `SQLWarning` class provides information about warnings generated during database access. It is derived as a subclass of `SQLException`, thereby inheriting many of the `SQLException` methods. An `SQLWarning` object contains the following information:

- The warning message as a `String` object. The message can be retrieved by using the `getMessage` method inherited by `SQLException`.
- The `SQLState` string identifying the warning according to the X/Open SQL specification. The `SQLState` can be retrieved using the `getSQLState` method.
- An error code that is specific to the vendor. This value can be retrieved using the `getErrorCode` method.
- A link to the next `SQLWarning` object, in case there is more than one warning. The next `SQLWarning` can be retrieved using the following method:

  ```
  public SQLWarning getNextWarning()
  ```

  which returns the next `SQLWarning` in the chain; it returns `null` if none.

## 5.8.3 The DataTruncation Class

The `DataTruncation` class, a subclass of `SQLWarning`, provides information about any truncations that happen to data that are read from or written to the database. Normally, truncation while reading from the database is reported as an `SQLWarning`, and truncation while writing to the database is classified as an `SQLException`. Since JDBC does not pose any restrictions on the size of data that are to be read from the database, data truncation does not occur during reads. However, data truncation is a real possibility while writing to the database. A `DataTruncation` object contains the following information:

- The string "Data Truncation" as the error/warning message to indicate that data truncation has taken place.
- The `SQLState` set to `01004`.
- A Boolean value indicating if a column or a parameter was truncated. This value is retrieved by invoking the following method:

  ```
  public boolean getParameter()
  ```

  which returns `true` if the value was a parameter and `false` if it was a column value.
- An integer value indicating the index of the column or parameter that was truncated. This value is retrieved by invoking the method

  ```
  public int getIndex()
  ```

  which returns the index of the truncated parameter or column value. This may be `-1` if the column or parameter index is unknown, in which case the `parameter` and `read` fields should be ignored.
- A Boolean value indicating if the data truncation happened on a read or a write. This value is retrieved by invoking the method

  ```
  public boolean getRead()
  ```

  which returns `true` if the value was truncated when read from the database and `false` if the data was truncated on a write.
- An integer value indicating the number of bytes that should have been transferred. This value is retrieved by invoking the method

  ```
  public int getDataSize()
  ```

which returns the number of bytes of data that should have been transferred. This number may be approximate if data conversions were being performed. The value may be `-1` if the size is unknown.

- An integer value indicating the number of bytes that were actually transferred. This value is retrieved by invoking the method

```
public int getTransferSize()
```

which returns the number of bytes of data actually transferred. The value may be `-1` if the size is unknown.

- A link to the next `SQLException` or `SQLWarning` object.

## 5.9 Scrollable ResultSets

The JDBC 2.0 specification adds new capabilities to the `ResultSet` class. `ResultSet` objects are now updatable and scrollable. In order to create updatable or scrollable `ResultSet` objects, the `Statement` object needs to be created using the following new method available in the `Connection` class:

```
Statement createStatement(int resultSetType,
                          int resultSetConcurrency)
```

The `resultSetType` parameter can take one of the following values:

- `ResultSet.TYPE_FORWARD_ONLY`. This is the default and the same as in JDBC 1.0. It allows only forward movement of the cursor, and columns can generally be read only once. When `rset.next()` returns `false`, the data are no longer available and the `ResultSet` is closed.
- `ResultSet.TYPE_SCROLL_INSENSITIVE`. This option enables the creation of a `ResultSet` object in which the cursor can move backward or forward, as well as in a random manner. Any changes made in the database to the rows selected in the current `ResultSet` object are not seen in the `ResultSet` object in Java memory.
- `ResultSet TYPE_SCROLL_SENSITIVE`. This option enables the creation of a `ResultSet` object in which the cursor can move backward or forward, as well as in a random manner. However, any changes in the database to the affected rows are immediately seen in the `ResultSet` object in Java memory.

The `resultSetConcurrency` parameter can take one of the following values:

- `ResultSet.CONCUR_READ_ONLY`. This is the default (and the same as in JDBC 1.0) and allows data only to be read from the database.
- `ResultSet.CONCUR_UPDATABLE`. This option allows for the Java program to make changes to the database based on the new methods and positioning ability of the cursor.

A scrollable `ResultSet` is obtained by calling the usual `executeQuery` method on a `Statement` object. The following code fragment illustrates how a scrollable `ResultSet` object can be created:

```
Statement stmt = conn.createStatement(
          ResultSet.TYPE_SCROLL_INSENSITIVE,
          ResultSet.CONCUR_READ_ONLY);
ResultSet rset = stmt.executeQuery("select * from cat");
```

Scrollable `ResultSet` objects can be manipulated and traversed using one of the following methods:

- `public boolean absolute(int row) throws SQLException`. If the given row number is positive, this method moves the cursor to the given row number (with the first row numbered 1). If the row number is negative, the cursor moves to a relative position from the last row. For example, the method call `absolute-(-1)` would move the cursor up one row, `absolute(-2)` up two rows, and so forth. If the row number is `0`, an `SQLException` will be raised.
- `public boolean relative(int row) throws SQLException`. This method call moves the cursor a relative number of rows, either positive or negative. An attempt to move beyond the last row (or before the first row) in the `ResultSet` positions the cursor after the last row (or before the first row).
- `public boolean first() throws SQLException`. This method call moves the cursor to the first row in the `ResultSet`.
- `public boolean last() throws SQLException`. This method call moves the cursor to the last row in the `ResultSet`.
- `public boolean previous() throws SQLException`. This method call moves the cursor to the previous row in the `ResultSet`.
- `public boolean next() throws SQLException`. This method call moves the cursor to the next row in the `ResultSet`.

- `public boolean beforeFirst() throws SQLException`. This method call moves the cursor to the front of the `ResultSet`, before the first row.
- `public boolean afterLast() throws SQLException`. This method call moves the cursor to the end of the `ResultSet`, after the last row.
- `public boolean isFirst() throws SQLException`. This method call indicates whether the cursor is at the first row.
- `public boolean isLast() throws SQLException`. This method call indicates whether the cursor is at the last row.
- `public boolean isAfterLast() throws SQLException`. This method call indicates whether the cursor is after the last row.
- `public boolean isBeforeFirst() throws SQLException`. This method call indicates whether the cursor is before the first row.
- `public int getRow() throws SQLException`. This method call retrieves the current row number. The first row is number 1, the second number 2, and so on.

Example 5.9.1 Consider the following relation, which stores data about books:

```
create table books (
   isbn varchar2(15),
   author varchar2(100) not null,
   title varchar2(128) not null,
   price number(7,2) not null,
   subject varchar2(30) not null,
   primary key (isbn)
);
```

The following Java program uses scrollable `ResultSet` objects to present a browsing interface for the books data. Initially, the program displays the first five rows from the table. After that, the user may look at the next five or previous five rows by entering `n<ENTER>` or `p<ENTER>`, respectively. The user may enter `q<ENTER>` to quit the program.

```
import java.sql.*;
import java.io.*;

public class browse {
  public static void main (String args [])
      throws SQLException, IOException {
```

```
// Load JDBC driver
try {
  Class.forName ("oracle.jdbc.driver.OracleDriver");
} catch (ClassNotFoundException e) {
    System.out.println ("Could not load the driver");
  }
// Make Connection
String user, pass;
user = "book";
pass = "book";
Connection conn =
  DriverManager.getConnection
   ("jdbc:oracle:thin:@tinman.cs.gsu.edu:1521:sid9ir2",
    user,pass);
// Create a Statement object for read-only and for
// insensitive scrolling result sets
Statement stmt = conn.createStatement(
    ResultSet.TYPE_SCROLL_INSENSITIVE,
    ResultSet.CONCUR_READ_ONLY );
// Create a result set for the query
ResultSet rset = stmt.executeQuery
 ("select isbn,author from books " +
  "where title like '%w%'");
// Get the number of rows and print it
rset.last();
int nRows = rset.getRow();
System.out.println("#rows in the result set is " +
                   nRows);
// Set up loop for browsing 5 rows at a time
int currentRow = 1;
while (currentRow==currentRow) {
  rset.absolute(currentRow);
  int n = 0;
  System.out.println("");
  // Display 5 rows
  for (int i=currentRow; i<=nRows; i++) {
    if (n == 5)
      break;
    System.out.println(rset.getString(1)+
                       " "+rset.getString(2));
```

```
          rset.next();
          n++;
        }
        // If toward end do not prompt for next 5
        if (currentRow == (((nRows/5)*5)+1)) {
          String opt =
           readEntry("\n p:previous 5, q:quit");
          if (opt.equals("q"))
            return;
          else if (opt.equals("p"))
            currentRow -= 5;
        }
        // If toward beginning do not prompt for previous 5
        else if (currentRow == 1) {
          String opt =
            readEntry("\n n:next 5, q:quit");
          if (opt.equals("q"))
            return;
          else if (opt.equals("n"))
            currentRow += 5;
        }
        // If in middle, prompt for next 5 and previous 5
        else {
          String opt =
            readEntry("\n n:next 5, p:previous 5, q:quit");
          if (opt.equals("q"))
            return;
          else if (opt.equals("n"))
            currentRow += 5;
          else if (opt.equals("p"))
            currentRow -= 5;
        }
      }
      conn.close();
    }
  }
```

The program uses a variable called `currentRow` that keeps track of where the user is in the set of rows. This value is updated appropriately when the user moves to the next five or previous five rows. End cases are taken care of appropriately. The `absolute(currentRow)` method call moves the cursor to the appropriate position.

# Exercises

## *Grade Book Database Problems*

5.1 Write a JDBC program that prompts the user for the term and line number of a course and prints a report containing the median scores for all the grading components for the course. The report should have the following format:

```
                Median Scores
            CSc 226, Programming I
          LineNo: 1231,  Fall 1996


EXAM1:  69
EXAM2:  64
HW:    126
QUIZ:   88
```

5.2 Write a JDBC program that produces a report consisting of the names of all the students in the database along with the number of A, B, C, D, and F grades earned by each student. The report should be sorted by student name. The format for the report is

```
          Grade Count Report
LNAME    FNAME    #A's  #B's  #C's  #D's  #F's
--------------------------------------------
Jones    Tony      3     0     0     0     0
Smith    Manny     1     3     2     0     0
Thomas   Tom       0     0     5     1     1
--------------------------------------------
```

5.3 Write a JDBC program that produces a report containing the 10 students with the highest enrollments in the database. The list should be sorted according to the number of courses in which the student is enrolled. The report format is

```
           Top 10 Enrollees
Rank      Name                    #Courses
-----------------------------------------
1.        Rajshekhar, Nandita        12
2.        Corn, Sydney               10
.
.
.
10.       Meyer, Malachi              2
-----------------------------------------
```

5.4 Assume that a particular course has several grading components, and from these the best subset of a particular size is to be chosen for the purposes of evaluation of the grade. For example, consider a course that has five components, called **quiz1**, **quiz2**, **quiz3**, **quiz4**, and **quiz5**. Each component is weighted 10% of the overall grade, and the three best scores are to be used to evaluate the overall grade. Assuming that all of these components are equally weighted, write a JDBC program that accomplishes the task of dropping these components and adding new ones corresponding to the subset chosen for grading purposes, with the best scores selected among the available scores. It is assumed that after this operation is performed, the sum of the weights of the components will equal 100.

The program should prompt the user for the term and line number of the course for which the manipulation is to be done. It should then prompt the user for the number of components (in the preceding example, five) and the names of the components to be considered (in the preceding example, five quizzes). Finally, it should prompt for the size of the subset of these components that is to be used in the final grade evaluation (in the previous example, three) and the names of the new components to be added (in the previous example, **bestquiz**, **secondbestquiz**, and **thirdbestquiz**). The tables to be manipulated in this problem are **components** and **scores**. Old components and their corresponding scores should be deleted, and the new components, along with the best scores, must be added.

5.5 Consider the following SQL query, which represents the `join` of four tables:

```
select   *
from   enrolls E, students S, components C, scores T
where S.sid = T.sid and
      S.sid = E.sid and
      E.term = C.term and
      E.lineno = C.lineno and
      E.term = T.term and
      E.lineno = T.lineno and
      C.compname = T.compname;
```

The select list in the preceding expression is deliberately left out. Write a JDBC program that prompts the user for a subset of the columns of `join` mentioned (number of columns and their names) and prints only those columns, instead of all the columns, in the `join`. For example, if the user entered **term**, **lineno**, and **sid**, only these three column values must be selected from the `join` and printed. The final results must be formatted properly, with column values lining up with the column names. This problem requires the use of metadata objects and methods.

## *Mail-Order Database Problems*

5.6 Write a JDBC program to process an order for a customer. The program should first prompt the user for a valid employee number. After this, it should determine whether this is a new customer. If the customer is new, pertinent information for the customer should be requested and an entry in the **`customers`** table should be made; otherwise, only the customer number is obtained from the user. After this, an order number should be generated internally, using the sequence **`orderseq`**. The part numbers and the quantities for each part should then be requested from the user. One row corresponding to this order should be inserted in the **`orders`** table, and several entries that correspond to this order should be inserted in the **`odetails`** table. At the end, the program should summarize the order and print it to screen. The program should be robust and should respond to all possible error situations.

5.7 Write a JDBC program that prompts the user for an order number and prints the invoice for this order, which includes the customer and employee details, as well as the parts in the order and their quantities and total price. The format of this report should be as follows:

```
Order Number: 1020
***********************************************
Customer: Charles          Customer Number: 1111
Street  : 123 Main St.
City    : Wichita
ZIP     : 67226
Phone   : 316-636-5555
-----------------------------------------------
Order No: 1020
Taken By: Jones (1000)
Received On: 10-DEC-94
Shipped  On: 12-DEC-94

Part No.  Part Name           Quan. Price  Sum
------------------------------------------------
10506     Land Before Time I     1   19.99  19.99
10507     Land Before Time II    1   19.99  19.99
10508     Land Before Time III   2   19.99  39.98
10509     Land Before Time IV    3   19.99  59.97
------------------------------------------------
                                  TOTAL:   139.93
************************************************
```

5.8 Write a JDBC program that will produce a report containing the 10 most ordered parts during a calendar year. The program should prompt for a year and then produce a report with the following format:

```
                YEAR: 1997

Rank PNO   Part Name            Quantity Ordered
-----------------------------------------------
1.   10506 Land Before Time I        98
2.   10507 Land Before Time II       87
.
.
.
10.  10900 Dr. Zhivago               24
-----------------------------------------------
```

5.9 Write a JDBC program that will update an incorrect zip code in the database. The program should prompt the user for the incorrect and then the correct zip code. It should then replace all the occurrences of the incorrect zip code with the correct zip code in all the tables.

To verify that the program did work, write another JDBC program that reads in a zip code and prints all the customers and employees living in that zip code. This program should be run before and after the previous program is executed, in order to verify the execution of the previous program.

5.10 Write a JDBC program that reads data from a text file and updates the **qoh** column in the **parts** table. The text file consists of several lines of data, with each line containing a part number followed by a positive quantity. The **qoh** value in the **parts** table for the part should be increased by the quantity mentioned next to the part number. Assume that the last line of the text file ends with a part number of `0` and a quantity of `0`. The **PreparedStatement** object should be used to accomplish this task.

## *Investment Portfolio Database Problems*

5.11 Write a JDBC program that caters to the following menu:

```
(1) Stock Split
(2) Merger
(3) Quit
```

The program should connect to the database and present this menu. Under the stock split option, the program should prompt the user for the security symbol and the split ratio. It should then make the necessary changes to the database to incorporate the stock split. Refer to Exercise 2.8(d) for details of the stock split. Under the merger option, the program should prompt the user for the symbols of the two companies, the new symbol and name under which the company will trade, and fractions of the new company shares to be assigned to each share of the old companies. The program should make the necessary changes to the database to incorporate the merger. The new price of the stock should be set to the larger of the two current prices of the old companies.

5.12 If you have read Chapter 5, convert the application into JDBC and compare the relative program sizes.

5.13 Write a JDBC program to view the ratings of a particular security. The program should prompt the user for the security symbol and produce the ratings list in the same format as Exercise 5.11.

### *Recursive Query Problem*

5.14 Recursive queries are easily expressed in rule-based languages such as Datalog or Prolog. Rules are generally of the form

```
P :- Q1, Q2, ..., Qn
```

and are interpreted as follows:

```
if Q1 and Q2 and ... and Qn then P
```

Consider the bill of materials (BOM) problem, a classical example of a recursive query. The problem is to find out the subparts at all levels of a given part, assuming that a table containing immediate subparts is given. Consider the following tables:

```
component(super_part,sub_part,quantity,part_type)
price(part,amount)
```

The `component` table consists of information about the immediate subparts of a part and the quantity and the type (basic or complex) of the subpart. The `price` table records the cost of each basic part. As an example, consider a part called `valve` consisting of one `gasket` (a basic part) and two `hangers` (a complex part). Assuming that the `hanger` consists of 5 `screws` (a basic part) and 10 `bolts` (a basic part), this information would be recorded in the `component` table as follows:

```
insert into component values
  ('valve','gasket',1,b).
insert into component values
  ('valve','hanger',2,c).
insert into component values
  ('hanger','screw',5,b).
insert into component values
  ('hanger','bolt',10,b).
```

The following rules define the notion of subparts at all levels for a part and, given a complex part, compute the total quantities of the basic components required to construct the complex component:

```
sub_part(X,Y,Q,T) :- component(X,Y,Q,T).
sub_part(X,Y,Q,T) :- component(Z,Y,Q2,T),
                     sub_part(X,Z,Q1,T1),
                     Q is Q1 * Q2.
basic_parts(P,Y,Q)   :- sub_part(P,Y,Q,b).
basic_comp(P,B,sum(<Q>)) :- basic_parts(P,B,Q).
```

The `sub_part` relation contains rows of the form `(X,Y,Q,T)`, where `Y` is a subpart (at any level) of `Z` in quantity `Q`, and `Y` is of type `T`. The `basic_parts` relation is defined to be a subset of the `sub_parts` relation in which the subpart is basic. The `basic_component` relation simply aggregates the quantities of each basic subpart for a complex part. Write a JDBC program that implements the following menu-based application for the bill of materials problem:

```
      MENU
(1) Given a part, find all its subparts at all levels.
(2) Given a part, list the quantities and total cost
    of the basic parts it contains.
(3) Given a basic part, list all the complex parts
    in which it is used.
(4) Find the cost of each complex part.
(5) Quit.
```

# CHAPTER 6

# SQLJ: Embedded SQL in Java

This chapter introduces SQLJ, a relatively new standard that many database vendors have already adopted. SQLJ differs from JDBC in that SQL statements can be embedded directly in Java programs and translation-time semantics checks can be performed. It is a powerful tool that complements JDBC access to databases. Programming in SQLJ is discussed in detail in this chapter, and an application program for the investment portfolio database is presented.

## 6.1 What Is SQLJ?

SQLJ is an emerging database programming tool that allows embedding of static SQL statements in Java programs, very much like Pro*C or Pro*C++. SQLJ is an attractive alternative to JDBC because it allows translation-time syntax and semantics checking of static SQL statements. As a consequence, application programs developed in SQLJ are more robust. SQLJ's syntax is also much more compact than that of JDBC, resulting in shorter programs and increased user productivity.

The SQLJ translator converts Java programs embedded with static SQL statements into pure Java code, which can then be executed through a JDBC driver against the database. Programmers can also perform dynamic SQL access to the database using JDBC features.

## 6.2 Simple Example

A simple program in SQLJ is presented in this section. This program illustrates the essential steps that are needed to write an SQLJ program. These steps follow:

1. *Import necessary classes.* In addition to the JDBC classes, `java.sql.*`, every SQLJ program will need to include the SQLJ run-time classes `sqlj.runtime.*` and `sqlj.runtime.ref.*`. In addition, to establish the default connection to Oracle, the `Oracle` class from the `oracle.sqlj.runtime.*` package is required. So, a typical set of statements to import packages would be:

```
import java.sql.*;
import sqlj.runtime.*;
import sqlj.runtime.ref.*;
import java.io.*;
import oracle.sqlj.runtime.*;
```

2. *Register the JDBC driver, if needed.* If a non-Oracle JDBC driver is being used, a call to the `registerDriver` method of the `DriverManager` class is necessary. For the purposes of this chapter, an Oracle JDBC driver is assumed. Therefore, this statement is not shown in any of the examples.

3. *Connect to the database.* Connecting to the Oracle database is done by first obtaining a `DefaultContext` object using the `getConnection` method (of the `Oracle` class[1]), whose specification is

```
public static DefaultContext getConnection
   (String url,String user,String password,boolean autoCommit)
throws SQLException
```

`url` is the database URL, and `user` and `password` are the Oracle user ID and password, respectively. Setting `autoCommit` to `true` would create the connection in autocommit mode, and setting it to `false` would create a connection in which the transactions must be committed by the programmer. A sample invocation is shown here:

```
DefaultContext cx1 =
  Oracle.getConnection("jdbc:oracle:oci8:@",
                       "book","book",true);
```

1. The `Oracle` class can be found in the package `oracle.sqlj.runtime.*`.

The `DefaultContext` object so obtained is then used to set the static default context, as follows:

```
DefaultContext.setDefaultContext(cx1);
```

This `DefaultContext` object now provides the default connection to the database.

4. *Embed SQL statements in the Java program.* Once the default connection has been established, SQL statements can be embedded within the Java program using the following syntax:

```
#sql {<sql-statement>}
```

where `#sql` indicates to the SQLJ translator, called `sqlj`, that what follows is an SQL statement and `<sql-statement>` is any valid SQL statement, which may include *host variables* and *host expressions*. Host variables are prefixed with a colon, much like in Pro*C/Pro*C++.

The following simple SQLJ program performs a query against the investment portfolio database. It reads a security symbol from the user and performs a simple query to retrieve information about the particular security. The program uses the `readEntry` method presented in Chapter 5.

```
import sqlj.runtime.*;
import sqlj.runtime.ref.*;
import java.sql.*;
import java.io.*;
import oracle.sqlj.runtime.*;

public class Simple1 {
  public static void main (String args[]) throws SQLException {

    DefaultContext cx1 =
      Oracle.getConnection("jdbc:oracle:oci8:@",
                           "book","book",true);
    DefaultContext.setDefaultContext(cx1);

    String cn;
    Double ap,bp,cp;
    String sym = readEntry("Enter symbol : ").toUpperCase();
```

```
        try {
          #sql {select cname,current_price,ask_price,bid_price
                into   :cn,:cp,:ap,:bp
                from   security
                where  symbol = :sym };
        } catch (SQLException e) {
            System.out.println("Invalid symbol.");
            return;
          }
        System.out.println("\n  Company Name   = " + cn);
        System.out.println("  Last sale at   = " + cp);
        if (ap == null)
          System.out.println("  Ask price      = null");
        else
          System.out.println("  Ask price      = " + ap);
        if (bp == null)
          System.out.println("  Bid price      = null");
        else
          System.out.println("  Bid price      = " + bp);
      }
    }
```

The program uses several Java variables (host variables) in the SQL query. It also checks to see if any of the values returned from the database are `nulls`. A `null` value returned by the query is indicated by a Java `null` reference for the host variable into which the database value is retrieved. This feature of SQLJ implies that whenever there is a possibility of a `null` value being retrieved into a host variable, the host variable's Java type should not be a primitive type.

## 6.3 Compiling SQLJ Programs

The SQLJ translator takes as input an SQLJ program file (with suffix `.sqlj`) and produces a `.java` file along with several other SQLJ profile files that contain the classes necessary to perform the SQL operations. The translator also automatically invokes the Java compiler to produce a `.class` file.

There are several command-line parameters that can be given to the SQLJ translator. For example, if the users want online semantics checking of SQL statements, they can specify the following command-line options in compiling the `Simple1.sqlj` program:

```
% sqlj -url = jdbc:oracle:oci8:@ \
      -user = book -password = book Simple1.sqlj
```

Online semantics checking is performed by the SQLJ translator by connecting to the Oracle database using the user ID and password provided as command-line parameters.

One other commonly used command-line parameter is the **-warn** parameter. This parameter takes as its value a comma-separated list of options that either enables or disables certain warnings from being generated by **sqlj**. For example, the command

```
% sqlj -warn = noprecision,nonulls Simple1.sqlj
```

will disable warnings concerning loss of precision or possible retrieval of a **null** value into a Java primitive type.

SQLJ allows the possibility of providing these command-line parameters in a properties file. This is convenient when there are many command-line parameters that have to be specified. By default, the properties file is called **sqlj.properties**. This default can be overridden by specifying the properties file name in the **-props=** command-line option. A sample **sqlj.properties** file is

```
sqlj.driver = oracle.jdbc.driver.OracleDriver
sqlj.url = jdbc:oracle:oci8:@
sqlj.user = book
sqlj.password = book
sqlj.warn = noprecision,nonulls
```

The options mentioned in this sample file are the JDBC driver name, the connect string URL, the Oracle user and password, and the warnings flags.

## 6.4 Multiple Connections

Application programs written in SQLJ can easily access data from several databases by creating one **DefaultContext** object for the default database connection and one nondefault connection context for each additional database connection that is required. A nondefault connection context class called **DbList** is declared as follows:

```
#sql context DbList;
```

This declaration is expanded by **sqlj** into a Java class called **DbList**, which can then be instantiated in the SQLJ program as follows:

```
DbList x2 = new DbList(Oracle.getConnection(
    "jdbc:oracle:oci8:@","book2","book2",true));
```

to create a new connection context. This connection context can then be used in embedded SQL statements as follows:

```
#sql [x2] {<sql-statement>};
```

The SQLJ translator also supports online SQL semantics checks on multiple connection contexts at translation time through command-line parameters that are optionally tagged with the connection context class name. For example, the `sqlj.properties` file for the previous multiple-connection scenario would be as follows:

```
sqlj.driver = oracle.jdbc.driver.OracleDriver
sqlj.warn = noprecision,nonulls
#
sqlj.url = jdbc:oracle:oci8:@
sqlj.user = book
sqlj.password = book
#
sqlj.url@DbList = jdbc:oracle:oci8:@
sqlj.user@DbList = book2
sqlj.password@DbList = book2
```

Any statements that are executed within the default connection context will be verified using the `book/book` schema connection, and any statements that are executed within the `DbList` connection context will be verified using the `book2/book2` schema connection.

The following SQLJ program illustrates multiple connections:

```
import sqlj.runtime.*;
import sqlj.runtime.ref.*;
import java.sql.*;
import java.io.*;
import oracle.sqlj.runtime.Oracle;

#sql context Book2Context;

public class Simple2 {
  public static void main (String args[])
      throws SQLException {
    DefaultContext x1 = Oracle.getConnection(
             "jdbc:oracle:oci8:@","book","book",true);
    DefaultContext.setDefaultContext(x1);
```

```
        Book2Context x2 = new Book2Context(
                 Oracle.getConnection(
                "jdbc:oracle:oci8:@","book2","book2",true));

        String dbname="";
        try {
          #sql [x2] { select db_name
                      into   :dbname
                      from   db_list
                      where  db_name like 'C%' };
        } catch (SQLException e) {
            System.out.println("Error:" + e.getMessage());
            return;
          }
        System.out.println("DB name is " + dbname);

        String cn = "";
        String sym =
                readEntry("Enter symbol : ").toUpperCase();
        try {
          #sql { select cname
                 into   :cn
                 from   security
                 where  symbol = :sym };
        } catch (SQLException e) {
            System.out.println("Invalid symbol.");
            return;
          }
        System.out.println("\n  Company Name  = " + cn);
      }
    }
```

In the preceding program, the `DefaultContext` object `x1` was designated as the default connection, and hence it was not necessary to include `x1` in the second query. It is assumed that a table called `db_list` with a column called `db_name` exists in the schema `book2/book2`. Note that the query would fail if the `db_list` table contained more than one row with the `db_name` value starting with the letter `C`. (An SQLJ iterator, introduced in Section 6.6, is necessary to process queries with multiple answers.)

## 6.5 Host Variables and Expressions

Host variables and expressions can be used in SQLJ to communicate values between the SQL statement and the Java environment. Host variables are either Java local variables, Java declared parameters, or Java class/instance variables. A host expression is any valid Java expression.

A host variable must be preceded by a colon (`:`) followed by `IN`, `OUT`, or `INOUT`,[2] depending on whether it is an input to the SQL statement, output to the SQL statement, or both. `IN` is the default for host variables and expressions (except in an `into` list) and may be left out. When using the `IN`, `OUT`, and `INOUT` tokens, the colon immediately precedes the token, and there must be a space between the token and the variable name. When not using the `IN` token for an input variable or the `OUT` token for an output variable, the colon can immediately precede the variable name. Two examples of host variables in SQL statements are

```
#sql {select a into :a1 from t where b = :b1};
#sql {select a into :OUT a1 from t where b = :IN b1};
```

In addition to host variables, Java host expressions such as arithmetic expressions, method calls with return values, instance or class variables, array elements, conditional expressions, logical expressions, and so on can be used in SQL statements. Complicated host expressions must appear within parentheses after the colon to ensure that they are interpreted properly by SQLJ. For example, the following embedded SQL statement updates the cash balance for a particular member to a value that is 100 more than the value of the variable `x`:

```
#sql {update member
      set    cash_balance = :(x+100)
      where  mid = :y };
```

At run time, the Java expressions are evaluated and then passed on to the SQL statement.

The host variables and expressions used in SQL statements must be compatible and be convertible to and from an SQL type. Figure 6.1 gives the mapping between commonly used Oracle data types and Java types.

The Java wrapper classes `Integer`, `Long`, `Float`, and `Double` should be used instead of their primitive counterparts when there is a possibility of a `null` value being communicated from or to the database. The use of Java wrapper classes is necessary because database `null` values are converted into Java `null` references

2. The `IN`, `OUT`, and `INOUT` tokens are not case sensitive.

**Figure 6.1** Mapping between Oracle data types and Java types.

| Oracle Type | Java Type |
|---|---|
| `number, number(n), integer, integer(n)` | `int, long` |
| `number, number(n), number(n,d)` | `float, double` |
| `char, varchar2` | `java.lang.String` |
| `date` | `java.sql.Date` |
| `cursor` | `java.sql.ResultSet` or SQLJ iterator objects |

and vice versa, and it is not possible for Java primitive types to be assigned **null** references.

## 6.6 SQLJ Iterators

Processing query results, especially when they contain more than one row, requires SQLJ *iterators*. An SQLJ iterator is basically a strongly typed version of a JDBC result set and is associated with the underlying database cursor defined by an SQL query.

An SQLJ iterator declaration specifies a Java class that is automatically constructed by SQLJ. The iterator class contains instance variables and access methods that correspond to the column types and, optionally, column names of the SQL query associated with the iterator. When an SQLJ iterator is declared, programmers can specify either just the data types of the selected columns (*positional iterators*) or both the data types and column names of the selected columns (*named iterators*).

An iterator object is instantiated by executing an SQL query, and the SQL data that are retrieved into the iterator object are converted to Java types specified in the iterator declaration.

### 6.6.1 Named Iterators

A named iterator is declared by specifying both the data types and the column names that correspond to the select list items of the query. The syntax for declaring a named iterator is as follows:

```
#sql iterator iterName
     (colType1 colName1, ..., colTypeN colNameN);
```

where **iterName** is a name given to the iterator, each **colTypeI** is a valid Java type, and each **colNameI** is a select list item name in the query to be associated with this iterator. It is important that the names and types in the iterator match the names and types in the SQL query. The select list items do not have to be in the same order as they appear in the iterator, but each select list item must appear in the iterator.

As an example, consider the problem of printing a monthly report of all transactions for a particular member in the investment portfolio database. The SQL query to produce such a listing is

```
select to_char(trans_date,'DD-MON-YYYY') tdate,
       trans_type ttype, symbol, quantity
       price_per_share, commission, amount
from   transaction
where  mid = :mmid and
       to_char(trans_date, 'MM') = :month and
       to_char(trans_date, 'YYYY') = :year;
```

where **:mmid** is the host variable holding the member ID and **:month** and **:year** are the host variables for the month and year for which the listing is to be produced. The SQLJ iterator for this query is defined[3] as follows:

```
#sql iterator TReport(String tdate, String ttype,
                      String symbol, double quantity,
                      double price_per_share,
                      double commission, double amount);
```

Notice that the SQL query select list items and their data types match the column names and types mentioned in the iterator. SQLJ automatically creates a class, called **TReport**, for the iterator. This class has methods to access the values of each of the columns mentioned in the iterator.

Once the named iterator has been declared, it can be instantiated and populated in the Java program with the following statements:

```
TReport t = null;
#sql t =
  {select to_char(trans_date,'DD-MON-YYYY') tdate,
          trans_type ttype, symbol, quantity,
          price_per_share, commission, amount
   from   transaction
```

3. The iterator declaration is typically made in the Java source file for the application that uses it. However, since the iterator declaration defines a separate Java class, it must be declared outside of the application class.

```
where  mid = :mmid and
       to_char(trans_date, 'MM') = :month and
       to_char(trans_date, 'YYYY') = :year };
```

The individual rows of the iterator can be accessed using the **next** method. Whenever **next** is called, it retrieves the next row from the iterator and returns **true**. If there is no next row, it returns **false**.

Once a row has been retrieved, the individual columns of the row can be accessed using the accessor methods that are automatically created by SQLJ. These accessor methods have the same names as the column names mentioned in the iterator declaration, which are also the names of the select list items.

The iterator is equipped with a **close** method, which should be called once the iterator has been processed.

The following is the **printReport** method, which prints a monthly report of transactions for a particular member. The member ID is an input parameter to this method. The method reads the month and year from the user and generates the monthly report of transactions.

```
private static void printReport(String mmid)
    throws SQLException, IOException {

  String mmid2;
  try {
    #sql { select distinct mid
           into   :mmid2
           from   transaction
           where  mid = :mmid };
  } catch (SQLException e) {
      System.out.println("No transactions");
      return;
    }
  String month = readEntry("Month(01 - 12): ");
  String year  = readEntry("Year(YYYY): ");

  TReport t = null;
  #sql t={select to_char(trans_date,'DD-MON-YYYY') tdate,
                 trans_type ttype, symbol, quantity,
                 price_per_share, commission, amount
          from   transaction
          where  mid = :mmid and
                 to_char(trans_date, 'MM') = :month and
                 to_char(trans_date, 'YYYY') = :year};
```

```
    // Print Report Header
    writeSpaces(15);
    System.out.println("MONTHLY TRANSACTION REPORT");
    writeSpaces(21);
    System.out.println(month + "/" + year);
    writeDashes(68); System.out.println();
    System.out.print("Date"); writeSpaces(9);
    System.out.print("Type"); writeSpaces(2);
    System.out.print("Symbol"); writeSpaces(5);
    System.out.print("Shares"); writeSpaces(5);
    System.out.print("PPS"); writeSpaces(4);
    System.out.print("Commission"); writeSpaces(2);
    System.out.println("Amount");
    writeDashes(68); System.out.println();

    while(t.next()) {
      System.out.print(t.tdate() + "  ");
      writeEntryRight(t.ttype(),6);
      writeSpaces(3);
      writeEntryLeft(t.symbol(),6);
      writeEntryRight(twoDigit(t.quantity()),10);
      writeEntryRight(twoDigit(t.price_per_share()),10);
      writeEntryRight(twoDigit(t.commission()),10);
      writeEntryRight(twoDigit(t.amount()),10);
      System.out.println();
    }
    writeDashes(68); System.out.println();
    t.close();
  }

  static String twoDigit(double f) {
    boolean neg = false;
    if (f < 0.0) {
      neg = true;
      f = -f;
    }
    long dollars = (long) f;
    int cents = (int) ((f - dollars) * 100);
    String result;
```

```
    if (cents <= 9)
      result = dollars + ".0" + cents;
    else
      result = dollars + "." + cents;
    if (neg)
      return "-" + result;
    else
      return result;
  }

  private static void writeEntryLeft(String text, int width) {
    System.out.print(text);
    for (int i = 0; i < (width - text.length()); i++)
        System.out.print(" ");
  }

  private static void writeEntryRight(String text, int width) {
    for (int i = 0; i < (width - text.length()); i++)
        System.out.print(" ");
    System.out.print(text);
  }

  private static void writeSpaces(int width) {
    for (int i = 0; i < width; i++)
      System.out.print(" ");
  }

  private static void writeDashes(int width) {
    for (int i = 0; i < width; i++)
      System.out.print("-");
  }
```

After the iterator has been populated using an SQL query, the `next` method is used to fetch the next row. For each row fetched, the accessor methods `t.tdate`, `t.symbol`, and so on are used to access the individual columns of the row.

The `printReport` method makes use of a dollar-formatting static method called `twoDigit`. It also uses other string-formatting methods including `writeSpaces`, `writeDashes`, `writeEntryLeft`, and `writeEntryRight`.

## 6.6.2 Positional Iterators

A positional iterator is declared in a manner similar to a named iterator, except that column names are not specified. The Java types into which the columns of the SQL query are retrieved must be compatible with the data types of the SQL data. The names of the SQL select list items are irrelevant.

Since the names of columns are not specified, the order in which the positional Java types are mentioned in the iterator must exactly match the order of the data types of the select list items of the SQL query.

The positional iterator is instantiated and populated in the same manner as a named iterator, but the manner in which the data are retrieved from the iterator is different. For a positional iterator, a `fetch into` statement is used along with a call to the `endFetch` method to determine if the last row has been reached. The syntax of the `fetch into` statement is as follows:

```
#sql { fetch :iter into :var1, ..., :vark };
```

where `iter` is the name of the positional iterator and `var1`, ..., `vark` are host variables of appropriate types that will receive values from the select list items. These variables must be in the same order as their corresponding select list items in the select list of the query.

The `endFetch` method, when applied to the iterator object, initially returns `true` before any rows have been fetched. It then returns `false` after each successful row fetch and finally returns `true` after the last row has been fetched. The call to `endFetch` must be done before the row is fetched, because the `fetch` does not throw an `SQLException` when trying to fetch after the last row.

As an example, consider the problem of printing the current, ask, and bid prices of a security, given a substring of the security name. The query to accomplish this task is

```
select symbol,cname,current_price,ask_price,bid_price
from   security
where  upper(cname) like :cn;
```

where `cn` is the substring of the security name. The positional iterator for this query is declared as follows:

```
#sql iterator PQuote(String,String,double,Double,Double);
```

Note that the Java data type corresponding to the `current_price` column is declared as `double` since this database column cannot contain `nulls`.

The method to get the price quote for a security given a substring of the company name is

```
public static void getPriceQuoteByCname(String cn)
      throws SQLException, IOException {
  double cp=0.0;
  Double ap=null,bp=null;
  PQuote p = null;
  String sym = "";

  #sql p = {select symbol, cname, current_price,
                   ask_price, bid_price
            from   security
            where  upper(cname) like :cn};
  #sql {fetch :p into :sym,:cn,:cp,:ap,:bp};
  if (!p.endFetch()) {
    System.out.print("Symbol"); writeSpaces(12);
    System.out.print("Company"); writeSpaces(17);
    System.out.print("Last Sale"); writeSpaces(4);
    System.out.print("Ask"); writeSpaces(7);
    System.out.println("Bid");
    writeDashes(74);
    System.out.println();
    while (!p.endFetch()) {
      writeEntryLeft(sym,9);
      writeEntryLeft(cn,30);
      writeEntryRight(twoDigit(cp),10);
      if (ap == null)
        System.out.print("      null");
      else
        writeEntryRight(twoDigit(ap.doubleValue()),10);
      if (bp == null)
        System.out.print("      null");
      else
        writeEntryRight(twoDigit(bp.doubleValue()),10);
      System.out.println();
      #sql {fetch :p into :sym,:cn,:cp,:ap,:bp};
    };
    writeDashes(74);
  } else {
      System.out.println("No company matches the name");
    }
  p.close();
}
```

## 6.7 Dynamic SQL Using JDBC

SQLJ by nature caters to static SQL. However, there are situations when dynamic SQL is needed. The dynamic SQL API for SQLJ is JDBC; hence, an SQLJ program may contain both SQLJ and JDBC code. Access to JDBC connections and result sets from an SQLJ program may be necessary for finer control. The two paradigms interoperate seamlessly with each other.

It is possible to extract a JDBC `Connection` object from an SQLJ default connection context as follows:

```
DefaultContext cx1 =
    Oracle.getConnection("jdbc:oracle:oci8:@","raj","raj",true);
DefaultContext.setDefaultContext(cx1);
Connection conn = DefaultContext.getDefaultContext()
                                 .getConnection();
```

and for an SQLJ connection context to be initialized with a JDBC connection as shown here:

```
#sql context PortDB;

Connection conn = DriverManager.getConnection(
        "jdbc:oracle:oci8:book/book");
PortDB cx2 = new PortDB(conn);
```

The following is an SQLJ program that performs dynamic SQL using JDBC. A JDBC `Connection` object is extracted from the SQLJ `DefaultContext` object and a dynamic query is performed.

```
import sqlj.runtime.*;
import sqlj.runtime.ref.*;
import java.sql.*;
import java.io.*;
import oracle.sqlj.runtime.*;

public class Dsqlj {
  public static void main (String args[])
     throws SQLException {

    DefaultContext cx1 =
        Oracle.getConnection("jdbc:oracle:oci8:@",
                             "book","book",true);
```

```
    DefaultContext.setDefaultContext(cx1);

    // Get a JDBC Connection object from an
    // SQLJ DefaultContext object
    Connection conn = DefaultContext.getDefaultContext()
                                    .getConnection();

    String sym = readEntry("Enter symbol substring: ")
                 .toUpperCase();
    String query =
      "select cname,current_price,ask_price,bid_price "+
      "from   security " +
      "where symbol like '%" + sym + "%'";
    Statement stmt = conn.createStatement();
    ResultSet rs = stmt.executeQuery(query);

    while (rs.next())  {
      System.out.println("\n  Company Name   = " +
                         rs.getString(1));
      System.out.println("  Last sale at   = " + rs.getString(2));
      String ap = rs.getString(3);
      if (rs.wasNull())
        System.out.println("  Ask price      = null");
      else
        System.out.println("  Ask price      = " + ap);
      String bp = rs.getString(4);
      if (rs.wasNull())
        System.out.println("  Bid price      = null");
      else
        System.out.println("  Bid price      = " + bp);
    }
    rs.close();
    stmt.close();
  }
}
```

JDBC result sets and SQLJ iterators can also be easily transformed from one to the other. To convert an SQLJ iterator into a JDBC result set, use the **getResultSet** method on an iterator object, as follows:

```
QueryIterator q;
#sql q = {<sql query>};
ResultSet rs = q.getResultSet();
```

To convert the result set back into an SQLJ iterator, use the **CAST** operator, as follows:

```
ResultSet rs = ....;
#sql q = {CAST :rs};
```

## 6.8 Calling PL/SQL from Within SQLJ

When using SQLJ with Oracle, it is possible to embed PL/SQL anonymous blocks in the Java program. For example, the following program, containing an anonymous PL/SQL block, populates a table called **squares**, defined as follows:

```
create table squares (n number, nsquared number);
```

with the first 10 squares of natural numbers.

```
import sqlj.runtime.*;
import sqlj.runtime.ref.*;
import java.sql.*;
import java.io.*;
import oracle.sqlj.runtime.*;

public class Anon {
  public static void main (String args[]) throws SQLException {
    DefaultContext cx1 =
        Oracle.getConnection("jdbc:oracle:oci8:@",
                             "book","book",true);
    DefaultContext.setDefaultContext(cx1);
    #sql {
      declare
        n number;
      begin
        delete from squares;
        n := 1;
        while (n <= 10) loop
          insert into squares values (n,n*n);
          n := n + 1;
        end loop;
```

```
      end;
    };
  }
}
```

It is also possible for SQLJ programs to make calls to PL/SQL stored procedures and functions. Consider the following PL/SQL stored procedure:

```
create or replace procedure latestTransactionDate
  (midd in member.mid%type, ldate out date) is
begin
  select max(trans_date)
  into   ldate
  from   transaction
  where  mid = midd;
end;
```

This stored procedure takes as input a member ID, `midd`, and returns the latest transaction date for that member in the output parameter `ldate`. This stored procedure can be called in an SQLJ program as follows:

```
String m = "10000";
java.sql.Date lastDate;
#sql {CALL latestTransactionDate(:in m, :out lastDate)};
```

Note the `IN` and `OUT` qualifiers for the parameters and also the data type matching between Java types and the corresponding PL/SQL types in the stored procedure. The whole SQLJ program that makes a call to the stored procedure is shown here:

```
import sqlj.runtime.*;
import sqlj.runtime.ref.*;
import java.sql.*;
import java.io.*;
import oracle.sqlj.runtime.*;

public class Plsql1 {
  public static void main (String args[]) throws SQLException {
    DefaultContext cx1 =
        Oracle.getConnection("jdbc:oracle:oci8:@",
                             "book","book",true);
    DefaultContext.setDefaultContext(cx1);

    String m = readEntry("Member ID: ");
```

```
        java.sql.Date lastDate;
        #sql {CALL latestTransactionDate(:in m, :out lastDate)};
        System.out.println("The last transaction date is " +
                           lastDate);
    }
}
```

PL/SQL stored functions are invoked in a similar manner as stored procedures, except that the **CALL** token is replaced by the **VALUES** token and the function call is enclosed within parentheses. Also, the result of the function call is assigned to a Java variable. Consider the PL/SQL stored function called **avgPP**, which takes as input a member ID and a security symbol and computes the average purchase price that the member paid for the current shares held in his or her portfolio. For all the **buy** transactions the member has for a particular security, a weighted average price is computed. Finally, a commission of 1% is applied to the total amount to compute the average purchase price. The PL/SQL stored function is

```
create or replace function avgPP(
    mid in member.mid%type,
    sym in security.symbol%type)
  return transaction.price_per_share%type as
  cursor c1 is
    select trans_type, quantity, price_per_share
    from transaction
    where mid = avgPP.mid and
          symbol = sym
    order by trans_date;
  q transaction.quantity%type := 0.0;
  a transaction.price_per_share%type := 0.0;
begin
  for c1_rec in c1 loop
    if (c1_rec.trans_type = 'buy') then
      a := ((q * a) +
            (c1_rec.quantity*c1_rec.price_per_share))/
           (q + c1_rec.quantity);
      q := q + c1_rec.quantity;
    else
      q := q - c1_rec.quantity;
    end if;
  end loop;
```

```
  return (1.01 * a);  -- Commission of 1%
end;
```

A call to the avgPP function in SQLJ is

```
String m = readEntry("Member ID: ");
String sym = readEntry("Symbol: ");
double pp;
#sql pp = { VALUES(avgPP(:in m, :in sym)) };
```

Notice the IN tokens, the VALUES token, and the assignment of the result of the function call to a Java variable. An SQLJ program that illustrates the stored function call is shown here:

```
import sqlj.runtime.*;
import sqlj.runtime.ref.*;
import java.sql.*;
import java.io.*;
import oracle.sqlj.runtime.*;

public class Plsql2 {
  public static void main (String args[])
     throws SQLException {
    DefaultContext cx1 =
        Oracle.getConnection("jdbc:oracle:oci8:@",
                             "book","book",true);
    DefaultContext.setDefaultContext(cx1);

    String m = readEntry("Member ID: ");
    String sym = readEntry("Symbol: ");
    double pp;
    #sql pp = { VALUES(avgPP(:in m, :in sym)) };
    System.out.println("The average purchase price " +
        "member " + m + " paid for security " +
        sym + " is " + pp);
  }
}
```

# 6.9 Investment Portfolio Database Application

In this section, an application program that interfaces with the investment portfolio database is presented. A few of the methods of this application have already been discussed earlier in the chapter. The remaining are presented here.

The program begins by presenting the following main menu:

```
(a) Member Login
(b) New Member Sign-in
(q) Quit
```

A new member can use option (b) to create a new account. This option prompts the new member for name, address, email, and password. It creates a new account and informs the new member of the account number.

An existing member can use option (a) to log into his or her account. The member is prompted for an account number and password. Upon successful login, the member is shown the following menu of options:

```
(a) View Portfolio
(b) Print Monthly Report
(c) Update Your Record
(d) Price Quote
(e) Buy a Stock
(f) Sell a Stock
(q) Quit
```

## *The* main *and* printMenu *Methods*

The main method, along with the printMenu method, are

```
public static void main (String args[])
  throws Exception,IOException,SQLException {

  String user = readEntry("userid  : ");
  String pass = readEntry("password: ");
  DefaultContext cx1 =
      Oracle.getConnection("jdbc:oracle:oci8:@",
                           user,pass,false);
  DefaultContext.setDefaultContext(cx1);

  boolean done = false;
  do {
```

```
      printMenu();
      String ch = readEntry("Type in your option: ");
      switch (ch.charAt(0)) {
        case 'a': memberLogIn();
                  break;
        case 'b': newMember();
                  break;
        case 'q': done = true;
                  break;
        default : System.out.println("Invalid option");
      }
    } while(!done);
  }

  private static void printMenu() {
    System.out.println("\nINVESTMENT PORTFOLIO " +
                       "TRACKING SYSTEM \n");
    System.out.println("(a) Member Log in ");
    System.out.println("(b) New Member Sign in ");
    System.out.println("(q) Quit. \n");
  }
```

After prompting the user for the Oracle user ID and password,[4] the **main** method opens a connection to the Oracle schema for the specified user and presents the main menu. Notice that the **autoCommit** mode is set to **false** in the **Oracle.getConnection** method call. It reads the user's option and calls the appropriate method.

## *The* memberLogin *and* printMenu1 *Methods*

The **memberLogIn** method prompts the user for an account number and password. It then verifies that the account number exists and that the password provided is correct. This is accomplished by a simple SQL query against the **member** table using the **select-into** statement. After the account number and password are verified, a member menu of options is presented. The program then reads the user's selected option and processes it appropriately by calling the corresponding method. The **memberLogIn** and **printMenu1** methods are

4. Note that there are two sets of user IDs and passwords. The first is the Oracle user ID and password, which enables the user to use the application program, and the second is the member's account ID and password, which enables the member to access his or her account.

```
private static void memberLogIn()
    throws SQLException, IOException {
  String mmid1,pass1;
  String mmid2 = readEntry("Account#: ");
  String pass2 = readEntry("Password: ");

  try {
    #sql {select mid, password
          into   :mmid1, :pass1
          from   member
          where  mid = :mmid2 and password = :pass2};
  } catch (SQLException e) {
      System.out.println("Invalid Account/Password");
      return;
    }

  boolean done = false;
  do {
    printMenu1();
    String ch = readEntry("Type in your option: ");
    switch (ch.charAt(0)) {
      case 'a': viewPortfolio(mmid1);
                break;
      case 'b': printReport(mmid1);
                break;
      case 'c': updateMember(mmid1);
                break;
      case 'd': getPriceQuote();
                break;
      case 'e': buyStock(mmid1);
                break;
      case 'f': sellStock(mmid1);
                break;
      case 'q': done = true;
                break;
      default : System.out.println("Invalid option ");
    }
  } while(!done);
}
```

```
private static void printMenu1() {
  System.out.println("\n    MEMBER OPTIONS \n");
  System.out.println("(a) View Portfolio ");
  System.out.println("(b) Print Monthly Report ");
  System.out.println("(c) Update Your Record ");
  System.out.println("(d) Price Quote ");
  System.out.println("(e) Buy a Stock ");
  System.out.println("(f) Sell a Stock ");
  System.out.println("(q) Quit \n");
}
```

### *The* newMember *Method*

The `newMember` method prompts the user for all the pertinent information and then performs an SQL `insert` statement. The sequence object `m_seq` is used to generate a new account number. The code for `newMember` is

```
private static void newMember()
     throws SQLException, IOException {
  String pass, fn, ln, addr, email;
  double cash;

  fn    = readEntry("Enter first name: ");
  ln    = readEntry("Enter last name: ");
  addr  = readEntry("Enter address: ");
  email = readEntry("Enter email: ");
  pass  = readEntry("Enter password : ");
  cash  = Double.valueOf(readEntry("Enter initial cash : "))
              .doubleValue();
  try {
    String mmid;
    #sql {select m_seq.nextval into :mmid from dual};
    #sql {insert into member values
              (:mmid,:pass,:fn,:ln,:addr,:email,:cash)};
    #sql {commit};
    System.out.println("\nYour Account Number is " + mmid);
  } catch (SQLException e) {
      System.out.println("Could not add member");
      System.out.println("Message:"+e.getMessage());
      return;
    }
}
```

### *The* `viewPortfolio` *Method*

The `viewPortfolio` method takes as input the member ID and prints the member's portfolio of stocks owned, their purchase prices, their current values, and the gain or loss. A summary for the entire portfolio is also produced. A sample portfolio view is shown in Figure 6.2.

**Figure 6.2** Portfolio view output.

```
                      MY PORTFOLIO

Symbol  Shares   Current    Market    Purchase    Gain    %Gain
                   PPS      Value       Price
-----------------------------------------------------------------
ORCL    100.00    23.25    2325.00   2708.06   -383.06   -14.14
SEG     100.00    30.00    3000.00   3244.62   -244.62    -7.53
-----------------------------------------------------------------
  Security Value:          5325.00   5952.68   -627.68   -10.54
  Cash Balance:           94047.33
  Account Value:          99372.33
-----------------------------------------------------------------
```

The query used to compute the current portfolio for a member is as follows:

```
select s.symbol, p.quantity, s.current_price,
       (p.quantity * s.current_price) MarketValue,
       (p.quantity * avgPP(:mid,p.symbol)) PurchasePrice
from   security s, portfolio p
where  p.mid = :mid and s.symbol = p.symbol;
```

This query uses the SQL view `portfolio`, defined in Section 2.5. It makes use of a PL/SQL stored function called `avgPP`, which was introduced in Section 6.8. The `viewPortfolio` method uses a named SQLJ iterator called `PView`, shown here:

```
#sql iterator PView(String symbol, double quantity,
   double current_price, double MarketValue,
   double PurchasePrice);
```

This iterator is used to retrieve all the stocks currently owned by the member, and the information retrieved is formatted and sent to the screen. The `viewPortfolio` method is shown next:

```
private static void viewPortfolio(String mid)
     throws SQLException, IOException {
  String mmid;
  try {
    #sql { select distinct mid
           into   :mmid
           from   portfolio
           where  mid = :mid };
  } catch (SQLException e) {
      System.out.println("Empty Portfolio");
      return;
    }

  PView p = null;
  #sql p =
    {select s.symbol,p.quantity,s.current_price,
            (p.quantity*s.current_price) MarketValue,
            (p.quantity*avgPP(:mid,p.symbol))
            PurchasePrice
     from   security s, portfolio p
     where  p.mid=:mid and s.symbol=p.symbol};

  double cash;
  #sql {select cash_balance
        into   :cash
        from   member
        where  mid = :mid};

  // Print Report Header
  writeSpaces(30);
  System.out.println("MY PORTFOLIO");
  System.out.print("Symbol"); writeSpaces(5);
  System.out.print("Shares"); writeSpaces(3);
  System.out.print("Current"); writeSpaces(4);
  System.out.print("Market"); writeSpaces(6);
  System.out.print("Purchase"); writeSpaces(6);
  System.out.print("Gain"); writeSpaces(7);
  System.out.println("%Gain"); writeSpaces(21);
  System.out.print("PPS"); writeSpaces(7);
  System.out.print("Value"); writeSpaces(8);
```

```
System.out.println("Price");
writeDashes(76); System.out.println();

double gainLoss, pGL;
double total_pp = 0.0, total_mv = 0.0;

while(p.next()) {
  writeEntryLeft(p.symbol(),8);
  writeEntryRight(twoDigit(p.quantity()),9);
  writeEntryRight(twoDigit(p.current_price()),9);
  writeEntryRight(twoDigit(p.MarketValue()),12);
  total_mv += p.MarketValue();
  writeEntryRight(twoDigit(p.PurchasePrice()),12);
  total_pp += p.PurchasePrice();
  gainLoss = p.MarketValue() - p.PurchasePrice();
  pGL = (gainLoss/p.PurchasePrice() ) * 100;
  writeEntryRight(twoDigit(gainLoss),12);
  writeEntryRight(twoDigit(pGL),12);
  System.out.println();
}

p.close();

writeDashes(76); System.out.println();
System.out.print("  Security Value: ");
writeSpaces(8);
writeEntryRight(twoDigit(total_mv),12);
writeEntryRight(twoDigit(total_pp),12);
writeEntryRight(twoDigit(total_mv - total_pp),12);
writeEntryRight(twoDigit(((total_mv - total_pp)/
                              total_pp)*100),12);
System.out.println();

System.out.print("  Cash Balance: ");
writeSpaces(12);
writeEntryRight(twoDigit(cash),10);
System.out.println();

System.out.print("  Account Value: ");
```

```
    writeSpaces(11);
    writeEntryRight(twoDigit(cash + total_mv),10);
    System.out.println();

    writeDashes(76);
  }
```

### *The* updateMember *Method*

The `updateMember` method allows the member to make changes to his or her password, address, or email. The method first performs a query to obtain the current password, address, and email of the member. It then prompts the user for new information and issues an SQL `update` statement to make the changes. The code follows:

```
  private static void updateMember(String mmid)
       throws SQLException, IOException {

    String password, address, email, answer;
    try {
      #sql { select password, address, email
             into   :password,:address,:email
             from   member
             where  mid = :mmid };
    } catch (SQLException e) {
        System.out.println("Invalid member account");
        return;
      }

    boolean change = false;
    System.out.println("password : " + password);
    answer = readEntry("Change password?(y/n):").toLowerCase();
    if (answer.equals("y")) {
      password = readEntry("Enter new password : ");
      change = true;
    }

    System.out.println("address : " + address);
    answer = readEntry("Change address?(y/n):").toLowerCase();
```

```
    if (answer.equals("y")) {
      address = readEntry("New address : ");
      change = true;
    }

    System.out.println("email : " + email);
    answer = readEntry("Change email?(y/n):").toLowerCase();
    if (answer.equals("y")) {
      email = readEntry("New email : ");
      change = true;
    }

    if (change) {
      #sql { update member
               set password = :password,
                   address = :address,
                   email = :email
               where mid = :mmid };
      #sql {commit};
      System.out.println("Updated successfully ");
    }
    else
      System.out.println("No changes made");
  }
```

## *The* getPriceQuote *and* getPriceQuoteBySymbol *Methods*

The **getPriceQuote** method allows the member to obtain a quote on a security based on the symbol or the company name of the security. It prompts the user for the option and calls the appropriate method for obtaining the quote. The **getPriceQuoteByCname** method, for obtaining a price quote for a security given a substring of the company name, was presented earlier in this chapter. The **getPriceQuoteBySymbol** method prompts the member for the exact security symbol and then performs a simple SQL query using the **select-into** statement. The code for these two methods follows:

```
  private static void getPriceQuote()
         throws SQLException, IOException {

    System.out.println("(a) Look up by symbol");
    System.out.println("(b) Look up by company name");
```

```
    String ch =
      readEntry("Type in your option: ").toLowerCase();

    String sym="",cn="";
    switch (ch.charAt(0)) {
      case 'a' :
        sym = readEntry("Enter symbol : ").toUpperCase();
        getPriceQuoteBySymbol(sym);
        break;
      case 'b' :
        cn = "%" + readEntry("Enter search string: ")
                   .toUpperCase() + "%";
        getPriceQuoteByCname(cn);
        break;
    }
  }

  public static void getPriceQuoteBySymbol(String sym)
         throws SQLException, IOException {
    double cp=0.0;
    Double ap=null,bp=null;
    String cn = "";

    try {
      #sql { select cname,current_price,ask_price,bid_price
             into   :cn,:cp,:ap,:bp
             from   security
             where  symbol = :sym };
    } catch (SQLException e) {
        System.out.println("Invalid symbol.");
        return;
      }
    System.out.println("\n  Company Name   = " + cn);
    System.out.println("  Last sale at   = " + cp);
    if (ap == null)
      System.out.println("  Ask price      = null");
    else
      System.out.println("  Ask price      = " + ap);
    if (bp == null)
      System.out.println("  Bid price      = null");
```

```
    else
      System.out.println("  Bid price      = " + bp);
  }
```

### *The* buyStock *and* buyConfirmation *Methods*

The `buyStock` method first prompts the member for the security symbol. It then obtains the current bidding price from the database. If the bidding price is `null`, it uses the current selling price. After this, the method obtains the number of shares from the user. Using this information, it computes the total cost of this transaction, including a 1% commission on the total value. The current cash balance for the member is obtained to see if the member has enough funds to pay for the transaction. The method then asks the member for a confirmation by calling the `buyConfirmation` method. Upon confirmation, a new row is added to the `transaction` table for this transaction. The cash balance in the `member` table is also updated. The code for `buyStock` and `buyConfirmation` follows:

```
  public static void buyStock(String mid)
      throws SQLException, IOException {

    double currentprice = 0.0;
    Double bidprice;

    String symbol  = readEntry("Symbol   : ");
    try {
      #sql { select current_price, bid_price
             into   :currentprice, :bidprice
             from   security
             where  symbol = :symbol };
    } catch (SQLException e) {
        System.out.println("Stock information not found");
        return;
      }

    double quantity =
      Double.valueOf(readEntry("Quantity: ")).doubleValue();

    double price,total, cash;
    if (bidprice == null)
      price = currentprice;
    else
```

```
    price = bidprice.doubleValue();

  double commission =
    Double.valueOf(twoDigit(0.01 * (price * quantity)))
          .doubleValue();
  total =
    Double.valueOf(twoDigit((price * quantity) + commission))
          .doubleValue();

  #sql { select cash_balance
         into   :cash
         from   member
         where  mid = :mid };

  if (total > cash) {
    System.out.println("Sorry, not enough money!");
    return;
  }

  if(!buyConfirmation(symbol,quantity,price)){
    System.out.println("Transaction was not processed");
    return;
  }

  #sql { insert into transaction values
           (:mid,:symbol,sysdate,'buy',:quantity,
            :price,:commission,:total) };
  #sql {commit};

  #sql { update member
         set    cash_balance = cash_balance - :total
         where  mid = :mid };
  #sql {commit};

  System.out.println("Successful Buy Transaction");
}

public static boolean buyConfirmation(
         String symbol, double quantity,
         double price_per_share) {
```

```
    double total = price_per_share * quantity;
    System.out.println("\n\t\tConfirmation:");
    System.out.println(quantity + " shares of " + symbol +
        " at $" + price_per_share + " per share.");
    System.out.println("\n");
    System.out.println("\tTotal price of shares:    " +
                       total+"\n");
    System.out.println("\tCommission:              +"
                        + (0.01 * total));
    System.out.println("\t                         " +
                       " -------------");
    System.out.println("\tTotal:                    $" +
                        (1.01 * total));
    System.out.println();
    for (;;) {
      String answer =
        readEntry("Accept?  (Y or N): ").toUpperCase();
      switch (answer.charAt(0)) {
        case 'Y': return true;
        case 'N': return false;
        default:   break;
      }
    }
  }
```

The `sellStock` and `sellConfirmation` methods are very similar.

# Exercises

## *Investment Portfolio Database Problems*

6.1 Write an SQLJ program that populates the `security` table by fetching data from the following Web address:

```
http://www.quicken.com/investments/quotes/?symbol=XXXX
```

where `XXXX` is the security symbol. This Web page contains information about the company in detail; however, only the name of the company and the current price need to be retrieved. The `ask_price` and `bid_price` values should be set to `null`. To solve this problem, you should import the **java.net** package and use the following Java method that fetches the HTML content of a Web page into a Java string variable:

```
private static String getHTMLContent(URL hp) throws Exception {
  BufferedReader data = new BufferedReader(new
    InputStreamReader(hp.openStream()));
  String line, sHtml="";

  while ((line = data.readLine()) != null)
    sHtml += line + "\n";
  data.close();
  return sHtml;
}
```

This method should be invoked as follows:

```
URL hp = new URL(
  "http://www.quicken.com/investments/quotes/?symbol="+XXXX);
String sHtml = getHTMLContent(hp);
```

where **XXXX** is a string variable containing the security symbol. To retrieve data for more than one security, you should create a constant array of security symbols within the Java program, loop through the array and, for each symbol in the array, fetch data from the Web page and store it in the database.

6.2 Write an SQLJ program that updates the **security** table for the current, ask, and bid prices by fetching data from the following Web address:

```
http://www.quicken.com/investments/quotes/?symbol=XXXX
```

where **XXXX** is the security symbol. This Web page contains a variety of information about the price quotes for the company. However, only the current, ask, and bid prices need to be retrieved.

6.3 Write an SQLJ program to implement the following menu for analysts:

```
(1) Rate a stock
(2) Update a stock rating
(3) Quit
```

The program should begin by prompting the analyst for an ID and password. After verifying the ID and password, the program should display the menu. To rate a stock, the program should prompt the analyst for the symbol and the rating. To update a stock rating, the program should prompt the analyst for the symbol, display the current rating by the analyst, and prompt the analyst for a new rating.

6.4 Implement the following two additional menu options for the `MEMBER OPTIONS` of the application presented in Section 6.9:

```
(g) View Ratings for a Security
(h) View Five Top-Rated Securities
```

The program should prompt the user for the security symbol for the view rating option and then display all the ratings by analysts for that symbol. The output should resemble the following:

```
Symbol: ORCL
Company: Oracle Corporation
Ratings:  Strong Buy  (rating = 1) : *****
          Buy         (rating = 2) : **
          Hold        (rating = 3) : **
          Sell        (rating = 4) :
          Strong Sell (rating = 5) :
          Consensus:       1.67
```

The number of stars after each rating is the number of analysts rating the security with that particular rating. The consensus mean is the weighted mean of the ratings. The View Five Top-Rated Securities option should display the top five securities based on the consensus mean value, in increasing order of consensus mean.

# CHAPTER 7

# Oracle Web Programming with Java Servlets

Java servlet technology provides Web application developers with a simple yet powerful means to extend a Web server's functionality. Servlets provide a platform-independent method for building Web-based applications, without the performance limitations of Common Gateway Interface (CGI) programs. In addition, servlets have access to the entire family of Java APIs, including the JDBC API to access relational databases. This allows for complicated Web applications to be designed and developed in a relatively quick and easy manner.

JavaServer Pages (JSP) technology is an extension of the servlet technology that makes it easier to combine fixed template data with dynamic content. JSP technology allows Web developers and designers to rapidly develop and maintain information-rich, dynamic Web pages. JSP technology separates the user interface from content generation, enabling designers to change the overall page layout without altering the underlying dynamic content. With JSP, the application or business logic can reside in server-based resources such as JavaBeans. This allows the separation of the presentation logic from the business logic, and as a consequence, JSP technology makes it faster and easier than ever to build Web-based applications.

Oracle9*i* provides an integrated environment to program Java servlets as well as JSP pages that access an Oracle database. Servlets are modules of Java code that run in a server application. Servlets are not tied to a specific client-server protocol, but they are most commonly used with HTTP, and the word "servlet" is often used to mean "HTTP servlet." Servlets make use of the Java standard extension classes in the packages `javax.servlet` (the basic servlet framework) and `javax.servlet.http` (the HTTP extension). Typical uses for HTTP servlets include processing data submitted by an HTML form, providing dynamic content available in a database to HTTP clients, and managing state information on top of the stateless HTTP. Servlets have a distinct advantage over traditional CGI programming in that they use an efficient process model. CGI programs spawn a separate process for each request, whereas servlets do not run in a separate process. Servlets also stay in memory between two requests and thus are more efficient than CGI programs.

This chapter introduces Web application development using Java servlet and JSP technologies in the context of Oracle databases. A Web shopping application that uses an Oracle9*i* database is used to illustrate servlet programming throughout the chapter. In this application, customers can become members, sign on to the Web application, search for products to purchase, add items of interest to a shopping cart, view and edit their shopping carts, and check out. Toward the end of the chapter, basic JSP programming is introduced via a series of examples.

## 7.1 A Simple Servlet

The following servlet illustrates the basic framework for writing servlet code. This servlet, called `Simple`, produces an HTML page with a message and the current time of day.

```
import java.io.*;
import javax.servlet.*;
import javax.servlet.http.*;

public class Simple extends HttpServlet {
   public static final String TITLE = "Hello World Servlet";

   public void doGet (HttpServletRequest request,
                      HttpServletResponse response)
        throws ServletException, IOException {
    // Set Content-Type header
    response.setContentType("text/html");

    // Get the channel with the requesting client
    PrintWriter out = response.getWriter();

    // Write the HTML code
    out.println("<HTML>");
```

```
      out.println("<HEAD>");
      out.println("<TITLE>" + TITLE + "</TITLE>");
      out.println("</HEAD>");
      out.println("<BODY BGCOLOR=\"#FFFFFF\">");
      out.println("<CENTER>");
      out.println("<H1>" + TITLE + "</H1>");
      out.println("<H3>The local time is: ");
      out.println("<font color='#FFBBCC'>" +
                  new java.util.Date() + "</font>");
      out.println("</H3>");
      out.println("</CENTER>");
      out.println("</BODY>");
      out.println("</HTML>");
    }
  }
```

Several points to note about the code are

- All servlets need to import the three packages `java.io`, `javax.servlet`, and `javax.servlet.http`. These contain all the basic classes required to develop a servlet.
- The `Simple` class being developed in this example extends the `HttpServlet` class. This is the standard way to develop servlets.
- The `HttpServlet`'s `doGet` method is overridden in the `Simple` class. This method is indirectly invoked by the `HttpServlet`'s `service` method. The `service` method is invoked each time the servlet is called from a client browser or program. Typically, the `service` method will process the HTTP request and call the appropriate `doXXX` method, where `XXX` may be either `Get`, `Post`, or one of the other HTTP request types.
- The `doGet` method has two parameters: `request`, of object type `HttpServletRequest`, and `response`, of object type `HttpServletResponse`. All information about the HTTP request being processed by the servlet is available in the `request` object, and it is the responsibility of the servlet to return an appropriate HTML response to the request in the `response` object.
- The first statement in the `doGet` method sets the `Content-Type` HTTP header to `text/html`. Next, the `doGet` method creates a `PrintWriter` object out of the `response` object. Subsequently, the method uses this `PrintWriter` object to send HTML code to the client requesting the service.

## 7.2 HTTP Servlet API Basics

The most commonly used classes and methods of the HTTP servlet API are introduced in this section.

### 7.2.1 The `HttpServlet` Class

The `HttpServlet` class is an abstract class that serves as a framework for developing HTTP servlets. This class is extended to create application-specific servlets. Methods available within the `HttpServlet` class are

- ```
  public void service(ServletRequest req,
                      ServletResponse res)
        throws ServletException, IOException
  ```

  This method is automatically invoked when an HTTP request is made from the browser. This method handles dispatching requests to the protected HTTP-specific `service` method.

- ```
  protected void doGet(HttpServletRequest req,
                       HttpServletResponse res)
           throws ServletException, IOException
  ```

  This method is automatically invoked by the `service` method when it receives a `GET` request from the client. Application-specific servlets must override this method to handle `GET` requests.

- `doPut`, `doPost`, `doOptions`, `doTrace`, and `doDelete`

  These methods have similar specifications to `doGet` and are also automatically invoked when a particular HTTP request is received. Application-specific servlets must override these methods to handle the corresponding HTTP requests. The `doPost` method is usually overridden by application-specific servlets that process the HTML form data being submitted. The other `doXXX` methods are rarely overridden.

- ```
  protected void service(HttpServletRequest req,
                         HttpServletResponse res)
           throws ServletException, IOException
  ```

  The public `service` method dispatches requests to this `service` method. This method dispatches requests to `doGet`, `doPost`, and other handler methods based on the type of request. If this method is overridden, no handlers are called.

- `protected long getLastModified(HttpServletRequest req)`
  ```

This method returns the date and time (expressed as milliseconds since midnight, January 1, 1970 GMT) at which the content produced by the servlet was last modified. Negative values indicate that the time is not known.

Application-specific servlets extend the `HttpServlet` class and, in most cases, override the `doGet` and `doPost` methods.

### 7.2.2 The `HttpServletRequest` Class

The `HttpServletRequest` class extends the basic `ServletRequest` class, providing additional functionality for HTTP servlets. It includes support for cookies and session tracking and access to HTTP header information. The `HttpServletRequest` object encapsulates information about a single client request, including request parameters and their values. Some of the important and commonly used methods available in the `HttpServletRequest` class are

- `public abstract String getParameter(String name)`. This method returns the value of the named parameter as a `String`. It returns `null` if the parameter does not exist and returns an empty string if the parameter exists but without a value. The value is guaranteed to be in its normal decoded form. If the parameter has more than one value, use the `getParameterValues` method instead.
- `public abstract Enumeration getParameterNames()`. This method returns the parameter names as an `Enumeration` of `String` objects. It returns an empty `Enumeration` object if the request has no parameters.
- `public abstract String[] getParameterValues(String name)`. This method returns all the values of the named parameter as an array of `String` objects. It returns `null` if the parameter does not exist. If the parameter has a single value, it is returned as an array of length 1.

Besides these three commonly used methods, a variety of other methods return information such as the method used in the request (`getMethod`), the remote client IP address (`getRemoteAddr`), and so on.

### 7.2.3 The `HttpServletResponse` Class

The `HttpServletResponse` class extends the basic `ServletResponse` class to allow manipulation of HTTP-specific data including response headers and status codes. Application-specific servlets use the `HttpServletResponse` object to send data back to the client. The servlet engine creates this object and passes it to the servlet's `service` method. To send character data (such as HTML code), one must use the `PrintWriter` object returned by the `getWriter` method. Two of the commonly used methods in the `HTTPServletResponse` class are

- `public abstract PrintWriter getWriter() throws IOException`. This method returns a `PrintWriter` object for writing character-based responses. This is the method used to obtain the communication channel to write HTML code to the client.
- `public abstract void setContentType(String type)`. This method sets the content type of the response to the specified type. For standard HTML responses, the value of `type` is `text/html`.

Besides these two methods, there are several other methods available to set HTTP headers, set status codes, and so on.

## 7.3 Web Shopping Application

A Web shopping application that accesses an Oracle9*i* database is introduced in this section. The mail-order database introduced earlier in this book has been adapted to suit the purposes of the Web shopping application. Several changes were made to the database schema: removed the `employees` table and any references to it, removed the `zipcodes` table and included the `city` column in the `customers` table, added several new columns to the `customers` table, added a new table called `cart` to hold a shopping cart, and added several new sequence objects. The portions of the mail-order schema that have been changed follow:

```
create sequence cust_seq start with 1000;

create table customers (
   cno      number(10) not null primary key,
   cname    varchar2(30),
   street   varchar2(50),
   city     varchar2(30),
   state    varchar2(30),
   zip      number(5),
   phone    char(12),
   email    varchar2(50),
```

```
   password varchar2(15),
   u_access varchar2(50),
   l_access Date);

create sequence cart_seq start with 1;

create table cart(
   cartno  number(10) not null,
   cno     number(10) not null references customers,
   pno     number(5) not null references parts,
   qty     integer check(qty >= 0) not null,
   primary key (cartno, pno));

create sequence o_seq start with 100;

create table orders (
   ono      number(5) not null primary key,
   cno      number(10) references customers,
   received date,
   shipped  date);
```

Customers of the Web shopping application use the Web shopping login page, shown in Figure 7.1, to sign on to the system. The HTML code that produces the login page is

```
<html>
<head>
<title>Web Shopping Application Login Page</title>
</head>
<body bgcolor="#FFFFCC">
<center>
<font size=5><font color=blue>
Welcome to the Web Shopping Application System</font>
<P><P><P>
<form action=
"http://tinman.cs.gsu.edu:7777/book/servletss/ProcesCustLogin"
method="POST">
<table border=1>
<tr>
```

**Figure 7.1** Web shopping application—customer login page.

```
<td>Customer Number:</td>
<td><INPUT TYPE="text" name="customerId" size=10
     maxlength=20 value=""></td>
</tr>
<tr>
<td>Password:</td>
<td><INPUT TYPE="password" name="password" size=10
     maxlength=20 value=""></td>
</tr>
</table>
<INPUT TYPE="submit" value="Proceed">
<P>
If you are not a customer, sign in
<A HREF="NewCustomer.html">here.</A>
</form>
</center>
</body>
</html>
```

After a successful login, the customer sees a three-frame Web page with the top frame containing a header, the left-hand frame containing a set of menu options, and the right-hand frame containing space to display the results of selected menu options. This three-frame Web page is shown in Figure 7.2.

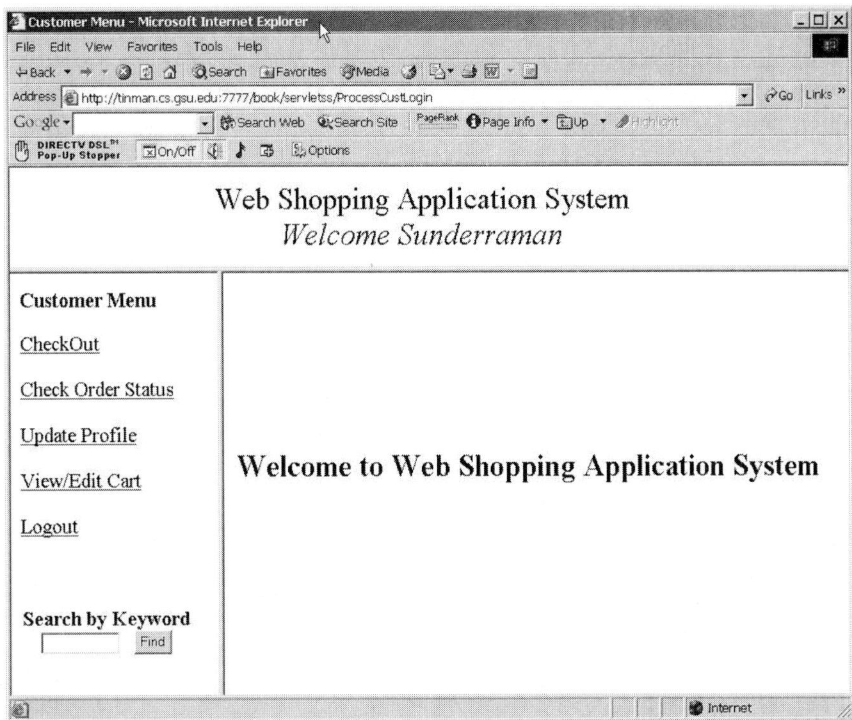


**Figure 7.2** Three-frame Web page—Web shopping application.

## 7.4 HTML Form Processing in Servlets

In this section, the `ProcessCustLogin` servlet is described. This servlet illustrates basic HTML form processing as well as typical authentication of users of online systems. The servlet code follows:

```
// Import relevant packages
import java.io.*;
import java.sql.*; // Import JDBC classes
import javax.servlet.*;
import javax.servlet.http.*;

// ProcessCustLogin subclasses HttpServlet
public class ProcessCustLogin extends HttpServlet {
```

```
public static Connection conn;
public static Statement stmt;
public static String uAccess;

// doGet passes request to doPost
public void doGet (HttpServletRequest request,
                   HttpServletResponse response)
            throws ServletException, IOException {
   doPost(request,response);
}

// doPost - main work of the servlet done here
public void doPost (HttpServletRequest request,
                    HttpServletResponse response)
            throws ServletException, IOException {

  // Set Content-Type header and obtain PrintWriter
  response.setContentType("text/html");
  PrintWriter out = response.getWriter();

  // Retrieve form parameters
  String cno[] = request.getParameterValues("customerId");
  String pwd[] = request.getParameterValues("password"); }

  // Load JDBC driver
  try {
    Class.forName("oracle.jdbc.driver.OracleDriver");
  } catch(ClassNotFoundException e)
      out.println("Error loading the Driver:");
      return;
    }

  // Make JDBC Connection to Oracle9i database
  Connection conn = null;
  try {
    conn = DriverManager.getConnection (
      MyUtilities.CONNECTSTRING,MyUtilities.ID,
      MyUtilities.PASSWORD);
  } catch (SQLException e1) {
      out.println("Error connecting to Oracle:");
```

```
    return;
  }
if (conn == null) {
  out.println("Null Connection");
  return;
}

// Create JDBC Statement object
Statement stmt = null;
try {
  stmt = conn.createStatement ();
} catch (SQLException e) {
    out.println("Error in createStatement");
    try {conn.close(); catch (SQLException e2) {};
    return;
  }

// Get password from customers table for given cno
ResultSet rset = null;
String query =
  "select password from customers where cno='"+
   cno[0]+"'";
try {
  rset = stmt.executeQuery(query);
} catch (SQLException e) {
    out.println("executeQuery " + e.getMessage());
    return;
  }

// If password available and correct, set u_access
// value in customers table to unique string; otherwise,
// return error messages
boolean OK = false;
try {
  if (rset.next()) {
    if (pwd[0].equals(rset.getString(1))) {
      OK = true;
      String update =
        "update customers set u_access ="+
        "to_char(sysdate, 'DDMONYYYYHHMISS'),"+
```

```
          "l_access = sysdate where cno='"+
           cno[0]+"'";
        int nrows;
        try {
          nrows = stmt.executeUpdate(update);
        } catch (SQLException e) {
            out.println("executeQuery");
            return;
          }
        } else {
            out.println("Invalid Password <br>");
          }
    } else {
        out.println("Invalid Customer Id <br>");
      }
  } catch (SQLException e) {
      out.println("Error in executeQuery");
      return;
    }

    // Get u_access value from database for passing to next
    // HTML page
    String query1 =
       "select u_access from customers where cno='"+
       cno[0]+"'";
    try {
      rset = stmt.executeQuery(query1);
    } catch (SQLException e) {
        out.println("executeQuery " + e.getMessage());
        return;
      }
    try {
      if (rset.next()) {
        uAccess = rset.getString(1);
      }
    } catch (SQLException e) {
        out.println("executeQuery");
        return;
      }
```

```
    // Close Statement and Connection objects
    try {
      stmt.close();
      conn.close();
    } catch (SQLException e) {
        out.println("executeQuery");
        return;
      }

   // If login OK, publish the three-frame member menu page.
   // Pass customerId and u_access values to servlets
   // (Banner and WSMenu) that publish individual frames.
   if (OK) {
     out.println("<html>");
     out.println("<head>");
     out.println("<title>Customer Menu</title>");
     out.println("</head>");
     out.println("<frameset rows=\"10%,*\">");
     out.println("<frame src=\"http://tinman.cs.gsu.edu:"+
           "7777/book/servletss/Banner?customerId="+
           cno[0]+ "&uAccess=" + uAccess + "\">");
     out.println("<frameset cols=\"25%,*\">");
     out.println("<frame src=\"http://tinman.cs.gsu.edu:"+
           "7777/book/servletss/WSMenu?customerId="+
           cno[0]+ "&uAccess=" + uAccess + "\">");
     out.println("<frame src=\"http://tinman.cs.gsu.edu"+
           "/~raj/WSWelcome.html\" name=\"view_window\">");
     out.println("</frameset>");
     out.println("</frameset>");
     out.println("</html>");
   }
   out.close();
 }

// This method returns information about this servlet
public String getServletInfo() {
   return "This Servlet processes Customer Login";
}
}
```

The `ProcessCustLogin` servlet overrides the `doGet` and `doPost` methods of `HttpServlet`. The `doGet` method simply passes the request off to `doPost`. The `doPost` method does all the work of processing the customer login. Since the HTML form invoking this servlet uses a `POST` method, it is not necessary to override the `doGet` method—it will not be called. However, it is a common practice among servlet programmers to override the `doGet` method anyway, as shown.

The `doPost` method obtains the HTML parameters `customerId` and `password` from the `HttpServletRequest` object. It also sets the response content type and obtains the `PrintWriter` object so that it can write HTML code to the client. After loading JDBC drivers and creating JDBC `Connection` and `Statement` objects, the `doPost` method makes a query to obtain the password for the particular customer from the database. It then compares the database password with the one submitted via the HTML form. If both match, the `customers` table is updated with a unique string for the `u_access` column and with the current `sysdate` value for the `l_access` column. This basically registers with the database that the customer has signed in. After this, the three-frame HTML page is published. Notice that two of the three frames require the `customerId` and `uAccess` values as parameters. These parameters are passed to the two servlets, `Banner` and `WSMenu`, as parameters within the URL itself. These servlets publish the individual frames as required.

## 7.5 SearchParts and AddToCart

In this section, two additional servlets, `SearchParts` and `AddToCart`, are discussed. These servlets illustrate further concepts in user authentication, session control, and handling dynamic HTML form parameters.

The `SearchParts` servlet responds to the Search by Keyword menu option available to the user in the left-hand frame of the three-frame Web page shown earlier. The servlet's responsibility is to list all the parts in the database whose names contain the keyword as a substring, as shown later in Figure 7.3. This listing also serves as a mechanism for the user to add items of interest to his or her shopping cart. Along with each part in the listing, a text box field is available for the user to make selections for the shopping cart.

The `SearchParts` servlet code is shown next. Each section of code is augmented with comments to make the servlet code easy to follow. Also, any piece of code that repeats from the previous servlet is not shown.

```
// Import relevant packages
   .
   .
   .
```

```
public class SearchParts extends HttpServlet {
   public static Connection conn;
   public static Statement stmt;
   public static String uAccess;

// Define the doGet method
.
.
.
// doPost handler; does the main work of the servlet
public void doPost (HttpServletRequest request,
                    HttpServletResponse response)
       throws ServletException, IOException {

  // Set the response Content-Type header and obtain
  // PrintWriter object from response object
  .
  .
  .
  // Extract HTML form parameters being submitted to this
  // servlet into local Java arrays

  String cno[] = request.getParameterValues("customerId");
  String uAccess[] = request.getParameterValues("uAccess");
  String keyword[] = request.getParameterValues("keyword");

  // Load JDBC driver
  // Create JDBC Connection object
  // Create JDBC Statement object
  .
  .
  .
  // Query database to get u_access value for customer
  ResultSet rset = null;
  String query0 = "select u_access from customers " +
                  "where cno='"+ cno[0]+"'";
  try {
    rset = stmt.executeQuery(query0);
  } catch (SQLException e) {
      out.println("Error executeQuery");
      return;
    }
```

```
// If no u_access value found or is not same as u_access
// HTML form parameter received from previous page,
// report error
try {
  if (!(rset.next())) {
    out.println("Not authorized to access this page");
    return;
  }
  else if (!(uAccess[0].equals(rset.getString(1)))) {
    out.println("Not authorized to access this page");
    return;
  }
  else { // u_access matched
    // Check to see if it has been more than 10 minutes
    // since user last accessed the system. If more than
    // 10 minutes have elapsed, expire session and
    // reset u_access value to null.
    String sTrack = "select 1440*(sysdate-l_access) "+
         "from customers where cno='" + cno[0] + "'";
    rset = stmt.executeQuery(sTrack);
    rset.next();
    if (rset.getDouble(1) > 10.0) {
      out.println("<html>");
      out.println("<head>");
      out.println("<title>Session Expired</title>");
      out.println("</head>");
      out.println("<body bgcolor=\"#FFFFCC\">");
      int nRows = stmt.executeUpdate("update customers "+
         "set u_access = null where cno='"+cno[0] + "'");
      out.println("Your session has expired!<BR> "+
          "Please login again to continue shopping.");
      out.println("</center>");
      out.println("</body>");
      out.println("</html>");
      return;
    }

    // Everything checked out fine; proceed to process
    // request. Set l_access value in customers table.
    int nRows = stmt.executeUpdate("update customers "+
```

```
   "set l_access=sysdate where cno='"+cno[0] + "'");

// Query for parts matching keyword
String query1 = "select pno,pname,price from parts "+
        "where upper(pname) like '%"+
         keyword[0].toUpperCase()+"%'";
try {
   rset = stmt.executeQuery(query1);
} catch (SQLException e) {
    out.println("Error executeQuery");
    return;
  }

// Publish HTML page containing search results.
// Create an HTML form that contains text boxes for
// customers to use to add items to shopping cart.
out.println("<html>");
out.println("<head>")
out.println("<title>Add To Cart</title>");
out.println("</head>");
out.println("<body bgcolor=\"#FFFFCC\">");
out.println("<center>");
out.println("<B>Search Results</B><BR><BR>");
out.println("<form method=\"POST\" action=\"" +
             MyUtilities.URLPREFIX + "AddToCart\">");
out.println("<input type = \"hidden\""+
    "name=\"customerId\" value=\"" + cno[0] + "\">");
out.println("<input type = \"hidden\""+
    "name=\"uAccess\" value=\""+uAccess[0]+"\">");
out.println("<table border=2>");
out.println("<tr>");
out.println("<th>PNO</th>");
out.println("<th>PNAME</th>");
out.println("<th>PRICE</th>");
out.println("<th>QTY</th>");
out.println("</tr>");
while (rset.next()) {
  out.println("<tr>");
  out.println("<td>" + rset.getString(1) + "</td>");
  out.println("<td>" + rset.getString(2) + "</td>");
```

```
          out.println("<td>" + rset.getString(3) + "</td>");
          out.println("<td><input type=\"text\" name=\"" +
             rset.getString(1)+"\" size=3 maxlength=10>"+
             </td>");
          out.println("</tr>");
        }
        out.println("</table><BR><BR>");
        out.println("<input type=\"submit\" " +
                    "value=\"Add to Cart\">");
        out.println("</form>");
        out.println("</center>");
        out.println("</body>");
        out.println("</html>");
      }
    } catch (SQLException e) {
        out.println("Error executeQuery");
        return;
      }

    // Close Statement and Connection objects
    .
    .
    .
  } // End of doPost
  } // End of SearchParts
```

The Web page produced by the **SearchParts** servlet is shown in Figure 7.3. The Web page contains an HTML form with an arbitrary number of text boxes, one for each part that was returned by the keyword search servlet. These text boxes are named with the part numbers.

The customer can enter quantities of parts they would like to add to the shopping cart and submit the HTML form to the **AddToCart** servlet, shown here:

```
  // Import relevant packages
  .
  .
  .
  import java.util.*;
  .
  .
  .
  public class AddToCart extends HttpServlet {
  .
  .
  .
```

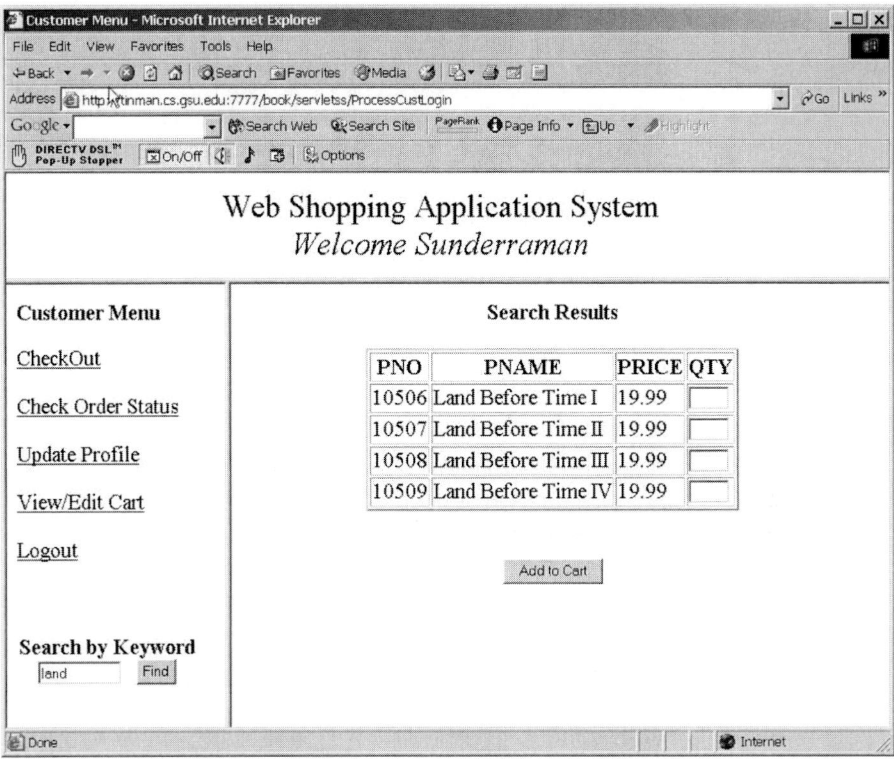


**Figure 7.3** `SearchParts` servlet output page.

```
public void doPost (HttpServletRequest request,
                    HttpServletResponse response)
      throws ServletException, IOException {
  // Code for extracting customerId and u_access values,
  // loading JDBC driver, creating Connection and Statement
  // objects, processing u_access value, etc., goes here.
  .
  .
  .
  // Since we do not know the number of parts and their
  // part numbers, we will use the getParameterNames
  // method on the request object and figure out what is
  // coming in as parameters.
  int numParams = 0;
  String parts[] = new String[100];
```

```
String pValues[] = new String[100];
Enumeration enum = request.getParameterNames();
while (enum.hasMoreElements()) {
  String x = (String) enum.nextElement();
  if (x.equals("uAccess") || x.equals("customerId"))
    continue;
  parts[numParams] = x;
  pValues[numParams] = request.getParameter(
                          parts[numParams]);
  numParams++;
}
// Print first part of Web page HTML code
out.println("<html>");
out.println("<head>");
out.println("<title>Add To Cart</title>");
out.println("</head>");
out.println("<body bgcolor=\"#FFFFCC\">");

rset = null;
String query1 = "select cartno from cart where cno='"+
                 cno[0]+"'";
rset = stmt.executeQuery(query1);
boolean hasCart = false;
int cartNum = 0;
if (rset.next()) { // cart exists for customer
  hasCart = true;
  cartNum = rset.getInt(1);
  for (int i = 0; i < numParams; i++) {
    if (pValues[i].equals(""))
      continue;
    String query11 = "select qty from cart where cno='"+
                     cno[0]+"' and pno=" + parts[i];
    rset = stmt.executeQuery(query11);
    if (rset.next()) { // Need to update
      String query12 = "update cart set qty = qty + " +
                       pValues[i] + " where cno = '" +
                       cno[0]+"' and pno = "+parts[i];
      nRows = stmt.executeUpdate(query12);
    }
    else { // Need to insert
```

```
              String query2 = "insert into cart values (" +
                              cartNum + ",'" + cno[0] + "'," +
                              parts[i] + "," + pValues[i] + ")";
              nRows = stmt.executeUpdate(query2);
            }
          }
        }
        else { // Create new cart for customer
          String query31 = "select cart_seq.nextval from dual";
          rset = stmt.executeQuery(query31);
          rset.next();
          cartNum = rset.getInt(1);
          for (int i = 0; i < numParams; i++) {
            if (pValues[i].equals(""))
              continue;
            String query32 = "insert into cart values ("+
                      cartNum + ",'" + cno[0] + "'," + parts[i] +
                      "," + pValues[i] + ")";
            nRows = stmt.executeUpdate(query32);
          }
        }

        out.println("Successfully added items to your cart<P>");
        out.println("If you would like to view/edit your cart,"+
           "please use the View/Edit Link<P>"+
           "If you are done shopping, please use "+
           "the CheckOut link<P>");
        out.println("</body>");
        out.println("</html>");
      } // else ends here

      } catch (SQLException e) {
          out.println("executeQuery");
          return;
        }
      // Code to close objects goes here
      .
      .
      .
      } // End of doPost
      } // End of AddToCart
```

The Web page produced after a successful addition to the cart is shown in Figure 7.4.

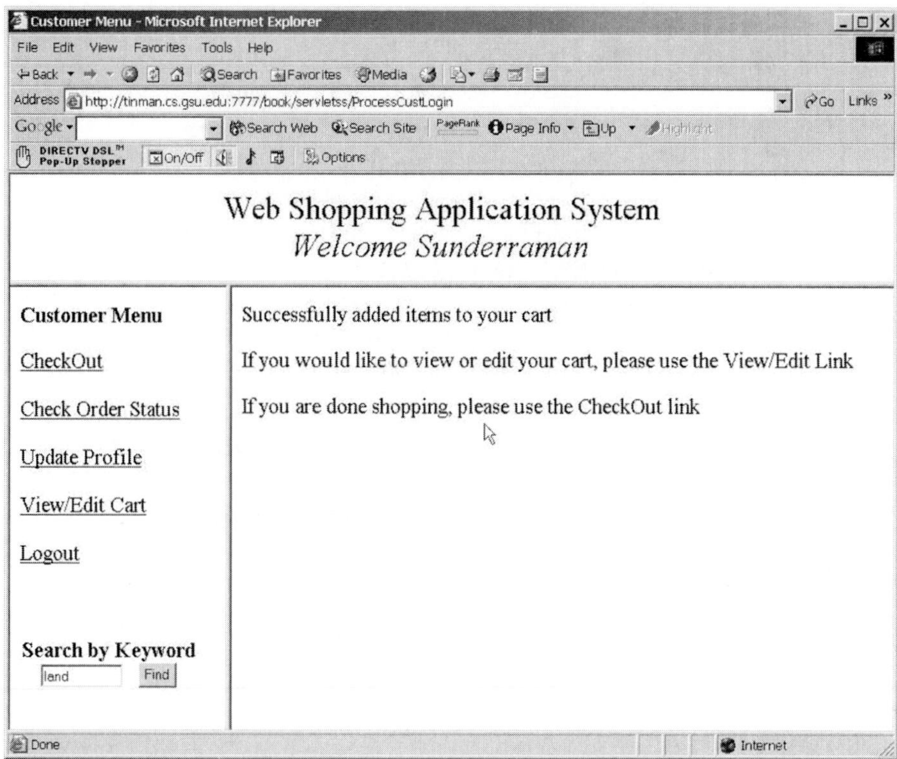


**Figure 7.4** Output of `AddToCart` servlet.

## 7.6 Oracle's Dynamic HTML Generation Package

In all of the previous examples, the HTML code generated by the servlets was sent to the `PrintWriter` object as Java `String` objects. This mechanism is a bit cumbersome, especially when the HTML code is complex and long. To alleviate some of the programmer's burden, Oracle provides a dynamic HTML generation package, called `oracle.html`. This package provides a means of creating HTML code in an object-oriented manner. It provides a set of classes that abstracts away the details of HTML (especially the HTML tags). In this approach, a Web page is viewed as an object that contains other HTML objects, such as a head and a body.

These objects in turn may contain other HTML objects—for example, the HTML body object may contain HTML list objects, HTML table objects, and so forth. This object-oriented approach simplifies the task of generating HTML and makes servlets easier to write and maintain.

## 7.6.1 A Simple Example

The following is a simple example illustrating the object-oriented construction of the HTML code generated by a servlet called `jwebTest`. This servlet receives three parameters, `firstName`, `lastName`, and `numIterations`, and prints a dynamic HTML page using the values of these parameters.

```
// Import relevant packages, including oracle.html
import java.io.*;
import javax.servlet.*;
import javax.servlet.http.*;
import oracle.html.*;

public class jwebTest extends HttpServlet {
  public void doGet(HttpServletRequest req,
                    HttpServletResponse res)
          throws ServletException, IOException {
    doPost(req,res);
  }
  public void doPost(HttpServletRequest req,
                     HttpServletResponse res)
          throws ServletException, IOException {

    // Retrieve parameters
    String firstName = req.getParameter("firstName");
    String lastName = req.getParameter("lastName");
    int numIter = Integer.parseInt(
                    req.getParameter("numIterations"));
    PrintWriter out = res.getWriter();
    res.setContentType("text/html");

    // Create HtmlHead and HtmlBody objects and use them
    // to create an HtmlPage object
    HtmlHead hd = new HtmlHead("Simple Example");
    HtmlBody bd = new HtmlBody();
```

```
HtmlPage hp = new HtmlPage(hd, bd);

// Add level-2 heading to HTML body object
bd.addItem(new SimpleItem(
     "This is a Heading (level2)").setHeading(2));

// Add simple text item in bold font to HTML body
// and add a line break <BR> tag
bd.addItem(new SimpleItem(
     "Good Day! "+firstName+" "+lastName).setBold())
  .addItem(SimpleItem.LineBreak);

// Add a horizontal line to HTML body
bd.addItem(SimpleItem.HorizontalRule);

// Write more text to HTML body; illustrates <em> tag
for (int i = 0; i < numIter; i++) {
  bd.addItem(new SimpleItem("This is Line ")
                 .setEmphasis())
                 .addItem(new SimpleItem(i))
                 .addItem(SimpleItem.LineBreak);
}

// Add a horizontal line to HTML body
bd.addItem(SimpleItem.HorizontalRule);

// Create a Preformat text object
Preformat pre = new Preformat();
pre.addItem("void main () (\n")
   .addItem("  int i;\n\n")
   .addItem("  i = 5;\n")
   .addItem("  printf(\"i = %d\n\",i);\n")
   .addItem("\n");

// Add Preformat object to HTML body followed by
// horizontal line
bd.addItem(pre);
bd.addItem(SimpleItem.HorizontalRule);

// Send HTML page to PrintWriter object for servlet
```

```
      // output and close PrintWriter object
      out.println(hp);
      out.close();
    }
  }
```

The general mechanism to create a dynamic HTML document is to create the following objects:

```
HtmlHead hd = new HtmlHead("Document Title");
HtmlBody bd = new HtmlBody();
HtmlPage hp = new HtmlPage(hd, bd);
```

Then, the `addItem` method can be used to add HTML elements to the `bd` object. Finally, when the page is ready to be printed, the following statement is used:

```
hp.print()
```

The `SimpleItem` object is used to create HTML lines of text. It is a subclass of the more general class `Item`. `SimpleItem` has three constants:

```
SimpleItem.Paragraph;
SimpleItem.LineBreak;
SimpleItem.HorizontalRule;
```

These three constants can be used to generate the paragraph, line break, and horizontal rule HTML elements, respectively. There are numerous constructors for the `SimpleItem` object, which take as input objects of most common data types, including `String`, `int`, and `float`. Many of the `Item` class methods can be applied to `SimpleItem` objects (e.g., `setBold`, `setEmphasis`, etc.).

The `Preformat` object is used to create preformatted HTML text. It is a subclass of the `CompoundItem` class, which in turn is a subclass of the `Item` class. The `addItem` method of the `CompoundItem` class can be used to add specific lines of text to the `Preformat` object, as was shown in the previous example.

## 7.6.2 HTML Form Processing

The `oracle.html` package provides the class

```
public class Form extends CompoundItem
```

for HTML form processing. Since the `Form` class has been defined as a subclass of `CompoundItem`, the `addItem` method can be applied to a `Form` object to populate it with various objects of the following types:

- CheckBox
- Radio
- Submit
- Reset
- TextField
- TextArea
- Select
- Hidden
- PasswordField

To create a Form object, the following steps must be taken:

1. Create a Form object, specifying the METHOD attribute (GET or POST) and the ACTION URL attribute.
2. Populate the Form object by creating one or more of the objects to be included in the form and then adding them to the form using the addItem method.
3. Add the Form object to the HtmlBody object.

Example 7.6.1 The following servlet, called params1, creates an HTML form with several form elements. Upon submission of the form, the form data are sent to a servlet called params2.

```
import java.io.*;
import javax.servlet.*;
import javax.servlet.http.*;
import oracle.html.*;
public class params1 extends HttpServlet {
  public void doGet(HttpServletRequest req,
                  HttpServletResponse res)
          throws ServletException, IOException {
    doPost(req,res);
  }
  public void doPost(HttpServletRequest req,
                   HttpServletResponse res)
          throws ServletException, IOException {

    PrintWriter out = res.getWriter();
    res.setContentType("text/html");
```

```
HtmlHead hd = new HtmlHead("Form Example");
HtmlBody bd = new HtmlBody();
HtmlPage hp = new HtmlPage(hd, bd);

// Create Form object
Form form1 = new Form("POST",
 "http://tinman.cs.gsu.edu:7777/raj/servlets/params2");

// Create Select object and add to form
Select select1 = new Select("sel");
select1.addOption(new Option("One"));
select1.addOption(new Option("Two"));
select1.addOption(new Option("Three"));
select1.addOption(new Option("Four"));
form1.addItem(select1);

// Introduce LineBreak and HorizontalRule tags
bd.addItem(SimpleItem.LineBreak);
form1.addItem(SimpleItem.HorizontalRule);

// Create CheckBox object and add to form
CheckBox cb1 = new CheckBox("chk", "1111");
CheckBox cb2 = new CheckBox("chk", "2222");
CheckBox cb3 = new CheckBox("chk", "3333");
CheckBox cb4 = new CheckBox("chk", "4444");
CheckBox cb5 = new CheckBox("chk", "5555");
CheckBox cb6 = new CheckBox("chk", "6666");
CheckBox cb7 = new CheckBox("chk", "7777");

form1.addItem(cb1); form1.addItem("1111");
form1.addItem(SimpleItem.LineBreak);
form1.addItem(cb2); form1.addItem("2222");
form1.addItem(SimpleItem.LineBreak);
form1.addItem(cb3); form1.addItem("3333");
form1.addItem(SimpleItem.LineBreak);
form1.addItem(cb4); form1.addItem("4444");
form1.addItem(SimpleItem.LineBreak);
form1.addItem(cb5); form1.addItem("5555");
form1.addItem(SimpleItem.LineBreak);
form1.addItem(cb6); form1.addItem("6666");
```

```
    form1.addItem(SimpleItem.LineBreak);
    form1.addItem(cb7); form1.addItem("7777");
    form1.addItem(SimpleItem.LineBreak);
    form1.addItem(SimpleItem.HorizontalRule);

    // Create Submit objects and add to form
    Submit submit1 = new Submit("opt","Option1");
    Submit submit2 = new Submit("opt","Option2");
    form1.addItem(submit1);
    form1.addItem(submit2);

    // Create Hidden parameter and add to form
    form1.addItem(new Hidden("sessionId","1234"));

    // Add form to body of HTML page
    bd.addItem(form1);

    out.println(hp);
    out.close();
 }
}
```

The form generated by the servlet `params1` contains the following objects:

- A pull-down select list, named `sel`
- Seven checkboxes, each named `chk`
- Two submit buttons, each named `opt`
- A hidden field, called `sessionId`

The user can select one of the values in the select list, check any number of checkboxes, and click one of the submit buttons to execute the form action. The Web page created by `params1` is shown in Figure 7.5.

The servlet (`params2`) that processes the form submitted by `params1` is

```
import java.io.*;
import javax.servlet.*;
import javax.servlet.http.*;
import oracle.html.*;
public class params2 extends HttpServlet {
```

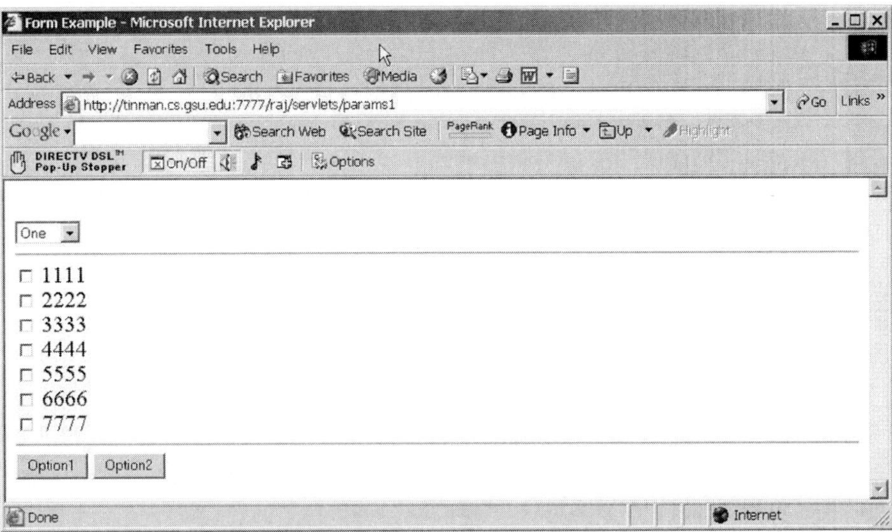


**Figure 7.5** Output of `params1` servlet.

```
public void doGet(HttpServletRequest req,
                  HttpServletResponse res)
        throws ServletException, IOException {
  doPost(req,res);
}
public void doPost(HttpServletRequest req,
                   HttpServletResponse res)
        throws ServletException, IOException {

  PrintWriter out = res.getWriter();
  res.setContentType("text/html");

  HtmlHead hd = new HtmlHead("Form Processing Output");
  HtmlBody bd = new HtmlBody();
  HtmlPage hp = new HtmlPage(hd, bd);

  // Retrieve form parameters
  String selPar[] = req.getParameterValues("sel");
  String chkPar[] = req.getParameterValues("chk");
  String optPar[] = req.getParameterValues("opt");
```

```
        String sessPar[] = req.getParameterValues("sessionId");

        // Add parameters received to body of HTML page
        for (int i=0; i<selPar.length; i++) {
          bd.addItem(new SimpleItem(selPar[i]))
            .addItem(SimpleItem.Paragraph);
        }

        for (int i=0; i<chkPar.length; i++) {
          bd.addItem(new SimpleItem(chkPar[i]))
            .addItem(SimpleItem.Paragraph);
        }

        for (int i=0; i<optPar.length; i++) {
          bd.addItem(new SimpleItem(optPar[i]))
            .addItem(SimpleItem.Paragraph);
        }

        bd.addItem(new SimpleItem(sessPar[0]))
          .addItem(SimpleItem.Paragraph);

        out.println(hp);
        out.close();
      }
    }
```

This servlet extracts the various parameters sent by **params1** and prints them to the output.

## 7.6.3 Formatting HTML Tables

The **oracle.html** package provides the **DynamicTable** class to construct HTML tables:

```
public class DynamicTable extends Table
```

**DynamicTable** is a subclass of the abstract class **Table**, which is a subclass of **Item**. Hence, a **DynamicTable** object can be included in a **CompoundItem** object such as a **Form** object or an **HtmlBody** object.

The `DynamicTable` object encapsulates a dynamically growing table. The `addRow` method is used to add new and dynamic rows to the table. To create a table, the following steps must be taken:

1. Create a `DynamicTable` object.
2. Create a `TableRow` object for each row in the table.
3. Create either a `TableDataCell` object or a `TableHeaderCell` object for each cell in a row.
4. Add cells to each row by using the `addCell` method.
5. Add all rows to the table by using the `addRow` method.

An example of dynamically creating HTML tables is shown here:

```
import java.io.*;
import javax.servlet.*;
import javax.servlet.http.*;
import oracle.html.*;

public class dtable extends HttpServlet {
  public void doGet(HttpServletRequest req,
                    HttpServletResponse res)
          throws ServletException, IOException {
    doPost(req,res);
  }
  public void doPost(HttpServletRequest req,
                     HttpServletResponse res)
          throws ServletException, IOException {

    int MAXNUM = 10;
    PrintWriter out = res.getWriter();
    res.setContentType("text/html");

    HtmlHead hd = new HtmlHead("Dynamic Table Demo");
    HtmlBody bd = new HtmlBody();
    HtmlPage hp = new HtmlPage(hd, bd);

    // Create DynamicTable object with two columns
    DynamicTable tab = new DynamicTable(2);
    tab.setBorder(2);
```

```
        // Create TableRow object and add two TableHeaderCells
        // Add row to table object.
        TableRow row = new TableRow();
        row.addCell(new TableHeaderCell("I"))
           .addCell(new TableHeaderCell("I-SQUARED"));
        tab.addRow(row);

        for (int i=1; i< MAXNUM; i++) {
          // Create TableRow object and add two TableDataCells.
          // Add row to table object.
          row = new TableRow();
          row.addCell(new TableDataCell(""+i))
             .addCell(new TableDataCell(""+i*i));
          tab.addRow(row);
        }

        // Add table object to HTML body object
        bd.addItem(tab);

        out.println(hp);
        out.close();
    }
  }
```

The preceding Java program creates an HTML table consisting of two columns with column headers and nine rows.

## 7.7 Java Server Pages

Java Server Pages is a Web scripting technology from Sun Microsystems, Inc., that allows Web developers to rapidly create dynamic Web pages. It is a presentation-layer technology sitting on top of the Java servlets model. It allows a Web developer to mix static HTML content with server-side scripting to produce dynamic output. A typical JSP script would contain HTML code with embedded Java code and other directives. JSP pages may be used in place of or in combination with Java servlets to build a Web application. JSP pages are used when there is a need for very rich presentation mixed with dynamic content. It is also quite possible to completely develop a Web application using JSP alone. In the rest of this section, JSP is introduced briefly, with several examples.

Example 7.7.1 The following is a very simple JSP script (**time.jsp**) that displays the time of day on a Web page:

```
<HTML>
<HEAD><TITLE>Time of Day</TITLE></HEAD>
<BODY>
Hello!  The time is now <%= new java.util.Date() %>
</BODY>
</HTML
```

In this script, a Java expression (**new java.util.Date()**) is enclosed within the symbols **<%=** and **%>**. In general, any valid Java expression may be included within HTML code in this manner, and its value will be evaluated at the time the JSP page is loaded. This script can be invoked on a Web browser using the URL

```
http://host:port/raj/time.jsp
```

Here, it is assumed that the JSP environment is already set up for a particular user with virtual path **/raj** and that the JSP script may be invoked by simply specifying the name of the file containing the script at the end of the URL.

One can also include entire blocks of Java code within a JSP script, as the next example shows.

Example 7.7.2 The following script receives two parameters, **name** and **num**, and displays the string "Hello, **name**" **num** times:

```
<HTML>
<HEAD><TITLE>Including Java in HTML</TITLE></HEAD>
<BODY>
<% String s = request.getParameter("name");
   int n = Integer.parseInt(request.getParameter("num"));
%>
<% for (int i=0; i<n; i++){%>
Hello, <%= s %> <BR>
<% } %>
</BODY>
</HTML>
```

The following features of JSP scripting are illustrated in this example:

- Java code can be included within JSP scripts within the symbols **<%** and **%>**. The Java code included in this manner is referred to as a *scriplet*. In this script, three fragments of Java code are included among the HTML code.

- JSP scripts can make use of four predefined variables: **request**, **response**, **out**, and **in**. These variables are the same variables that are defined within servlets.
- Java programming constructs such as **for** loops, **if-then** conditional statements, and so forth can be broken into pieces, and HTML code can be interspersed between these pieces. In this example, the **for** loop's ending brace (}) is separated from the rest of the loop, and an HTML string is included between the two pieces.

Example 7.7.3 The following JSP script contains Java code that connects to an Oracle database, performs an SQL query, and displays the results in an HTML table:

```
<HTML>
<HEAD><TITLE>JSP and Database Access Example</TITLE></HEAD>
<BODY>
<%@ page import="java.sql.*" %>
<H1>JSP Example</H1>
<H3>Querying STUDENTS table</H3>
<% try {
     Class.forName("oracle.jdbc.driver.OracleDriver");
     java.sql.Connection conn;
     conn = DriverManager.getConnection(
       "jdbc:oracle:thin:@tinman.cs.gsu.edu:1521:sid9ir2",
       "book","book");
     Statement stmt = conn.createStatement();
     ResultSet rs = stmt.executeQuery(
                         "select * from students");
%>

<TABLE BORDER=2 CELLPADDING=5 CELLSPACING=5>
   <TR><TH>SID</TH><TH>LNAME</TH><TH>FNAME</TH></TR>
<% while (rs.next()) {
     String sid   = rs.getString(1);
     String lname = rs.getString(2);
     String fname = rs.getString(3);
%>
   <TR><TD><%= sid%></TD>
       <TD><%= lname%></TD>
       <TD><%= fname%></TD>
   </TR>
<%   } // End while
     rs.close();
```

```
        stmt.close();
        conn.close();
%>
</TABLE>
<%
   } catch (Exception e) {
%>
Begin Exception Dump<P>
<% e.getMessage();
   e.printStackTrace();
%>
<%= e %>
<P>End Exception
<%
   } // End catch
%>
<HR>
</BODY>
</HTML>
```

In this example, Java code fragments for loading the JDBC driver, making a JDBC connection, executing an SQL query, and processing the result set are included within the script. The script also includes the following JSP `page` directive:

```
<%@ page import="java.sql.*" %>
```

All JSP directives are included within the symbols `<%@` and `%>`. The `page` directive with the `import` attribute is needed in the script because the JDBC API is used within the embedded Java code. Another commonly used directive is the `include` directive, which enables the inclusion of another static HTML file or another JSP script file. The syntax for the `include` directive is

```
<%@ include file="filename" %>
```

In JSP scripts, one can also include declarations of variables and methods. The next example illustrates the inclusion of a method declaration as well as an invocation of the method to process a database query.

Example 7.7.4 The following script declares a method, `processQuery`, which takes the `HttpServletRequest` object as input, extracts the parameter `price`, and queries the `parts` table of the mail-order database for all parts costing less than `price`. It then returns the rows, formatted as an HTML table, as a `String` value. The Java declarations are included within the symbols `<%!` and `%>`.

```
<%@ page import="java.sql.*" %>
<%!
  String processQuery(HttpServletRequest req)
                    throws Exception {
    String p = req.getParameter("price");
    String result =
      "<table border=2 cellpadding=5 cellspacing=5>";
    try {
      Class.forName("oracle.jdbc.driver.OracleDriver");
      java.sql.Connection conn;
      conn = DriverManager.getConnection(
        "jdbc:oracle:thin:@tinman.cs.gsu.edu:1521:sid9ir2",
        "book","book");
      Statement stmt = conn.createStatement();
      ResultSet rs = stmt.executeQuery(
        "select * from parts where price < " + p);
      result += "<tr> <th>PNO</th> <th>PNAME</th>"+
                "<th>PRICE</th> </tr>";
      while (rs.next()) {
        String pno   = rs.getString(1);
        String pname = rs.getString(2);
        String price = rs.getString(3);
        result += "<tr><td>" + pno + "</td>";
        result += "<td>" + pname + "</td>";
        result += "<td>" + price + "</td> </tr>";
      }
      result += "</table>";
      rs.close();
      stmt.close();
      conn.close();
    } catch (SQLException e) return "ERROR";
    return result;
  }
%>
<HTML>
<BODY>
<%= processQuery(request) %>
</BODY>
</HTML>
```

The preceding example is a JSP script that is almost all Java code (method declaration and invocation). To separate Java code from HTML presentation code within a JSP script, it is a good idea to encapsulate the Java code in a Java object and have the JSP script instantiate and use that object. The JSP framework provides this ability by allowing us to define *Java beans* and use them within JSP scripts. A Java bean is essentially a Java class that encapsulates data and code. The JSP framework provides the following tags to use Java beans:

- `<jsp:useBean>`. Used to instantiate a Java bean within a JSP script. The syntax is

  ```
  <jsp:useBean id="name" scope="scopeName" class="x" />
  ```

  The `id` attribute is used to name the bean instance. The `scope` attribute may have one of the following values: `page`, `request`, `session`, or `application`. The `page` value means that the bean is associated with this particular request to this page. The `request` value means that the bean is associated with this current client request, with a forwarded request, or with another included JSP script. The `session` value means that the bean is available throughout the current session, across multiple requests. The `application` value means that the bean is available in any JSP page within the same Web application. The default value for the `scope` attribute is `page`. The `class` attribute names the class file corresponding to the bean.

- `<jsp:setProperty>`. Used to set the values of bean properties. The values can be set explicitly using the syntax

  ```
  <jsp:setProperty name="beanName" property="pname" value="val" />
  ```

  The bean property values can also be set implicitly to `request` parameter values by specifying

  ```
  <jsp:setProperty name="myBean" property="*" />
  ```

- `<jsp:getProperty>`. Used to retrieve the values of bean properties. The syntax is

  ```
  <jsp:getProperty name="myBean" property="pname" />
  ```

  Usage of Java beans is illustrated in the following example.

Example 7.7.5 A JSP script that implements an SQL interpreter on the Web is developed here. The JSP script, when invoked on a Web browser, shows a text area where the user can enter an SQL query or an `update` statement. When the form is submitted, the script displays the results to the query or performs the updates and shows the same text area for the next query or update. The following is the Java bean code, which contains the **get** and **set** methods for all its variables. In addition, it implements a **getQueryResult** method that takes the SQL query or update and returns the result of the query as an HTML table–formatted string or performs the update.

```
package sqlInterpreter;
import java.sql.*;
public class sqlInterpreter {
  private String sql = ""; // Will hold SQL query or update
  private String userName = "";
  private String password = "";
  private String connectionUrl;
  private int columnCount= 0;
  // get and set methods
  public void setSql(String sql) {
    if (sql!=null)
      this.sql = sql;
  }
  public String getSql() {
    return sql;
  }
  public void setUserName(String userName) {
    if (userName!=null)
      this.userName = userName;
  }
  public String getUserName() {
    return encodeHtmlTag(userName);
  }
  public void setPassword(String password) {
    if (password!=null)
      this.password = password;
  }
  public String getPassword() {
    return encodeHtmlTag(password);
  }
  public String getConnectionUrl() {
    return encodeHtmlTag(connectionUrl);
  }
  public void setConnectionUrl(String url) {
```

```
    connectionUrl = url;
  }
  public String getQueryResult() {
    if (sql==null || sql.equals(""))
      return "";
    StringBuffer result = new StringBuffer(1024);
    try {
      Connection con = DriverManager.getConnection(
           connectionUrl, userName, password);
      Statement s = con.createStatement();
      if (sql.trim().toUpperCase().startsWith("SELECT")) {
        // Start HTML table; execute query
        result.append("<table border=1>");
        ResultSet rs = null;
        try {
          rs = s.executeQuery(sql);
        } catch(SQLException ee) {
        result.append("<br>Not well formed query<br>");
          }
        ResultSetMetaData rsmd = rs.getMetaData();
        // Write HTML table headings
        columnCount = rsmd.getColumnCount();
        result.append("<tr>");
        for (int i=1; i<=columnCount; i++) {
          result.append("<th>" + rsmd.getColumnName(i) +
                        "</th>\n");
        }
        result.append("</tr>");
        // For each row in result, produce HTML row
        while (rs.next()) {
          result.append("<tr>");
          for (int i=1; i<=columnCount; i++) {
            result.append("<td>" +
               encodeHtmlTag(rs.getString(i)) + "</td>" );
          }
          result.append("</tr>");
        }
        rs.close();
        result.append("</table>");
```

```
      }
      else { // Perform update
        int i = s.executeUpdate(sql);
        result.append("Record(s) affected: " + i);
      }
      s.close();
      con.close();
      result.append("</table>");
    }
    catch (SQLException e) {
      result.append("<B>Error</B>");
      result.append(sql + "<BR>");
      result.append(e.toString());
    }
    catch (Exception e) {
      result.append("<B>Error</B>");
      result.append("<BR>");
      result.append(e.toString());
    }
    return result.toString();
  }

  private static String encodeHtmlTag(String tag) {
  // This method encodes special HTML characters
    if (tag==null)
      return null;
    int length = tag.length();
    StringBuffer encodedTag = new StringBuffer(2 * length);
    for (int i=0; i<length; i++) {
      char c = tag.charAt(i);
      if (c=='<')
        encodedTag.append("&lt;");
      else if (c=='>')
        encodedTag.append("&gt;");
      else if (c=='&')
        encodedTag.append("&amp;");
      else if (c=='"')
        encodedTag.append("&quot;");
      else if (c==' ')
```

```
          encodedTag.append(" ");
        else
          encodedTag.append(c);
      }
      return encodedTag.toString();
    }
  }
```

The preceding code can be independently compiled, and the corresponding Java class file needs to be placed in the appropriate directory so that the JSP server can locate it.

The JSP script that uses the previous Java bean follows:

```
<%-- Instantiate sqlInterpreter Bean --%>
<jsp:useBean id="myBean"
             class="sqlInterpreter.sqlInterpreter">
</jsp:useBean>
<%-- Set Bean Properties --%>
<jsp:setProperty name="myBean" property="userName"
                 value="book"/>
<jsp:setProperty name="myBean" property="password"
                 value="book"/>
<jsp:setProperty name="myBean" property="connectionUrl"
 value="jdbc:oracle:thin:@tinman.cs.gsu.edu:1521:sid9ir2"/>
<jsp:setProperty name="myBean" property="sql"/>
<%-- Define jspInit() to Load JDBC Driver --%>
<%!
  public void jspInit() {
    try {
      Class.forName("oracle.jdbc.driver.OracleDriver");
    } catch (ClassNotFoundException e) {
      System.out.println(e.toString());
    }
  }
%>
<%-- Start HTML Code --%>
<html>
<head>
```

```
<title>SQL Interpreter on the Web</title>
</head>
<body>
<h1>SQL Interpreter on the Web</h1>
<br>Please enter your SQL statement:
<!-- Include HTML Form with textarea Element -->
<br><form method=post>
<textarea name=sql cols=40 rows=7>
</textarea>
<br>
<input type=submit>
</form>
<br>
<hr>
<!-- Invoke getQueryResult() on Bean -->
<jsp:getProperty name="myBean" property="sql"/>
<%= myBean.getQueryResult() %>
</body>
</html>
```

The script begins with instantiating a Java bean from the `sqlInterpreter` class. It then sets the properties of the bean and defines the `jspInit` method to load the JDBC driver. Then it displays the HTML code for the page, which includes an HTML form with a `textarea` element for the user to enter an SQL statement (query or update). Below the form, the `getQueryResult` method is invoked and the results are displayed. The `<jsp:getProperty>` tag is used to retrieve the query string from the bean and is displayed in the HTML page just before the query results are displayed. Here are a few points to note about the script:

- There are two types of comments included: those included between `<%--` and `--%>` (not sent to browser) and those included within `<--` and `-->` (sent to browser).
- The HTML form does not contain an `ACTION` attribute. This is because the script invoked when the form is submitted is the same script in which the form appears.

The Web page produced by this script is shown in Figure 7.6.

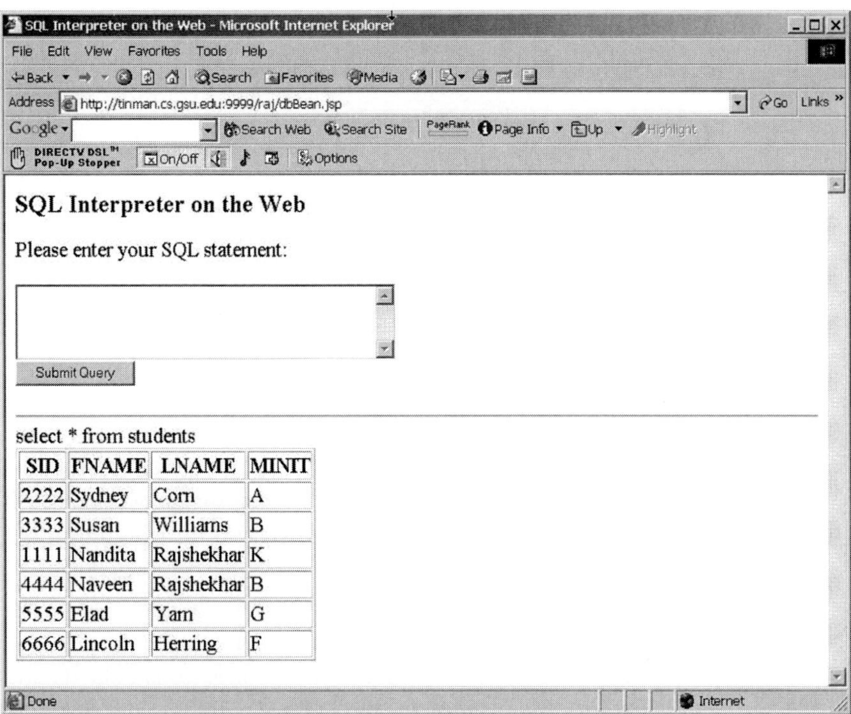


**Figure 7.6** SQL interpreter page (generated by `dbBean.jsp`).

# Exercises

7.1 Write Java servlets/JSP programs that allow a set of presenters to sign up for a seminar in a semester-long course (16 weeks) that meets once a week. Assume that the number of presenters is less than or equal to the number of weeks in a semester. The data are stored in the following two tables:

```
create table presenters (
   name varchar2(20) primary key
);
create table schedule (
   when date primary key,
   who  varchar2(20),
   foreign key (who) references presenters
);
```

Sample data in these tables is shown below:

```
insert into presenters values ('Jones');
insert into presenters values ('Smith');
.
.
.
insert into schedule(when) values('21-AUG-2002');
insert into schedule(when) values(
                    to_date('21-AUG-2002')+7);
.
.
.
```

The first servlet, called **DisplaySchedule**, should display a list consisting of a seminar date followed by the name of the person who has signed up to make a presentation on that date or a pull-down list of names of people who have not yet signed up for a presentation. The initial value in the pull-down list should be blank. The list should be followed by a submit button for signing up. A presenter who has not yet signed up will visit the page displayed by this servlet and choose his or her name against the date when he or she would like to present the seminar. After choosing the date, the presenter will submit his or her choice. A second servlet, called **ProcessSchedule**, should take this choice, update the database, and display the updated schedule confirming the choice of the presenter.

7.2 Write Java servlets/JSP programs to implement a best **n** out of m grading components problem for the grade book database. Assume that a particular course has several similar grading components, such as **quiz1**, **quiz2**, . . . , **quizm**, each weighted equally. The best **n** of these m scores is to be considered for the purpose of evaluating the final grade. Assume that the weight of the original quiz is w. The weight of each of the new components will be (m/**n**)*w. The database manipulation will involve two steps: (1) reduce to 0 the weights of the original components, and (2) add **n** new components and populate the scores for these new components with the **n** best scores from the old components.

A series of servlets/JSP programs need to be designed for this problem. The first servlet/JSP page will display a pull-down list of term and line number values for courses in the database. The term and line number values should appear as one string separated by a colon. The user will choose one course and submit the HTML form. The second servlet/JSP page will receive the term/line number string and display a list of component names along with their weights, with a checkbox prefixing each component name. At the end, the servlet/JSP page will display a text box labeled Best How Many and a submit button. The user will check each component of the group of components that he or she wants to manipulate and enter a number in the text box that is less than the number of components in the group. Upon submission of this form, a third servlet or JSP page will perform the manipulation requested by the user and report a success. Appropriate error handling should be incorporated in each of the servlets or JSP pages.

7.3 Write Java servlets/JSP programs to implement the following features of an online portfolio management system based on the **Portfolio** database:

- *New member registration.* This servlet/JSP page should collect all new member information (including the password chosen by the user) from an HTML form and update the database. It should create a unique member ID and inform the user of this ID.
- *Member sign-in.* This servlet/JSP page reads ID and password information from an HTML form and authenticates it with the database. If the ID and password are correct, it should display a two-frame web page with menu options in the left-hand frame for Price Quote, Trade, and View Portfolio. The right-hand frame should be used for subsequent display of intermediate and final screens for the three menu options.
- *Price quote.* This servlet/JSP page reads the symbol from a text box HTML element (which the user enters before clicking the Price Quote menu option). It then queries the database for the ask, bid, and last trade prices and displays the information in the right-hand frame.
- *Trade.* Upon choosing this menu option, the user is shown a form in the right-hand frame containing a text box in which to enter the symbol of the security to trade, two radio buttons (for buy and sell), and a text box in which to enter the number of shares. A submit button labeled Trade also appears in the form. Another servlet/JSP page reads this information and executes the trade. Appropriate error processing should be undertaken.
- *View portfolio.* Upon choosing this menu option, the user's portfolio should be displayed in a nicely formatted manner in the right-hand frame.

7.4 Consider the bibliography database represented by the following two tables:

```
create table articles (
     aid varchar2(20),     -- article ID
     jname varchar2(200), -- journal name
     vol number(2),        -- volume
     num number(2),        -- number
     spage number(4),      -- start page
     epage number(4),      -- end page
     title varchar2(256), -- title of the article
     primary key (aid)
);
create table authors (
```

```
        aid varchar2(20),      -- article ID
        aname varchar2(50),    -- author name
        primary key (aid,aname),
        foreign key (aid) references articles
);
```

The **articles** table stores information about articles appearing in journals. Since an article may have more than one author, a separate **authors** table keeps track of the authors of each article. Write Java servlets/JSP pages to implement a bibliography data browser. The initial page produced in this browser application should consist of a list of hyperlinks, one per journal. Upon clicking the hyperlink for a particular journal, a new Web page should be generated that contains a listing of hyperlinks, one per volume. Upon clicking a particular volume hyperlink, a new Web page should be generated with a listing of all the articles for that volume categorized under volume numbers (all articles under volume 1 listed first, under the heading Volume 1, followed by articles under volume 2, etc.). The articles should be formatted as follows: list of authors, followed by title, followed by start and end page numbers separated by a dash (–). A sample article listing is

Tony Jones, Larry Smith, and Jim Jones. *Negated information in relational databases, pages 112–126.*

7.5 Consider the mail-order database. Write a Java servlet or JSP page that produces a Web page containing a pull-down listing of order numbers and a submit button labeled Print Invoice. Upon choosing an order number and submitting the HTML form, a second servlet or JSP page should produce a well-formatted invoice for this order. The invoice should contain the customer information at the top, followed by a tabular listing of all parts ordered within this order, the quantity, unit price, and total price for each part, with a total price for the whole order at the end. A sample invoice is shown here:

```
Order Number: 1001
Order Taken By: Sam Snead

Customer:
John Jones
123 Main St.
Atlanta, GA 33333
```

| Part Number | Part Name | Price | Quantity | Total Price |
|---|---|---|---|---|
| 100 | Nut | 1.00 | 20 | 20.00 |
| 101 | Bolt | 2.00 | 24 | 48.00 |
| | | | | 68.00 |

# CHAPTER 8

# Oracle XML

The eXtensible Markup Language (XML) is a data representation and exchange standard adopted by the World Wide Web Consortium (W3C) to enable diverse networked applications to share and exchange data over the Internet. It is a text-based representation of data that uses extensible user-defined tags to demarcate individual data components. XML was designed specifically to describe content rather than presentation. It differs from HTML in several aspects: (a) users can define new tags at will to provide meaningful annotations to data elements, (b) structures can be nested to arbitrary depth, and (c) an optional description of the structure of data can be provided. These differences allow semantically meaningful information to be incorporated into XML documents.

XML has already become a universal data exchange format, and many software vendors have built tools for importing and exporting XML data. Various APIs, such as Simple API for XML (SAX) and Document Object Model (DOM) parsers, have been proposed, and several implementations of these APIs exist. Numerous tools to manipulate, query, and transform XML data are also available in the market. XML is being used to describe configuration parameters for system software such as Apache Web servers and servlet engines such as the Apache Tomcat server, and it is the language used in the recently introduced Web services framework (messages sent from clients to remote Web services are coded in XML, and results are packaged in XML for delivery back to clients). Numerous other technologies are also using XML as the format for data representation.

XML has become an extremely important technology, and Oracle has provided strong XML support in its current Oracle9*i* release. This chapter begins by introducing the bascis of XML syntax and Document Type Definitions (DTDs), followed by XML parsing using the SAX and DOM parser APIs. Finally, Oracle's XML-SQL Utility (XSU) and the **XMLType** object type are presented.

# 8.1 Basic Syntax

XML represents data in textual form and encloses pieces of data with meaningful user-defined tags. The data can be nested to arbitrary levels, and there are no strict rules on the structuring of data compared to database systems. XML data may also be accompanied by a grammar that describes the allowable structure of data. The basic syntax of XML data or documents is presented next.

## 8.1.1 XML Elements

The basic building block of an XML document is called an *element*. An XML element encapsulates a piece of data within matching tags such as **<state>**, called the *start tag*, and **</state>**, called the *end tag*. The data within these tags may be primitive string data or nested elements. For example, the following XML element that describes a state contains two subelements, each of which encapsulates textual data:

```
<state>
   <sname>Georgia</sname>
   <scode>GA</scode>
</state>
```

The tags must be balanced—i.e., start tags must be closed with corresponding end tags in the inverse order in which they were opened, much like balanced parentheses. Tags in XML are user defined, unlike in HTML. It is possible for an element to be empty (i.e., contain no data). Such elements have the syntax **<tag></tag>** and may be abbreviated as **<tag/>**. Collections of similar data are represented in XML using repeated structures. For example, the collection of U.S. states can be represented using the following repeated structure enclosed within **<states>** and **</states>** tags:

```
<states>
   <state>
      <sname>Alabama</sname>
      <scode>AL</scode>
   </state>
```

```
   <state>
      <sname>Alaska</sname>
      <scode>AK</scode>
   </state>
   .
   .
   .
</states>
```

## 8.1.2 XML Attributes

An XML attribute is used to describe some properties of an XML element. Attributes are expressed as name-value pairs within the start tag of the XML element they are describing. The value part of the name-value pair is enclosed within double quotes. For example,

```
<state region="Mid West">
   <sname>Iowa</sname>
   <scode>IA</scode>
</state>
```

In the preceding element, the XML attribute **region** describes a property of the state. The attribute names are also user defined, and an XML element may have any number of attributes.

Sometimes it is confusing to differentiate between attributes of an element and subelements of an element. For example, the **region** attribute may also be represented as a subelement, as follows:

```
<state>
   <region>Mid West</region>
   <sname>Iowa</sname>
   <scode>IA</scode>
</state>
```

Whether to use attributes or subelements is a matter of preference as well as semantics. However, attributes and subelements have two important differences. First, one cannot have two attributes with the same name within the same tag, but one can have multiple subelements with the same name within a single element. Second, attribute values are always string data, whereas element values may be string data or other subelements.

The XML data model can be viewed as an object-oriented data model. Each element (or subelement) is an object with an implicit object identifier. It is possible to make these object identifiers explicit by using the special attributes **id**, **idref**, and **idrefs**. The attribute **id** is used to define an object identifier, whereas the attributes **idref** and **idrefs** are used as object references. Examples of object identifiers and references are shown in the following XML fragments:

```
<state id="georgia">
   <scode>GA</scode>
   <sname>Georgia</sname>
   <capital idref="atlanta"/>
   <citiesin idref="atlanta"/>
   <citiesin idref="columbus"/>
   <citiesin idref="savannah"/>
   <citiesin idref="macon"/>
   <nickname>Peach State</nickname>
   <population>6478216</population>
</state>

<city id="atlanta">
   <ccode>ATL</ccode>
   <cname>Atlanta</cname>
   <stateof idref="georgia"/>
</city>

<city id="columbus">
   <ccode>CLB</ccode>
   <cname>Columbus</cname>
   <stateof idref="georgia"/>
</city>
```

The **state** element defines an object identifier **id="georgia"** as an XML attribute, and the **city** subelement **stateof** references this object identifier using the XML attribute **idref="georgia"**. Also note that the **citiesin** subelement of the **state** element references the object identifiers defined in the **city** element. Instead of having multiple **citiesin** subelements, the following alternate subelement using the **idrefs** attribute could have been used:

```
<citiesin idrefs="atlanta columbus savannah macon"/>
```

The **idrefs** attribute can be used when one or more references are present.

### 8.1.3 Mixing Elements and Textual Data

The XML syntax allows for free-flowing textual data/notations to appear along with subelements within an element. For example,

```
<state region="Mid West">
   This describes the state of Iowa
   <sname>Iowa</sname>
   <scode>IA</scode>
</state>
```

From a database perspective this seems unnatural, but if XML is viewed from the document perspective, it is quite reasonable.

### 8.1.4 Miscellaneous Constructs

The XML format allows for comments, version indicators, and escape sequences. Comments are included as follows:

```
<!--This is a comment  -->
```

An XML document usually starts with an indication of the version being used:

```
<?xml version="1.0">
```

XML also provides the `CDATA` construct to escape strings that contain special characters. For example,

```
<![CDATA[<ename>employee name goes here</ename>>
```

will treat the string data being specified as simply string data, even though it contains a start and an end tag.

## 8.2 Document Type Definitions

XML documents may optionally include a Document Type Definition (DTD) that serves as a grammar for the underlying data. DTDs serve the role of schemas for XML data and are easy to specify. The following is a DTD for the states example introduced previously in this chapter:

```
<!DOCTYPE states [
   <!ELEMENT states(state+)>
```

```
    <!ELEMENT state(sname,scode)>
      <!ATTLIST state region CDATA #REQUIRED>
    <!ELEMENT sname (#PCDATA)>
    <!ELEMENT scode (#PCDATA)>
]>
```

The first line of the DTD declares the root element name. Subsequent lines describe the structure of the XML elements and details of any attributes the elements may have. Here, the root element, `states`, consists of one or more subelements named `state`. The regular expression `state+` is used to denote one or more occurrences. Each `state` subelement consists of two subelements, `sname` and `scode`, and one attribute named `region`. The `sname` and `scode` subelements are character data (denoted by `#PCDATA`). Other regular expressions that are allowed in DTDs are: `e*` (zero or more occurrences), `e?` (zero or one occurrence), `e1 | e2` (alternation), and `e1.e2` (concatenation).

DTDs can be used as schemas for data. For example, the relational data represented within the three tables `emp(eno,ename,addr)`, `dept(dno,dphone)`, and `works(eno,dno)` can be captured using the following DTD:

```
<!DOCTYPE db [
    <!ELEMENT db(emp*,dept*,works*)>
    <!ELEMENT emp(eno,ename,addr)>
    <!ELEMENT dept(dno,dphone)>
    <!ELEMENT works(eno,dno)>
    <!ELEMENT eno (#PCDATA)>
    <!ELEMENT ename (#PCDATA)>
    <!ELEMENT addr (#PCDATA)>
    <!ELEMENT dno (#PCDATA)>
    <!ELEMENT dphone (#PCDATA)>
]>
```

This DTD captures the structure shown in the following instance:

```
<db>
    <emp>
        <eno>1111</eno>
        <ename>Jones</ename>
        <addr>123 Main St</addr>
    </emp>
    <dept>
        <dno>d1</dno>
        <dphone>111-1234</dphone>
```

```
    </dept>
    <works>
        <eno>1111</eno>
        <dno>d1</dno>
    </works>
</db>
```

The data are constrained by the DTD to have all `emp` elements precede elements. However, note that DTDs do not have the ability to specify data types.

An alternative DTD that allows the `emp`, `dept`, and `works` elements to be arbitrarily interspersed would define the `db` element as

```
<!ELEMENT db((emp | dept | works)*)>
```

DTDs can be specified either within an XML document instance (immediately after the first XML version line and before the data instance begins) or in a separate file (say, `dbschema.dtd`), with a reference to the file included in the XML instance document as

```
<!DOCTYPE db SYSTEM "dbschema.dtd">
```

The DTD file may even be a reference URL, such as

```
<!DOCTYPE db
    SYSTEM "http://tinman.cs.gsu.edu/~raj/dbschema.dtd">
```

## 8.3 XML Parsing in Java

XML documents are often created and used by networked applications, so support for parsing such documents is absolutely essential. The W3C has provided specifications for two types of XML parsers: the SAX parser and the DOM parser. The SAX parser is an event-based parser; it does not store the entire XML document in memory and hence is suitable for read-only applications and applications in which only one pass of the input XML document is necessary. On the other hand, the DOM parser uses a tree-based model to view the XML document and stores the entire DOM tree structure in memory. Hence, it is more memory intensive, but it allows updating of the XML document as well as any number of passes through the XML document. Oracle provides an XML parser package in Java, called `oracle.xml.parser.v2`, that contains implementations of both the SAX and DOM parser specifications. For a detailed description of the Oracle XML parser, consult the documentation that comes with the parser.

## 8.3.1 SAX Parsing

SAX is an event-based API for parsing XML documents. Certain events and data encountered while reading the XML document can be reported by callback functions to the application program, and, by appropriately defining/redefining the callback event handler methods in the Java application, one can process individual elements or data in the XML document. The SAX parser does not store the XML document tree in memory, which makes it very efficient. However, as only a single pass is made over the input XML document, SAX parsing is not suitable when it may be necessary to look at the same XML fragment more than once or to modify the XML document. In such instances, the DOM parser must be used. The two important classes in the SAX API are `SAXParser` and `HandlerBase`.

- The `SAXParser` class implements the XML SAX parser specification. Once a `SAXParser` object is instantiated within a Java program, the programmer can register a SAX handler to receive notifications of various parser events. The method to create a new `SAXParser` object is

  ```
  public SAXParser()
  ```

  Once a `SAXParser` has been created, one can register a document event handler using the following method:

  ```
  public void setDocumentHandler(DocumentHandler handler)
  ```

  A similar method is available to register an error handler:

  ```
  public void setErrorHandler(ErrorHandler handler)
  ```

- The `HandlerBase` class is a default base class for event handlers. This class implements the default behavior for the various handlers, such as `DocumentHandler` and `ErrorHandler`. Application writers can extend this class by rewriting any of the following event handler methods:

  - `public void startDocument() throws SAXException`. This method receives notification of the beginning of the document. Application programmers can rewrite this method to include preparsing statements such as opening files and allocating space, opening database connections, and so on.
  - `public void endDocument() throws SAXException`. This method receives notification of the end of the document. Application programmers can rewrite this method to include postparsing statements such as closing files, deallocating space, closing database connections, and so on.
  - `public void startElement(String name, AttributeList attributes) throws SAXException`. This method receives notification of the

start of an element. Application writers may override this method to take specific actions when encountering a particular element, such as creating a node or writing output to a file. The **name** parameter contains the name of the element, and the **attributes** parameter contains attributes of the element.

- **public void endElement(String name) throws SAXException**. This method receives notification of the end of an element. Application writers may override this method in a subclass to take specific actions at the end of each element, such as finalizing a tree node or writing output to a file. The **name** parameter contains the name of the element.
- **public void characters(char ch[], int start, int length) throws SAXException**. This method receives notification of character data within an element. Application writers may override this method to take specific actions for each chunk of character data, such as adding the data to a node or buffer or printing it to a file. **ch** contains the character data, **start** is the start position in the character array, and **length** is the number of characters to use from the array.
- **public void warning(SAXParseException e) throws SAXException**. This method receives notification of a parser warning. Application writers may override this method to perform any specific actions.
- **public void error(SAXParseException e) throws SAXException**. This method receives notification of a parser error. Application writers may override this method to perform any specific actions.
- **public void fatalError(SAXParseException e) throws SAXException**. This method receives notification of a fatal SAX parser error. The default implementation throws a **SAXParserException**. Application writers may override this method to perform their own error-processing tasks. The program should terminate when a fatal error is encountered, since the XML document being parsed is no longer reliable.

In a typical SAX parser application, the application writer will extend the **HandlerBase** class and override many of the methods discussed earlier. The steps involved in writing such an application are

1. Create an instance of the parser:

   ```
   Parser parser = new SAXParser();
   ```

2. Create the handler object (instance of the class being developed):

   ```
   SampleApp app = new SampleApp();
   ```

3. Set the handlers in the parser:

```
parser.setDocumentHandler(app);
parser.setErrorHandler(app);
```

4. Parse the XML document URL:

```
parser.parse(url);
```

5. The application will also involve method overrides.

To illustrate the use of the SAX parser, let's look at an example.

**Example 8.3.1** Consider an XML document containing bibliographic information about articles published in journals. The XML document is deeply nested. The top-level `Journals` element consists of one or more `Journal` elements. Each `Journal` element consists of a `JournalName` subelement (`PCDATA`) and a `Volumes` subelement. The `Volumes` element consists of one or more `VolumeEntry` subelements. The `VolumeEntry` element consists of a `Volume` subelement (`PCDATA`) and a `Numbers` subelement. The `Numbers` element consists of a `Number` subelement (`PCDATA`), a `Date` subelement (`PCDATA`), and an `Articles` subelement. The `Articles` element consists of one or more `Article` subelements. The `Article` element consists of an `Authors` subelement, a `Title` subelement (`PCDATA`), a `StartPage` subelement (`PCDATA`), and an `EndPage` subelement (`PCDATA`). The `Authors` element consists of one or more `Author` subelements (`PCDATA`). A portion of the XML document is shown here:

```
<Journals>
 <Journal>
  <JournalName>ACM Transactions on Database Systems (TODS)
                             </JournalName>
  <Volumes>
    <VolumeEntry>
     <Volume>20</Volume>
     <Numbers>
       <NumberEntry>
        <Number>1</Number>
        <Date>March 1995</Date>
        <Articles>
         <Article>
          <Authors>
           <Author>Alexander Aiken</Author>
           <Author>Joseph M. Hellerstein</Author>
           <Author>Jennifer Widom</Author>
```

```
            </Authors>
            <Title>Static Analysis Techniques for Predicting
              the Behavior of Active Database Rules.</Title>
            <StartPage>3</StartPage>
            <EndPage>41</EndPage>
           </Article>
             .
             .
             .
          </Articles>
         </NumberEntry>
           .
           .
           .
       </Numbers>
      </VolumeEntry>
        .
        .
        .
    </Volumes>
   </Journal>
     .
     .
     .
  </Journals>
```

The SAX parser is illustrated via a Java program that reads/parses the preceding XML file, extracts PCDATA values, and uses them to form SQL **insert** statements. The SQL **insert** statements can then be used to populate a relational database with the following schema:

```
create table articles (
   aid varchar2(20),
   jname varchar2(200),
   vol number(2),
   num number(2),
   spage number(4),
   epage number(4),
   title varchar2(256),
   primary key (aid)
);

create table authors (
   aid varchar2(20),
   aname varchar2(50),
```

```
    primary key (aid,aname),
    foreign key (aid) references articles
);
```

The `articles` table stores information about each article in the XML document, except for the author information. The `aid` column is generated from the XML data by concatenating the journal code (the text within parentheses in the journal name), the volume, the number within the volume, and the start page number. These values are separated by colons. For example, the `aid` value for the article shown previously is `TODS:20:1:3`. The `authors` table stores the names of the authors of each article.

The Java application subclasses the `HandlerBase` class and redefines various handler methods. The code is

```
// Import necessary classes
import java.io.*;
import java.net.*;
import org.xml.sax.*;
import oracle.xml.parser.v2.SAXParser;

// Extend the HandlerBase class
public class CreateBibData extends HandlerBase {
  String elementEncountered;
  String journalName, journalCode, vol, num,
         startPage, endPage, title;
  String authorNames[];
  int numRows;
  int numAuthors;
  static public void main(String[] argv) {
    try {
      if (argv.length != 1) {
        // Must pass in the name of the XML file
        System.println("Usage: CreateBiBData filename");
        System.exit(1);
      }
      // Create a new handler for the parser
      CreateBibData createData = new CreateBibData();

      // Get an instance of the parser
      Parser parser = new SAXParser();

      // Set handlers in the parser
```

```
    parser.setDocumentHandler(createData);
    parser.setErrorHandler(createData);

    // Convert file to URL and parse
    try {
      parser.parse(createURL(argv[0]).toString());
    } catch (SAXParseException e) {
        System.out.println(e.getMessage());
      }
      catch (SAXException e) {
        System.out.println(e.getMessage());
      }
  } catch (Exception e) {
      System.out.println(e.toString());
  }
}

public void startDocument() {
  // Print SQL comment, initialize variables
  System.out.println("--Start of SQL Insert Statements");
  authorNames = new String[20];
  numRows=0;
}

public void endDocument() throws SAXException {
  // Print SQL comment and print message
  System.out.println("--End of SQL Insert Statements");
  System.out.println("--Just generated "+numRows+
                     " SQL insert statements");
}

public void startElement(String name, AttributeList atts)
                 throws SAXException {
  // Set variable to name of element just encountered.
  // This variable will be examined on other events.
  elementEncountered = name;
  // Reset author count to 0 if Authors element
  // encountered
  if (name.equals("Authors")) {
    numAuthors=0;
```

```
  }
}

public void endElement(String name) throws SAXException {
  // If end of Article element then print SQL insert
  // statements
  if (name.equals("Article")) {
    String aid=journalCode+":"+vol+":"+num+":"+startPage;
    System.out.println("insert into articles values ('"+
        aid +"','" + journalName+"',"+ vol+","+ num+","+
        startPage+","+ endPage+",'"+ title+"');");
    numRows++;
    for (int i=0; i<numAuthors; i++) {
      System.out.println("insert into authors values('"+
          aid+"','"+authorNames[i]+"');");
      numRows++;
    }
    numAuthors=0;
  }
  elementEncountered=null;
}

public void characters(char[] cbuf, int start, int len) {
  // Depending on the element encountered recently,
  // extract character data into a Java variable
  if (elementEncountered.equals("JournalName")) {
    journalName = new String(cbuf,start,len);
    int ii = journalName.indexOf("(");
    int jj = journalName.indexOf(")");
    journalCode=journalName.substring(ii+1,jj);
  }
  else if (elementEncountered.equals("Volume")) {
    vol=new String(cbuf,start,len);
  }
  else if (elementEncountered.equals("Number")) {
    num=new String(cbuf,start,len);
  }
  else if (elementEncountered.equals("Title")) {
    title=new String(cbuf,start,len);
  }
```

```
    else if (elementEncountered.equals("StartPage")) {
      startPage=new String(cbuf,start,len);
    }
    else if (elementEncountered.equals("EndPage")) {
      endPage=new String(cbuf,start,len);
    }
    else if (elementEncountered.equals("Title")) {
      title=new String(cbuf,start,len);
    }
    else if (elementEncountered.equals("Author")) {
      authorNames[numAuthors++]=new String(cbuf,start,len);
    }
  }

  public void warning (SAXParseException e)
              throws SAXException {
    System.out.println("Warning:"+e.getMessage());
  }

  public void error (SAXParseException e)
              throws SAXException {
    throw new SAXException(e.getMessage());
  }

  public void fatalError (SAXParseException e)
              throws SAXException {
    System.out.println("Fatal error");
    throw new SAXException(e.getMessage());
  }

  // Helper method to create URL from file name
  static URL createURL(String fileName) {
    URL url = null;
    try {
      url = new URL(fileName);
    } catch (MalformedURLException ex) {
        File f = new File(fileName);
        try {
          String path = f.getAbsolutePath();
          String fs = System.getProperty("file.separator");
```

```
                if (fs.length() == 1) {
                  char sep = fs.charAt(0);
                  if (sep != '/')
                    path = path.replace(sep, '/');
                  if (path.charAt(0) != '/')
                    path = '/' + path;
                }
                path = "file://" + path;
                url = new URL(path);
              } catch (MalformedURLException e) {
                  System.out.println("Cannot create url for: "+
                                     fileName);
                  System.exit(0);
                }
          }
        return url;
      }
    }
```

## 8.3.2 DOM Parsing

DOM, the Document Object Model, is a W3C specification for the tree structure of an XML document. The DOM tree of an XML document basically consists of nodes corresponding to elements/subelements and textual data. The DOM parser stores the entire tree in memory, allowing the programmer to traverse the tree structure and extract individual node information. The parser also has methods to create nodes, change the contents of nodes, and remove nodes from the DOM tree. The important classes and methods of the DOM parser are summarized next.

- The `DOMParser` class implements the XML 1.0 parser to parse an XML document and produce a DOM tree. The class comes with a constructor

  ```
  public DOMParser()
  ```

  that creates a new parser object. Besides the constructor, other important methods in this class are

  - `public void setValidationMode(boolean yes)`. Setting the `yes` parameter to `true` instructs the parser to validate the XML document against a DTD.

  - **`public final void parse(URL url) throws XMLParseException, SAXException, IOException`**. The **`parse`** method parses the XML document pointed to by the given URL and creates the corresponding XML document hierarchy. This method must be invoked to proceed further with DOM parsing.
  - **`Public XMLDocument getDocument()`**. After the DOM tree is produced using the **`parse`** method, the **`getDocument`** method should be invoked to obtain the **`XMLDocument`** object.

- The `XMLDocument` class is one of the central classes in the XML parser package. This class stores the XML document tree and provides access to the individual parts of the DOM tree. An `XMLDocument` object is usually created by using the `getDocument` method on a `DOMParser` object. Some of the methods in this class are

  - **`public NodeList getElementsByTagName(String tagname)`**. This method returns a `NodeList` of all the elements with a given tag name in the order in which they would be encountered in a preorder traversal of the document tree.
  - **`public void print(OutputStream out) throws IOException`**. This method prints the XML document to the output stream specified.

- The `NodeList` class provides an abstraction for an ordered collection of nodes. It has two methods:

  - **`public abstract Node item(int i)`**. This method returns the item at index **`i`** in the collection. If the index is greater than or equal to the number of nodes in the list, this returns **`null`**.
  - **`public abstract int getLength()`**. This method returns the number of nodes in the list. The range of valid child node indexes is `0` to **`length-1`**, inclusive.

- The `NamedNodeMap` class represents a collection of DOM nodes that can be accessed by name. No particular order of nodes is assumed, although a convenient access by index is allowed. This class contains the following useful methods:

  - **`public abstract int getLength()`**. This method returns the number of nodes in the map.
  - **`public abstract Node item(int i)`**. This method returns the `i`th node in the map.
  - **`public abstract Node getNamedItem(String name)`**. This method retrieves the node with the specified name.

- The `XMLNode` class implements the DOM `Node` interface and serves as a primary data type for the entire Document Object Model. It represents a single node in the DOM tree. The following are some of the access methods of this class:
  - `public Node getFirstChild()`. This method returns the first child of this node. If there is no such node, it returns `null`.
  - `public Node getNextSibling()`. This method returns the next sibling node. If there is no such node, it returns `null`.
  - `public String getNodeName()`. This method returns the name of this node.
  - `public String getNodeValue()`. This method returns the value of this node.
  - `public String valueOf(String pattern) throws XSLException`. This method returns the value of the first node from the tree that matches `pattern`. `pattern` is typically a tag name.
  - `public void print(OutputStream out) throws IOException`. This method prints the contents of the node to the output stream specified.
  - `public NamedNodeMap getAttributes()`. This method returns a `NamedNodeMap` object containing the attributes of this node.

The use of the DOM parser is illustrated through the following example.

Example 8.3.2 Consider the following XML document (in the file `geo.xml`) containing data about states and cities of the United States:

```
<?xml version="1.0" standalone="no"?>
<!DOCTYPE geography SYSTEM "geo.dtd">
<geography>
  <state id="georgia">
    <scode>GA</scode>
    <sname>Georgia</sname>
    <capital idref="atlanta"/>
    <citiesin idref="atlanta"/>
    <citiesin idref="columbus"/>
    <citiesin idref="savannah"/>
    <citiesin idref="macon"/>
    <nickname>Peach State</nickname>
    <population>6478216</population>
  </state>
  <city id="atlanta">
    <ccode>ATL</ccode>
```

```
    <cname>Atlanta</cname>
    <stateof idref="georgia"/>
  </city>
  <city id="columbus">
    <ccode>CLB</ccode>
    <cname>Columbus</cname>
    <stateof idref="georgia"/>
  </city>
  <city id="savannah">
    <ccode>SVN</ccode>
    <cname>Savannah</cname>
    <stateof idref="georgia"/>
  </city>
  <city id="macon">
    <ccode>MCN</ccode>
    <cname>Macon</cname>
    <stateof idref="georgia"/>
  </city>
</geography>
```

This XML document refers to a DTD stored in a separate file called **geo.dtd**, shown here:

```
<!ELEMENT geography (state|city)*>
<!ELEMENT state(scode,sname,capital,citiesin*,
               nickname, population)>
  <!ATTLIST state id ID #REQUIRED>
<!ELEMENT scode (#PCDATA)>
<!ELEMENT sname (#PCDATA)>
<!ELEMENT capital EMPTY>
  <!ATTLIST capital idref IDREF #REQUIRED>
<!ELEMENT citiesin EMPTY>
  <!ATTLIST citiesin idref IDREF #REQUIRED>
<!ELEMENT nickname (#PCDATA)>
<!ELEMENT population (#PCDATA)>
<!ELEMENT city (ccode, cname, stateof)>
  <!ATTLIST city id ID #IMPLIED>
<!ELEMENT ccode (#PCDATA)>
<!ELEMENT cname (#PCDATA)>
<!ELEMENT stateof EMPTY>
  <!ATTLIST stateof idref IDREF #REQUIRED>
```

As the DTD suggests, the root element is called **geography** and contains zero or more **state** or **city** subelements. Each **state** and **city** element has an **ID** attribute defining its object identifier. These identifiers are referred to in other appropriate places in the XML document. One of the subelements of the **state** element is called **capital**. This is an empty element (i.e., containing no textual information), but it contains a reference to the **city** object corresponding to the capital city of the state identified in the containing **state** element. The **state** element also has zero or more subelements called **citiesin** that are similar to the **capital** subelement, except that they contain references to all the major cities within the state. Note that the capital city reference is duplicated in the data.

The data contained in the XML document are to be processed within a Java program and stored into an object-relational database with the following schema:

```
create type city_type as object (
  ccode     varchar2(15),
  cname     varchar2(50)
);
create type cities_in_table as table of city_type;

create table state (
  scode      varchar2(15),
  sname      varchar2(50),
  nickname   varchar2(100),
  population number(30),
  capital    city_type,
  cities_in  cities_in_table,
  primary key (scode))
  nested table cities_in store as cities_tab;
```

This is a simple schema describing an object-relational table called **state**. This table contains one row per state and has a column for the capital city that is an object type. The table also contains a column that contains a nested table of cities. The following program, written in Java, uses the DOM XML parser provided by Oracle to read the XML file and extract various elements. It then uses JDBC to insert the data into the object-relational table, **state**.

```
// Import basic packages
import java.io.*;
import java.net.*;
// Import DOM classes
import org.w3c.dom.*;
import org.w3c.dom.Node;
```

```
// Import Oracle's XML parser classes
import oracle.xml.parser.v2.*;
// JDBC import
import java.sql.*;

public class CreateGeoData {
  static public void main(String[] argv)
      throws SQLException {

    // Load JDBC driver
    try {
      Class.forName("oracle.jdbc.driver.OracleDriver");
    } catch (ClassNotFoundException e) {
        System.out.println("Error");
        return;
      }

    // Create JDBC Connection and Statement objects
    Connection conn = null;
    try {
      conn = DriverManager.getConnection (
        "jdbc:oracle:thin:@tinman.cs.gsu.edu:1521:sid9ir2",
        "book", "book");
    } catch (SQLException e1) {
        System.out.println("Error");
        return;
      }
    if (conn == null) {
      System.out.println("Null Connection");
      return;
    }
    Statement stmt = conn.createStatement();

    try {
      // Make sure XML input file is specified
      if (argv.length != 1) {
        System.err.println(
            "Usage: java createGeoData xmlfilename");
        System.exit(1);
      }
```

```
// Get an instance of the parser
DOMParser parser = new DOMParser();

// Generate a URL from file name using helper method
URL url = createURL(argv[0]);

// Set various parser options: DTD validation on,
// warnings shown
parser.setValidationMode(true);

// Parse the document
parser.parse(url);

// Obtain the document
XMLDocument doc = parser.getDocument();

// Extract list of state and city nodes
NodeList sl = doc.getElementsByTagName("state");
NodeList cl = doc.getElementsByTagName("city");
int len = sl.getLength();

String scode = null, sname = null, nickname = null;
long population = 0;

// Set up loop to process each state node
for (int j=0; j < len; j++) {
  // Extract jth state item from list and extract
  // simple subelement values
  XMLNode e = (XMLNode) sl.item(j);
  scode = e.valueOf("scode");
  sname = e.valueOf("sname");
  nickname = e.valueOf("nickname");
  population =
     Long.parseLong(e.valueOf("population"));
  // Look for child node labeled "capital"
  XMLNode child = (XMLNode) e.getFirstChild();
  while (child != null) {
    if (child.getNodeName().equals("capital"))
      break;
    child = (XMLNode) child.getNextSibling();
```

```
}
// Get attributes of capital element
NamedNodeMap nnm = child.getAttributes();
XMLNode n = (XMLNode) nnm.item(0);
String cname=null, ccode=null;
// Invoke helper method to get city name and code
// values returned as one string with ":" separator.
String x = GetCityNameAndCode(cl,n.getNodeValue());
int kk = x.indexOf(":");
String capName = x.substring(0,kk);
String capCode = x.substring(kk+1);

// Get children nodes labeled "citiesin" and
// invoke helper method to get city name and code
child = (XMLNode) e.getFirstChild();
String cCode[] = new String[10];
String cName[] = new String[10];
int count = 0;
while (child != null) {
  if (child.getNodeName().equals("citiesin")) {
    nnm = child.getAttributes();
    n = (XMLNode) nnm.item(0);
    x = GetCityNameAndCode(cl,n.getNodeValue());
    kk = x.indexOf(":");
    cName[count] = x.substring(0,kk);
    cCode[count++] = x.substring(kk+1);
  }
  child = (XMLNode) child.getNextSibling();
}

// Prepare SQL insert statement
String insert =
   "insert into state values ('" +
   scode +"', '" + sname + "', '" +
   nickname + "', " + population + ", " +
   "city_type('"+capCode+"', '"+capName + "'), ";

String insert += "cities_in_table(";
for (int i = 0; i < count; i++) {
  if ( i == count-1) {
```

```
                insert += "city_type('" + cCode[i] +
                          "', '" + cName[i] + "')))";
                break;
              }
              insert += "city_type('"+ cCode[i] +
                        "', '" + cName[i] + "'), ";
            }

            // Execute insert statement
            int nrows = 0;
            try {
              System.out.println(insert);
              nrows = stmt.executeUpdate(insert);
            } catch (SQLException e2) {
                System.out.println("Could not insert row");
                System.out.println(e2.getMessage());
              }
          }
     } catch (Exception e) {
         System.out.println(e.toString());
       }
    }

    // Helper method to extract city name and code
    static String GetCityNameAndCode(NodeList cl, String cid) {

    // Go through each city element and see if given cid
    // value matches. Upon match, extract city name and code
    // and concatenate with ":" separator and return string.
      try {
        int len = cl.getLength();
        for (int j=0; j < len; j++) {
          XMLNode e = (XMLNode) cl.item(j);
          NamedNodeMap nnm = e.getAttributes();
          XMLNode n = (XMLNode) nnm.item(0);
          if (n.getNodeValue().equals(cid)) {
            return
             (e.valueOf("cname") + ":" + e.valueOf("ccode"));
          }
        }
```

```
            return null;
         } catch (Exception e) {
            System.out.println(e.toString());
            return null;
         }
      }
   }
```

## 8.4 The Oracle XML-SQL Utility

Oracle 9*i*'s XML-SQL Utility (XSU) provides the programmer with the ability to (a) transform data obtained from object-relational tables/views into XML; (b) extract relevant data from an XML document and, using a canonical mapping between XML and SQL, insert data into database tables; and (c) extract relevant data from an XML document and use it to delete/update data in database tables. The XSU capabilities are available as Java and PL/SQL APIs. Oracle also provides a Java command-line front end to perform XSU actions.

### 8.4.1 Canonical SQL-to-XML Mapping

Data stored in a relational or object-relational table can easily be mapped into XML as follows. The rows returned by the SQL query are enclosed within a **ROWSET** element, which is also the root element of the generated XML document. The **ROWSET** element contains one or more **ROW** elements. Each of these **ROW** elements contains the data from one of the returned rows from the query. Specifically, each **ROW** element contains one or more elements whose names and content are those of the database columns specified in the select list of the SQL query. And finally, these elements corresponding to the database columns contain the data from the columns.

The following shell command executes the Java command-line front end available with Oracle XSU. The Java front-end utility, called **OracleXML**, takes several command-line parameters, including user ID and password, JDBC connect string, and so on. The **getXML** parameter is used for extracting data from the database into XML form.

```
[~/ows/xml/xsu][9:28pm] java OracleXML getXML \
 -user "book/book" \
 -conn "jdbc:oracle:thin:@tinman.cs.gsu.edu:1521:sid9ir2" \
  "select * from state where scode='GA'"
```

```
<?xml version = '1.0'?>
<ROWSET>
   <ROW num="1">
      <SCODE>GA</SCODE>
      <SNAME>Georgia</SNAME>
      <NICKNAME>Peach State</NICKNAME>
      <POPULATION>6478216</POPULATION>
      <CAPITAL>
         <CCODE>ATL</CCODE>
         <CNAME>Atlanta</CNAME>
      </CAPITAL>
      <CITIES_IN>
         <CITIES_IN_ITEM>
            <CCODE>ATL</CCODE>
            <CNAME>Atlanta</CNAME>
         </CITIES_IN_ITEM>
         <CITIES_IN_ITEM>
            <CCODE>CLB</CCODE>
            <CNAME>Columbus</CNAME>
         </CITIES_IN_ITEM>
         <CITIES_IN_ITEM>
            <CCODE>SVN</CCODE>
            <CNAME>Savannah</CNAME>
         </CITIES_IN_ITEM>
         <CITIES_IN_ITEM>
            <CCODE>MCN</CCODE>
            <CNAME>Macon</CNAME>
         </CITIES_IN_ITEM>
      </CITIES_IN>
   </ROW>
</ROWSET>

[~/ows/xml/xsu][9:28pm]
```

Each row of the `state` table is mapped into a `ROW` element enclosed within a `ROWSET` element. The individual column values of simple data types are mapped as simple elements whose tag names are the same as the column names. In the case of an object type column, a nested element duplicating the nested structure of the object type is included. An example of this is the `CAPITAL` element, which has two subelements, `CCODE` and `CNAME`. When a column is a nested table, a nested element with several subelements (one per row in the nested table) is created. In the preceding example, the `CITIES_IN` element illustrates the nested structure produced for a column value that is a nested table type. Each subelement is labeled with the tag `CITIES_IN_ITEM`. Other points to note in the mapping from SQL to XML are that the `ROW` element contains a `ROWNUM` attribute indicating the row number for the particular row and that `null` value columns are left out entirely in the XML output.

It is also possible to retrieve data from the database as attributes rather than elements in XML. For example, the following invocation of the command-line utility:

```
$java OracleXML getXML -user "book/book"
 -conn "jdbc:oracle:thin:@tinman.cs.gsu.edu:1521:sid9ir2" \
 "select scode "@scode",sname,nickname,capital from state"
```

will produce the XML data

```
<?xml version = '1.0'?>
<ROWSET>
   <ROW num="1" scode="GA">
      <SNAME>Georgia</SNAME>
      <NICKNAME>Peach State</NICKNAME>
      <CAPITAL>
         <CCODE>ATL</CCODE>
         <CNAME>Atlanta</CNAME>
      </CAPITAL>
   </ROW>
</ROWSET>
```

Notice that the database column value that is to be extracted as an XML attribute (`scode`) is labeled `"@scode"` in the `select` clause of the query. All such columns will be extracted as XML attributes. It is important to note that all attributes must appear before any nonattribute. It is currently not possible to load XML data stored in attributes.

## 8.4.2 Canonical XML-to-SQL Mapping

XML to SQL mapping is a more difficult mapping, since XML documents can be arbitrarily nested and structured. However, when the target relational table or object-relational table structure is known, the process is just the reverse of the SQL-to-XML mapping. In case the XML document is not in the format required by this mapping, one can always transform the XML document to suit the format required. The following two examples illustrate how to exploit the mapping from XML to SQL to load Oracle tables with data from an XML file.

Example 8.4.1 Consider the following relational table structure from the grade book database:

```
create table students (
   sid   varchar2(5),
   fname varchar2(20),
   lname varchar2(20),
   minit char
);
```

and the following XML data file:

```
<STUDENTS>
  <STUDENT>
    <SID>1111</SID>
    <FNAME>Tony</FNAME>
    <LNAME>Jones</LNAME>
    <MINIT>A</MINIT>
  </STUDENT>
  <STUDENT>
    <SID>1111</SID>
    <FNAME>Tony</FNAME>
    <LNAME>Jones</LNAME>
    <MINIT>A</MINIT>
  </STUDENT>
</STUDENTS>
```

The data in the XML file can be loaded into the **students** table with the default mapping using the command-line utility (the **putXML** parameter is used to load the database with XML data):

```
$java OracleXML putXML -user "book/book" \
 -conn "jdbc:oracle:thin:@tinman.cs.gsu.edu:1521:sid9ir2" \
 -rowTag "STUDENT" -fileName student.xml "students"
successfully inserted 2 rows into students
```

Example 8.4.2 Consider the following object-relational table structure for the `state` table:

```
create type city_type as object (
  ccode     varchar2(15),
  cname     varchar2(50)
);
```

```
create type cities_in_table as table of city_type;

create table state (
  scode      varchar2(15),
  sname      varchar2(50),
  capital    city_type,
  cities     cities_in_table,
  nickname   varchar2(100),
  population number(30)
) nested table cities store as cities_tab;
```

The object-relational table, `state`, contains an object type column (`capital`) and a nested table column (`cities`). The following XML data file consists of data that fits the object-relational structure:

```
<ROWSET>
  <ROW>
    <SCODE>GA</SCODE>
    <SNAME>Georgia</SNAME>
    <CAPITAL>
      <CCODE>ATL</CCODE>
      <CNAME>Atlanta</CNAME>
    </CAPITAL>
    <CITIES>
      <CITIES_ITEM>
        <CCODE>CLB</CCODE>
        <CNAME>Columbus</CNAME>
      </CITIES_ITEM>
      <CITIES_ITEM>
        <CCODE>ATL</CCODE>
        <CNAME>Atlanta</CNAME>
      </CITIES_ITEM>
      <CITIES_ITEM>
        <CCODE>SVN</CCODE>
        <CNAME>Savannah</CNAME>
      </CITIES_ITEM>
      <CITIES_ITEM>
        <CCODE>MCN</CCODE>
        <CNAME>Macon</CNAME>
      </CITIES_ITEM>
    </CITIES>
```

```
    <NICKNAME>Peach State</NICKNAME>
    <POPULATION>6478216</POPULATION>
  </ROW>
</ROWSET>
```

The data in the XML file can be loaded into the `state` table with the default mapping using the command-line utility

```
$ java OracleXML putXML -user "book/book" \
-conn "jdbc:oracle:thin:@tinman.cs.gsu.edu:1521:sid9ir2" \
-fileName sgeo.xml "state"
successfully inserted 1 row into state
```

## 8.4.3 The XSU Java API

The XSU Java API allows generation of XML data from an Oracle9*i* database as well as insertion of data from an XML document into an Oracle9*i* database. One can also perform deletes and updates in the database based on data available in an XML document. The two classes in this API are

- `oracle.xml.sql.query.OracleXMLQuery`. This class provides capabilities to extract data from an Oracle9*i* database in XML format. The typical steps involved are
  1. Create a JDBC `Connection` object.
  2. Create an `OracleXMLQuery` instance by supplying an SQL query string or a JDBC `ResultSet` object.
  3. Set options in the `OracleXMLQuery` object.
  4. Obtain the result as either a DOM tree or an XML string.
- `oracle.xml.sql.dml.OracleXMLSave`. This class provides methods to insert the XML data into Oracle9*i* tables, update existing tables with the XML document, and delete rows from the table based on the XML element values. The typical steps involved are
  1. Create a JDBC `Connection` object.
  2. Create an `OracleXMLSave` object, providing the `Connection` object and the name of the table to be updated as input.
  3. Set options in the `OracleXMLSave` object.
  4. Invoke the appropriate method to insert, delete, or update.

The XSU Java API is illustrated with examples in the next section. For a detailed description of the API, please consult the Oracle9*i* documentation.

## *Extracting XML*

The following Java program performs a simple query on the database and returns the results as an XML string:

```
// Import relevant classes
import oracle.jdbc.driver.*;
import oracle.xml.sql.query.OracleXMLQuery;
import java.lang.*;
import java.sql.*;

public class xsuGet {
  public static void main(String[] argv)
            throws SQLException {
    // Load JDBC driver
    try {
      Class.forName ("oracle.jdbc.driver.OracleDriver");
    } catch (ClassNotFoundException e) {
        System.out.println ("Could not load the driver");
        return;
      }
    // Create Connection object
    Connection conn =  DriverManager.getConnection(
        "jdbc:oracle:thin:@tinman.cs.gsu.edu:1521:sid9ir2",
        "book","book");

    // Create the OracleXMLQuery object
    OracleXMLQuery qry = new OracleXMLQuery(conn,
                "select * from cat");

    // Get the XML string
    String str = qry.getXMLString();

    // Print the XML output
    System.out.println(str);
    qry.close();
    conn.close();
  }
}
```

A sample output from this program is:

```
<?xml version = '1.0'?>
<ROWSET>
  <ROW num="1">
    <TABLE_NAME>ARTICLES</TABLE_NAME>
    <TABLE_TYPE>TABLE</TABLE_TYPE>
  </ROW>
  <ROW num="2">
    <TABLE_NAME>AUTHORS</TABLE_NAME>
    <TABLE_TYPE>TABLE</TABLE_TYPE>
  </ROW>
.
.
.
</ROWSET>
```

Instead of obtaining the XML data as a string, one can also retrieve it as a DOM tree. The following Java program fragment retrieves the same data as the previous example, but as a DOM tree. It then traverses the tree and prints only the table names.

```
// Get the XML data as a DOM tree
XMLDocument doc = (XMLDocument) qry.getXMLDOM();

// Extract all ROW elements
NodeList tl = doc.getElementsByTagName("ROW");
int len = tl.getLength();

// Set up loop to process each ROW node
for (int j=0; j < len; j++) {
   // Extract jth ROW item from list and extract
   // table name value and print
   XMLNode e = (XMLNode) tl.item(j);
   String tname = e.valueOf("TABLE_NAME");
   System.out.println("Table Name = "+tname);
}
```

## *Insert Processing*

To insert data from an XML document into a table or view, simply supply the table or view name and then the XML document file. The XSU parses the document and creates an **insert** statement using the values in the XML document.

By default, the XSU inserts values into all the columns of the table or view, and an absent element is treated as a `null` value. Consider the following XML data about students:

```
<ROWSET>
<STUDENT>
  <SID>1111</SID>
  <FNAME>Tony</FNAME>
  <LNAME>Jones</LNAME>
  <MINIT>A</MINIT>
</STUDENT>
<STUDENT>
  <SID>2222</SID>
  <FNAME>Robert</FNAME>
  <LNAME>Smith</LNAME>
</STUDENT>
</ROWSET>
```

The following Java program inserts the preceding data into the **`students`** table:

```
// Import necessary classes
import java.sql.*;
import java.net.*;
import java.io.*;
import oracle.xml.sql.dml.OracleXMLSave;

public class xsuInsertStudent {
  public static void main(String argv[])
     throws SQLException {
    // Load JDBC driver
    try {
      Class.forName ("oracle.jdbc.driver.OracleDriver");
    } catch (ClassNotFoundException e) {
        System.out.println ("Could not load the driver");
        return;
      }
    // Create Connection object
    Connection conn = DriverManager.getConnection(
        "jdbc:oracle:thin:@tinman.cs.gsu.edu:1521:sid9ir2",
        "book","book");
    // Create OracleXMLSave object
```

```
        OracleXMLSave sav = new OracleXMLSave(
                          conn, "book.students");
        // Set some options
        sav.setRowTag("STUDENT");
        // Create file URL using command-line parameter
        URL u = createURL(argv[0]);
        // Invoke the insertXML method with the URL
        sav.insertXML(u);
        // Close objects
        sav.close();
        conn.close();
    }
  }
```

The preceding program produces and executes the following SQL **insert** statements:

```
insert into students values(1111,'Tony','Jones','A');
insert into students values(2222,'Robert','Smith',null);
```

It is also possible to insert data into certain specified columns. For example, the following code fragment:

```
String [] colNames = new String[3];
colNames[0] = "SID";
colNames[1] = "FNAME";
colNames[2] = "LNAME";
// Set column names to be used in insert
sav.setUpdateColumnList(colNames);

URL u = createURL(argv[0]);
sav.insertXML(u);
```

will take data in the following XML file:

```
<ROWSET>
<STUDENT>
  <SID>6666</SID>
  <FNAME>Shyam</FNAME>
  <LNAME>Sunder</LNAME>
</STUDENT>
<STUDENT>
  <SID>7777</SID>
```

```
    <FNAME>Ram</FNAME>
    <LNAME>Sunder</LNAME>
    <MINIT>T</MINIT>
  </STUDENT>
  </ROWSET>
```

and insert only the SID, FNAME, and LNAME column values (even though a MINIT value is specified in the XML data!). The preceding program fragment produces and executes the following SQL insert statements:

```
insert into students(SID,FNAME,LNAME)
      values(6666,'Shyam','Sunder');
insert into students(SID,FNAME,LNAME)
      values(7777,'Ram','Sunder');
```

If a required column value is missing, a null value is inserted. Nonrequired column values are ignored.

## *Update Processing*

Update processing requires the programmer to specify the key columns, which are then used in the where clause generated by XSU. All columns specified in the XML data (except for the key columns) are updated in the database. Consider the following XML document, containing new values for the FNAME column for one student and new values for the FNAME and MINIT columns for the other student:

```
<ROWSET>
<STUDENT>
  <SID>6666</SID>
  <FNAME>Shyamala</FNAME>
</STUDENT>
<STUDENT>
  <SID>7777</SID>
  <FNAME>Rammohan</FNAME>
  <MINIT>T</MINIT>
</STUDENT>
</ROWSET>
<ROWSET>
```

The following Java program fragment takes the data in the given XML document and updates the students table with the new values:

```
OracleXMLSave sav =
   new OracleXMLSave(conn, "book.students");
```

```
sav.setRowTag("STUDENT");
URL u = createURL(argv[0]);

// Set key columns
String [] keyColNames = new String[1];
keyColNames[0] = "SID";
sav.setKeyColumnList(keyColNames);

sav.updateXML(u);
```

This program fragment will produce the following SQL **update** statements:

```
update book.students set FNAME='Shyamala' where SID=6666;
update book.students set FNAME='Rammohan', MINIT='T'
       where SID=7777;
```

It is also possible to update only a certain specified set of columns. As an example, the following Java code fragment:

```
OracleXMLSave sav =
   new OracleXMLSave(conn, "book.students");
sav.setRowTag("STUDENT");
URL u = createURL(argv[0]);
// Specify key columns
String [] keyColNames = new String[1];
keyColNames[0] = "SID";
sav.setKeyColumnList(keyColNames);
// Specify columns to update
String[] updateColNames = new String[1];
updateColNames[0] = "MINIT";
sav.setUpdateColumnList(updateColNames);

sav.updateXML(u);
```

will update only the `MINIT` column, using the values in the XML data file. For the following XML document:

```
<ROWSET>
<STUDENT>
  <SID>6666</SID>
  <MINIT>X</MINIT>
</STUDENT>
<STUDENT>
```

```
    <SID>7777</SID>
    <FNAME>Rammohan</FNAME>
    <MINIT>Y</MINIT>
  </STUDENT>
  </ROWSET>
```

the Java code fragment will produce and execute the following SQL `update` statements:

```
update book.students set MINIT='X' where SID=6666;
update book.students set MINIT='Y' where SID=7777;
```

The `FNAME` value is ignored by XSU, since it is not specified as a column to be updated.

## *Delete Processing*

By default, delete processing uses all the values given in the XML document in the `where` clause of the SQL `delete` statement. As an example, the following Java code fragment deletes rows from the `students` table using the data in the XML file:

```
OracleXMLSave sav =
   new OracleXMLSave(conn, "book.students");
sav.setRowTag("STUDENT");
URL u = createURL(argv[0]);

sav.deleteXML(u);
```

If the XML file contained the following:

```
<ROWSET>
<STUDENT>
  <FNAME>Shyam</FNAME>
</STUDENT>
<STUDENT>
  <MINIT>T</MINIT>
</STUDENT>
</ROWSET>
```

the following SQL `delete` statements would be produced and executed by the Java code fragment:

```
delete from students where FNAME='Shyam';
delete from students where MINIT='T';
```

It is also possible to delete based on specified key values, as the following code fragment illustrates:

```
OracleXMLSave sav =
   new OracleXMLSave(conn, "book.students");
sav.setRowTag("STUDENT");
URL u = createURL(argv[0]);
// Specify key columns
String [] keyColNames = new String[1];
keyColNames[0] = "SID";
sav.setKeyColumnList(keyColNames);

sav.deleteXML(u);
```

The preceding code fragment, when executed with the following XML data file:

```
<ROWSET>
<STUDENT>
  <SID>7777</SID>
</STUDENT>
<STUDENT>
  <SID>9999</SID>
</STUDENT>
</ROWSET>
```

will produce and execute the following SQL **delete** statements:

```
delete from students where SID=7777;
delete from students where SID=9999;
```

## 8.5 XMLType

Oracle9*i* supports **XMLType**, a new system-defined object type. **XMLType** has built-in member functions that offer a powerful mechanism to create, extract, and index XML data. **XMLType** can be used as a data type for columns in tables. Variables of **XMLType** can be used in PL/SQL stored procedures as parameters and return values. Columns of type **XMLType** can be easily accessed within SQL statements via the many access functions and methods available with **XMLType**.

### 8.5.1 XMLType Columns in a Table

The following is an example of a table definition that defines a column of type **XMLType**. This is a table that contains address book information such as names, addresses, email addresses, and phone numbers of people of interest. Besides normal columns, such as the name of the person and the date when the entry was made, the table also contains a column of type **XMLType** called **card**. This column can contain as its value an XML datagram.

```
CREATE TABLE addrbook(
  name varchar2(20),
  card SYS.XMLTYPE,
  creationDate Date
);
```

The **createXML** method can be used to create instances for **XMLType**, as the following three SQL **insert** statements illustrate:

```
insert into addrbook values
  ('Roger', sys.XMLType.createXML(
            '<ACARD CREATEDBY="raj">
               <EMAIL>roger12@yahoo.com</EMAIL>
               <WPHONE>111-1234</WPHONE>
               <WPHONE>111-5678</WPHONE>
               <CELL>111-3342</CELL>
               <ADDRESS>
                 <LINE1>123 Main St.</LINE1>
                 <CITY>Atlanta</CITY>
                 <STATE>GA</STATE>
                 <ZIP>33333</ZIP>
               </ADDRESS>
               <COMMENT>Works the night shift</COMMENT>
             </ACARD>'),
   sysdate);
insert into addrbook values
  ('Bobby', sys.XMLType.createXML(
            '<ACARD CREATEDBY="raj">
               <EMAIL>bob@aol.com</EMAIL>
               <WPHONE>111-2900</WPHONE>
               <ADDRESS>
                 <LINE1>200 Oak St.</LINE1>
```

```
                    <CITY>Atlanta</CITY>
                    <STATE>GA</STATE>
                    <ZIP>33330</ZIP>
                  </ADDRESS>
                </ACARD>'),
   sysdate);
insert into addrbook values
  ('Tommy', sys.XMLType.createXML(
            '<ACARD CREATEDBY="raj">
               <EMAIL>tom200@yahoo.com</EMAIL>
               <WPHONE>333-8000</WPHONE>
               <CELL>111-9000</CELL>
             </ACARD>'),
   sysdate);
insert into addrbook values
  ('Abe', sys.XMLType.createXML(
          '<ACARD CREATEDBY="raj">
             <EMAIL>abe1212@yahoo.com</EMAIL>
             <WPHONE>111-2000</WPHONE>
             <CELL>111-3344</CELL>
             <ADDRESS>
               <LINE1>125 Main St.</LINE1>
               <CITY>Savannah</CITY>
               <STATE>GA</STATE>
               <ZIP>33300</ZIP>
             </ADDRESS>
             <COMMENT>Kids: John, Jamie</COMMENT>
           </ACARD>'),
   sysdate);
insert into addrbook values
  ('Tony', sys.XMLType.createXML(
           '<ACARD CREATEDBY="ram">
              <EMAIL>anthony1@yahoo.com</EMAIL>
              <WPHONE>111-1000</WPHONE>
              <CELL>111-3000</CELL>
              <ADDRESS>
                <LINE1>123 Elm St.</LINE1>
                <CITY>Savannah</CITY>
                <STATE>GA</STATE>
                <ZIP>33300</ZIP>
```

```
              </ADDRESS>
              <COMMENT>Works for CNN</COMMENT>
            </ACARD>'),
    sysdate);
insert into addrbook values
  ('Frank', sys.XMLType.createXML(
            '<ACARD CREATEDBY="ram">
               <EMAIL>francisco@yahoo.com</EMAIL>
               <WPHONE>123-1234</WPHONE>
               <ADDRESS>
                 <LINE1>123 Grant St.</LINE1>
                 <CITY>Atlanta</CITY>
                 <STATE>GA</STATE>
                 <ZIP>33333</ZIP>
               </ADDRESS>
               <COMMENT>Dog name: Fife</COMMENT>
             </ACARD>'),
    sysdate);
```

The `createXML` method checks for the well-formed property of the XML datagram. If the XML datagram is not well formed, the `insert` statement is rejected.

## 8.5.2 Querying XML Data

The `getClobVal`, `getStringVal`, and `getNumberVal` functions on `XMLType` columns return the XML data as a `CLOB` (Character Large Object), `varchar`, or `number`, respectively. Following is an example of the use of the `getClobVal` function:

Query 1: Extract the XML datagram for "Roger" as a `CLOB` value.

```
set long 1000

select a.card.getClobval() as Address
from   addrbook a
where  name = 'Roger';

ADDRESS
------------------------------------------------------------
<ACARD CREATEDBY="raj">
               <EMAIL>roger12@yahoo.com</EMAIL>
               <WPHONE>111-1234</WPHONE>
```

```
        <CELL>111-3342</CELL>
        <ADDRESS>
          <LINE1>123 Main Street</LINE1>
          <CITY>Atlanta</CITY>
          <STATE>GA</STATE>
          <ZIP>33333</ZIP>
        </ADDRESS>
      </ACARD>

ADDRESS
-----------------------------------------------------------
```

XMLType data can be queried using the existsNode and extract methods, both of which use a limited form of XPath expressions to traverse the XML tree. XPath is a W3C standard for querying XML data. Applying an XPath expression to an XML tree results in a set of internal nodes, each representing an XML element. Some of the common constructs used in XPath are

- The / expression is used to represent the root of the XML tree, and hence /ACARD would represent the ACARD elements of the tree.
- The / expression is also used as a path separator to represent child nodes, and hence /ACARD/ADDRESS/ZIP would represent the ZIP element within the ADDRESS element within the ACARD element.
- The // expression represents all descendants of a node, and hence ACARD//ZIP would represent all ZIP elements that are descendants of the ACARD element at any level below.
- The * expression is used as a wild card, and it matches any element. Hence, /ACARD/*/ZIP would match ZIP elements, which are grandchild nodes of ACARD elements.
- The [] expression is used for predicate expressions. For example, the expression /ACARD[EMAIL="roger12@yahoo.com"]/ADDRESS selects all the ADDRESS elements of each ACARD element whose subelement EMAIL has the specified value. The [] expression is also used to denote an index within a list. For example, the expression /ACARD/WPHONE[2] denotes the second WPHONE element in a list of WPHONE elements within the ACARD element.

The existsNode and extract methods are illustrated in the following queries:

Query 2: Get the names and email addresses of all individuals.

```
select a.name, a.card.extract('/ACARD/EMAIL') as email
from   addrbook a;

NAME     EMAIL
-----    ---------------------------------
Roger    <EMAIL>roger12@yahoo.com</EMAIL>
Bobby    <EMAIL>bob@aol.com</EMAIL>
Tommy    <EMAIL>tom200@yahoo.com</EMAIL>
Abe      <EMAIL>abe1212@yahoo.com</EMAIL>
Tony     <EMAIL>anthony1@yahoo.com</EMAIL>
Frank    <EMAIL>francisco@yahoo.com</EMAIL>
6 rows selected.
```

In this query, the `extract` method is invoked in the `select` clause on the `XMLType` column. This method takes an XPath expression as input and returns an XML fragment containing the email addresses. The `text` function allows the text within an element to be extracted. So, the query can be reworded as follows to extract the email addresses without the enclosing tag:

```
select a.name, a.card.extract('/ACARD/EMAIL/text()') as email
from   addrbook a;
```

Query 3: Find the name and the second work phone number of all persons who have a second work phone.

```
select a.name, a.card.extract('/ACARD/WPHONE[2]/text()')
                as secondphone
from   addrbook a
where  a.card.existsNode('/ACARD/WPHONE[2]') = 1;

NAME     SECONDPHONE
----     -------------
Roger    111-5678
```

In this query, the `existsNode` method is invoked in the `where` clause to determine if the current person has a second phone number. If so, that person's name and second phone number (extracted using the `extract` method) are listed.

Query 4: Find the name and address of the person with a given email address.

```
select a.name, a.card.extract(
       '/ACARD[EMAIL="roger12@yahoo.com"]/ADDRESS') as
```

```
       rogeraddress
from   addrbook a
where  a.card.existsNode(
         '/ACARD[EMAIL="roger12@yahoo.com"]') = 1;

NAME   ROGERADDRESS
----   ------------------------------
Roger <ADDRESS>
        <LINE1>123 Main St.</LINE1>
        <CITY>Atlanta</CITY>
        <STATE>GA</STATE>
        <ZIP>33333</ZIP>
      </ADDRESS>
```

In this example, the predicate expression feature of XPath is used to select only those elements with a particular subelement based on the subelement value.

Query 5: Find the names and email addresses of persons whose entries were created by ram.

```
select a.name, a.card.extract('/ACARD/EMAIL/text()')
       as ramaddresses
from   addrbook a
where  a.card.extract('/ACARD/@CREATEDBY').getstringval() =
       'ram';

NAME    RAMADDRESSES
-----   --------------------
Tony    anthony1@yahoo.com
Frank   francisco@yahoo.com
```

The **where** clause in this query includes an XPath expression to extract the value of an XML attribute.

The next example illustrates the use of **XMLType** from within PL/SQL. It is possible to declare PL/SQL variables of **XMLType** and manipulate these variables within a PL/SQL program. Consider the following relational table definition:

```
create table abook (
  name      varchar2(20),
  email     varchar2(50),
  address   varchar2(200),
  primary key (name)
);
```

The following PL/SQL anonymous block takes the data stored in the table **addrbook** (which has an **XMLType** column), converts it into purely relational form, and stores it into the **abook** table:

```
declare
  email varchar2(50);
  street varchar2(100);
  city varchar2(30);
  state varchar2(30);
  zip number(5);
  address varchar2(200);
  cursor c1 is  -- Cursor to get all rows of addrbook
    select name, card
    from   addrbook;
  c1_rec c1%rowtype;
begin
  for c1_rec in c1 loop
    -- c1_rec.card is of XMLType; apply extract() method
    email := c1_rec.card.extract(
             '/ACARD/EMAIL/text()').getstringval();
    street := c1_rec.card.extract(
             '/ACARD/ADDRESS/LINE1/text()').getstringval();
    city := c1_rec.card.extract(
             '/ACARD/ADDRESS/CITY/text()').getstringval();
    state := c1_rec.card.extract(
             '/ACARD/ADDRESS/STATE/text()').getstringval();
    zip := c1_rec.card.extract(
             '/ACARD/ADDRESS/ZIP/text()').getnumberval();
    address := street || ', ' || city || ', ' || state ||
               ', ' || zip;
    insert into abook values (c1_rec.name,email,address);
  end loop;
end;
/
show errors
```

The anonymous block processes each row from the **addrbook** table, extracts relevant information from the XML data, and uses the data to create a row in the **abook** table.

### 8.5.3 Updating and Deleting XML Data

Replacing the entire XML datagram with a new datagram is done using the usual syntax of SQL. For example, to update the email address for Roger, the following `update` statement can be used:

```
update addrbook
set card = sys.XMLType.createXML(
            '<ACARD CREATEDBY="raj">
               <EMAIL>roger12@earthlink.net</EMAIL>
               <WPHONE>111-1234</WPHONE>
               <WPHONE>111-5678</WPHONE>
               <CELL>111-3342</CELL>
               <ADDRESS>
                 <LINE1>123 Main St.</LINE1>
                 <CITY>Atlanta</CITY>
                 <STATE>GA</STATE>
                 <ZIP>33333</ZIP>
               </ADDRESS>
               <COMMENT>Works the night shift</COMMENT>
             </ACARD>'),
    creationDate = sysdate
where name = 'Roger';
```

Note that the whole XML datagram denoting information about the individual is repeated with the new email address. Updating data within the XML datagram without repeating all of the data are not currently possible but is expected to be a feature in coming releases of Oracle.

Deleting rows from tables containing XML data are done in the usual manner, as the following example illustrates:

```
delete addrbook a
where  a.card.extract(
   '/ACARD/ADDRESS/ZIP/text()').getnumberval() = '33333';
```

This `delete` statement deletes all rows that correspond to individuals whose addresses have zip codes of `33333`.

# Exercises

8.1 Consider the following XML data representing orders taken for the mail-order database:

```
<orders>
  <order>
    <orderNumber>1020</orderNumber>
    <takenBy>1000</takenBy>
    <customer>1111</customer>
    <receivedDate>10-DEC-94</receivedDate>
    <items>
      <item>
        <partNumber>10506</partNumber>
        <quantity>1</quantity>
      </item>
      .
      .
      .
    </items>
  </order>
  .
  .
  .
</orders>
```

Write a Java program that parses the preceding XML data using a SAX parser and populates the mail-order database. The program should handle appropriate error processing.

8.2 Consider the following XML data representing information about movies:

```
<movies>
  <movie>
    <title>Godfather, The</title>
    <year>1972</year>
    <directors>
      <director>Francis Ford Coppola</director>
    </directors>
    <genres>
      <genre>Action</genre>
      <genre>Drama</genre>
    </genres>
```

```
      <plot>the plot goes here</plot>
      <cast>
        <performer>
          <actor>Marlon Brando</actor>
          <role>Don Vito Corleone</role>
        </performer>
        .
        .
        .
      </cast>
    </movie>
    .
    .
    .
  </movies>
```

Carry out the following:

1. Write a DTD for the XML data.
2. Design a relational database to store the XML data.
3. Write a Java program that uses a DOM parser to read data from the XML file and populates the relational database of (1).

8.3 Consider the mail-order database. Assume that all the information about orders and order details is stored in a single table called **xorder** with the following schema:

```
create table xorders(
  ono      number(5) primary key,
  orderr   SYS.XMLType
);
```

The following **insert** statement shows the data about order number 1020:

```
insert into xorders values
  (1020,sys.XMLType.createXML('
<order>
  <takenBy>1000</takenBy>
  <customer>1111</customer>
  <receivedDate>10-DEC-94</receivedDate>
  <shippedDate>12-DEC-94</shippedDate>
  <items>
    <item>
      <partNumber>10506</partNumber>
      <quantity>1</quantity>
    </item>
```

```
    <item>
      <partNumber>10507</partNumber>
      <quantity>1</quantity>
    </item>
    <item>
      <partNumber>10508</partNumber>
      <quantity>2</quantity>
    </item>
    <item>
      <partNumber>10509</partNumber>
      <quantity>3</quantity>
    </item>
  </items>
</order>'));
```

Write SQL **select** statements to answer the following queries:

1. Get the names and street addresses of customers who have placed orders.
2. Get the numbers and names of customers who have ordered part 10506.
3. Get the numbers and names of customers who have ordered parts from an employee from Wichita.
4. Get the numbers and names of customers who have ordered only from employees from Wichita.
5. Get the numbers and names of employees who have not taken a single order.

8.4 Consider the following relation about movies:

```
create table xmovies(
  mno     number(5) primary key,
  movie   SYS.XMLType
);

insert into xmovies values(1,sys.XMLType.createXML('
<movie>
  <title>Godfather ,The</title>
  <year>1972</year>
  <directors>
    <director>Francis Ford Coppola</director>
  </directors>
  <genres>
    <genre>Crime</genre>
    <genre>Drama</genre>
```

```
  </genres>
  <plot>Son of a Mafia boss takes over when his father is
        critically wounded in a mob hit.</plot>
  <cast>
    <performer>
      <actor>Marlon Brando</actor>
      <role>Don Vito Corleone</role>
    </performer>
    <performer>
      <actor>Al Pacino</actor>
      <role>Michael Corleone</role>
    </performer>
    <performer>
      <actor>Diane Keaton</actor>
      <role>Kay Adams Corleone</role>
    </performer>
    <performer>
      <actor>Robert Duvall</actor>
      <role>Tom Hagen</role>
    </performer>
    <performer>
      <actor>James Caan</actor>
      <role>Sonny Corleone</role>
    </performer>
  </cast>
</movie>'));
```

Write SQL `select` statements to answer the following queries:

1. Get the titles and years of all crime movies.
2. Get the names of persons who have acted in a movie and also been the sole director of the same movie.
3. Get the titles and years of movies in which James Caan has acted.

# CHAPTER 9

# Projects

This chapter presents some project suggestions that can be developed by the reader to get a better understanding of the material presented in this book. Each project will typically go through the following phases:

- *Phase 0.* Design the database (using entity-relationship diagrams).
- *Phase 1.* Create the tables, including constraints such as primary keys, foreign keys, check constraints, and `not null` constraints.
- *Phase 2.* Create triggers and active elements to maintain the integrity of the database and to perform appropriate actions on database updates.
- *Phase 3.* Populate the database using SQL `insert` statements or by writing programs in Java or Pro*C/CH.
- *Phase 4.* Write application programs in Java and/or Pro*C/CH and/or PL/SQL.
- *Phase 5.* Document the project.

The application programs will have to implement some form of user interface. The simplest user interface is terminal based and involves menus and submenus. However, there are several tools and languages that support the development of fancier user interfaces, such as the `curses` package in Unix, the Java AWT toolkit, and the X-Windows libraries. The reader may choose to develop the user interfaces using these tools and languages.

The rest of this chapter discusses several application areas for which a database application can be developed. For each application area, a brief description of the application is followed by a description of the relational tables and a sketch of the application program requirements in the form of menus and submenus. The reader is encouraged to use the ideas presented as a starting point for the definition of the problem and to modify it according to his or her understanding of the problem.

## 9.1 Airline Flight Information System

The airline flight information database consists of information relating to the operations of the airline industry. One possible design of the database results in the following relational tables:

```
AIRPORT(AIRPORT_CODE,name,city,state)
FLIGHT(NUMBER,airline,weekdays)
FLIGHT_LEG(FLIGHT_NUMBER,LEG_NUMBER,
  departure_airport_code,scheduled_departure_time,
  arrival_airport_code,scheduled_arrival_time)
LEG_INSTANCE(FLIGHT_NUMBER,LEG_NUMBER,LEG_DATE,
  number_of_available_seats,airplane_id,
  departure_airport_code,departure_time,
  arrival_airport_code,arrival_time)
FARES(FLIGHT_NUMBER,FARE_CODE,amount,restrictions)
AIRPLANE_TYPE(TYPE_NAME,max_seats,company)
CAN_LAND(AIRPLANE_TYPE_NAME,AIRPORT_CODE)
AIRPLANE(AIRPLANE_ID,total_number_of_seats,
  airplane_type)
SEAT_RESERVATION(FLIGHT_NUMBER,LEG_NUMBER,DATE,
  SEAT_NUMBER,customer_name,customer_phone)
```

*Note:* The primary key columns are shown in uppercase.

Each `FLIGHT` is identified by a `FLIGHT_NUMBER` and consists of one or more `FLIGHT_LEG`s with `LEG_NUMBER`s 1, 2, 3, and so on. Each leg has many `LEG_INSTANCE`s, one for each date on which the flight flies. `FARES` are kept for each flight, and `SEAT_RESERVATION`s are kept for each `LEG_INSTANCE`. Information about airports is kept in the `AIRPORT` table, and information about individual airplanes is kept in the `AIRPLANE` table. `AIRPLANE_TYPE` records the information about the airplane type, and the `CAN_LAND` table keeps information about which airplane type can land in which airport.

The following is an outline for the application program to be developed for the airline reservation system. It includes a main menu of options and several submenus.

```
        MAIN MENU
(1) Customer functions
(2) Reporting functions
(3) Administrative functions
(4) Quit

        CUSTOMER FUNCTIONS MENU
(1) Make a reservation
(2) Cancel a reservation
(3) Confirm a reservation
(4) Print trip itinerary
(5) Locate fare
(6) Quit

        REPORTING FUNCTIONS MENU
(1) Print flight roster
(2) Print flight schedule (based on several criteria
    such as airline, departure city, arrival city)
(3) Print flight performance report
    (Given airline, print on-time and delayed flights)
(4) Quit

        ADMINISTRATIVE FUNCTIONS MENU
(1) Add/drop flight
(2) Add airport
(3) Update fares
(4) Create leg instance
(5) Update leg instance (departure/arrival times)
(6) Quit
```

## 9.2 Library Database Application

Consider the operations of a public library system in a city. The library has many patrons who borrow books from one of its many branches. Each branch of the library holds a number of copies of a particular book. Books that are not returned on time are fined at a rate of 25 cents for each day after the due date. One possible design of a database for the public library system results in the following relational tables:

```
BOOKS(BOOK_ID,title,publisher_name)
BOOK_AUTHORS(BOOK_ID,AUTHOR_NAME)
PUBLISHERS(NAME,address,phone)
```

```
BOOK_COPIES(BOOK_ID,BRANCH_ID,no_of_copies)
BRANCHES(BRANCH_ID,branch_name,address)
BOOK_LOANS(BOOK_ID,BRANCH_ID,CARD_NO,
  date_out,date_due,date_returned)
BORROWERS(CARD_NO,name,address,phone,unpaid_dues)
```

*Note:* The primary key columns are shown in uppercase.

The `BOOKS` table records information about all the books that are available in the library system. Each book has a unique `BOOK_ID`. Information about the authors of books is kept in the table `BOOK_AUTHORS`, and information about the publishers is kept in the table `PUBLISHERS`. The number of copies of each book in a particular library branch is recorded in the `BOOK_COPIES` table. The branch information is kept in the `BRANCHES` table. Information about the patrons of the library is kept in the `BORROWERS` table, and the loaned books are recorded in the `BOOK_LOANS` table.

The following is an outline for an application program to be developed for a library database:

```
     MAIN MENU
(1) Patron functions (ask for card number,
     then show submenu)
(2) Administrative functions
(3) Quit


     PATRON FUNCTIONS MENU
(1) Book checkout
(2) Book return
(3) Pay fine
(4) Print loaned books list
(5) Quit


     ADMINISTRATIVE FUNCTIONS MENU
(1) Add a book
(2) Update book holdings
(3) Search book
(4) New patron
(5) Print branch information
(6) Print top 10 frequently checked-out books
(7) Quit
```

## 9.3 University Student Database

Consider the data that are usually maintained by a typical university concerning students, courses, and enrollments. Students are admitted to the university, and they pursue a degree program in a particular department. The university catalog consists of courses that are offered every term. Students choose courses to take and enroll in them during registration. Instructors are assigned courses to teach, and they in turn assign grades. A possible database design results in the following relational tables:

```
COURSES(CNO,ctitle,hours,dept_id)
DEPARTMENTS(DEPT_ID,dept_name,college)
INSTRUCTORS(LAST_NAME,FIRST_NAME,
  dept_id,office,phone,email)
SECTIONS(TERM,LINENO,cno,instr_lname,instr_fname,
  room,days,start_time,end_time,capacity)
STUDENTS(SID,last_name,first_name,class,phone,
  street,city,state,zip,degree,dept_id,hours,gpa)
ENROLLMENT(SID,TERM,LINENO,grade)
```

*Note:* The primary key columns are shown in uppercase.

The `COURSES` table maintains the list of courses in the university catalog. Information about departments, instructors, and students is maintained in the `DEPARTMENTS`, `INSTRUCTORS`, and `STUDENTS` tables, respectively. Notice that some of the columns in the `STUDENTS` table are computed columns (`gpa`, `hours`)—i.e., their values are determined by other values in other tables. The `SECTIONS` table maintains information about the schedule of classes for each term. These are the sections of the various courses that are offered each term. The `ENROLLMENT` table keeps information about the enrollment of students in sections.

The following is an outline of a possible application program for the student database:

```
     MAIN MENU
(1) Student functions
(2) Administrative functions
(3) Reporting functions
(4) Quit

     STUDENT FUNCTIONS MENU
(1) Register for courses
(2) Add/drop a course
(3) Request transcript
(4) Pay fees (get a fee report)
(5) Quit
```

```
     ADMINISTRATIVE FUNCTIONS MENU
(1) Create a new course/drop course
(2) Prepare term schedule (add sections)
(3) Add/drop instructors
(4) Alter term schedule (add/drop/update sections)
(5) Add/drop students
(6) Quit

     REPORTING FUNCTIONS MENU
(1) Print schedule of classes (for a term)
(2) Print the catalog
(3) Print the honors list of students for a department
(4) Quit
```

## 9.4 Video Chain Database

Consider the operations of a video rental and sales chain. Such a company purchases videos from vendors and stocks them in one of many stores. Each store has several employees who rent or sell these movies to members. Members are required to return the rented movies by the due date; otherwise, a fine is imposed. Commissions are awarded to employees based on their sales volume. One possible design of a database for this application results in the following relational tables:

```
STORE(STORE_NUM,address)
EMPLOYEES(EID,name,store_num,commission_rate)
MOVIES(VID,STOCK_NUM,title,cost,category,rent_price,
       sale_price,purchase_date,vendor_name,qoh)
MEMBERS(MID,lname,fname,address,bonus_points)
RENTALS(RENTAL_TRANSACTION_NUMBER,mid,stock_num,
        vid,eid,date_out,frequency,date_in)
SALES(SALE_TRANSACTION_NUMBER,mid,stock_num,vid,eid,
      sale_date)
VENDORS(VENDOR_NAME,address,phone)
```

*Note:* The primary key columns are shown in uppercase.

The `STORE` table records the store numbers and addresses of the individual stores. The `EMPLOYEES` table records information about the employees and the store with which they are associated. The `MOVIES` table contains information about all the videos in the company. The `STOCK_NUM` column may indicate the store to which each videocassette belongs. Information about the members is kept in the `MEMBERS` table. Members are given some bonus points each time they rent a movie. The accumulated points are recorded in this table. Members are eligible for a free rental after accumulation of a certain number of bonus points. The **RENTALS** and **SALES** tables record each transaction made. For the rental of movies, the date checked out, the duration of the checkout (how many days?), and the date returned are recorded. The **VENDORS** table records information about vendors from whom the videos are purchased.

A possible application program for the video company is outlined in the following menu/submenus:

```
      MAIN MENU
(1) Member functions
(2) Reporting functions
(3) Administrative functions
(4) Quit

      MEMBER FUNCTIONS MENU
(1) Video checkout
(2) New member signup
(3) List of outstanding videos
(4) Membership cancellation
(5) Video purchase
(6) Quit

      ADMINISTRATIVE FUNCTIONS MENU
(1) Video return
(2) Add/delete employee
(3) Process new shipment of videos
(4) Open new store
(5) Quit

      REPORTING FUNCTIONS MENU
(1) Print catalog (arranged by categories)
(2) Print due list of videos
(3) Print employee commission report
(4) Print rental summary
    (sorted based on frequency of rental)
(5) Quit
```

## 9.5 Banking Database

Consider the operations of a typical banking enterprise. A bank normally has many branches, and customers can open accounts at any of these branches. It is normal for more than one customer to have the same account and for one customer to have multiple accounts. The bank offers various types of services—from savings and checking accounts to loans. A possible design for the banking enterprise results in the following relational tables:

```
BRANCHES(BRANCH_NUM,branch_name,address)
CUSTOMERS(CUSTOMER_NUM,name,address,phone)
CHECKING_ACCOUNTS(ACCOUNT_NUM,branch_num,date_opened,
  balance,overdraft_amount,check_limit)
SAVINGS_ACCOUNTS(ACCOUNT_NUM,branch_num,date_opened,
  balance,interest_rate)
LOAN_ACCOUNTS(ACCOUNT_NUM,branch_num,date_opened,
  loan_type,interest_rate)
HAS_ACCOUNT(CUSTOMER_NUM,ACCOUNT_TYPE,ACCOUNT_NUM)
TRANSACTIONS(ACCOUNT_TYPE,ACCOUNT_NUM,TRANS_DATE,
  TRANS_AMT,TRANS_TYPE,trans_comments)
```

*Note:* The primary key columns are shown in uppercase.

The `BRANCHES` table keeps information about all the branches of the bank, and the `CUSTOMERS` table records information about all the customers of the bank. There are three tables for the three different types of accounts. Each has an `ACCOUNT_NUM` column, which may or may not be unique across the accounts. Hence, the table `HAS_ACCOUNT`, which keeps information about which customers own which accounts has the column `ACCOUNT_TYPE` to indicate what types of account the customers own. The `TRANSACTIONS` table records all the transactions that occur within the accounts.

The following is a sketch of an application for the banking enterprise:

```
      MAIN MENU
(1) Customer functions
(2) Administrative functions
(3) Reporting functions
(4) Quit

      CUSTOMER FUNCTIONS MENU
(1) Deposit
(2) Withdraw
(3) Transfer
```

```
(4) Loan payment
(5) Quit

      ADMINISTRATIVE FUNCTIONS MENU
(1) Process checks
    (assume a file containing checks received
     by the bank)
(2) Add/drop customer
(3) Open/close account
(4) Quit

      REPORTING FUNCTIONS MENU
(1) Print monthly statement
(2) Print loan payment schedule
(3) Print yearly tax statement (interest earned)
    (to be mailed out for each customer)
(4) Quit
```

## 9.6 BibTEX Database

Consider the TEX word processing system and the way it handles bibliography information. The bibliographic entries are created in a text file in a particular format and are consulted by the BibTEX program when processing the entries referenced in a document.[1] The problem is to keep the collection of bibliographic entries in an Oracle database and to allow manipulation of these entries via an application program.

The bibliographic entries are classified into various categories: `article`, `book`, `inbook`, `proceedings`, `inproceedings`, `techreport`, `manual`, `conference`, and so on. An entry in each of these categories has some required fields and some optional fields. Each entry is identified by a unique `citekey`.

One possible design of a relational database results in the following tables:

```
MASTER_ENTRIES(CITE_KEY,entry_type)
ARTICLE(CITE_KEY,author,title,journal,volume,number,
  pages,month,year,note)
BOOK(CITE_KEY,author,editor,title,publisher,address,
  volume,edition,series,month,year,note)
```

1. See Leslie Lamport, *LaTeX User's Guide and Reference Manual* (Reading, MA: Addison-Wesley, 1986), for details on this format and other specifics regarding the BibTEX program.

```
PROCEEDINGS(CITE_KEY,editor,title,publisher,
  organization,address,month,year,note)
INBOOK(CITE_KEY,author,editor,title,publisher,address,
  volume,edition,series,chapter,pages,month,year,note)
INPROCEEDINGS(CITE_KEY,author,editor,title,booktitle,
  publisher,organization,address,pages,month,year,note)
.
.
.
REQUIRED_FIELDS(ENTRY_TYPE,FIELD)
```

*Note:* The primary key columns are shown in uppercase.

The MASTER_ENTRIES table contains the citekey and the type of entry (article, book, etc.) for all the bibliographic entries. There is one table for each entry type that maintains all the entries under that particular category. For example, the table ARTICLE contains all the bibliographic entries that are articles. The REQUIRED_FIELDS table records information about the required fields for each type of entry. This information will have to be consulted when creating a new bibliographic entry.

An application program that manipulates the preceding database is sketched out here:

```
     MAIN MENU
(1) Update functions
(2) Search functions
(3) Reporting/utility functions
(4) Quit

     UPDATE FUNCTIONS MENU
(1) Add an entry
(2) Modify an entry
(3) Delete an entry
(4) Quit

     SEARCH FUNCTIONS MENU
(1) Search based on author
(2) Search based on keyword in title
(3) Search based on multiple search criteria
(4) Quit

     REPORTING/UTILITY FUNCTIONS MENU
(1) Print summary reports
(2) Read .bib files and load database
(3) Write all entries to .bib file
(4) Write selected entries to .bib file
(5) Quit
```

## 9.7 Music Store Database

Consider the operations of a company that sells prerecorded compact discs and related items. The company has many outlets in several states. Each outlet has been assigned a number and has its own manager, employees, inventory, sales, and returns. Company-wide product and customer lists are maintained. Based on this information, the following relational tables constitute one possible design of the database:

```
OUTLET(OUTLET_NUMBER,address,city,state,zip,phone)
EMPLOYEE(OUTLET_NUMBER,EMP_NUMBER,emp_name)
PRODUCT(PRODUCT_CODE,artist,title,cost,sale_price)
CUSTOMER(CUSTOMER_ID,customer_name,address,city,
  state,zip,phone)
MANAGER(OUTLET_NUMBER,emp_number)
INVENTORY(OUTLET_NUMBER,PRODUCT_CODE,quantity)
SALES(OUTLET_NUMBER,EMP_NUMBER,CUSTOMER_ID,PRODUCT_CODE,
  SALE_DATE,SALE_TIME,quantity)
RETURNS(OUTLET_NUMBER,PRODUCT_CODE,CUSTOMER_ID,
  RETURN_DATE,RETURN_TIME,quantity,reason,restock)
```

*Note:* The primary key columns are shown in uppercase.

The following is a sketch of an application program interface using menus and submenus:

```
      MAIN MENU
(1) Sale/return processing
(2) Outlet/employee/customer/product maintenance
(3) Reports
(4) Quit

      SALES/RETURNS MENU
(1) Process a sale
(2) Process a return
(3) View a sale (given date and customer id)
(4) View a return (given date and customer id)
(5) Quit

      MAINTENANCE MENU
(1) Add/modify/drop outlet
(2) Add/modify/drop employee
(3) Add/modify/drop customer
(4) Add/modify/drop product
```

```
(5) Process new shipment of products for an outlet
(6) Process returns
(7) Quit

     REPORTS MENU
(1) Produce yearly sales report for outlet
(2) Produce sales report for employee
(3) Produce the list of top 10 selling items
(4) Quit
```

## 9.8 Online Auctions Database

Consider the operations of an online auction company that offers members the opportunity to buy and sell computer-related hardware and software items. The seller lists the item for sale. A description of the item, along with the starting price and bid increments, is specified by the seller. Various other information, such as shipping mode and charges, category of the item, when the auction ends, and so on, is also provided at the time of the listing. Buyers make bids for the items they are interested in buying. The person placing the highest bid at the time of the end of the auction is declared the winner and a transaction between the buyer and seller may proceed soon after. Buyers and sellers can leave feedback regarding their experience with a purchase or sale on the system. This feedback is available for every member to view.

Based on this information, the following relational tables constitute one possible design of the database:

```
MEMBERS(USERID,password,name,address,phone,email)
ITEMS(INO,category,title,description,sellerID,quantity,
      startPrice,bidIncrement,lastBidReceived,closeTime)
SHIPPING(INO,SHIPTYPE,SHIPPRICE)
BID(BUYERID,INO,PRICE,QTYWANTED,BIDTIME)
RATING(INO,BUYERID,SELLERID,sComment,bComment,sScale,bScale)
```

*Note:* The primary key columns are shown in uppercase.

The `MEMBERS` table records information about all the members of the online auction company. These include both buyers and sellers, and the same member can be the seller of one item and the buyer of another item. The `ITEMS` table keeps track of items that are on the auction block. Each item is assigned a unique item number. The seller's user ID is included in this table. For each item on auction, there can be several shipping modes, and the `SHIPPING` table keeps track of this information. The bids placed by members for items are recorded in the `BID` table. The `RATING` table records the ratings placed by buyers or sellers for a transaction. The rating includes a descriptive comment as well as a numeric value (say, -1 for a negative experience, 0 for a neutral experience, and +1 for a positive experience).

The following is a sketch of an application program interface using menus and submenus:

```
      MAIN MENU
(1) Member registration
(2) Member login
(3) Quit

      MEMBER MENU
(1) Place an item for auction
(2) Bid on an item
(3) Search for items
(4) Place a rating
(5) View rating
(6) Quit
```

## 9.9 Oracle Data Dictionary Browser

Oracle maintains information about all the database objects in its data dictionary, as briefly described in Section 2.8. The data dictionary includes the names and structures of all tables, constraints, indexes, views, synonyms, sequences, triggers, stored functions, procedures, and packages. Each individual Oracle user has access to the portion of the data dictionary that pertains to his or her schema, via predefined views. Some of these views are

```
user_objects  : description of user's objects
user_tables   : description of user's tables
user_indexes  : description of user's indexes
user_sequences: description of user's sequences
user_synonyms : description of user's synonyms
user_source   : description of user's stored
                functions, procedures, and packages
user_triggers : description of user's triggers
user_views    : description of user's views
```

This project involves providing a convenient and powerful way for users to search and browse their database objects.

The following is a sketch of an application program interface for the data dictionary browser using menus and submenus:

```
      MAIN MENU
(1) Oracle user login
(2) Quit

      ORACLE USER MENU
(1) View tables
(2) View functions/procedures/packages
(3) View synonyms
(4) View sequences
(5) View indexes
(6) View triggers
(7) View views
(8) View objects
(9) Quit
```

To implement this project, the reader must get familiar with Oracle's data dictionary. Within SQL*Plus, issuing the `describe` command on each of the predefined views lists the data dictionary table structure for that view.

## 9.10 Oracle Data Browser on the Web

Using the PL/SQL Web Toolkit or Java servlets, implement an Oracle Data Browser. The Oracle Data Browser is a Web application that allows a user to examine his or her schema and data contents. The initial login screen should allow the user to enter a user schema name and password. After authenticating the name and password, the user is presented with a three-frame Web page, shown in Figure 9.1.

The top frame is always fixed. The right-hand frame is the work area where results are displayed. The left-hand frame contains the following five menu options:

- *Tables*. This option presents the user with a pull-down list of the tables in his or her schema. Upon choosing one and submitting it, the table schema should be displayed in the right-hand frame, as shown in Figure 9.2.

  The table schema display includes one checkbox per column of the table and a submit button. The user may choose zero or more checkboxes and click the submit button. The contents of the table (only those columns chosen or all columns if none of the checkboxes is chosen) should be displayed in the same frame upon submission.

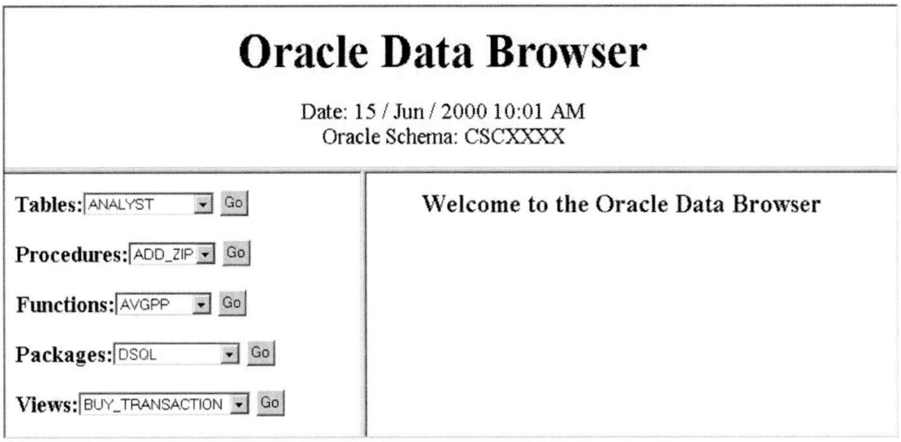

# Oracle Data Browser

Date: 15 / Jun / 2000 10:01 AM
Oracle Schema: CSCXXXX

**Tables:** ANALYST Go

**Procedures:** ADD_ZIP Go

**Functions:** AVGPP Go

**Packages:** DSQL Go

**Views:** BUY_TRANSACTION Go

**Welcome to the Oracle Data Browser**

**Figure 9.1** Three-frame initial Web page—Oracle Data Browser.

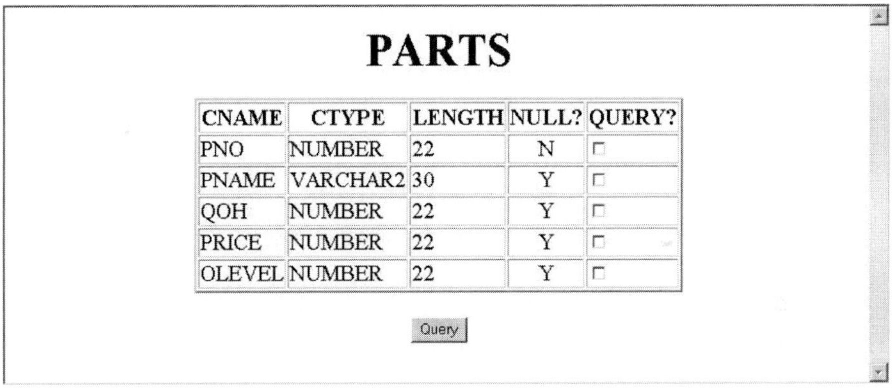

# PARTS

| CNAME | CTYPE | LENGTH | NULL? | QUERY? |
|---|---|---|---|---|
| PNO | NUMBER | 22 | N | ☐ |
| PNAME | VARCHAR2 | 30 | Y | ☐ |
| QOH | NUMBER | 22 | Y | ☐ |
| PRICE | NUMBER | 22 | Y | ☐ |
| OLEVEL | NUMBER | 22 | Y | ☐ |

Query

**Figure 9.2** Table schema display—Oracle Data Browser.

- *Procedures.* This option presents the user with a pull-down list of the stored procedures in his or her schema. Upon choosing one and submitting it, the stored procedure source code should be displayed in the right-hand frame.
- *Functions.* Similar to Procedures.
- *Packages.* Similar to Procedures, except that only the package specification should be displayed, along with a submit button labeled with the string "Get Package Body." Upon submission, the package body should be displayed in the same frame.

- *Views*. This option presents the user with a pull-down list of the views in his or her schema. Upon choosing one and submitting it, the view definition should be displayed in the right-hand frame, along with a submit button labeled with the string "Get Current View." Upon submission, the view should be calculated and the result should be displayed in tabular form.

## 9.11 QBE Interface on the Web

This project implements a subset of Query By Example (QBE) query language using Java servlets. QBE is a visual query language that uses a two-dimensional syntax in which the user expresses a query using example elements and variables. You can learn about QBE from any standard database text. The initial login screen should allow the user to enter an Oracle schema name and password. After authenticating the name and password, the user is presented with a two-frame Web page, shown in Figure 9.3.

The left-hand frame consists of a list of each of the tables in the user's schema, along with a pull-down list of the integers 0, 1, 2, and 3. The right-hand frame contains a welcome message and will be used to display the results of any subsequent form submits.

To express a query, the user first chooses an integer for each of the tables (representing the number of copies of the table the query refers to) and clicks the submit button. Upon submission, table skeletons are shown in the right-hand frame, as shown in Figure 9.4.

A special *condition box* is also shown in the right-hand frame. The condition box is used to express conditions that are not easily expressed in the skeletons themselves. In general QBE, some queries do need more than one row in table skeletons; however, for this assignment, only one row in each skeleton is sufficient.

The user expresses the query by entering form elements in the skeletons and condition box. There are four types of elements: `P.`, `P._Variable`, `Constant`, and

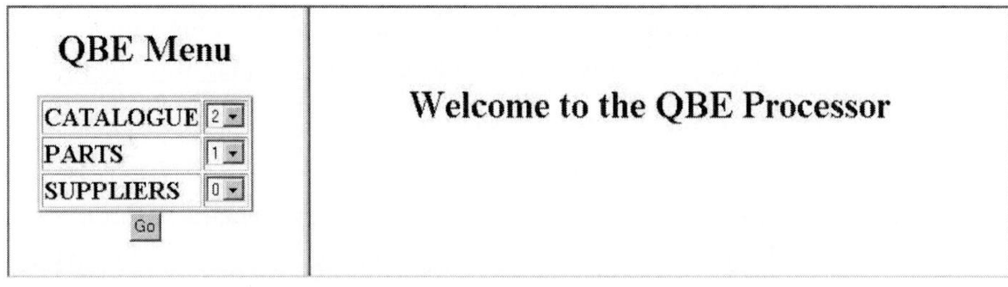


**Figure 9.3** Two-frame initial Web page—QBE interface.

**PARTS:0**

| PID(NUMBER) | PNAME(VARCHAR2) | COLOR(VARCHAR2) |
|---|---|---|
| _Z | P. | P. |

**CATALOGUE:0**

| SID(NUMBER) | PID(NUMBER) | COST(NUMBER) |
|---|---|---|
| _X | _Z | |

**CATALOGUE:1**

| SID(NUMBER) | PID(NUMBER) | COST(NUMBER) |
|---|---|---|
| _Y | _Z | |

**Condition Box** _X <> _Y

Query

**Figure 9.4** Table skeletons—QBE interface.

`_Variable`. Upon submission, the system should produce the results of the query along with the SQL statement obtained by translating the QBE query, as shown in Figure 9.5.

**SQL QUERY IS:**

```
select  parts_0.pname, parts_0.color
from    parts parts_0, catalogue catalogue_0, catalogue catalogue_1
where   parts_0.pid = catalogue_0.pid and
        parts_0.pid = catalogue_1.pid and
        catalogue_0.pid = catalogue_1.pid and
        catalogue_0.sid <> catalogue_1.sid
```

**QUERY RESULT IS:**

| PNAME | COLOR |
|---|---|
| nut | red |
| bolt | green |
| screw | red |

**Figure 9.5** SQL query and query results—QBE interface.

## 9.12 A Web Survey Management System

Using PL/SQL or Java servlets, implement a Web application that manages the creation and deployment of online surveys. The system has two types of users: *surveyors* and *survey takers*. Surveyors should be able to create, edit, and delete surveys. Each survey consists of a set of questions, and each question contains a question number, a question description, its answer type (one of four possible GUI elements: text box, text area, radio button, or select list), and an answer description (properties of the GUI elements such as width of text box, values associated with the radio buttons, etc.). Surveyors should also have the ability to assign surveys to survey takers. Survey takers should be able to take surveys that are assigned to them. They usually will be given a deadline before which they should submit each survey. They may take a survey any number of times before the deadline and save their responses each time. They will have an option of submitting the survey; however, once a survey is submitted, they should not be able to take the survey again. The system should also provide the ability to display results of a survey to the surveyors.

The data associated with the system is stored in the following relational database:

```
CREATE TABLE surveyors ( -- surveyor information
  vno  NUMBER(10)   PRIMARY KEY,
  name  VARCHAR2(30) NOT NULL,
  email  VARCHAR2(50) UNIQUE,
  password VARCHAR2(20) NOT NULL
);

CREATE TABLE surveys ( -- information about surveys
  sno  NUMBER(10) PRIMARY KEY,
  sname      VARCHAR2(100) UNIQUE,
  firstDate DATE,
  lastDate DATE,
  vno  NUMBER(10) REFERENCES surveyors
);

CREATE TABLE questions( -- questions for each survey
  sno  NUMBER(10) REFERENCES surveys,
  qno  NUMBER(10) CHECK(qno>=1),
  question VARCHAR2(150),
  answtype VARCHAR2(15),
  answdesc VARCHAR2(400),
  PRIMARY KEY (sno, qno)
);
```

```
CREATE TABLE takers ( -- survey takers
  tno  NUMBER(10) PRIMARY KEY,
  email  VARCHAR2(50) UNIQUE,
  password VARCHAR2(20)
);

CREATE TABLE takesurveys ( -- records survey takers for each survey
  tno  NUMBER(10) REFERENCES takers,
  sno  NUMBER(10) REFERENCES surveys,
  finishdate DATE,
  isdone      CHAR CHECK(isdone IN ('Y', 'N')),
  PRIMARY KEY (sno, tno)
);

CREATE TABLE answers( -- records responses to survey questions
  sno  NUMBER(10),
  tno  NUMBER(10),
  qno  NUMBER(10),
  answer VARCHAR2(200),
  PRIMARY KEY (sno, tno, qno),
  FOREIGN KEY (sno, tno) REFERENCES takesurveys,
  FOREIGN KEY (sno, qno) REFERENCES questions
);
```

Some examples of rows in the question table are

```
insert into questions values
(1,1,'How old are you?','TextField','2,3');
```

Here, the first question in survey 1 is being described as a `TextField` question (a text box with a maximum of three characters and with the displayed width being two). An example of a text area question is

```
insert into questions values
(1,2,'Enter your comments','TextArea','80,5');
```

Here, the second question in survey 1 is being described as a `TextArea` question (a text area box with five rows and 80 columns). An example of a radio button question is

```
insert into questions values
(1,2,'Your Class','RadioButton','Freshman,Sophomore,Junior,Senior');
```

Here, a `RadioButton` question is being described with four possible values listed in the `answdesc` column (separated with commas). The user may choose

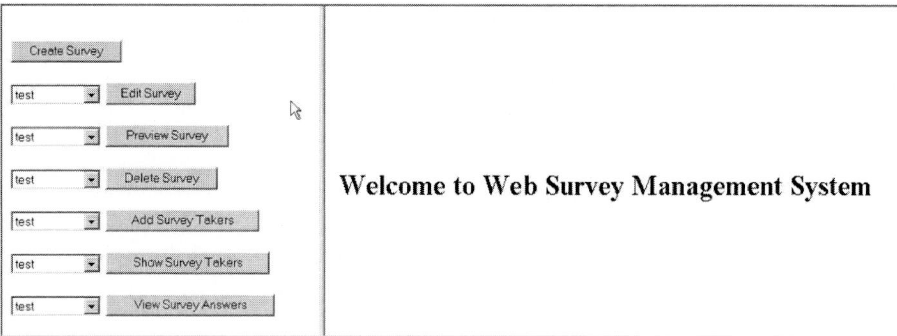


**Figure 9.6** Two-frame initial Web page—Web survey (surveyor).

exactly one of these possibilities as an answer. A `SelectList` question is similar to a `RadioButton` question, except that the user may choose one or more of the options listed when answering this type of question.

There should be two different sign-in Web pages for the two types of users in the system. Once a surveyor has signed in successfully, the surveyor should be shown the two-frame Web page shown in Figure 9.6.

The right-hand frame is used as a workspace. The seven menu options in the left-hand frame are

- *Create Survey.* The user is able to name the survey and specify survey questions using the screen (shown in Figure 9.7) that appears in the right-hand frame when this option is chosen.

  Subsequent question screens will not have the survey name field.

Survey Name:
First date to take survey: JAN 1 2003
Last date to take survey: JAN 1 2003

| Index | Question | Answer Type | Answer Description |
|---|---|---|---|
| 1 | | Text Field<br>Radio Button<br>Select List<br>Text Area | |

Save and Add Next Question

**Figure 9.7** Create survey—Web survey management.

- *Edit Survey.* The user is able to edit questions using the screen (shown in Figure 9.8) that appears in the right-hand frame when this option is chosen.

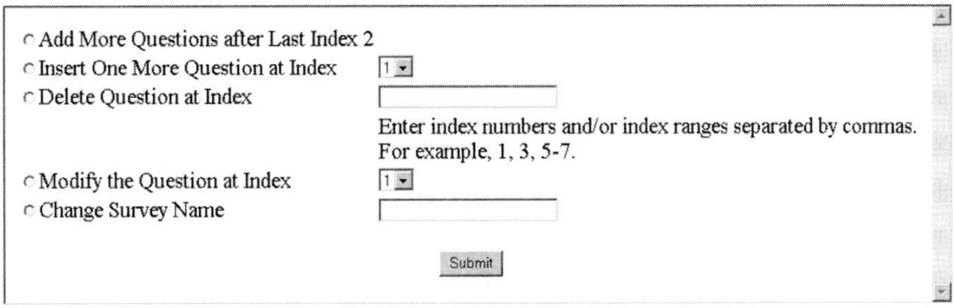

○ Add More Questions after Last Index 2
○ Insert One More Question at Index [1 ▾]
○ Delete Question at Index [ ]
Enter index numbers and/or index ranges separated by commas. For example, 1, 3, 5-7.
○ Modify the Question at Index [1 ▾]
○ Change Survey Name [ ]
[Submit]

**Figure 9.8** Edit survey—Web survey management.

- *Preview Survey.* This option should display the survey as seen by the survey taker.
- *Delete Survey.* This option should delete the survey, including all its questions.
- *Add Survey Takers.* This option should allow the user to add emails of survey takers to the survey. An automatic email should be sent to the survey takers, giving them the URL to follow to take the survey, the deadline for taking the survey, and a system-generated password to use to sign in to the system to take the survey.
- *Show Survey Takers.* This option should display a list of current survey takers for the particular survey.
- *View Survey Answers.* This option should display the answers to the questions in a suitable format.

The sign-in page for survey takers contains text boxes for email and password and a submit button. Upon successfully signing in, the survey taker is shown a pull-down list of surveys assigned to him or her. The survey taker chooses one of the surveys and submits the request. The survey taker is then shown the survey questions along with two submit buttons labeled Save and Submit.

# SUGGESTED READINGS

Koch and Loney (2002) provide comprehensive coverage of all of Oracle9*i*'s features, including a detailed discussion of all Oracle9*i* SQL commands and statements. This is a must-have reference for any serious Oracle programmer. There are numerous books covering SQL. Among the more interesting ones are Bowman, Emerson, and Darnovsky (2001), Melton and Simon (1993) covering SQL-92, Melton, Simon, and Gray (2001) covering SQL-1999, Melton (2002) covering object-relational features of SQL-1999, and Pratt (2000). Embedded SQL in C/C++ is covered in McClanahan (1996), Melton and Simon (1993), and Melton, Simon, and Gray (2001). Three widely cited and used books on PL/SQL are Urman (2001), Urman and Smith (1996), and Feuerstein and Pribyl (2002). PL/SQL Web programming is covered in Boardman, Caffrey, Morse, and Rosenzweig (2002) and Brown, Niemiec, and Trezzo (1996). Price (2002), Reese (2000), and White, Fisher, Cattell, Hamilton, and Hapner (1999) focus on JDBC, and a good reference for SQLJ is Melton, Eisenberg, and Cattell (2000). Java servlet programming is covered in detail in Hall (2000) and Hunter (2001). Oracle XML is discussed in Chang, Scardina, and Kiritzov (2001) and Muench (2000). Relational database concepts are covered in academic database textbooks such as those by Elmasri and Navathe (2000), O'Neil, O'Neil, and Gray (2000), Silberschatz, Korth, and Sudarshan (2001), and Ullman and Widom (2001).

Boardman, S., M. Caffrey, S. Morse, and B. Rosenzweig. *Oracle Web Application Programming for PL/SQL Developers*. Prentice Hall PTR, 2002.

Bowman, J. S., S. L. Emerson, and M. Darnovsky. *The Practical SQL Handbook: Using SQL Variants*, 4th ed. Addison-Wesley, 2001.

Brown, B. D., R. J. Niemiec, and J. C. Trezzo. *Oracle Web Application Server Web Toolkit Reference*. McGraw-Hill Osborne Media, 1998.

Chang, B., M. Scardina, and S. Kiritzov, *Oracle9i XML Handbook*. McGraw-Hill Osborne Media, 2001.

Elmasri, R. and S. B. Navathe. *Fundamentals of Database Systems*, 3rd ed. Addison-Wesley, 2000.

Feuerstein, S. and B. Pribyl. *Oracle PL/SQL Programming*, 3rd ed. O'Reilly, 2002.

Hall, M. *Core Servlets and JavaServer Pages (JSP)*. Prentice Hall PTR, 2000.

Hunter, J. *Java Servlet Programming*, 2nd ed. O'Reilly, 2001.

Loney, K. and G. Koch. *Oracle9i: The Complete Reference*. McGraw-Hill Osborne Media, 2002.

McClanahan, D. Oracle Developer's Guide, Oracle Press, Osborne/McGraw-Hill, 1996.

Melton, J. *SQL: 1999—Understanding Object-Relational and Other Advanced Features*. Morgan-Kaufmann, 2002.

Melton, J., A. Eisenberg, and R. Cattell. *Understanding SQL and Java Together: A Guide to SQLJ, JDBC, and Related Technologies*. Morgan-Kaufmann, 2000.

Melton, J. and A. R. Simon. *Understanding the New SQL: A Complete Guide*. Morgan-Kaufmann, 1993.

Melton, J., A. R. Simon, and J. Gray. *SQL: 1999—Understanding Relational Language Components*. Morgan-Kaufmann, 2001.

Muench S. *Building Oracle XML Applications*. O'Reilly, 2000.

O'Neil, P., E. O'Neil, and J. Gray. *Database: Principles, Programming and Performance*, 2nd ed. Morgan-Kaufmann, 2000.

Pratt, P.J. *A Guide to SQL*, 5th ed. Course Technology, 2000.

Price, J. *Oracle9i JDBC Programming*. McGraw-Hill Osborne Media, 2002.

Reese, G. *Database Programming with JDBC and Java*, 2nd ed. O'Reilly, 2000.

Silberschatz, A., H. F. Korth, and S. Sudarshan. *Database Systems Concepts*, 4th ed. McGraw-Hill, 2001.

Ullman, J. D. and J. Widom. *A First Course in Database Systems*, 2nd ed. Prentice Hall, 2001.

Urman, S. *Oracle9i PL/SQL Programming*. McGraw-Hill Osborne Media, 2001.

Urman, S. and T. Smith. *Oracle PL/SQL Programming*. Oracle Press, Osborne/McGraw-Hill, 1996.

White, S., M. Fisher, R. Cattell, G. Hamilton, and M. Hapner. *JDBC API Tutorial and Reference: Universal Data Access for the Java2 Platform*, 2nd ed. Addison-Wesley, 1999.

# INDEX